TRI-CITY PUBLIC LIBRARY DISTRICT

3 7740 00005 5341

S0-AIN-168

LIFE IN CIVIL WAR AMERICA

Michael O. Varhola
Foreword by Eric J. Wittenberg • Photo appendix by Maureen A. Taylor

Tri-City Public Library
Buffalo, IL

FAMILY
TREE
BOOKS

Cincinnati, Ohio
shopfamilytree.com

LIFE IN CIVIL WAR AMERICA. Copyright ©1999 and 2011 by Michael O. Varhola. Manufactured in the United States of America. All rights reserved. No other part of this book may be reproduced in any form or by any electronic or mechanical means including information storage and retrieval systems without permission in writing from the publisher, except by a reviewer, who may quote brief passages in a review. Published by Family Tree Books, an imprint of F+W Media, Inc., 4700 East Galbraith Road, Cincinnati, Ohio 45236. (800) 289-0963. Second edition. For more genealogy resources, visit <shopfamilytree.com>.

Library of Congress Cataloging has cataloged the Writer's Digest first edtion as follows:

Varhola, Michael J.

  Everyday life during the Civil War / by Michael J. Varhola.

    p.   cm.

  Includes bibliographical references and index.

    ISBN 0-89879-922-8 (pbk.: alk. paper)

    1. United States—History—Civil War, 1861-1865—Social aspects. 2. United States—Social life and customs—1783-1865. I. Title.

E468.9 .V37 1999

973.7 1 21—dc21   99-045940

                                                                                                              CIP

ISBN 13: 978-1-4403-1086-7

15 14 13 12 11   5 4 3 2 1

Distributed in Canada
by Fraser Direct
100 Armstrong Ave.
Georgetown, Ontario, Canada L7G 5S4
Tel: (905) 877-4411

Distributed in the U.K
and Europe by F+W Media International
Brunel House, Newton Abbot, Devon, TQ12 4PU,
England
Tel: (+44) 1626-323200,
Fax: (+44) 1626-323319
E-mail: postmaster@davidandcharles.co.uk

Distributed in Australia
by Capricorn Link
P.O. Box 704, Windsor, NSW 2756 Australia
Tel: (02) 4577-3555

EDITED BY **Jacqueline Musser**
DESIGNED BY **Christy Miller**
PICTURE RESEARCHER **Regina B. McNeely**
PRODUCTION COORDINATED BY **Mark Griffin**

DEDICATION

To my daughters Lindsey and Hayley,
each of whom inspires me in her own way.

ACKNOWLEDGMENTS

A number of people deserve thanks for the roles they played in the completion of this book.

Foremost among them is my wife, Diane, who, together with other things, carried the weight of household responsibilities so that I could devote the necessary time and effort to this project.

Teacher and reenactor Les Albers provided invaluable guidance in my research for the additional material that appears in this revised and expanded edition of this book. He is notable for also having helped me with my research on the original edition back in 1999.

Other people who deserve recognition for their assistance include editor Jacqueline Musser, who helped guide this project during the four months from when she initially contacted me about it until it was finished; author Eric J. Wittenberg, who very generously agreed to write the foreword to this edition of the book; Megan Irvine, whose expertise as a seamstress of historical clothing helped her provide me with some tips on Chapter 8: Clothing and Dry Goods; and Ted Savas of Savas Beatie LLC, who provided some useful advice.

I would also like to thank all of the editors, colleagues, family members, and friends who patiently waited for me to fulfill my obligations to them while I was focusing so much of my attention on this project.

If there is anyone I have left out, I sincerely beg their forgiveness and thank them for their help as well.

ABOUT THE AUTHOR

Michael O. Varhola is an author, editor, publisher, and lecturer who lives outside of San Antonio, Texas, in the heart of the state's Hill Country. He runs gaming company Skirmisher Publishing LLC.

Other books Varhola has written include *Texas Confidential: Sex, Scandal, Murder, and Mayhem in the Lone Star State*; *Shipwrecks and Lost Treasures: Great Lakes*; *Ghosthunting Maryland*; *Ghosthunting Virginia*, and *Fire and Ice: The Korean War, 1950–1953*. Books he has co-authored include *Armchair Reader: Civil War*; *The Writer's Complete Fantasy Reference*; and *D-Day: The Invasion of Normandy, June 6, 1944*.

Publications Varhola has founded include *Living History* magazine and the d∞ ("d-Infinity") quarterly gaming supplement. He has contributed to *Civil War Times*, *Renaissance*, and pop-culture magazine *Brutarian*.

Varhola studied at Metropolitan State College in Denver, Colorado, and at the American University of Paris in Paris, France, before earning a B.S. in journalism from the University of Maryland, College Park.

He is an eight-year veteran of the U.S. Army who served as an infantryman with the 1st Infantry Division (Forward) in Stuttgart, Germany, during the Cold War and as part of a Civil Affairs team attached to the 3rd Armored Division during the First Gulf War.

Varhola has lived throughout the United States and Europe and traveled worldwide. He regularly speaks on cruise ships and to classes, Civil War Roundtables, and other groups.

Varhola also has an active online presence, notably on Facebook, through his TravelBlogue **<varhola.blogspot.com>**, and on a variety of other blogs, forums, and sites.

Contents

Attempts to document the day-to-day lives and routines of Civil War soldiers began almost as soon as the volunteer forces mustered into service. Numerous Northern and Southern newspapers published letters by soldiers—often written pseudonymously—detailing their day-to-day activities. Because the soldiers knew that their friends and families at home would read these letters, they were usually very accurate and very reliable, and they were typically contemporaneous to the events they described.

After the war, hundreds of memoirs were published, many by high-ranking officers, but also many written by common soldiers. The historiography of the Civil War is filled with superb first-person accounts, such as Sam Watkins' iconic *Co. Aytch: Maury Grays, First Tennessee Regiment or, A Side Show of the Big Show*, which provides a humorous but detailed view of life in a Confederate regiment, or Wilbur Hinman's fine book, *Corporal Si Klegg and His "Pard": How They Lived and Talked, and What They Did and Suffered, While Fighting for the Flag*, which provides an accurate picture of life in a Northern regiment. John D. Billings' wonderful memoir, *Hardtack and Coffee: The Unwritten Story of Army Life*, also provides the same sort of insight and humor.

Modern historians have also tried to capture the same essence, using modern historical methods and drawing on the vast array of sources that exist. Two of the best-known examples are Bell I. Wiley's two classic studies, *The Life of Johnny Reb: The Common Soldier of the Confederacy* and *The Life of Billy Yank: The Common Soldier of the Union*, both of which set the standard for this sort of study. Prof. James M. McPherson's *For Cause and Comrades: Why Men Fought in the Civil War* endeavors to understand what motivated men to leave their homes and families to go off and fight for a cause that they believed in. Civil War historiography is replete with solid modern studies that shed a great deal of light on the plight of the common soldier.

Few, though, have done it as well as Michael O. Varhola's 1999 book, *Everyday Life During the Civil War: A Guide for Writers, Students, and Historians.* Unlike so many others of its genre, Varhola's book is intended to be a handbook for those engaged in the study of the Civil War. It includes almost every conceivable category of information, glossaries of the terminology, descriptions of the applicable technology of the era, a timeline of pertinent events, and, perhaps most useful of all, a detailed bibliography and suggestions of other resources to pursue if the reader is interested in learning more about a given topic. In short, Varhola's book is an extremely useful and extremely valuable resource for anyone interested in learning more about almost any aspect of the Civil War.

And now, Mike Varhola has prepared a second edition of his book that substantially improves upon the original version. He has added and updated the contents, has created new chapters, and has made a valuable resource even more valuable by expanding and improving what was already a fine resource. Varhola's new edition is even more indispensable than was the first edition, and it should find a place on the bookshelf of any serious student of the Civil War, as well as the bookshelf of anyone interested in gaining a better understanding of the daily travails of the men who fought for causes that they believed in. I commend the new edition of Mike's book to you.

Eric J. Wittenberg » Columbus, Ohio

For a variety of reasons, the American Civil War has captivated the interest of people in the United States and beyond more than any other episode in U.S. history. Over the course of four years, this conflict escalated from political turmoil into a massive total war that claimed the lives of some 625,000 Americans (more than all the U.S. personnel killed in World War I, World War II, the Korean War, and the Vietnam War combined). In the process, the Civil War did more to influence the course of our nation than any other single event.

This fascination with the Civil War has persisted now for a full 150 years and is not likely to fade any time soon. Today, an extraordinary number of people remain interested in the War Between the States, fueling the creation of movies, documentaries, history books, and novels about it. Movies like *Gettysburg* and *Glory* gained instant followings when they were released; Ken Burns' PBS documentary *The Civil War* is still widely considered one of the best documentaries ever made; and novels about the Civil War, such as *The Killer Angels* and *Cold Mountain*, are regularly on the bestseller lists. Indeed, starting even before the Civil War ended in 1865, more nonfiction books and novels have been written about it than about any other conflict involving the United States.

One reason for this fervent interest is, perhaps, the proximity of the war's events to the everyday lives of so many modern Americans. Reminders of the war are provided by streets still bearing the names that appear in period accounts of its events, by towns contested by the opposing armies, and by cities and military posts named for the rival commanders. People in Pennsylvania, Maryland, Virginia, North Carolina, South Carolina, Georgia and Washington, DC, drive on many of the same roads that massive armies marched along some 150 years ago. Boaters cruise the same inland waterways, coasts, and rivers that U.S. Navy ships guarded, desperate blockade runners plied by night, and armored gunboats patrolled. Inhabitants of the Mississippi River Valley live within hours of the savage raids and battles of the war in the West. Citizens of places like Baltimore, Atlanta, and New Orleans live in cities that were under military occupation. Indeed, the greatest, most destructive war ever seen in North America was fought on ground many of those citizens walk across every single day.

Today, too, the incivility that has become commonplace in political discourse has sparked in some a practical interest in what can happen if the voices of moderation and common sense are unable to prevail. As enjoyable and interesting as a study of the subject can be, people should never forget or ignore what a terrible thing any civil war is.

Life in Civil War America is a broad-based introduction to the day-to-day conditions, attitudes, and events of the period from just before the conflict until a dozen years after its conclusion. While the Civil War was fought from 1861 to 1865, it is a bit contrived to imagine this period can be removed from the broader era in which it existed. Thus, the years before and after are also covered to some extent, notably from abolitionist John Brown's raid on Harpers Ferry, Virginia, through the end of Reconstruction and the Federal occupation of Southern states.

In addition to being a standalone book devoted to the topics it covers, *Life in Civil War America* is also designed to serve as a companion volume to other books on the struggle — especially those dedicated to specific battles or other elements — and to provide useful definitions or explanations of terms or concepts to which they refer (for example, terms like "regiment" are often used freely with little clarification of what they mean).

In any event, as a general work, there are practical limits to the depth of this book, and entire volumes have been written about any of the topics covered in a single chapter here. Those seeking additional information are thus encouraged to seek larger and more detailed works, and this book therefore provides some guidance in this regard.

Subject matter covered in this book includes an overview of the North and the South before, during, and after the war; descriptions of life during the war, including what people ate, what they wore, the sort of work they did, how they entertained themselves, how they worshipped, and where they got their information; the state of education during the era of the war; an overview of the opposing military forces and the personnel who fought in them; a timeline that describes the major events and battles of the war and its aftermath in chronological order; examples of songs and poems composed during the Civil War; and resources readers can use to do further research into specific aspects of the war.

When the first edition of this book was released as *Everyday Life During the Civil War* in 1999, it was recognized as a work that covered ground in a way that no other single volume did. This revised and re-titled edition of that book is, nonetheless, superior to its predecessor in every way (if only because its author is a better writer today than he was more than a decade ago). It has been reedited, reorganized, expanded, corrected as needed, and had added to it two completely new chapters, those on Education and Religion.

Enjoy! We are confident that this book will be an invaluable tool in your explorations into one of the most fascinating episodes in American history.

Michael O. Varhola

DISCOVERING YOUR CIVIL WAR ANCESTORS
Adapted from *Family Tree Magazine*

C ould you have Civil War veterans in your family tree? Now, a century-and-a-half since that great conflict, it is never been easier to start researching your Blue or Gray soldier ancestor. Not only can you search for the basic facts of his military service, you also can delve into the details of his regiment and battles he may have fought in, trace the unit's movements on historical maps, and perhaps even find an image of him with his comrades. Pension files and other records could provide long-sought details about your soldier's spouse and children, helping you win your own battle to understand your family's past.

The Civil War produced voluminous documents about the more than 3.5 million men (and a few hundred women) who fought both for the Union and the Confederacy. Understanding a few key facts about these documents and a handful of essential resources can unlock a wealth of information about your Civil War ancestor. Follow these nine simple steps and you will soon be immersed in the epic struggle of North and South—and your family's role in that drama.

Step 1: Look in the index.

First, you want to confirm your ancestor was in the war and learn some basic facts about his service. The Civil War Soldiers and Sailors System (CWSS) <www.itd.nps.gov/cwss>—a massive project by the National Park Service with the Genealogical Society of Utah and the Federation of Genealogical Societies—puts basic information on 6.3 million soldier names just a click away. How can there be 6.3 million records in this online index, you ask, when only three million fought in the Civil War? If a soldier served in more than one regiment, he will be listed multiple times; the same is true for men who served under more than one name or whose records are separated by spelling variations.

The CWSS contains transcribed information from General Index Cards, created beginning in the 1880s by Maj. Gen. Fred C. Ainsworth's staff to determine veterans' eligibility for military pensions. Happily, the staff examined Confederate records, even though Rebel soldiers were not eligible to draw federal pensions. The names on the index cards were drawn from muster rolls, usually kept on the company level and updated about every two weeks. The original cards are now at the National Archives and Records Administration (NARA) <archives.gov> in Washington, DC.

Searching the CWSS could not be easier. Click on Soldiers, then fill in as many blanks in the search form as you can: last name, first name, Union or Confederate, state or place of origin, unit, function (infantry, cavalry, artillery, sharpshooters, or engineers). Don't worry—you do not have to know your ancestor's unit. In fact, that is one of the key pieces of data you can learn from CWSS.

If you know the unit but cannot find your soldier, click on Regiments to search for a specific unit. You will get a brief regimental history and a link to a list of all soldiers in that unit. A successful search will confirm your ancestor served in the Civil War and retrieve his name (as listed in related records), side (Union or Confederate), regiment and company, initial rank and final rank, and the microfilm location of the original index card. The index also might contain an alternate name or notes. You can find the same information on microfilm or in two series edited by Janet B. Hewett, both from Broadfoot Publishing: *The Roster of Union Soldiers, 1861-1865* (33 volumes) and *The Roster of Confederate Soldiers*, 1861-1865 (16 volumes).

You face a bigger challenge for sailor ancestors. Naval records are not microfilmed or well-organized for either side. To date, only the records of 18,000 African-American Union sailors are indexed in CWSS.

Step 2: Go on record.

Now you are ready to get a copy of your ancestor's Compiled Military Service Record (CMSR). Every soldier has a CMSR for each regiment he served in, so if your ancestor was in more than one, seek out all his CMSRs. The CMSR envelope, with contents compiled from original muster rolls and other records, contains various cards typically recording whether the soldier was present during a period of time, facts of enlistment and discharge, and any wounds or hospitalization. (Note that you usually cannot prove from a CMSR that a soldier was present in a particular battle, unless he was injured or captured.) His place of birth may be noted; only the country is listed for foreign-born men. The CMSR also may include an internal jacket of "personal papers," such as his enlistment documents and any prisoner of war records. According to NARA's Civil War records guide **<archives.gov/genealogy/military/civil-war>**, CMSRs "were so carefully prepared that it is rarely necessary to consult the original muster rolls and other records from which they were made."

What might you learn from an ancestor's CMSR? NARA's guide gives the example of Pvt. William P. Western, Company D, 106th New York Volunteer Infantry Regiment: He enlisted July 29, 1862, at DeKalb, New York. He was 26 years old, born in Stockholm, New York, and stood 5 feet, 8 inches, with gray eyes and brown hair. The CMSR follows Western as he was taken prisoner at Fairmont, Virginia, April 29, 1863. After his parole, Western suffered "remittant fever" and "chronic diarrhea," and was hospitalized in Virginia and Washington, DC. During his service, he received $95 in clothing, $27 in advanced bounty and pay through August 31, 1864; he owed $1.27 for a "painted blanket" and $23.96 for transportation.

Confederate records tend to be sparser and less detailed, though some CMSRs from Louisiana, Mississippi, and Alabama units list battles in which the soldier fought. Most Union CMSR files are not microfilmed, but you can access microfilmed Confederate records at NARA or the Church of Jesus Christ of Latter-day Saints' Family History Library (FHL) **<www.familysearch.org>**. Visit your local FamilySearch Center (find it using FamilySearch.org) to rent FHL microfilm. Study original Union or Confederate CMSRs at NARA in Washington, DC, or request copies: On the Web, go to Order Online **<eservices.archives.gov/orderonline>** and click Order Reproductions.

If you learn your ancestor, like Western, was a prisoner-of-war, check Selected Records of the War Department Relating to Confederate Prisoners of War, 1861-1865, on NARA or FHL microfilm. On CWSS, click Prisoners to search its index of Confederate prisoners held at Fort McHenry and Union prisoners at Andersonville.

Step 3: Draw on pensions.

If your ancestor fought for the Union, it is likely he, his widow, or his minor children later applied for a pension. Surprisingly, these pension files often contain richer information about a soldier's service than his CMSR does, including a medical history if he lived for a number of years after the war. Pension files can be a genealogical gold mine for researching the family, too: Widows had to supply evidence of marriage, and applicants on behalf of minor children had to prove their birth and the soldier's marriage. Western's pension file, for example, details his death and burial in October 1864, his marriage to Ulisa Daniels; the birth of their daughter, Rosena; and Ulisa's remarriage to Patrick Curn.

Union pension records are indexed on 544 rolls of NARA microfilm called General Index to Pension Files, 1861-1934 (T288), which also are available from the FHL. The index is arranged by place, then by the veteran's or widow's name. You can also search it online at with a paid subscription to Ancestry.com <ancestry.com> or free at libraries offering Ancestry Library Edition. Footnote's <www.footnote.com> free search is generous with transcribed information. The actual pension files are not microfilmed, but you can request copies from NARA's Order Online service. Ask for copies of all the documents in the file, or you will receive only selected pages.

The victorious federal government was not too eager to pay pensions to those who had fought against it, so Confederate pensions fell to the states. Some paid only to indigent or disabled veterans, widows, and orphans. A qualifying veteran could apply to the state where he lived, even if he served in another state's unit. NARA does not keep Confederate pension records, but does provide a guide to locating them <archives.gov/genealogy/military/civil-war/confederate/pension.html>. Most Confederate pension files are on FHL microfilm, and several states have put indexes or applications online including:

FLORIDA <www.floridamemory.com/collections/pensionfiles>
GEORGIA <content.sos.state.ga.us/cdm4/pension.php>
LOUISIANA <www.sos.louisiana.gov/Default.aspx?tabid=637>
OKLAHOMA <www.odl.state.ok.us/oar/docs/pension.pdf>
SOUTH CAROLINA <archives.sc.gov/information/confederate/>
TENNESSEE <www.tennessee.gov/tsla/history/military/pension.htm>
TEXAS <www.tsl.state.tx.us/arc/pensions/introcpi.html>
VIRGINIA <www.lva.virginia.gov/public/guides/opac/conpenabout.htm>

Many former Confederate states also built soldiers homes for needy veterans. Records of homes in Arkansas, Georgia, Louisiana, Missouri, Tennessee, Texas, and Virginia are available on FHL microfilm—run a keyword search of the online catalog on the state name and *soldiers home*.

Step 4: Draft your ancestors.

Not all Union soldiers were volunteers, of course. In 1863, Congress enacted the nation's first military draft; it applied to men ages 20 to 45. Draft records, which are not microfilmed, are at NARA in record group 110, Records of the Provost Marshal General's Bureau. They include much genealogical data, even if your ancestor never actually served. Consolidated Lists show each man's name, residence, age, occupation, marital status, place of birth, and any previous military service. Descriptive Rolls include physical description, birthplace, and whether the person was enlisted. Both listings are organized by state, then congressional district, then surname. To find your ancestral county's 1863 congressional district, consult *United States Congress, Congressional Directory for the Second Session of the Thirty-Eighth Congress of the United States of America*, available on FHL film 1425543 (Item 6, Official Congressional Directory).

The Enrollment Act of 1863 granted your Union ancestor the option to avoid military service by giving a substitute $300 but, in practice, this fee escalated. With a little digging in draft records, you can find out if your ancestor followed the example of, for instance, then-future president Grover Cleveland, who paid 32-year-old Polish immigrant George Beniski to take his place in the 76th New York Volunteer Infantry Regiment.

If you have already found your ancestor's CMSR and pension files, there is little extra to be gleaned from draft records. But if you strike out in the former, draft records may provide otherwise-elusive answers.

Step 5: Enlist the census.

The federal census sometimes holds clues about Civil War service. The 1890 census included a special enumeration of Union veterans and widows. Most of that census was lost to fire, but those special schedules survived for states alphabetically from Kentucky through Wyoming. You can access census records on FHL and NARA microfilm, and on Ancestry.com. The 1910 census also asked whether a person was a survivor of the Union Army (abbreviated UA) or Navy (UN), or the Confederate Army (CA) or Navy (CN). Some postwar state censuses, such as the 1865 New York and 1885 Wisconsin enumerations, also identified Union veterans (both of those state censuses are on FHL microfilm; veterans from the latter one are in a digitized book at <www.wisconsinhistory. org/turningpoints/search.asp?id=1539>). Several Southern states took censuses of Confederate veterans. Those available on FHL microfilm include Alabama in 1907, 1921, and 1927; Arkansas in 1911; and Louisiana in 1911.

Step 6: Join the club.

After the war, many Union veterans joined organizations, such as the Grand Army of the Republic (GAR)—by 1890, some 40 percent of Union veterans were GAR members. The records of local GAR posts, including rosters and meeting minutes, often provide genealogical information about members. Look for them in state historical societies, archives, and libraries. They are on FHL microfilm for some states, including Iowa, South Dakota, Michigan, Nebraska, Oregon, and Utah.

See a listing of GAR posts by state at **<loc.gov/rr/main/gar>**. Union officers formed the Military Order of the Loyal Legion of the United States **<suvcw.org/mollus.htm>**, which exists today as a hereditary group. Other hereditary organizations include the Daughters of Union Veterans of the Civil War **<www.duvcw.org>** and the Sons of Union Veterans of the Civil War **<suvcw.org>**, both of which offer historical information on their websites.

Confederate veterans established the United Confederate Veterans in 1889. Records of the organization are available on FHL microfilm, and the Library of Virginia has an online index to names in Confederate Veteran magazine. Confederate hereditary groups include Sons of Confederate Veterans **<www.scv.org>** and United Daughters of the Confederacy **<www.hqudc.org>**.

Step 7: Visit the cemetery.

Whether it happened during the war or years later, all Civil War veterans have passed on—and cemetery records yield more ancestral clues. About 200,000 Union soldiers who died in the war are recorded in the twenty-seven volume *Roll of Honor* available from Genealogical Publishing Co. and on FHL microfilm. It is arranged by burial place, so first check *Index to the Roll of Honor* by Martha and William Reamy and its addendum, *The Unpublished Roll of Honor* by Mark Hughes, both from Genealogical Publishing Co. If you think your Civil War ancestor is buried in a government cemetery, start your search at the Department of Veterans Affairs' National Gravesite Locator **<gravelocator.cem.va.gov>**. This site indexes burial locations of veterans and their families in VA national cemeteries, state veterans cemeteries, and other military and Department of Interior cemeteries.

An 1879 act of Congress authorized the government to provide headstones to soldiers and veterans buried in private cemeteries. The cards recording these 166,000 headstones—honoring Union soldiers and veterans who died between 1861 and about 1903—are on NARA microfilm M1845; the FHL has copies. You'll get the name, rank, company and regiment, date of death, place of burial, and grave number, if any.

No single source lists all the 250,000-some Confederate soldiers who died during the Civil War, but the FHL has several useful references. Two book series compiled by Raymond W. Watkins are good starting places: *Confederate Burials* (twenty-eight volumes) and *Deaths of Confederate Soldiers in Confederate Hospitals* (fifteen volumes). CWSS eventually will contain an index to all the burials in the National Park Service's fourteen national cemeteries. To date, you will find data and headstone images only from Virginia's Poplar Grove National Cemetery at Petersburg.

Step 8: Follow the regiment.

Once you have researched your ancestor's military records, you can learn much more about his Civil War experiences by studying his regiment and company. For a quick regimental history, including major battles, just click on the CWSS site's Regiments link. It covers four thousand Union and Confederate units, with links to soldiers' names and detailed battle histories.

Civil War buffs and soldiers' descendants have written volumes of printed and online histories. Search the Library of Congress for books about your ancestor's regiment. The ultimate information source for Civil War events—though it rarely names individual soldiers—is the "OR." That's the War Department's seventy-volume *The War of the Rebellion: A Compilation of the Official Records of the Union and Confederate Armies*. Many large public and university libraries have these books, which also are on NARA and FHL microfilm. Even better, you'll find a searchable version of the OR at **<library5.library.cornell.edu/moa>** (click Browse, then look under Browse Civil War Documents).

You will also want to consult the unit histories in *Supplement to the Official Records of the Union and Confederate Armies* compiled by Janet B. Hewett (fifty-one volumes, Broadfoot Publishing). It is drawn from two NARA regimental records microfilm collections: The 225-roll Compiled Records Showing Service of Military Units in Volunteer Union Organizations and its 74-roll Confederate counterpart.

For additional background on the war, see if your library subscribes to the Civil War Era database from ProQuest Information and Learning. The service includes complete runs of eight newspapers from the North, South, and border states spanning 1840 to 1865, as well as nearly two thousand opinion pamphlets from leaders of the era.

Step 9: Use visual aids.

Nothing brings your ancestors' world alive like images. Photographers, such as the legendary Mathew Brady, made the Civil War the first military conflict captured in pictures, showing uniforms, weapons, camp life, and battle aftermath. Maps let you trace the movements and battlefield positions of your soldier's unit. NARA has a wealth of Civil War images, including maps and Brady's work. Access the archive's war-related holdings through its Archival Research Catalog **<archives. gov/research/arc>**. The Library of Congress' American Memory site offers digitized Civil War maps and photos from its own and other repositories' collections; browse or search from **<memory. loc.gov>**. Its photographic holdings are cataloged at **<loc.gov/rr/print>**. Another key resource for photos and maps is the U.S. Army Heritage and Education Center in Carlisle, Pa. **<www.carlisle. army.mil/ahec>**.

Whatever you learn about your ancestor's part in the great drama of the Civil War—whether he turns out to be a Yankee or a Rebel, a hero or a deserter—finding how your family fits into this American epic will illuminate that era as no schoolbook lesson can.

NORTH AND SOUTH:
ONE NATION, TWO PEOPLES

"Prior to my installation here, it had been inculcated that any State had a lawful right to secede from
the national Union, and that it would be expedient to exercise that right whenever the devotees of the
doctrine should fail to elect a President to their own liking; and, accordingly, so far as it was legally possible,
they had taken seven States out of the Union, had seized many of the United States forts, and had fired upon
the United States flag, all before I was inaugurated, and, of course, before I had done any official
act whatever. The Rebellion thus begun soon ran into the present Civil War ... "
— President Abraham Lincoln, in a June 12, 1863, open letter to prominent Albany, New York, Democrat Erastus Corning

When the Civil War erupted in early 1861, people in the North and the South had long regarded themselves as separate. Indeed, the customs, economies, and philosophies of the two peoples were markedly different. Nonetheless, the two portions of the country had developed alongside each other and were bound in ways that did not become apparent until they were locked in total war against each other. During the war, the combined population of the two opposing nations was a bit more than thirty-one million people (by comparison, the population of the United States today, in the second decade of the twenty-first century, is ten times as large at more than 310 million). From this relatively small population base, the North ultimately put two million men into uniform, the South one million. With three million men under arms, the combined Union and Confederate militaries were proportionately about twenty times larger than the active duty U.S. armed forces today, which number somewhat more than 1.4 million personnel at this writing (i.e., nearly 10 percent of the population during the Civil War vs. about half of one percent of the population today).

By May 1861, the country was divided into 23 states that had either declared loyalty to the Union or at least not done so with regard to the Confederacy (including five slave-holding border states that did not secede but to one extent or another tried to maintain some semblance of neutrality until 1863); eleven Confederate states; and a number of large, unorganized U.S. government territories, the number of which varied during the war, as new territories or states were partitioned from larger ones.

Two additional states were admitted to the Union after the war began, West Virginia in 1863 and Nevada in 1864, raising the number of states within the Union to twenty-five.

UNION STATES: California, Connecticut, Delaware, Illinois, Indiana, Iowa, Kansas, Kentucky, Maine, Maryland, Massachusetts, Michigan, Minnesota, Missouri, Nevada (1864), New Hampshire, New Jersey, New York, Ohio, Oregon, Pennsylvania, Rhode Island, Vermont, West Virginia (1863), and Wisconsin.

Nearly 10 percent of the population engaged in military service during the Civil War.

CONFEDERATE STATES (with their dates of secession): South Carolina (December 20, 1860), Mississippi (January 9, 1861), Florida (January 10, 1861), Alabama (January 11, 1861), Georgia (January 19, 1861), Louisiana (January 26, 1861), Texas (February 1, 1861), Virginia (April 17, 1861), Arkansas (May 6, 1861), Tennessee (May 7, 1861), and North Carolina (May 20, 1861).

TERRITORIES (with their years of existence): Arizona Territory (1863-1912), Colorado Territory (1861-1876), Dakota Territory (1861–1889), Idaho Territory (1863–1890), Indian Territory (1834-1907), Montana Territory (1864–1889), Nebraska Territory (1854–1867), Nevada Territory (1861–1864), New Mexico Territory (1850–1912), Utah Territory (1850–1896), and Washington Territory (1853–1889).

The North

More than twenty-two million of the thirty-one million people living in America when the Civil War broke out lived in states that remained loyal to the Union.

The North was far more industrialized than the South and had within its borders some 100,000 factories, including almost all of the nation's shipyards and means of arms production. More than one million workers were employed in these factories. The Union also controlled most of the components of industry, which included almost all of the country's coal mines, which produced the fuel needed to run factories and steamships, and most of the canals, needed to transport coal and other heavy goods. And naturally, the North also controlled most of the fruits of industrialization, including 70 percent of the country's railroads (22,385 miles) and about 95 percent of its rolling stock and railway equipment.

Despite the fact that it was so industrialized, the North was also largely self-sufficient in agriculture and produced more than the South in every agricultural category except for cotton. It was thus not dependent upon the seceding states for food to feed its people.

Financially, the Union controlled more than 80 percent of the total U.S. bank deposits, about $189 million, and about 60 percent of the total gold reserves, or about $56 million worth of gold. These factors immeasurably helped the North finance a successful war effort.

The South

Only about nine million of the thirty-one million people living in the United States at the time of the Civil War lived in the South, and a third of them were slaves. This was a relatively small population for a region that, while smaller than the North, was still bigger than all of Western Europe, and totaled about 750,000 square miles in size.

Industrially, the South was far behind the North, with only 20,000 factories employing some 100,000 workers (as compared to 100,000 factories employing more than a million workers in the North). Only 30 percent of the nation's railroads lay within the Confederacy, somewhat more than 9,000 miles of them, along with a mere 5 percent of its rolling stock and railway equipment (which still made the C.S. railroad system the third largest of any nation in the world in 1861). While the South was not highly industrialized, it wasn't poor, either, and its major cash crop, cotton, afforded a high standard of living for many of its people. Nonetheless, at the outbreak of war the Confederacy controlled just under 20 percent of the country's total bank deposits, about $47 million, and about 40 percent of the total gold reserves, worth some $37 million. Lack of industrialization and financing contributed greatly to the ruination of the South and its defeat during the Civil War.

> Only about nine million of the thirty-one million people living in the United States at the time of the Civil War lived in the South, and a third of them were slaves.

Also, a short-sighted policy early in the war of withholding cotton from European markets in an attempt to make the European states support the Confederacy in exchange for an uninterrupted supply of the crop backfired and deprived the South of much-needed revenue. Some cloth manufacturers in Great Britain had to shut down mills and fire workers, causing some elements to call for backing of the South to keep the peace among English workers and mill owners. Ultimately, however, Europe looked to other sources for cotton, such as Egypt. And, by the time the Confederacy reversed its policy, the Federal naval blockade ensured that little cotton could be successfully exported anyway.

The Union States

Following are brief overviews of the states that remained loyal to the Union during the Civil War. One particularly interesting note is how many of the states on either side were settled or granted statehood only a few years before the war, a reminder that in the 1860s much of the United States was still unsettled frontier and sparsely-populated farm country. America's greatest cities also had distinct characteristics at the time of the Civil War and information on

The 176th New York Volunteer Infantry Regiment, also known as the "Ironsides Regiment" was recruited from the entire state of New York.

some of them is included in the descriptions of states. Slave states that remained within the Union are marked with an (S).

California

California was the westernmost state at the time of the Civil War. U.S. forces had invaded the region, then controlled by Mexico, in 1846, and officially acquired California two years later through the **Treaty of Guadalupe Hidalgo**. Although much of southern California was in favor of slavery, the entire state remained loyal to the Union during the war, which had little direct effect on the state.

While no troops were raised for combat in the East, five hundred California volunteers served with a Massachusetts unit. Volunteer regiments were raised to provide security within the state, fight in Arizona and New Mexico, and garrison outposts in Washington and Oregon.

On January 24, 1848, gold was discovered at Sutter's Mill in northern California, sparking a gold rush that brought thousands of "Forty-niners" into the state; by 1850, the state's non-Indian population had more than tripled to 93,000 inhabitants, and by 1860 was nearly 380,000, about 4,000 of whom were free blacks.

California was admitted to the Union in 1850 as a free state under the **Compromise of 1850**. Gold production declined in the early 1850s, and in the 1860s fruit, grain, and wine making became important components of the state economy. In 1869, the first transcontinental railroad, linking Sacramento with the rest of the country, was completed.

Connecticut

Connecticut abolished slavery in 1848 and most of its citizens opposed it at the start of the Civil War. About fifty-five thousand men from Connecticut fought for the Union during the war (eight thousand of them of Irish descent), and the state provided blankets, ammunition, firearms, and several ships to the war effort. At the start of the war, the state's total population was around 460,000. About 8,600 of these people were free blacks.

Connecticut's economy grew markedly during the nineteenth century, with industry surpassing agriculture by the 1850s. Commerce, insurance, and shipping were important components of the state's economy; Connecticut also manufactured brasswork, clocks, rubber goods, and textiles. Industry continued to grow in the postwar years.

(S) Delaware

As one of the Mid-Atlantic states, it is fitting that in 1860 Delaware was a synthesis of the urbanized, industrial North and the more rural, agricultural South. Although a slave state, on the eve of the war, Delaware had only about 1,800 slaves and more than ten times as many free blacks, out of a total population of more than 112,000. While its people remained divided over the issue of slavery during the war, most of them were moderates who supported the Union, and many soldiers from Delaware fought in the Union armed forces. After the war, economic growth continued in Delaware, concentrated in the Wilmington area. Like many Southern states in the postwar years, Delaware vigorously opposed black rights through a variety of corrupt political tactics, including an 1873 **poll tax**.

Illinois

Illinois, home to U.S. President Abraham Lincoln, was populated by many first-and second-generation Southerners at the time of the Civil War, creating divided loyalties within the state. Like many Midwestern states, it was a hotbed of Copperhead sentiment (see chapter eleven for more information about copperheads).

Nonetheless, many Illinoisans were proud of their connection with Lincoln, and the state sent some 257,000 soldiers to fight for the Union, out of a total population of about 1,712,000 (it has been estimated that one-seventh of these soldiers died during the war). Illinois was also a major Northern source of iron products, meat, and grain.

Indiana

Indiana had supported intensive development of its infrastructure in the decades prior to the Civil War, especially canals and railroads, nearly bankrupting itself in the process. In 1851, lawmakers responded by amending the state constitution to require the government to have a balanced budget at the end of each fiscal year.

Although many Indianans were of Southern origin, the state supported the Union war effort with materiel and more than 208,000 troops, out of a total population of about 1,350,000. Little action took place on Indiana soil, the major event being an 1863 raid led by Confederate Brig. Gen. John Hunt Morgan.

After the Civil War, farming, forestry, and mining emerged as mainstays of the state's economy. Industrialization was facilitated by European immigrants, who helped launch local glass, furniture, brick, steel, and tile manufacturing industries.

Iowa

Iowa entered the Union as a state in 1846 and, at the time of the Civil War, had a population of about 675,000 (a decade later, it nearly doubled to 1,194,000). All of the state's major communities, such as Cedar Falls and Iowa Falls, were built along rivers, railroads, or both.

Initially Democratic, Iowa became staunchly Republican and abolitionist in 1856. In keeping with this tradition, many Iowans participated in the **Underground Railroad**, and the state sent a larger proportion of its men to fight in the Civil War than any other state except Massachusetts, nearly eighty thousand of them. No battles, however, were fought on Iowan soil.

Agriculture and commerce were dual mainstays of Iowa's economy in the mid-nineteenth century, and from its earliest days, the state was commercially linked to the rest of the country. A preponderance of the state's citizens were settlers, and many eventually moved westward again. Iowa became fully settled after the war and the railroads improved, moving the state toward commercial rather than subsistence farming. Agrarian activity, such as the **Granger movement**, was a reaction to widespread distrust of banks and politicians and price gouging by the railroads.

Kansas

Kansas was largely uninhabited by whites until the mid-1850s, when the local Indians were relocated to Indian Territory in what is now Oklahoma and the U.S. government opened it to settlement under the provisions of the 1854 **Kansas-Nebraska Act**. The act stipulated that the question of whether a territory would be admitted as a slave state or a free state would be decided by a popular referendum.

Abolitionist and proslavery organizations each began pushing for immigration by sympathizers to their causes, and by 1855 the proponents of these rival camps had established opposing governments. Violence eventually broke out between the two factions and escalated, a series of events dubbed "**Bleeding Kansas**" (prior to his final battle at Harpers Ferry, Virginia, rabid abolitionist John Brown had been deeply involved in this violence).

Conflict continued both within the territory and in the U.S. Congress until January 29, 1861, when Kansas was finally admitted to the Union as a free state. Savage guerrilla raids characterized the Civil War in Kansas, directed against soldiers and civilians alike along the border with Missouri. These peaked with the Lawrence Massacre on August 21, 1863, when Confederate guerilla leader William C. Quantrill and his raiders sacked and razed the town of Lawrence, slaughtering as many as 200 men and boys in the process.

About 107,000 people lived in Kansas at the outbreak of the Civil War. Thousands of immigrants flocked to the state in the 1870s, including many Germans, Swedes, and Russians, sparking a major land boom. German-Russian Mennonites brought winter wheat to Kansas, transforming the face of agriculture in the state.

(S) Kentucky

Kentucky, a slave state on the border between the North and South, tried to stay neutral during the Civil War. Its strategic positioning and the divided loyalties of its citizens, however, made it impossible for the state to stay out of the conflict.

Agriculture was the basis of Kentucky's economy at the start of the Civil War. Farmers, who wanted access to the port of New Orleans via the Mississippi River, opposed secession because they believed commerce would be impeded by it. On the other hand, plantation owners and advocates of states' rights favored separation from the Union. As a result, the Civil War really was a "brothers' war" for Kentucky, which sent regiments of troops to fight for both the Union and the Confederacy. From a population of just over 1,155,000, about 75,000 Kentuckians served in the Union forces, while about 35,000 fought for the Confederacy (marking Kentucky as a Rebel state in the eyes of many Northerners).

A Confederate army invaded Kentucky in 1861 but was driven out of the state in October 1862. After that, the Confederacy contested ownership of the state largely through cavalry raids and guerilla warfare tactics.

Kentucky changed both economically and socially after the war ended. Hemp was replaced by tobacco as the major cash crop, expansion of the railroads stimulated coal mining in the eastern part of the state, and major urban areas grew as manufacturing and industry increased in the northern end of the state.

Maine

Maine was a prosperous shipbuilding area and center of commerce at the time of the Civil War, conducting a brisk seaborne trade in lumber with Asia, Europe, and the West Indies.

At the outbreak of the war, Maine had a population of about 628,000. About 73,000 of its men served in the Union military during the Civil War (some 6,700 in the Navy and Marine Corps), and nearly one in ten of them was killed. Maine also contributed significant amounts of supplies for the Union cause during the war.

After the Civil War ended, the mainstays of Maine's economy shifted from the coastal regions and agriculture, shipping, and lumbering, to manufacturing in the interior. State, local, and private interests expanded the state's infrastructure, notably roads and streets, lighting and electricity, libraries and education, and public transportation and communication systems. Population growth slowed during this period, despite the considerable numbers of French Canadians and Irish who immigrated to the state.

(S) Maryland

Maryland was a synthesis of the North and South during the Civil War. Like many Southern states, it had a rural economy—based on large tobacco plantations in the east and small farms in the west—but like Northern states it thrived on trade and manufacturing. Baltimore was a vital port, becoming a shipbuilding and industrial center that rivaled Boston, New York, and Philadelphia; the city had a population of more than 170,000 at the time of the Civil War and, overall, the state had a population of about 687,000. Equal numbers of free and enslaved blacks lived within the state.

Maryland had strong Southern sympathies and was leaning toward secession in 1861. Maryland in general, and Baltimore in particular, was incredibly important to the Federal war effort because of its role as a major port and rail hub and because of its proximity to Washington, D.C.; if the state were lost to the Confederacy, the U.S. capital would be completely surrounded. To prevent its loss to the Union, Lincoln garrisoned Baltimore with soldiers throughout the war. Fort McHenry, site of the British siege that inspired Francis Scott Key to compose the national anthem, was occupied by Federal troops and used as a stronghold to control the city. Baltimoreans responded with civil unrest and rioting, and on more than one occasion troops were attacked in the streets, resulting in both civilian and military casualties.

Confederate destruction of Maryland property cooled sympathy for the Southern cause amongst those financially affected by such actions. In June 1861, for example, Confederate Maj. Gen. Joseph Johnston ordered the destruction in the Shenandoah Valley of forty-two locomotives and 386 cars owned by the Baltimore and Ohio Railroad, ostensibly to keep them from falling into Union hands. This devastation inflicted total losses of more than $1 million on the railroad company and its stockholders.

Some of the heaviest fighting of the war took place on Maryland soil, including the 1862 battles of South Mountain and Antietam and the Battle of Monocacy in 1864.

Industrialization expanded rapidly after the war and eventually became the mainstay of the state's economy. Thousands of rural blacks and immigrants from Germany, Greece, Italy, Poland, and Russia came to Baltimore seeking jobs in the city's factories.

Massachusetts

Massachusetts enjoyed a period of prosperity in the decades leading up to the Civil War. Agriculture remained important during this period and continued to spread into the state's hilly interior. All of its main cities were connected by toll roads, canals, or railroads, and its textile and shoe industries began to grow and dominate the state's economy.

Large numbers of Irish immigrants arrived in the state in the 1840s and took jobs in the textile mills, which had originally been operated by people recruited from the state's farms. Many factory towns doubled their populations in less than a decade. As natural water power proved inadequate for the needs of the mills, it was increasingly replaced with coal-powered steam engines. Living and working conditions in mill towns were often substandard, and unrest began to grow among many factory workers.

Massachusetts, long a center of abolitionism, entered the Civil War enthusiastically. Many troops from the state fought for the Union cause, including the now-famous 54th Massachusetts Volunteer Infantry Regiment, the first all-black unit—except for officers—sanctioned by the government. Altogether, about 160,000 men served in the Union army, plus more in the navy than from any other state except New York. Massachusetts also provided huge numbers of blankets, guns, tents, and shoes to the Federal war effort.

Michigan

Michigan sent more than 90,000 military-age men to fight for the Union during the Civil War, and about 14,000 of them were killed during the conflict. The labor shortages this created fostered many labor-saving devices in the state's industries, laying the way for large-scale industrialization.

During and after the war, staples of Michigan's economy included farming of wheat, potatoes, and hops, sheep raising, and lumbering. Loggers in Michigan cleared vast tracts of timber in the years following the Civil War, annihilating the state's virgin forests in just a few decades.

Public education has been important in Michigan since 1787, when the Northwest Ordinance called for the state to "encourage education." America's first state primary school fund was established in 1837, free primary schooling was made available in 1869, and in 1874, the state supreme court upheld the legality of using local taxes to pay for the establishment of high schools. The Detroit News was one of the state's principal newspapers in the mid-nineteenth century.

Minnesota

Minnesota, admitted to the Union as a state in 1858, had a population of about 172,000 at the time of the Civil War and an economy based on lumbering, milling, and wheat farming. Altogether, more than twenty thousand Minnesotans fought for the Union.

While no battles against Confederate forces took place on Minnesota soil, the state did suffer from Indian uprisings during the war. During the 1850s, the local Indians were forced to give up claims to their homelands and move onto reservations. In 1862, food and money promised to the reservations was diverted to the Union war effort, leading to an armed uprising in the state. Over a period of several days, angry Sioux killed more than four hundred white settlers before the rebellion was quashed and the Indians captured. Some 306 of the Sioux were sentenced to death and eighteen to prison before Abraham Lincoln intervened and commuted the death sentences of all but thirty-nine of them, an action resented by most of the white settlers.

(S) Missouri

Missouri had for many years been a jumping-off point for innumerable expeditions to the West because of its central location and access to navigable waterways—notably the Mississippi and Missouri rivers—which had been plied by steamboats from the 1820s onward. Some 1,182,000 people lived in the state when the war began.

Many people in largely-agricultural Missouri, particularly in the Ozarks, were subsistence farmers and woodsmen, and the state's plantations tended to be much smaller than those of the Deep South. By the 1850s, slavery was becoming uneconomical, and the demographics began to shift as many German and Irish immigrants came to the state.

Slavery became a controversial issue in the state in the 1850s. Dred Scott vs. Sandford, the lawsuit in which the U.S. Supreme Court, in 1857, ruled that blacks were not and could never be U.S. citizens, originated in Missouri, and the moderate abolitionist stance of longtime Missouri Senator Thomas Hart Benton destroyed his political career.

Nonetheless, a Missouri state convention voted in 1861 to remain within the Union rather than secede. While 110,000 Missourians fought under the United States flag, some 40,000 of them served in the Confederate forces. A number of major battles took place in the state during the ensuing Civil War, and conflict in Missouri was characterized by savage guerrilla warfare that led to the destruction of entire towns.

After the war, anti-black extremist groups caused trouble, and many former guerrillas, most notably Jesse James, turned to banditry and continued to plague the state with violence. By the 1870s, however, stability had largely been restored in the state. Railroad building was expanded and movement toward the American West once again ensued.

Nevada

Nevada was part of land granted to the United States by the 1848 Treaty of Guadalupe Hidalgo and was initially part of the Utah Territory. Mormons founded the first permanent settlement at Genoa in the Carson Valley in 1849 and established a mission in the Las Vegas Valley in 1855. Monthly mail service across the northern part of the state began in 1853, and the Pony Express crossed central Nevada from 1860 until it was replaced by telegraphy in 1861.

Nevada's economy boomed with the discovery of the Comstock Lode of gold and silver ore in 1858, and between 1860 and 1870 the population grew sixfold, from seven thousand to forty-two thousand. Nevada separated from the Utah Territory in 1861 and was admitted to the Union on October 31, 1864; it is sometimes said to have been "Battle Born" for becoming a state in the midst of a great national war.

Nevada's major contribution to the Union during the Civil War was gold and silver bullion, used by the U.S. government as collateral for credit. This earned Nevada the nickname the "Silver State." The state raised thirteen companies of troops. One served with a California regiment and the others fought against local tribes of hostile Indians; none of the companies saw action against Confederate troops.

Mining continued to flourish in the postwar years. The first transcontinental railroad was completed across Nevada in 1869, and the Central Pacific Railroad gained the lucrative freight concession from the Comstock mines. Cattle ranching also started in the 1860s, followed by sheep herding in the 1870s. Both activities were pursued by the state's Spanish immigrant population.

New Hampshire

New Hampshire, with a population of about 326,000, was a highly-industrialized manufacturing state by the time the Civil War began. A great number of textile mills had been established from the 1810s onward, and by the 1830s, railroad lines stretching into the breadbasket of the Midwestern states eroded the role of agriculture in the local economy. Farmland was reclaimed by forest and stone walls that once marked fields and pastures crumbled. After the war, large-scale shoe factories joined the textile mills as important industries.

New Hampshire sent eighteen regiments of troops to fight for the United States, and about thirty-nine thousand men from the state served in the Union forces during the war.

New Jersey

New Jersey was divided during the Civil War, with many of its citizens having Southern sympathies. A largely Democratic state, New Jersey did not support Abraham Lincoln for reelection in 1864, casting its votes instead for former U.S. Gen. George B. McClellan, a Democrat and a son of the state who campaigned on a platform of peace even if it meant dissolution of the Union. Nonetheless, about 88,000 men from New Jersey fought under the Federal flag during the war.

New Jersey's wartime population of 672,000 people was predominantly of northern European extraction until after the Civil War, when many blacks migrated from the South in search of unskilled factory work, along with overseas immigrants from Southern and Eastern Europe.

During the nineteenth century, New Jersey gained a reputation as the home of several important inventors. In the early 1800s, John Stevens built the world's first steam ferry line and America's first steam locomotive, and later in the century Thomas Alva Edison set up shop at Menlo Park.

New York

New York has been known as the Empire State since its earliest years. At the time of the Civil War, it had the largest population of any state in the Union, swelled in part by immigrants to more than 3,880,000, and led the way in industry and manufacturing.

New York society had become more liberalized through the 1840s, abolishing slavery and seeking reform in the areas of women's rights, temperance, and education. A strong abolitionist movement had developed in New York during this period. Some 500,000 New Yorkers fought for the Union during the war, and one in ten of them was killed. Support for the war was not universal throughout the state, however, and dissent against the war effort was demonstrated most dramatically by the 1863 draft riots.

After the war, New York's economy developed rapidly, as did the state's urban areas, inflated by the vast waves of European immigrants flowing into the state. Political corruption, unjust labor practices, and inadequate social services attended these expansions.

Ohio

Ohio was strongly identified with abolitionist sentiment before and during the Civil War. The Underground Railroad was active on Lake Erie and along the Ohio River, and by 1848, the state had repealed its **black laws**. Nearly 320,000 men from the state fought for the Union. It did, nonetheless, still have a significant amount of pro-Southern Copperhead activity.

During the war, Confederate Brig. Gen. John Hunt Morgan led a cavalry raid-in-force into Ohio on July 13, 1863. Two weeks later, on July 26, Morgan and his men were captured and imprisoned as horse thieves, rather than soldiers.

At the time of the Civil War, Ohio was well-known nationally as a prosperous agricultural and industrial state and was home to about 2,400,000 people. An efficient railroad network had been growing since 1850 when the Dayton-Sandusky line opened, which had increased farm income and land values in the northern and western farming areas and encouraged development of the Ohio coal industry. Ohio was the boyhood home of U.S. General and President Ulysses S. Grant (as well as six other future U.S. presidents) and became influential on a national level as an industrial state in the decades following the Civil War.

Oregon

Oregon entered the Union as a state in 1859. At that time, it had a white population of only about fifty-two thousand and was almost completely unaffected by the hostilities. A half-dozen companies of troops were raised for local security duties but did not see action outside of the region.

Most settlers to the region came with the intention of pursuing agriculture, including beekeeping. In 1849, however, some of them were drawn to California by the discovery of gold, and others by the discovery of gold in southwestern Oregon a year later; another rush ensued in 1860, when gold was discovered in eastern Oregon. Farming and ranching were stimulated by the role of gold in the economy, and Oregon eventually began to export wheat and beef. After the war, railroad building allowed Oregon's timber and fruit to be exported across the country.

Pennsylvania

Pennsylvania contributed heavily to the Union cause during the Civil War in terms of troops and materiel. Out of a total population of around 2,906,000, some 338,000 men served in the U.S. Army and about 14,000 in the U.S. Navy.

Key routes led into Pennsylvania from the South, enticing Gen. Robert E. Lee to lead his Army of Northern Virginia into the state in 1863. His army encountered Union forces at Gettysburg, leading to a major Confederate defeat and one of the bloodiest battles of the war. Nearly a third of the Federal troops who fought in the Battle of Gettysburg were native Pennsylvanians.

Pennsylvania's steel production expanded dramatically after the war ended and, by 1870, Pittsburgh had become the primary center of the U.S. steel industry, producing more than 65 percent of the national total.

Rhode Island

Rhode Island was one of America's most industrialized states by the time of the Civil War, following a trend established by the construction in 1790 of the first factory in America, a textile mill in the Blackstone Valley. Nearly 24,000 Rhode Island men, out of a population of about 175,000, fought for the Union during the Civil War, and more than one in ten of them was killed or injured during the hostilities.

Jewelry and silverware manufacturing, whaling, and overseas trade were also important to Rhode Island. Foreign trade, however, began to decline in the 1840s and demand for whale oil waned after the discovery of mineral oil in America. In the postwar years, mills producing woolen goods began to proliferate, and the area soon became the nation's largest source of them.

Vermont

Vermont, the only New England state without a seacoast, was the region's most productive agricultural state at the time of the Civil War and had a population of about 315,000. In 1823, the Champlain Canal connected Lake Champlain with the Hudson River, allowing Vermont farmers to ship goods to New York City. This stimulated agriculture, wool production, and, in the 1860s, dairy farming, which eventually dominated the local economy.

About thirty-five thousand men from Vermont served in the U.S. forces during the war, and more than one in seven of them died during the hostilities.

In 1864, the northernmost Confederate raid into the United States occurred at St. Albans, during which twenty-two Confederate soldiers ventured across the international border from Quebec, robbed several banks, then fled back into Canada.

West Virginia

West Virginia entered the Union as a new state in 1863 after a preponderance of the citizens of western Virginia opposed secession from the Union and counter-seceded from the mother state in 1861. Its population was about 423,000.

During the Civil War, many rural West Virginians from both the lowest and highest levels of society fought for the Confederacy (about ten thousand), while the more urbanized middle classes (generally of Scots-Irish descent) tended to be typical of those who fought for the Union (about thirty-two thousand).

During the war, Union sympathizers supported by the Republican party had pushed for state-hood and made the northern panhandle city of Wheeling the capital. After the war ended, pro-Southerners gained political control of the state and made Charleston the capital in 1870. Power shifted again in 1875, when Wheeling became the capital again, until 1885, when Charleston regained the status permanently.

Wisconsin

Strong anti-slavery sentiment predominated in Wisconsin in the years leading up to the Civil War and some of its leaders actually proposed seceding from the United States if the Federal govern-ment would not make slavery illegal.

Wisconsin itself was fairly new to the Union at the beginning of the war, having become the thirtieth state on May 29, 1848. When the war began, the state had a population of about 775,000, about 300,000 of whom were recent immigrants, more than 100,000 of them from Germany. Many of these immigrants balked at volunteering to fight for their new country, and Wisconsin resorted to a draft to fill its troop quotas.

Nonetheless, some of the most stalwart units of the war came from Wisconsin, including three regiments (the Second, Sixth, and Seventh) of the legendary Iron Brigade. Altogether, the state sent more than ninety-one thousand men to fight for the Union.

War also interrupted the state's economic growth, and Wisconsin did not change or develop much from 1860 to 1870. In the following decade, however, farming expanded northward in the state, helped by the replacement of oxen with horses for draft animals, and technological innova-tions, such as the reaper. A local dairy industry also began to grow in the mid-1870s and eventually lead the state to a national reputation for cheese making.

The Confederate States

A general overview is provided for each of the Confederate states, presented in the order of their secession from the Union.

South Carolina

South Carolina had strong tendencies toward independence from the U.S. government for decades and, in 1832, a special state convention had nullified the Federal Tariff Act. President Andrew Jack-son responded with the Force Act and, although the crisis was resolved through compromise, a states'-rights movement began to grow in South Carolina.

On December 20, 1860, South Carolina became the first Southern state to secede from the Union. On April 12, 1861, South Carolinian forces fired on Union-held Fort Sumter, sparking the

Division of Maps
SEP 15 1946
Library of Congress

This map and text outline defense plans for smaller ports and inlets in South Carolina during the Civil War. It was created by Gabriel E. Manigault.

Civil War. At that time, the state was home to more than 703,000 people.

Beyond the effects of the Union blockade, some relatively minor land actions and the capture by Federal forces of Beaufort and Port Royal on November 7, 1861, the impact of war was not heavily felt in South Carolina until Union Maj. Gen. William Tecumseh Sherman invaded the state in early 1865. Throughout the course of the war, some sixty-three thousand South Carolinians fought for the Confederacy, about a quarter of whom were killed.

Reconstruction was long and hard in South Carolina, which suffered from state debt created by corrupt officials. In 1876, Reconstruction in the state ended with the election of Governor Wade Hampton (a former Confederate general) and the departure of Federal troops.

Mississippi

Mississippi left the Union on January 9, 1861, the second state to do so. Mississippi politician Jefferson Davis—a West Point graduate, member of Congress and former secretary of war—became the only president of the Confederacy.

Several Civil War actions took place in Mississippi, including much of the crucial Vicksburg campaign, which concluded in Confederate defeat in December 1863, ending Southern control over the Mississippi River Valley. Over the course of the war, about 80,000 Mississippians fought for the Confederacy, out of a population of about 791,000. After the war, Reconstruction and Federal government rule lasted until 1870, when Mississippi was readmitted to the Union.

Like other Deep South states, Mississippi's economy was based on cotton plantations.

Mississippi did not change much in the years following cessation of hostilities, and on the eve of the twentieth century, social attitudes and positions in the state were much the same as they had been before the Civil War. Freed blacks became sharecroppers, but their status and treatment remained much the same as it had been under slavery.

Florida

Florida seceded from the Union on January 10, 1861, after entering it as a slave state on March 3, 1845. In 1861, Florida's population was around 140,000, and about 63,000 of its residents were black.

Revered by some in the South as a hero, but by even more in the North as a villain, C.S. President Jefferson Davis led the Confederacy of Southern states during its four long, hard years.

Union forces captured most of the state's coastal towns early in the war, but not Tallahassee, which the Confederacy never lost during the war. Fort Jefferson, a massive fortification on the Dry Tortugas islands, served as a Union military prison during and after the war. One of the Confederacy's last victories, the Battle of Olustee, was fought in Florida on February 20, 1864. About fifteen thousand Floridians served in the Confederate forces.

In 1868, Florida adopted a new constitution that authorized voting rights for blacks and a statewide system of public education, upon which the state was readmitted to the Union. As with many Southern states during Reconstruction, Republicans held political power until 1876, when the Democrats once again took power.

Florida did not experience much economic growth until the 1880s, when phosphate deposits were discovered, citrus groves were planted, swampland was drained for farmland, and railroads were built throughout the state.

Alabama

Alabama, on the eve of the Civil War, was a predominantly rural state, and Mobile, a growing seaport, was its only sizable city. Like other Deep South states, Alabama's economy was dominated by large cotton plantations and, of its 964,000 inhabitants, 435,000 were slaves. Most of its citizens viewed slavery as an integral part of Alabama's economic and social systems. It became the fourth state to secede from the Union on January 11, 1861.

In February 1861, the Confederate States of America was established at Montgomery, which was subsequently named capital of the Confederacy (it had been the state capital since 1847); it served in that capacity until May, when Virginia seceded and the capital was moved to Richmond. A handful of land battles were fought in Alabama throughout the war. Union forces captured the Tennessee Valley in 1862 and occupied Montgomery in 1865.

One of the most dramatic actions took place in August 1864, however, when Union Flag Officer David G. Farragut led his warships into Mobile Bay—reputedly proclaiming "Damn the torpedoes, full speed ahead!"—and won a major naval victory. Some 100,000 troops from the state of Alabama fought for the Confederacy during the Civil War. About a quarter of these soldiers were killed during the conflict.

Reconstruction was a difficult period for Alabama, which refused to ratify the Fourteenth Amendment and was placed under military rule in 1867. Alabama was readmitted to the Union in 1868 after it ratified the constitutional amendment and guaranteed citizenship for blacks. Black and white Republicans wielded considerable power in the state until 1874, when white Democrats, who included among their ranks many former secessionists, regained control of the state. In the decades following the end of Reconstruction, legislators in Alabama wrote racial segregation into many state and local laws.

Prior to and during the Civil War, waterways were the primary means of transportation in Alabama; the state also had about 683 miles of railroad. One of Alabama's main newspapers during the war was the *Mobile Register*, founded in 1813.

Georgia

Georgia was a state with social, economic, and political structures that at the time of the Civil War were based largely on the needs of large-scale rice and cotton farming. Out of a total population of about 1,057,000 residents, more than 462,000 were slaves.

Increased demand for cotton had spurred settlement and plantation building in Georgia through about 1840, creating a demand for land, slaves, and removal of the local Indian population. From 1832 to 1838, the U.S. government removed Cherokees to lands in the western territories, the final segment of which became known as the Trail of Tears. As a result, much of southern Georgia was sparsely populated until well after the end of the war.

Georgia, which seceded on January 19, 1861, suffered severely during the Civil War. Its heaviest blow came when the sixty-thousand-man army of Union Maj. Gen. William Tecumseh Sherman crossed the state in 1864. Sherman's troops burned Atlanta in November and moved toward Savannah, reaching it a month later and leaving across the state a swath of destruction sixty miles wide. About seventy-five thousand Georgians fought for the Confederacy.

During Reconstruction, Georgia's state legislature refused to ratify the Fourteenth Amendment, and the Federal government placed the state under military rule until 1870, when it was readmitted to the Union.

Although slavery had been abolished, Georgia's planters, like those in several other Southern states, adopted a tenancy system that kept many blacks and whites alike in servile poverty. Georgia was largely untouched by the waves of immigrants that came to America in the decades following the war, leaving its demographics and social status quo largely unchanged.

PICKING COTTON ON A GEORGIA PLANTATION.

At the start of the Civil War, slaves made up nearly 44 percent of Georgia's population.

Louisiana

Louisiana, which seceded on January 26, 1861, occupied a strategic position on the Mississippi River, making it a Union target early in the war. On April 25, 1862, a Federal naval assault smashed through Confederate defenses on the Mississippi and captured the critical port of New Orleans. Ironically, Union control of New Orleans allowed for trade directly with the North, making it an even more important economic zone than it otherwise would have been.

Louisiana had been under French control until 1803, when it was acquired by the United States as part of the Louisiana Purchase. In 1861, the state was home to about 708,000 people, more than 331,000 of whom were slaves. Its economy was largely agricultural, with large plantations run by slave labor on one end of the scale and subsistence farming by people of Scots-Irish descent in the hills and Cajuns in the south on the other end. Waterways were the traditional transportation routes in the state since it was settled. By 1860, travel by steamboat peaked, and many communities in the state could be reached by such vessels.

Union occupation and Reconstruction took a heavy toll on Louisiana, which, along with slow moves toward industrialization, hampered the economic recovery of the state. Railroads began to improve after the war, causing the importance of the traditional steamboats to decline.

Texas

Texas entered the Union in 1845, with the former independent republic claiming all the territory from the mouth of the Rio Grande River to its source in Colorado. This claim was vigorously

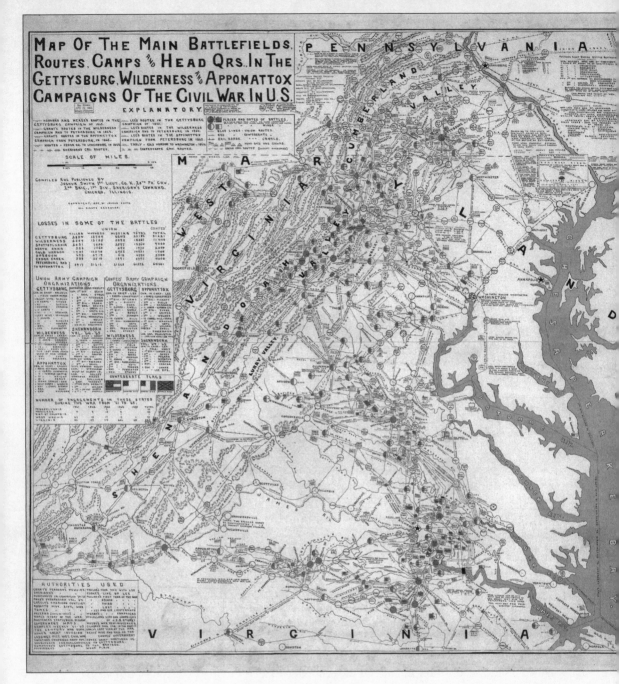

The majority of the major Civil War battles were fought on Virginia soil. This map shows the main battlefields, routes, camps, and headquarters in the Gettysburg, Wilderness, and Appomattox campaigns of the war.

Richmond, capital of the Confederacy and a constant target of Union invasions, was almost completely destroyed in the last few months of the war.

opposed by those who wanted to exclude slavery from the territories recently acquired from Mexico. In 1850, Texas relinquished its claim to parts of Colorado, Wyoming, Oklahoma, Kansas, and half of what is now New Mexico in exchange for $10 million, as part of the Compromise of 1850.

On February 23, 1861, Texas withdrew from the Union and joined the Confederacy. While the state raised ten regiments of troops for the Confederacy, some two thousand Texans volunteered for service with the Union. Little fighting took place on Texas soil. The capture and subsequent recapture of Galveston, a major supply port for the Confederacy, were the most important actions, and the Battle of Palmito Ranch, fought after the Rebel surrender at Appomattox, was the last land battle of the war.

When the Civil War ended, Texas was subjected to military rule and flooded with carpetbaggers. It was readmitted to the Union on March 30, 1870, however, after ratifying the Thirteenth, Fourteenth, and Fifteenth Amendments to the Constitution. Cattle ranching became increasingly important to the state's economy in the postwar years, and huge herds were driven over the Chisholm Trail to the railhead in Kansas.

Virginia

Virginia played a critical role during the Civil War, serving as the capital of the Confederacy and having more major battles fought on its soil than any other state. At the beginning of the war, it had a population of about 1,596,000; after its western portion became the new state of West Virginia, its population was reduced to about 1,173,000.

Virginia seceded from the Union on April 17, 1861, after Confederate forces attacked Fort Sumter and Abraham Lincoln called for mobilization of state militia forces. Soon after joining the Confederacy, Richmond became the new capital of the Confederacy, replacing Montgomery, Alabama.

Major actions on Virginia soil included the battles of First and Second Bull Run; Union Gen. George B. McClellan's Peninsular Campaign; the battles of Fredericksburg, Chancellorsville, the Wilderness, and Spotsylvania; the siege of Petersburg; and constant combat in the Shenandoah

Valley. Virginia was utterly ravaged by the end of the war and, unlike other states, actually lost a large part of its territory as a result of the Civil War, when the western part of the state counter-seceded and entered the Union as the state of West Virginia in 1863.

As in many other Southern states, radical Republicans ran the state government during Recon-struction but were replaced by more conservative politicians as soon as possible. In 1870, Virginia was readmitted to the Union.

In the nineteenth century, as today, the state was sometimes referred to as the Old Dominion, because of the decision of Charles II to make Virginia a fourth dominion of his realm, after Eng-land, Scotland, and Ireland.

Arkansas

Arkansas was acquired by the United States in 1803 as part of the Louisiana Purchase and became the twenty-fifth state in 1836.

When the Civil War began, Arkansas had a population of about 435,000, of whom 111,000 were slaves. Eastern and southern Arkansas had an economy based on cotton plantations, farmed by slaves, while northern and western Arkansas had an economy based on subsistence farming. These two halves were divided in their loyalty to the Union, the plantation owners opting for secession and the small farmers opposing it. In March 1861, the state legislature voted to remain within the Union, but this decision was reversed amidst much dissension on May 6, 1861, when the legislature voted to secede. Over the course of the ensuing war, more than fifty thousand Arkansans served in the Confederate forces, while some thirteen thousand—many black—served in the Union forces.

On March 7–8, 1862, Union forces defeated Confederate troops in an especially bloody battle at Pea Ridge, Arkansas. The Federal government took over Little Rock in 1863 and used it as a base to control the rest of the state. A new state capital was established in Washington, in southern Arkan-sas, and by early 1864 Confederate forces were confined to this part of the state.

From 1866 to 1867, Southern sympathizers in control of the Arkansas legislature passed a num-ber of measures restricting the rights of freed blacks, which led to the state being placed under Federal military rule. In mid-1868, Arkansas ratified a new state constitution and was readmitted to the Union. Republicans controlled the state government from 1867 until 1874, when the Demo-crats once again took power, for nearly a century.

Tennessee

Tennessee, torn by almost unanimous support of the Confederacy in its slave-holding middle and west, and equally fervent support for the Union in its east, was one of the last Southern states to secede, and did so on June 8, 1861.

Because of its position as a border state, Tennessee was ravaged by the Civil War. More battles were fought on its soil than any other state but Virginia, the most devastating being the Battle of Shiloh. From its population of about 1,110,000, Tennessee sent 186,652 men to fight for the Confed-eracy and 31,092 to fight for the Union.

After the Union victory at Fort Donelson on February 16, 1862, Tennessee was placed under military rule, with Andrew Johnson as military governor.

When the war ended, Tennessee was the first Confederate state to be readmitted to the Union, but Reconstruction still proved to be difficult. Agriculture made a slow revival as the mainstay of Tennessee's economy in the postwar years, coupled with moves toward industrialization.

In 1870, Democrat John C. Brown was elected governor, ending Reconstruction in the state and beginning nearly a century of Democratic domination of state politics. In 1878, while losses from the war could still be felt, a yellow fever epidemic nearly wiped out the entire population of Memphis.

North Carolina

North Carolina was a relatively progressive Southern state with an economy based largely on agriculture and tobacco plantations on the eve of the Civil War. Its population was more than 992,000.

From 1815 to 1835, the state had stagnated politically and economically, the reform-minded western portion of the state controlled by the more conservative east. In 1835, however, a reapportionment allowed the western part of the state to gain control of the state house of representatives, while the eastern part retained control of the senate. As a result, progress in education, tax reform, transportation, and women's rights, as well as agricultural expansion and greater prosperity, continued until 1860, reversing a downward economic and political spiral and discouraging a trend toward emigration to the west and south.

War brought these improvements to an end. Pro-Union sentiment stalled secession and, on May 20, 1861, North Carolina became the last state to secede. Nonetheless, 125,000 North Carolinians, more than the number of registered voters, fought for the Confederacy, and about 40,000 of them died during the course of the war. Notable Civil War events in North Carolina included the battles of Fort Hatteras, Plymouth, Fort Fisher, and Bentonville; Union Maj. Gen.l William Tecumseh Sherman's 1865 invasion; and Confederate Gen. Joseph Johnston's surrender to Sherman near Durham on April 26, 1865.

Reconstruction exacerbated the wartime political and social disruptions that had existed in the state. In 1870, the Democratic party regained legislative control and, in 1876, reelected wartime Gov. Zebulon B. Vance, ending the Reconstruction period in North Carolina.

United States Territories

In addition to the states that had been admitted to the Union, the country possessed several vast territories. These were administered loosely, if at all, and inhabited largely by Indians, pioneers, soldiers, prospectors, explorers, adventurers, outlaws, and escaped slaves.

Arizona Territory

Northern Arizona was acquired from Mexico in 1848 under the provisions of the Treaty of Guadalupe Hidalgo and, in 1853, the **Gadsden Purchase** acquired southern Arizona. Both were part of what was then the New Mexico Territory.

Much of southern Arizona had been settled by Southerners, particularly Texans, and when the Civil War broke out most Arizonans supported the Confederacy. Rebel troops occupied Tucson in February 1862, making southern Arizona a Confederate territory. Two months later, in April 1862, the one battle of the war fought on Arizona soil took place at Picacho Peak. In May 1862, U.S. Army Col. James Carlson led his California Column into Arizona, recapturing it for the United States.

President Abraham Lincoln was certain that Arizona gold and silver could be used to finance the Union war effort, and on February 24, 1863, Arizona was proclaimed a separate U.S. territory. By 1864, the white population of the territory was only about 4,500.

In the postwar years, violence broke out between settlers in the territory and the local Apaches, led by Geronimo, Cochise, and Mangas Coloradas, and continued throughout the mid-1880s.

Colorado Territory

In 1858, gold was discovered in the northern part of the Kansas Territory. On August 1, 1858, the local settlers met and established the Territory of Jefferson, roughly corresponding to what is now Colorado. Embroiled in the controversy over slavery, Congress refused to consider a partition of the Kansas Territory. Nonetheless, the local convention proceeded to adopt a constitution for the Jefferson Territory on October 24.

In February 1861, Congress formed the Territory of Colorado, superseding the illegal local government, which had been unable to effectively govern the region.

Colorado raised eleven companies of U.S. troops during the war but nearly as many men from the territory fought for the Confederacy.

Dakota Territory

In 1803, the United States acquired the Dakota Territory from France as part of the Louisiana Purchase. Trading posts like Fort Pierre, established in 1817, thrived with the fur trade. In 1859, the first permanent white settlement was founded at Yankton, made possible by a treaty with the Yanktonai Sioux. When the Civil War broke out, the territory was home to only about 2,400 whites and, in 1862, Yankton was made its capital. A number of settlements were established along the Missouri River and its tributaries over the following decade, multiplying rapidly with the arrival of the railroad in the 1870s.

In 1874, Lt. Col. George Armstrong Custer led an expedition into the Black Hills and discovered gold, which spurred settlement of the territory and the foundation of towns such as Deadwood. Conflicts with the Sioux intensified as settlers increasingly encroached on land granted to the Indians by treaty. In 1876, Custer led his troops against the Sioux, and he and nearly a third of Seventh Calvary serving under him was killed at the Battle of the Little Bighorn.

Indian Territory

Prior to the 1830s, the term "Indian Territory" was loosely applied to vast areas of the western United States occupied by Indians. In the 1830s, however, a number of laws were passed, including the 1830 Indian Removal Act and the 1834 Indian Intercourse Act, which defined Indian Territory as the area of what is now Oklahoma, Kansas, Nebraska, and the Dakota —areas into which Indians were being moved by force.

In 1854, the Kansas-Nebraska Act further curtailed Indian Territory, reducing it to the area of what is now Oklahoma, an area occupied by the Five Civilized Tribes. Justifiably unhappy with their treatment at the hands of the Federal government, these tribes allied themselves with the Confederacy during the Civil War. After the war ended, a series of 1866 treaties forced the tribes to give up the western half of their land, which became part of the new Oklahoma Territory.

Nebraska Territory

In 1803, the United States acquired the Nebraska Territory from France as part of the Louisiana Purchase. It was a vast area that encompassed what is now Montana, North Dakota, South Dakota, Wyoming, and Nebraska. It was considered part of various territories from 1803 until 1854, when the Kansas-Nebraska Act defined it as the Nebraska Territory. A territorial legislature first met on January 16, 1855.

Part of the territory was admitted to the Union as the state of Nebraska in 1867. In the 1820s, expeditions through the area led by Stephen H. Long had described Nebraska (as well as Colorado and other parts of the region) as unfit for agriculture and dismissed it as a part of the "Great American Desert." Because of this, the territory was largely ignored in favor of settlement further west. Nonetheless, enough settlers remained that Nebraska's population exploded after the Civil War, from a mere 2,732 in 1854 to more than 122,000 in 1870.

New Mexico Territory

U.S. Army Gen. Stephen Kearny captured Santa Fe and acquired New Mexico for the United States in 1846 during the Mexican War. In 1850, the Territory of New Mexico was organized. It was expanded in 1853, when the Gadsden Purchase added a strip of land in its south. In 1863, the territory was divided to create the Arizona Territory, which reduced New Mexico to its present-day boundaries.

At the start of the Civil War, Confederate forces seized much of the territory. In March 1862, however, Union troops decisively defeated the Confederates at Glorieta Pass, near Santa Fe, and the rebel forces soon withdrew from New Mexico.

When the war ended, cattle ranching became an important industry in New Mexico, leading to conflicts between cattle ranchers and sheep herders.

Utah Territory/State of Deseret

Utah was first settled in 1847 by Mormons fleeing persecution in Illinois. When they arrived, the area was still owned by Mexico. It became part of the United States in 1848, at which time the Mormons declared it the State of Deseret—which encompassed an area from Oregon to Mexico—and requested admission to the Union.

Congress refused to recognize Deseret or its boundaries, however, and created the Territory of Utah instead, roughly corresponding to the current states of Utah and Nevada, with Mormon leader Brigham Young as governor. Violence broke out between the Mormons and the local Indians, notably the Ute, and continued until 1867, when the Ute were settled on a reservation.

In 1857, the Utah War broke out between the Mormons and the U.S. government, which was opposed to the Mormon practice of polygamy, and continued until 1858, when U.S. President James Buchanan sent soldiers and a new governor to Utah. The territory was partitioned in 1861 and Nevada was granted statehood in 1864.

A wave of new settlers, many of them non-Mormons, followed the linking of the transcontinental railroad in 1869, sparking agriculture, industrialization, and the mining of gold, silver, and lead.

Washington Territory

White settlements were established in what is now Washington in the 1840s and 1850s, a period marked by constant warfare with the indigenous Indian population. In 1853, Washington was made a U.S. territory, narrowly missing being named the Columbia Territory.

Peace treaties were signed with the local Indian tribes in the following years, most notably the 1855 Treaty of Point Elliott. Settlers had been allowed by the Donation Act since before 1850 to file claims up to 320 acres for single people or 640 acres for married couples. By the early 1860s, most of the territory's accessible land was owned and occupied. When the Civil War began, the local white population was about twelve thousand.

Lumbering, mining, and salmon fishing emerged as state industries during and after the Civil War, and an area dubbed the "Inland Empire" was established for these purposes and was increasingly serviced with railroad lines.

Terms

BLACK LAWS, BLACK CODES: State and local laws regulating the behavior and status of free blacks, before, during, and after the Civil War (laws governing slaves were called slave codes). Under such laws, blacks were generally prevented from bearing arms, meeting in unsupervised groups, or testifying in court unless party to a legal proceeding. Such laws also specified harsher legal penalties for blacks than for whites, criminal rather than civil liability for some actions (such as breaking labor contracts), discriminatory vagrancy laws, and forced "apprenticeships" for black children, which were little better than slavery.

BLEEDING KANSAS: Term applied to events in Kansas during the period 1854 to 1861, in which a savage war was fought between pro- and anti-slavery factions. This border war was sparked by the Kansas-Nebraska Act of 1854, which left the question of whether Kansas or Nebraska should be slave states a matter of popular choice.

COMPROMISE OF 1850: Five laws enacted by the U.S. Congress that provided for the admission of California to the Union as a free state; organization of New Mexico and Utah as territories that could enter the Union with or without slavery; the settlement of the Texas boundary claims with the federal government assuming ten million dollars in debts contracted by the Republic of Texas; the prohibition of the slave trade—though not slavery—in the District of Columbia; and a more stringent Fugitive Slave Law. These laws were aimed at ending sectional disputes seen as threats to the Union.

GADSDEN PURCHASE: Name given to a strip of land in southern Arizona and New Mexico purchased by the U.S. government from Mexico in 1853 as an adjustment to the Treaty of Guadalupe Hidalgo. On December 30, 1853, U.S. diplomat James Gadsden signed a treaty that called for Mexico to cede a rectangular strip of about thirty thousand square miles to the United States in exchange for ten million dollars. One practical effect of the treaty would have been a railroad route to the Pacific for the South, plans that were interrupted by the Civil War.

GRANGER MOVEMENT: A movement of the 1860s and 1870s in which farmers in Minnesota, Iowa, Illinois, and Wisconsin organized to have laws passed limiting the power of railroad and warehouse monopolies.

KANSAS-NEBRASKA ACT: A May 30, 1854, act of the U.S. Congress that established the territories of Kansas and Nebraska and repealed the 1820 Missouri Compromise. Passage of the act, however, reopened controversy over the expansion of slavery in the western territories. Sectional differences between North and South were eventually aggravated to the point that reconciliation was virtually impossible, driving the country closer to the Civil War.

POLL TAX: A uniform tax that had to be paid by all adults in the taxed area. Poll taxes were used after the Civil War to prevent free blacks, who often could not afford to pay them, from voting.

TREATY OF GUADALUPE HIDALGO: Treaty signed February 2, 1848, ending the Mexican War. It recognized U.S. dominion over Texas, with the Rio Grand River as its southern border, and called for Mexico to cede to the United States what is now California, New Mexico, and Arizona. In return, the United States agreed to pay Mexico fifteen million dollars, grant citizenship to any Mexicans living in the area, assume any claims of U.S. citizens against Mexico, and recognize previous land grants in the region. Some parts of the negotiated boundary between the United States and Mexico were unsurveyable and had to be adjusted by the 1853 Gadsden Purchase.

WHERE PEOPLE LIVED:
LIFE IN CITY, TOWN, AND COUNTRY

"Throughout the ages, big cities have fascinated people because they concentrate many ways of life, displaying splendor and misery on a stage for the entire world. In nineteenth century America, the drama of the scene increased when intensified urbanization and rapid industrialization exposed people to modern life." — Gunther Barth, *City People*

America was not a widely urbanized country at the time of the Civil War but, as a result of the **Industrial Revolution**, its cities were multiplying and expanding. In the decades after the war, technology advanced rapidly, allowing farms to be tended by fewer people and creating more factory jobs in urban areas. These factors caused the nation to move toward becoming an urban, rather than a rural, society.

Where People Lived in the North

Northern society was more urbanized than the South in the middle of the nineteenth century. Virtually all of the nation's largest cities were located in the North, including the three largest, Chicago, New York, and Philadelphia, along with Boston, Cincinnati, Baltimore, and St. Louis (although the latter two were in "border states" with populaces that had significant pro-Southern sympathies). Some 5.5 million Northerners were city dwellers, about a quarter of the 22 million people living in the Union states. Most of the balance, about 16.5 million people, lived in towns or villages or on farms.

Where People Lived in the South

Southern society was far less urbanized than in the North, and only about 10 percent of the population, less than a million people, lived in cities, while the balance, just over eight million, lived in small towns and villages and on plantations and farms.

Southern cities, such as Charleston, New Orleans, and Richmond, tended to be smaller, less industrialized, and less congested than urban areas in the North.

Country Life

At the onset of the Civil War, rural people lived on farms as well as in small communities such as plantations, villages, and communes.

In 1860, the average American farm was about sixty acres in size and about a half mile away from a neighboring farm. This distance varied widely by region; farms in the West tended to be farther away from each other than farms in the East, and in newly-settled states or the territories it was often possible to go many miles without encountering any sort of homestead.

People settled in the new states and territories for a wide variety of reasons, often because land was cheap and plentiful. While many settlers embraced the isolation of rural life, many others suffered from loneliness, and periodic social events with their neighbors became very important. Another way people tried to offset the solitude and isolation of rural life in the nineteenth century, especially in the decades after the Civil War, was through the foundation of small villages, sometimes referred to as "rural neighborhoods."

Farmhouses

Far too many regional and economic differences allow for a brief description of a "typical" nineteenth-century farmhouse but there are a number of general characteristics that could be found in many of them.

For one thing, because air conditioning had not yet been invented, houses were generally constructed with lots of

FARMHOUSE FEATURES

A Nineteenth century farmhouse often included these features:

» wooden construction
» narrow rooms and lots of windows (for good air circulation)
» multiple exterior doors (for air circulation and to serve as emergency fire exits)
» a summer kitchen
» a root cellar

Godey's Lady's Book was famous for house plans. This is a modest cottage.

windows and narrow rooms to encourage air circulation. For the same reason, many houses also included summer kitchens in outbuildings or well-ventilated areas separate from the main house, in order to keep the home and main kitchen from getting too hot during the summer months.

Houses were also generally constructed with several exterior doors, and even a modest home might have one door on each side. One reason for this was because, as with ample windows, a number of doors helped facilitate good ventilation. Just as important, however, was that wooden houses were prone to catching fire and people wanted plenty of ways to get out of them. While there were fire departments in some cities at this point in time, country folk were on their own if faced with such a calamity.

Many houses were also built with root cellars, which were used primarily for storing the vegetables that families would eat during the winter.

The most large and prosperous of such dwellings generally included a ground-level bedroom that functioned as a "birthing room" when necessary but was otherwise rented to travelers for the night. Such rooms tended to be far more popular than village inns, which were often much less clean or hospitable.

Villages and Towns

Mid-nineteenth century American towns were as diverse as the people who lived in them. Their style and atmosphere ranged from neat, orderly, prosperous communities in the farm country of the West, to raw, vital boomtowns in frontier areas, to sleepy, decaying former state capitals such as Williamsburg, Virginia. The average number of people living in a town ranged from several hundred to a few thousand. Such communities often served as a center of commerce for outlying farms and smaller villages.

Town streets and sidewalks were generally not paved, nor were there streetlights. Buildings visitors were likely to find included residences, inns, taverns, general stores, churches, cemeteries, tradesmen's workshops, doctors' and lawyers' offices, or pharmacists' shops, as well as public areas where people could meet, such as town greens or commons and market squares.

Other possible features of small communities included militia armories, warehouses (especially in port or rail towns), theaters (not cinemas), hospitals or sanitariums, and town, county, or district courthouses. Also, most towns had some sort of school or educational center, and some had several (for example, Williamsburg, Virginia, had nine private schools and colleges). While there were not likely to be any public parks, there tended to be considerably more shade trees than in contemporary cities.

Facilities not likely to be present in many towns during or immediately after the Civil War included banks, telegraph offices, and railway stations (unless the town had deliberately been built along a rail line).

AROUND TOWN

At the start of the Civil War, many villages and towns included:

» inns and taverns
» general stores
» churches and cemeteries
» tradesmen's workshops
» lawyers' and doctors' offices
» pharmacists' shops
» public space such as a square or green

Leading citizens of the town generally included gentleman farmers, doctors, lawyers, and the most prosperous merchants. Other typical inhabitants included laborers, slaves, servants, lesser merchants, tavern owners, tradesmen, and innkeepers.

In areas heavily contested during the war, many towns changed hands between Federal and Confederate forces several times over the course of the hostilities, having a profound effect upon the lives of the residents of those communities. When soldiers of the same side took control of the town, the inhabitants cheered them, opened their houses to the soldiers, and provided them with food and other amenities, or even returned if they had previously fled. When enemy soldiers took control, people sometimes fled, shut up their houses, hid their food or valuables, and generally avoided the invaders as much as possible.

Most plantations had a labor force of fewer than fifty black slaves. About half of all enslaved Southern blacks were "plantation negroes."

Plantations

Plantations, one of the most characteristic institutions of the antebellum South, were large-scale agricultural ventures overseen by an owner or managers who used large slave-labor forces to produce cash crops for export. Plantations in America originated in Virginia and soon spread elsewhere, mainly to the South and West.

Plantations shared many aspects of villages, the main differences being that they were generally owned by a single individual, family, or organization and that the land around them were worked not by free white farmers but instead by black slaves. Many plantations even looked like villages. Besides a main house, plantations included buildings such as slave quarters, barns, stables, storage buildings, mills, workshops, and anything else they required. A plantation's occupants included the master and his family; overseers, who were sometimes cousins or other relatives of the owners; and a labor force of black slaves, up to several hundred on the largest plantations but fewer than fifty on most.

Many Southern plantations specialized in a single crop, usually cotton, rice, sugarcane, corn, or tobacco, as dictated by regional conditions. Cotton and sugarcane were the primary crops along the lower Mississippi River. South Carolina lead the country in rice production at the time of the war.

"During the summer months, rice crops waved over fields of thousands of acres in extent, and upon a surface so level and unbroken, that in casting one's eye up and down the [Santee] river, there was not for miles, an intervening object to obstruct the sight," one visitor wrote in *The American Monthly Magazine* in 1836, revealing the intense level of agriculture the plantation system allowed.

Plantation owners reaped the rewards of this system and were often able to use their wealth to build large houses, lead extravagant lifestyles, and dominate the economic, social, and political life of the antebellum South. This wealth and power was acquired, of course, at the expense of others, and about half of all enslaved Southern blacks were "plantation negroes."

In addition to planting and harvesting crops, plantation slaves were required to do many other activities. These included clearing land, cutting and hauling wood, digging ditches, slaughtering livestock, and repairing tools and buildings. Some slaves were taught other trades or skills needed on the plantation and served as carpenters, blacksmiths, machinists, drivers, and in other capacities. Inside the plantation house, slaves served as maids, butlers, cooks, nannies, wet nurses, and in all the other roles needed to run a large household.

America's plantation system was dealt a mortal blow by the Civil War, which ended slavery. After the war, plantation owners tried to maintain their way of life by using the sharecropping and tenancy systems to exploit free but impoverished blacks and whites alike. Eventually, however, machinery replaced mass labor and ended the viability of plantations as they had existed.

Communes

In the latter part of the eighteenth century and into the nineteenth century, various religious groups and intellectual movements in America had established and lived in communal villages, where they practiced farming and sometimes other industries. Most of the early communes were founded by conservative Christian sects, such as Mennonites, Moravians, and Shakers.

One of the most notable examples was the Amana Society, a conservative, pacifistic religious community that held all property in common. In 1842, some eight hundred members of the Amana group migrated to the United States from Germany. They settled initially in Ebenezer, New York, but eventually moved on to Iowa. The community still exists today and is known for making kitchen appliances.

Another good example are the Shakers, who established a small community at Watervliet, New York, in 1776. By 1830, some six thousand Shakers lived in communities in eight states. Shaker communes were marked by industry and became noted for manufacturing high-quality furniture. Unlike many other contemporary religious communes, the Shakers did not shun technology, and were noted for their technological innovations.

After the first quarter of the century and into the decades following the Civil War, various other groups founded communes throughout

Prior to the invention of the elevator, buildings could not practically be more than five or six stories tall and, as a result, the skylines of American cities were much lower during the war than they were by the end of the century. In 1857, Elisha Graves Otis introduced the first passenger elevator.

the country, including socialists, anarchists, Hutterites, Bohemians, Christian socialists, Theosophists, and Jews. A notable example is Robert Owen's utopian New Harmony commune in Indiana, which he founded in 1825.

Most communes lasted only a few years and then dissolved, especially in the years following the Civil War, when revivalism declined. Those based on conservative religious principles tended to enjoy the most longevity.

City Life

In the years leading up to the Civil War, increasing numbers of Americans and immigrants were being drawn to the large cities for the financial and social benefits they offered.

In the North, drafts were one of the war's most profound effects upon city dwellers. Industry, however, flourished, providing jobs for increasing numbers of immigrants.

In the South and border regions, where several cities were occupied by Federal troops (including Baltimore, New Orleans, and Charleston) or almost completely destroyed (as were Atlanta and Richmond), the war was felt much more directly. Destruction and occupation created a refugee problem, making it difficult to find adequate living space in many Southern cities. In one case, for example, six Southern families shared an eight-room house for two and one-half years.

Characteristics of Cities

American cities were generally divided up by function, into areas for industry and manufacturing; shopping, business, and entertainment; worship; education; and living.

With very few exceptions, American cities did not have any central organization. They were generally laid out on a rigid "gridiron" of city blocks, which usually did not take the natural geography in to account. These squares were further divided into lots that were owned by businesses, individuals, and other interests.

This lack of central planning was in striking contrast to most major European cities. However, Europe was a land of kings, emperors, strong central governments, and limited personal freedoms. While there were limitations, American landowners had an amazing amount of freedom in what they could do with their land. And, for the most part, the government was not empowered to direct the development of urban areas. According to Gunther Barth, author of City People, Americans "recognized neither prince, priest, nor planner as guide," even though many were subsequently "dismayed by the chaotic scenes that the free use of space produced."

A few American cities, built for specific purposes, did come into being as the result of central planning. These included Savannah, Georgia, founded in 1733 by James Oglethorpe as a mercantile and shipping center; Washington, D.C., selected by George Washington as the site of the nation's capital in 1790 and the seat of the Federal government since 1800; and Salt Lake City, Utah, founded in 1847 by Brigham Young and the Mormon church as the seat of their religion.

Prior to the invention of the elevator, buildings could not practically be more than five or six stories tall and, as a result, the skylines of American cities were much lower than they were by the

If their families did not live nearby, young and single middle- and working-class people tended to rent rooms from families who had extra space. Maiden aunts, grandparents, and orphaned nieces and nephews were far more likely to live with relatives, if possible, than on their own or as wards of the state.

end of the century. In 1857, Elisha Graves Otis introduced the first passenger elevator and, by the late 1870s, his sons had developed a hydraulic elevator with a speed of eight hundred feet per minute (a working electric elevator was introduced in 1889). Such devices encouraged the construction of much taller buildings than ever before.

The first skyscrapers were built in the years following the Civil War and included the New York Tribune Building in New York City, completed in 1875 and designed by architect Richard Morris Hunt. It was Chicago, however, that became most closely associated with skyscrapers in the decades following the Civil War.

By 1870, Chicago had a population of nearly 300,000 and had become a major American center of commerce. In October 1871, a fire broke out in a barn and quickly spread out of control, destroying a third of the city in two days. Because of elevators, architects no longer faced the same height limitations on the building designs, and a new "Chicago school of architecture" was created as designers moved toward rebuilding the city with structures that reached skyward. By 1890, the city was full of nine- and ten-story buildings.

Transportation

In the middle of the nineteenth century, the disparate areas of the city, along with its suburbs, were increasingly linked with various forms of transportation. Streetcars and horse-drawn omnibuses were among the most common forms of public transportation prevalent along major downtown streets. Horsecars were an important means of linking the cities with the middle-class suburbs, particularly in the decades immediately following the Civil War.

Areas of the city often developed in response to the sort of transportation accessible from it. This is especially true of industrial areas. Warehouse districts, for example, grew up near railway terminals, and factories were built in the corridors along railway lines.

Residential Areas

Residential areas, or neighborhoods, were divided up like everything else in the city, in their case along class lines. Living conditions between upper-, middle-, and lower- and working-class peoples were much more striking in cities than in small towns or the country, and the various classes of society reacted to the expansion of urban areas in different ways.

Wealthy families either lived in affluent enclaves in or near the city center, or moved out of the city altogether to estates accessible by the main rail lines. Middle-class people became unable to afford houses within the city and increasingly left to live in small houses in the growing suburbs accessible by streetcars or railroads or, less often in the mid-nineteenth century, rented apartments. And the poor, who could neither afford property within the city nor afford to commute from the suburbs for their menial jobs in workshops, factories, and industrial areas, lived increasingly in subdivided tenant houses and tenements.

At the time of the Civil War, more than half a million people lived in tenements in New York City alone, reaching a population density of 290,000 to the square mile in some areas.

Upper-Class Neighborhoods

The richest people lived in large houses or mansions, often built in the newest architectural styles, such as Gothic Revival and Greek Revival (see Architectural Styles on page 56), and surrounded by sweeping lawns, gardens, and outbuildings, such as carriage houses. Their exclusive neighborhoods were characterized by broad, well-lit streets, Parisian-style parks, and features like art museums. Such neighborhoods, however, represented a distinct minority and were vastly outnumbered by lower-class living areas.

Middle-Class Neighborhoods

Middle-class families tended to live in rowhouses, freestanding wood-frame houses or, less often in the 1860s, in apartments (generally known in mid-nineteenth-century America as "French Flats"). The size and stylishness of such homes varied widely depending on the incomes of their occupants; the families of prosperous merchants might live in attractive brownstone rowhouses, while those of clerks tended to live on long streets of small, identical homes with tiny front yards.

Young and single middle- and working-class people did not live alone as frequently during the 1860s as they do today. If their families did not live nearby, they tended to rent rooms from families who had extra space. Likewise, in an era of extended families, maiden aunts, grandparents, and orphaned nieces and nephews were far more likely to live with relatives, if possible, than on their own or as wards of the state. And, in contemporary cities, a majority of homeowners with spare rooms would rent them out to single boarders, often in conjunction with board or an arrangement to share common areas, such as a kitchen or parlor.

Lower- and Working-Class Neighborhoods

The poorest strata of society, which comprised about half the people in many cities, lived either in small, shabby wood-frame houses or, increasingly, in tenant houses and tenements. Working-class people in planned industrial communities, such as Lowell, Massachusetts, also lived in company-owned boarding houses, dormitories, and rowhouses.

"The first tenement New York knew bore the mark of Cain from its birth," wrote journalist Jacob August Riis in 1890 of the once-fashionable houses along the East River that were subdivided into tenant rooms in the first decades of the century. The large rooms of these dwellings were divided into numerous smaller rooms, the rate of rent being determined by the size of the partitioned space. The higher it was above the street, the lower the rent.

Racing was America's most popular spectator sport prior to the rise of professional baseball, and tracks had existed since before the Civil War.

Specially-built tenant buildings, even worse than subdivided houses, were wooden structures two to four stories high built behind houses in spaces once used for gardens. Such rear tenant houses were often unsound and subject to collapse or fire. Often, more rental space was realized by the upward expansion of the front houses, although, in the words of a contemporary observer, adding such levels "often carried [the building] up to a great height without regard to the strength of the foundation walls."

Tenements were the worst of the dwellings available to the poor. Distinct from any other sort of housing, tenements were often warrens of tiny spaces partitioned from huge abandoned hulks, such as churches or warehouses, or from entire city blocks. A description of the tenement from a nineteenth-century court case cited by Riis in *How the Other Half Lives* captures its spirit all too well.

"It is generally a brick building from four to six stories high on the street, frequently with a store on the first floor, which, when used for the sale of liquor, has a side opening for the benefits of the inmates and to evade the Sunday law," the brief states. "Four families occupy each floor, and a set of rooms consists of one or two dark closets, used as bedrooms, with a living room twelve feet by ten. The staircase is too often a dark well in the center of the house, and no direct through ventilation is possible, each family being separated from the other by partitions. Frequently, the rear of the lot is occupied by another building of three stories high with two families on a floor."

At the time of the Civil War, more than half a million people lived in tenements in New York City alone, reaching a population density of 290,000 to the square mile in some areas. There were numerous examples of tenement houses in which were lodged several hundred people with barely two square yards of living space each.

Most of the people who lived under such squalid conditions were recent immigrants, largely Irish, Italians, Scandinavians, Germans, and Dutch. Most of them were industrious people who lived in tenement conditions because of their desire to work, which they could do only if they lived in the city; in the absence of automobiles or public transportation into the suburbs, people were unable to live outside of the city and commute into work, as so many do today.

Rent for tenements was usually paid a month in advance. Ironically, the cost of renting such miserable rooms was often 30 or 40 percent higher than it would be to rent small, clean, country cottages. However, jobs for the masses were available only in the cities, so people were forced to pay extortionate rates to live under wretched conditions. De facto slavery, then, was a fact of life in the North as well as the South. In light of this, it is more comprehensible, while no less tragic, that Irish laborers rioting in the summer of 1863 took out their anger against blacks, whom they saw as beneficiaries of the war against the South.

Death was a daily fact for people in the worst tenement districts. Infant mortality rates were as high as one in ten in some areas (i.e., considerably worse than many developing countries today). Suicide was also not uncommon. One sad episode involved a young immigrant couple who occupied a room less than ten feet by ten feet; they drank poison together rather than continue their dreary existence. And disease, which often left upper-class districts of the city untouched, could kill nearly 20 percent of the people in the most congested areas. In New York City, the general mortality rate for the city as a whole was 1 in 41.83 in 1815. With the rise of the tenement, this general rate rose to 1 in 27.33 in 1855.

Pigs, the most common urban scavengers, were among the hazards people had to deal with in the worst parts of the city. Such beasts could be aggressive and dangerous, especially to women and children, and their presence persisted on New York City streets until the winter of 1867, when city ordinances were passed prohibiting them from being allowed to roam in built-up areas.

Urban Recreation Areas

As urban areas expanded in the early and mid-nineteenth century—and as property values increased—green spaces within cities shrank and disappeared. As a result of this, city dwellers began to crave areas reminiscent of the country. This, in conjunction with a variety of other factors, led to the rise of public parks.

Unfortunately, people's use of public parks for leisure activities took a toll upon the grass, trees, and other plants. This led to officials spending an inordinate amount of time and energy in preventing people from actually using, and thus damaging, public parks. To a great extent, this diminished the value of parks to many city dwellers.

In the absence of parks, cemeteries became popular places for people to meet and walk. Venues for spectator sports that included green areas, such as racetracks and baseball parks, were also very popular with city dwellers, certainly to some extent because of their appearance, as well as for what they were used for. Racing was America's most popular spectator sport prior to the rise of professional baseball, and tracks had existed since before the Civil War. And, while baseball had been growing in popularity since the 1840s, it was usually played in parks, fields, and empty lots until after the Civil War, when specialized parks began to be built for the sport.

City Water and Sewage Systems

Indoor plumbing depended on municipal water systems, something that had only come into existence in America a few decades before the Civil War and was still not widespread by 1861. Crowding in urban areas, however, spurred by the Industrial Revolution, had necessitated development of city water and sewage systems.

While most urban areas were equipped with storm drains, disposal of human waste into them had generally been prohibited, but as city populations swelled, it became more and more difficult to prevent the drains from being abused in this way. In the absence of adequate means for providing fresh water and carrying away filth, sewage flowed into lakes, rivers, and tidal estuaries. The bodies of water and shallow wells from which people drew their drinking water became heavily contaminated with disease-bearing organisms.

Waterborne diseases like cholera spread unchecked in some cities. In the years following the Civil War, one particularly savage outbreak in Chicago, caused by sewage accidentally flowing into the water system, killed a quarter of the population, some 75,000 people. Chicago responded by developing one of the most advanced water systems in the country, and the threat of such outbreaks prompted administrators in other cities to create adequate water supply systems.

URBAN WATER WORKS In the early 1800s, the invention of the steam engine meant that pumps could be used for maintaining water pressure in city water supply systems. In 1820, Philadelphia was the first American city to finish building municipal water works and, in 1823, Boston completed the first American sewer system.

New York City provides an excellent example of an early water supply and transmission system. Begun in 1830 with the construction of the Croton Reservoir—an impoundment of the Croton River that was completed in 1842—the system conveyed water to the city through a massive system of gravity tunnels that were long considered one of America's greatest engineering feats.

Water filtration systems were first installed in America in Poughkeepsie, New York, in the 1870s (although even by 1900, only ten filtration plants were in operation throughout the entire country).

TOILETS AND THE LIKE Prior to the existence of plumbing, people had generally used outhouses. An outhouse was known as such in the mid-nineteenth century, and might also be called a "privy," "privy house," **"jake," "joe"** or **"john"** by rural or lower-class people, and as a "house of office," "necessary house" or "necessary" in more polite society. When separate outhouses were available for men and women, the door to the men's was often marked with a sun and the women's with a crescent moon.

Many middle class Americans lived in small wood-frame houses or cottages.

Chamber pots were also kept indoors, usually under the bed, for use at night, by the sick, or in case of emergencies. Other common names for these implements included "piss pot" and "potty" (for a small chamber pot, as for one used by a child). In the homes of affluent people, a chamber pot was sometimes embellished to look like something else and was referred to as a "commode" or a *"chaise perce."*

In the mid-1700s, privies began to appear inside of upper-class homes. Initially, these were little more than small rooms containing a chair with a hole in the seat and a chamber pot beneath it (which still had to be emptied, of course). Such a privy was referred to as a "water closet," "closet stool," or "close stool." Actual toilets, sometimes called "**quinces**," did not come into use until the 1820s, and only then in areas where municipal sewage existed. Toilet covers followed by the late 1830s. By the 1850s, urinals were being used by men in urban areas.

Toilet paper did not become available until the 1880s. Prior to that, people used materials like leaves, corn shuckings, and old newspapers.

BATHING By the 1830s, many Americans were bathing on a weekly basis, generally on Saturday night so they would be clean for Sunday services. This was a radical departure from even a generation earlier, when it was only the wealthy or the eccentric who bathed regularly. A generation before that, bathing had been considered immodest, uncomfortable, and unnecessary, and many people went their entire lives without ever bathing.

In the 1830s, people generally bathed in large wood or tin tubs in front of a fireplace or kitchen stove where water could easily be heated. During this period, the term "bathroom" was used to refer to a room used only for bathing and which did not contain a toilet, as today.

By the mid-1850s, the homes of some affluent people included bathrooms in the modern sense, with both a bathtub and a toilet (one of the first was installed in 1855 in the New York City mansion of George Vanderbilt).

The trend toward bathing more frequently continued after the end of the Civil War. In 1865, Vassar College made it mandatory for girls to bathe twice a week. By the 1880s, an estimated 15 percent of all American city folk had indoor bathrooms of some sort.

Architectural Styles

Several distinct styles of architecture predominated in America during the 1860s and could be found in the country's homes, churches, government buildings, memorials, and other structures. Naturally, some of these styles persisted from earlier decades (e.g., Georgian), as homes and public buildings were not torn down and replaced just because new styles developed.

As a loose rule, the styles that predominated in the eighteenth century had their origins in England and those that developed during the nineteenth century were characterized by Romantic revivals and eclecticism.

In the years leading up to, during, and following the Civil War, the Georgian, Neoclassic, Greek Revival, Corporate, Egyptian Revival, Italianate, Second Empire Baroque, High Victorian Gothic, and Richardsonian Romanesque were all major influences on American architecture. These styles are further described below, along with a few examples of each (mostly public buildings, with which people are more likely to be familiar).

Georgian

Georgian (1714–1776) was an English-inspired style of architecture that predominated in America until the Revolution. Named for England's King George I, who ascended the throne in 1714, this style of architecture showed a greater concern for style and higher standards of comfort than earlier styles. Georgian architecture, however, carried the taint of British imperialism and colonialism, and it was abandoned after independence was achieved. Georgian-style buildings proliferated throughout the New England and the Southern colonies, and good examples include the Old North Church (1723) and the Old State House (1712), both in Boston.

Neoclassicism

Neoclassicism (1750–1850), influenced heavily by Thomas Jefferson, supplanted Georgian architecture in America and came to represent the political and social identity of the new nation. It included several variations, including Federalist, Idealist, Rationalist, and Greek Revival.

FEDERALIST architecture, heavily influenced by English models, was especially prevalent in New England and was used for many official structures. A good example is the State House in Boston (1795–1798), designed by architect Charles Bulfinch.

IDEALIST architecture was an intellectual and moral approach to classicism that was at first inspired by Roman models. Symbolism played an important role in this style, an excellent example of which is Thomas Jefferson's Monticello (1770–1809) in Charlottesville, Virginia.

RATIONALIST architecture emphasized classical structure and building techniques, such as stone vaulting and domes.

GREEK REVIVAL became the first truly national American style of architecture and, being very adaptable, appeared in all sorts of buildings, public and private, throughout every part of the country. One reason this style became so popular was that it was strongly associated with classical traditions and democracy, making it ideal for the buildings of a young republic. Examples include the

Italianate-style villas were popular as both country and city residences for well-to-do families.

Ohio State Capitol, Columbus, Ohio (1838–1861), designed predominantly by painter Thomas Cole; and the Treasury Building, in Washington, D.C. (1839–1869), designed by architect Robert Mills. This style was also used for many mansions and Southern plantation houses.

Corporate

Corporate (1800–1900) architecture was a practical style used for commercial and industrial structures, especially factories, and, in its time, was considered to be a "style-less style."

Egyptian Revival

Egyptian Revival (1820–1850) was used primarily for memorials, cemeteries, prisons, and, later, warehouses. The most famous American example of this architectural style is the Washington Monument, an Egyptian-style obelisk.

Gothic Revival

Gothic Revival (1820–1860) architecture, based on English and French styles of the twelfth to fifteenth centuries, was strongly associated with religion and nature and was used for both ecclesiastic and residential structures, from urban churches to rural cottages. Good examples include St. Patrick's Cathedral (1858–1879) in New York City, designed by architect James Renwick, and the "wedding cake" house, built around 1850 in Kennebunkport, Maine.

Italianate

Italianate (1840–1860), or Italian Villa Mode, was an architectural style inspired by Renaissance models that was used for domestic structures, notably country houses and villas.

Large, well-built farmhouses were evidence of the prosperity of many American farmers both before and after the Civil War.

Second Empire Baroque

Second Empire Baroque (1860–1880) originated in France and was largely influenced by the additions to the Louvre in the 1850s and the construction of the Paris Opera. In America, this style was used for both public and residential structures. Good examples include the State, Navy, and War Building in Washington, D.C., designed by architect Alfred B. Mullet, and City Hall in Philadelphia (1868–1901), designed by architect John MacArthur.

High Victorian Gothic

High Victorian Gothic (1860–1880), which originated in England and was named for Queen Victoria I, was used for public, religious, and residential buildings. Good examples include the Pennsylvania Academy of Art (1876), in Philadelphia, designed by architect Frank Furness, and the First Church (1868) in Boston, designed by architects William Ware and Henry Van Brunt.

Richardsonian Romanesque

Richardsonian Romanesque (1870–1895), named for designer Henry Hobson Richardson, was a revival style based on French and Spanish Romanesque styles of the eleventh century. Structures built in this style are somber and dignified and characterized by massive stone walls, dramatic semicircular arches, and a dynamism of interior space that was new at the time. Richardsonian Romanesque was the last major style to influence American architecture in the years immediately after the Civil War and eclipsed all others for a time. Good surviving examples are Grace Church (1867–1869) in Medford, Massachusetts, and Trinity Church in Boston (1872–1877), both designed by Richardson himself.

Costs of Homes and Housing

What it cost to buy a home or rent living space varied widely from city to country and from North to South during the Civil War. Following, however, are some examples of what it cost to buy or rent a home. Some of the costs for homes are from contemporary catalogs and publications, and editorials of the day sometimes derided them as being overpriced.

	COST IN THE 1840S	COST IN THE 1850S
prairie-style farmhouse:	$800 to $1,000	
large but modest farmhouse		$2,000 to $3,000
larger, nicer farmhouse		$3,000 to $6,000
large, extravagant country house		$3,000 to $14,000

	COST
house	$500 per year (In areas affected by wartime housing shortages, this price was at least doubled.)
room and board in a boarding house	$30 to $40 per month (1862).
furnished house	$80 per month (1863)
third-story front room, without carpeting or gas for heat or light	$60 per month (1863)
sleeping/dining room, plus use of parlor	$60 per month plus one-half the gas bill (1863)
room and board in a rooming house	$50 or more per month (1863)
furnished rooms	$25 to $110 per room, per month (1864)
Rooms in a tenement for a family (in a rear building divided up for ten families, worth $800 altogether)	$5 per month
Stable, rented as a dwelling (one of twenty on a fifty foot by sixty foot lot, worth $600 altogether)	$15 per year

Terms

INDUSTRIAL REVOLUTION: The shift from an agrarian into an industrial society that began in America at the end of the eighteenth century and continued throughout the nineteenth century. A central aspect of the revolution was a radical increase in per capita production, facilitated by the mechanization of manufacturing.

....

JAKE, JOE, JOHN: Slang terms used primarily by men to refer to either outhouses or chamber pots.

....

QUINCY: slang term for a toilet that originated in 1825, when a toilet was first installed in the White House during the presidency of John Quincy Adams, an event that prompted much debate and many jokes.

....

3

EDUCATION:
FROM SCHOOLHOUSES TO UNIVERSITIES

"Education is that which discloses to the wise and disguises from the foolish their lack of understanding." — Ambrose Bierce

While opportunities for education of various sorts were widespread throughout the United States during the era of the Civil War, they were by no means uniformly available or of the same quality from region to region, nor were they available to people of all races or economic means. Many changes in education took place in the decades leading up to the conflict, and these changes impacted the people who lived during the war by shaping their knowledge base.

Most education, both public and private, was geared toward preparing an elite few for college. Curricula and educational materials were classical in nature and tended to stress the importance of morality and civic duty, and an ability to read and write in Greek and Latin was emphasized (although German and French predominated as acceptable second, modern languages).

The first schools in America were founded in the 1600s, the earliest in Massachusetts, starting in 1635 with the Boston Latin School and followed a year later by Harvard University. Within a few decades, all of the

New England colonies had established some sort of mandatory education programs for boys, the emphasis generally being on grammar schools intended to prepare the sons of relatively affluent families for college. Educational prospects for girls or the sons of the less privileged were considerably more rare.

In the 1700s, "**common schools**," began to appear throughout the country. These typically did not grade students in any way and, while they were generally supported by the community, were typically not free and charged some sort of tuition. And, while some public support for female education did exist in New England by 1767, such programs were optional and many communities were reluctant to underwrite either female schooling or institutions that would benefit poor families. In communities where everyone was taxed to support schools, desire to support them was generally limited while in communities that assessed school taxes only against those who had children, there was typically widespread support for programs that would benefit boys and girls of all social classes.

> Teaching children was not a prestigious occupation in the early nineteenth century. Many teachers during this era were not especially well-qualified.

Various religious denominations founded most early American colleges for the purposes of training clergymen and, in New England in particular, literacy was a priority so that people would be able to read the Bible. Most of the institutions of higher education that began operating between 1640 and 1750 are members of what has since become known as the Ivy League (a term that did not come into widespread use until the 1950s), including Brown, Columbia, Harvard, the University of Pennsylvania, Princeton, and Yale.

Education flourished in some quarters in the years following the American Revolution, especially in the North. Private academies sprung up in cities and towns across the country, and Americans overall had one of the highest rates of literacy in the world at the time of the Civil War. In rural areas, however—especially in the South— there were few schools established prior to the 1880s.

Teaching children was not a prestigious occupation in the early nineteenth century and many of the most educated people of the time were not interested in doing so, meaning that many teachers during this era were not especially well-qualified. Local school boards were responsible for verifying the credentials of the teachers they hired but, as often as not, the board's primary concerned was to not overspend tax dollars. Starting in 1823, however, with the foundation of the Columbian School in Concord, Vermont, an increasing number of two-year normal schools—institutions designed to train teachers to provide primary education—were established throughout the country. In the decades leading into and following the Civil War, a growing number of elementary-school teachers received training from such schools.

Starting in the late 1830s, particularly in the North, more private academies were established throughout the country for the purposes of educating girls beyond primary school, and some of these offered a classical curriculum similar to that provided for boys. Starting in 1840, the national census conducted once every ten years included questions related to education and literacy, and the responses indicated that of the 1.88 million boys and 1.8 million girls between the ages of five and fifteen, somewhat more than half attended some sort of primary schools or academies.

Nationwide, the school system was largely private and unorganized until two decades before the onset of the Civil War, when the Federal government began to play a larger role in education. However, public secondary schools did not begin to outnumber private academies until the beginning of the twentieth century.

One-room schoolhouses with one teacher were common in rural areas.

Throughout the nineteenth century, one-room schoolhouses in which a single teacher provided all the primary and secondary education for the school were a phenomenon of rural areas that had low population densities but a high proportion of young people. Spread-out farming communities without central areas sometimes had anywhere from two to a half-dozen such facilities. Schools were placed so that children would not have to travel too far to attend them and so that children could be home in time to do their afternoon chores. Sessions at such schools were also most likely to be conducted in the cold-weather months, when students had less work on family-run farms.

In the five decades between the end of the Civil War and the beginning of World War I, the growth of urban areas, influx of foreign immigrants, and national spirit of reform all played a role in transforming the character of American education. More high schools were established and their curriculum was modified to prepare students for the expanding private and state colleges and universities. Education also began to shift away from a classical nature to more a vocational and utilitarian style.

Educational Movements

A number of educational movements occurred in the years leading up to, during, and after the Civil War that affected the education people received during the era. These included the establishment of common and normal schools throughout the country, the concept of "republican motherhood," and the establishment of **land-grant institutions**.

Common and Normal Schools

In 1837, Horace Mann became secretary of education in Massachusetts and set about creating a statewide system of "**normal schools**" to train professional teachers. He also established "common schools" for primary and secondary education. Common schools were developed from a model used in Prussia that was based on the idea that everyone was entitled to a uniform education.

Mann postulated that universal public education was the best means of transforming the country's undisciplined youth into conscientious citizens of the republic, and his ideas were widely accepted by progressives and fellow Whigs.

Establishment of public common and normal schools in accordance with Mann's guidelines began to spread throughout the North, especially in New England, and most states eventually adopted something at least reminiscent of the system of schools he had established.

Republican Motherhood

In the early nineteenth century, a number of influential female writers in New England began proffering the idea that, as the people tasked with taking care of children, women were the best qualified to serve as their teachers. Especially popular in urban areas, this concept of "republican motherhood" was an early family-values movement that linked the success of the burgeoning nation with the virtue of its families.

By the 1840s, these apologists for republican motherhood had begun to successfully make the case that educational opportunities for women and girls should be expanded and improved and that they should be granted greater access to subjects previously offered only to males. Such subjects, including philosophy and mathematics, became increasingly essential elements in the curricula for girls at both public and private schools. In the years during and following the Civil War, such institutions were increasingly spreading and bolstering a growing tradition of women as the teachers and overseers of American ethical and moral values.

These ideas became widespread throughout the country and went a long way toward enhancing the status of women and convincing people of the need for girls to be educated so that they could become effective and virtuous teachers and mothers of good citizens.

While these ideas had their genesis in the North, they caught on in the South as well, and private female academies—made possible through donations and community spirit—were established in towns throughout the region. Plantation owners in particular were interested in educating their daughters, not least of all because a complete education could make them more marriageable and even serve as a substitute for dowry payments.

Such Southern female academies had a broad, structured curriculum that emphasized proficiency in writing, penmanship, arithmetic, and foreign languages. By the 1840s, these schools were producing a refined and literate body of women well-suited to serve as the wives and mothers of the upper crust of Southern society.

The "republican motherhood" movement promoted the idea that women were the best suited to teach.

Land-Grant Institutions

Passed by the U.S. Congress during the Civil War, the Land-Grant Colleges Act of 1862, also called the Morrill Act, provided federal funds for states to establish educational institutions that specialized in agriculture, engineering, and military studies. Such facilities were known as "land-grant" institutions.

Some of the first schools to be established under these provisions included Kansas State University (1863), Cornell University in New York (1865), the University of California (1868), Purdue University (1869) in Indiana, The Ohio State University (1870), and Texas A&M University (1871). Michigan State University and Pennsylvania State University were both founded as state land-grant schools ahead of the Morrill Act, in 1855.

Such schools were generally intended to bolster the declining importance of agrarian values in America. Another goal was to teach farmers more effective agricultural techniques, and students were often expected to cover part of their expenses and strengthen their character by performing agricultural labor. This requirement was increasingly dropped at land-grant institutions; many such schools did not have well-developed agricultural curricula anyway. In practice, few alumni became farmers. Instead they moved on to middle-class, white-collar occupations of various sort, which lead many contemporary politicians to criticize such schools as expensive and useless experiments.

Where the land-grant institutions proved their value, however, was in training the cadre of industrial engineers and agricultural scientists who, for the half-century following the Civil War, led the rapid expansion and industrialization of the country and its establishment as a technology-based world power.

> Students attending land-grant universities were often expected to cover part of their expenses and build character by performing agricultural labor, but few alumni became farmers, instead moving on to middle-class, white-collar occupations.

Education in the North

Public primary education was fairly widespread in the Northern states, especially in urbanized areas. Many institutions of higher education had existed in these states since Colonial times, and new colleges continued to be established throughout the nineteenth century. As a result, Northerners enjoyed a relatively high level of education and literacy.

New England in particular was on the cutting edge of education for the country in general, and communities across both the North and the South adopted many of the improvements developed there in one form or another, as illustrated by Massachusetts' normal school and common school models.

A great number of educational institutions that were founded in the nineteenth century were subsequently renamed and expanded in the decades or century following their initial establishment, but their beginnings shaped the minds of the Civil War generation.

California

California's 1849 constitution called for free statewide public education. One of the first colleges established in the state was the Contra Costa Academy in Oakland in 1853, founded for purposes of training its students to establish a Christian college. They did so in 1855 with the foundation of the College of California, a private institution that was merged with the public Agricultural, Mining, and Mechanical Arts College in 1868 to form the University of California, one of the country's earliest land-grant institutions (which, in 1873, was relocated from Oakland to Berkeley).

Other institutions of higher education in California included Santa Clara University, a private Jesuit school that is the oldest university in the state; the University of the Pacific, a private university that was affiliated with the United Methodist Church at the time of its establishment (1851); Mills College, an independent liberal arts women's college (1852); and the University of San Francisco, another private Jesuit university (1855).

Connecticut

Influenced to a great extent by its neighbor to the north, Connecticut adopted a system of normal and common school in 1849 similar to those established by Horace Mann in Massachusetts.

Historic institutions of higher education in the state include Yale University (1701), the American School for the Deaf (1817), Trinity College (1823), and Wesleyan University (1831). It was also home to Litchfield Law School, the country's first law school, which operated from 1773 to 1833.

Boarding schools operational during the era of the Civil War would have included Cheshire Academy (1794), Suffield Academy (1833), Miss Porter's School (1843), the Gunnery (1850), and Loomis Chaffee (1874).

Private day schools included Hopkins School in New Haven (1660), the Norwich Free Academy in Norwich (1854), and King Low Heywood Thomas in Stamford (1865).

Hartford Public High School (1638) is the second oldest secondary school in the United States and the Hopkins School (1660) is the fifth oldest.

Delaware

Delaware had established public primary and secondary education in 1829, but it was underfunded, uneven in quality, and excluded blacks.

The University of Delaware was chartered in 1833 and grew out of a Presbyterian "Free School" that had originally been founded some ninety years earlier during the Colonial era and was operated out of the home of minister Francis Alison (and had evolved into the Academy of Newark by 1769). Other institutions included the Wilmington Conference Academy (1873, renamed Wesley Collegiate Institute in 1918).

Illinois

Educational institutions active during the era of the Civil War in Illinois include private North-western University, founded in 1851 by nine Chicago businessmen to serve the people of what had just a generation before been the Northwest Territory; Illinois State University, the oldest public university in the state and the legal documents for which were drawn up by lawyer Abraham Lincoln; Illinois Industrial University, founded in 1867 as a land-grant school and the basis of what would eventually become the University of Illinois at Urbana-Champaign, the second-oldest public university in the state; and Saint Ignatius College, a Jesuit institution founded in 1870 that became Loyola University Chicago.

Indiana

In 1816, the Indiana constitution was the first in the nation to establish a state-funded public school system, and it also allocated a township for development into a public university. These plans were too ambitious for a frontier society, however, and there was initially not enough of a tax base to support them. A new state constitution in 1851 included provisions for supporting such educational institutions and, while the development of a system of public schools was impeded by legal red tape, a number of elementary schools were open by 1870.

America's first free kindergarten, trade school, and coeducational teaching system were nonetheless founded in New Harmony in the first half of the nineteenth century. In 1801, Jefferson Academy was founded and it subsequently became Vincennes University; the Indiana State Seminary was founded in 1820 and became the basis for Indiana University; the University of Notre Dame was founded as an all-male Catholic school in 1842; Taylor University was founded in 1846, the first evangelical Christian college in the country; Indiana Asbury University was founded in 1837 and went on to become DePauw University; Moores Hill College was founded in 1854 and subsequently became the University of Evansville; Butler University, one of the country's first higher education institutions to admit women, was opened in 1855; and Purdue University was established as a land-grant institution in 1869.

Iowa

One of the most significant educational institutions at the time of the Civil War was the Iowa Agricultural College and Model Farm, founded in 1858 in Ames, reclassified in 1864 as the nation's first land-grant institution, and eventually renamed Iowa State University of Science and Technology. Other public institutions included the University of Iowa, founded in 1847, and the University of Northern Iowa, founded in 1876.

Kansas

Kansas' first colleges were chartered by acts of the Kansas Territorial legislature and signed by the territorial governor in February 1858, and, of the ten institutes of higher education established at that time, three survive in some form. These include Baker University, the oldest continuously-operating college in the state; Highland University, now Highland Community College; and Blue Mont Central College, now Kansas State University. Other institutions of higher education included the University of Kansas (1866) and Emporia State University (1863).

Kansas' public universities were among the first in the nation to become coeducational, Kansas State University being the third and the University of Kansas (1869) the fifth.

Kentucky

Kentucky's first school opened in 1775, and a public school system was established by the state legislature in 1838. Higher education institutions included Transylvania Seminary, chartered in 1780 and the oldest university west of the Allegheny Mountains; the University of Louisville, founded in 1798; and the University of Kentucky, established in 1865 as a land-grant institution. It is also home to Berea College (1855), the first coeducational institution of higher learning in the South to admit both black and white students, which it did starting from when it was founded.

Maine

Maine had a well-established tradition of higher education by the time of the Civil War. Its public institutions of higher learning included Western State Normal School (1864), a teaching school that eventually became the University of Maine at Farmington, and the Maine College of Agriculture and the Mechanic Arts (1865), a land-grant institution that became the University of Maine.

Maine's private institutions of higher education included Bowdoin College (1794), Colby College (1813), Bangor Theological Seminary (1814), and Bates College (1855). One of the most famous Union heroes of the Civil War, Maj. Gen. Joshua Chamberlain, was a professor of rhetoric at Bowdoin when the war began, and he took a leave of absence from teaching to serve in the 20th Maine Volunteer Infantry Regiment.

Maryland

Statewide education was established in Maryland in 1826 but excluded blacks because Maryland was a slave state. In 1867, a separate school system was established for black students.

The University of Maryland in Baltimore is the state's oldest public institution of higher learning and was founded in 1807. The Maryland Agricultural College was established in 1856, became a land-grant institution in 1864, and is today better known as the University of Maryland College Park. Southern sympathies were strong in Maryland throughout the war and, when Confederate troops briefly occupied this campus, it was noted how well its administrators got along with the invaders.

Johns Hopkins

One of the most significant private institutions of higher education in the state is Johns Hopkins University (1876), founded with a grant from the Baltimore entrepreneur for whom it is named.

Massachusetts

Education at every level—from primary to university—had been important in Massachusetts since its earliest days, and the state was undoubtedly the leader in American schooling by the time of the Civil War; in 1642, the Massachusetts Bay Colony made "proper" education compulsory and nearly every system of teaching currently used in the United States originated in Massachusetts before or during the nineteenth century.

Boston Latin School, both the nation's first public secondary school and oldest-existing school in the United States, opened in 1635; Harvard, the first college, was founded in 1636; the Roxbury Latin School opened in Boston in 1645; Boston started the first public high school in the country in 1821; the first high school for girls was established in 1826; and the first public normal school in the nation, the Framingham Normal School, was founded in 1839.

Massachusetts passed a compulsory attendance law for primary and secondary education in 1852, ensuring that all children would receive at least some formal education.

Michigan

Public education had been important in Michigan since 1787, when the Northwest Ordinance called for the future state to "encourage education." America's first state primary school fund was established in 1837, free primary schooling was made available in 1869, and in 1874 the state supreme court upheld the legality of using local taxes to pay for the establishment of high schools.

Public institutions of higher education during the era of the Civil War included the University of Michigan Ann Arbor (originally founded as the Catholepistemiad in Detroit in 1817, two decades before Michigan even became a state); Michigan State University (1855), a state land-grant institution; and Detroit Medical College (1868), the oldest part of what is now Wayne State University.

Private institutions at the time of the war included Grand Traverse College (1858), which later changed its name to Benzonia College and closed its doors in 1918 (and which was the alma mater of noted Civil War historian Bruce Catton).

Minnesota

In 1849, Minnesota's territorial government established provisions for school districts and declared that common schools were to be open to all people between the ages of four and twenty-one, supported by a general sales tax and part of the proceeds from fines and licenses. However, by the early 1850s, only about 250 children were enrolled in three privately-operated schools. In 1858, the state legislature established a normal school in Winona.

Public institutions of higher education during the era of the Civil War included the University of Minnesota, which was founded in 1851 but, because of financial problems and the onset of the Civil War, was unable to actually begin enrolling students until 1867.

Private institutions included Northfield College (1866), now known as Carleton College; Augsburg College (1869) in Minneapolis; and St. Olaf College (1874), also in Northfield.

Missouri

Before the Civil War, primary and secondary education in Missouri took place mainly in private institutions. In the years following the war, however, free public education became available in most parts of the state.

Higher education institutions included St. Louis University (1818), the University of Missouri (1839, the first state university west of the Mississippi), Washington University (1853), and Lincoln University (1866).

Nevada

Established by the state's constitution, the University of Nevada in is the oldest institution of higher learning in the state and was opened in 1874 in Elko as a land-grant university (and was eventually relocated to Reno).

New Hampshire

The first high schools in New Hampshire, the Boys' High School and the Girls' High School in Portsmouth, were established between 1827 and 1830.

Many colleges and universities existed in New Hampshire in the mid-nineteenth century, including Dartmouth College (founded in 1769) and the University of New Hampshire (1866, a land-grant institution).

America's first free public library, the Juvenile Library, was established in 1822 in Dublin, and the first free library supported by public funds was opened in Peterborough in 1833.

New Jersey

In 1871, statewide public education was established in New Jersey, and an 1875 amendment to the state constitution required that free public schooling be provided for all children between the ages of five and eighteen.

Public colleges in the state during the era of the war included the New Jersey State Normal School (1855), now the College of New Jersey, in Ewing Township; the Newark Normal School (1855), now Kean University; and Rutgers College (1825), originally established as Queen's College in 1766 and now known as Rutgers University.

Private institutions of higher learning established by the time of the Civil War included Princeton University (1746), one of nine colleges in the country founded prior to the American Revolution; Seton Hall University (1856), a Catholic institution in South Orange; and Rider University in Lawrenceville (1865).

New York

Since 1784, education in New York has been the responsibility of the sixteen regents of the University of the State of New York.

Institutions of higher learning included the Collegiate School (1628) in Manhattan; the U.S. Army Military Academy at West Point, founded in 1802 at the site of a military fortification overlooking the Hudson River; New York University, established in 1831; Fordham University, founded by Jesuits in 1841; and Cornell University, founded in 1865 as a land-grant institution.

Ohio

An 1825, state law required Ohio counties to fund public education.

Public institutions of higher learning included Cincinnati College and the Medical College of Ohio (1819), the former half of which is now the University of Cincinnati; the Cincinnati Conservatory of Music (1867), established as part of a girls' finishing school and now also part of the University of Cincinnati; The Ohio State University (1870), a land-grant institution; and the University of Toledo (1872).

Private colleges operating soon after the war ended included Buchtel College (1870), a Universalist institution that is now the public University of Akron.

Libraries of significance in the state include the Cincinnati Public Library, which opened in 1853 and evolved from a subscription library established a half-century earlier, and the Columbus Metropolitan Library, which opened in 1873.

Oregon

Educational institutions in the state established soon after the conclusion of the Civil War included Lewis and Clark College (1867), a private institution founded in Albany (and eventually relocated to Portland); Oregon State University, a land-grant institution founded in 1868; and the University of Oregon, founded in 1876.

Pennsylvania

Public primary and secondary education had existed in Pennsylvania since 1790, developing slowly but being well-established by the time of the Civil War. At this time, there were also more than a dozen institutions of higher education throughout the state, including the private University of Pennsylvania (1740); the public University of Pittsburgh (1787); and Pennsylvania State University (1855), which was founded initially as a state land-grant institution even before the passage of the Morrill Act of 1862.

Rhode Island

Public higher education in Rhode Island began with the founding of the Henry Barnard School of Law in 1845. Other public institutions included Rhode Island Normal School (1854), now known as Rhode Island College.

Weeping Willow Schoolhouse, Chester County, Pennsylvania, circa 1860.

Private institutions operating during or soon after the Civil War included Brown University (1764), Bryant College (1863), and Rhode Island School of Design (1877).

Another institution of note, although not established until nearly two decades after the conclusion of the war, in 1884, is the Naval War College in Newport.

Vermont

In 1777, Vermont became the first state to constitutionally mandate funding for universal public education. The state enjoyed a level of prosperity high enough to back up this lofty ideal. By 1850, academies and grammar schools had been established throughout the state and some were providing to both boys and girls a level of education comparable to that available at contemporary colleges. While many of these schools were private institutions and remained so, most nonetheless received funding from municipal governments to educate local students and a number eventually became public schools.

Several of Vermont's grammar schools eventually became colleges, including Addison County Grammar School, which became Middlebury College in 1800; Lamoille County Grammar School, which became Johnson State College in 1828; Orange County Grammar School, which became Vermont Technical College in 1866; and Rutland County Grammar School (1787), which became Castleton State College in 1867. A number of grammar schools were also converted into normal schools in order to meet a growing need for qualified teachers.

Other higher educational institutions operating at the time of the war included the University of Vermont at Burlington, founded in 1791.

West Virginia

When it was founded in 1863, West Virginia did not have as many educational institutions as Virginia, the state from which it had seceded, and those that it had were generally not as large or old. Many of those still in existence now were founded in the years immediately following the war.

Private institutions of higher education operational during the era of the Civil War or founded soon after included Marshall Academy, a private secondary school that evolved into Marshall University; Bethany College (1840); and Broaddus College, a Baptist college established in Winchester in 1871 and named for a minister prominent during the conflict;

Public institutions included West Liberty State College (1837); West Virginia Normal School (1865), now known as Fairmont State University; the Agricultural College of West Virginia (1867), a land-grant institution that is now West Virginia University; Shepherd University (1871); Concord University (1872); and Glenville State College (1872).

Wisconsin

Wisconsin's 1848 state constitution provided for free public education and, in the years following the Civil War, the state was one of the leaders in the establishment of higher-education institutions in the Midwest.

Public institutions that had been founded by or during the era of the war included the University of Wisconsin (1848), which became a land-grant institution in 1866; Platteville Normal School (1866), the state's first institution for training teachers and now the University of Wisconsin—Platteville; and Oshkosh State Normal School (1871), the first normal school in the United States with a kindergarten, and now the University of Wisconsin—Oshkosh.

Private colleges included Carroll College (1846), now known as Carroll University, which was forced by the war and financial problems to suspend its operations during the 1860s; Beloit College (1846), founded by the Friends for Education, a group of four settlers from New England; and Ripon College (1851).

Education in the South

Although public primary and secondary education had been established to some extent in the South—and while some of the country's oldest colleges were in the South, notably Virginia—such institutions were much less widespread than in the North. Plantation owners and other members of the upper class typically either sent their children to private schools or hired tutors to teach them.

In consequence, levels of education and literacy were considerably lower throughout the South than in the North. This is even more profound if the one-third of Southerners who were uneducated slaves is taken into consideration; while some Southern blacks did manage to become literate or achieve some level of education, the Confederate states had laws prohibiting schooling for blacks.

During the period of Reconstruction, the biracial governments of the defeated Southern states established public school systems designed to serve the needs of all children, but these were universally segregated. After the pendulum swung back toward white-controlled government in the years following Reconstruction, black schools tended to be sorely underfunded (although, in general, the postwar South had not distinguished itself as a bastion of education for any of its citizens).

Alabama

Public institutions of higher education in Alabama included Auburn University (1856), which closed during the Civil War when most of its faculty and students joined the Confederate military forces; the Lincoln Normal School (1856), which in 1874 was reclassified as Alabama State University, the nation's first state-supported university for blacks; and Alabama Agricultural and Mechanical University (1875), a historically black land-grant university located in Normal.

Private institutions of higher education included Spring Hill College (1830), a Jesuit school in Mobile; and Talladega College (1867), the state's oldest historically black college, founded by two former slaves with the assistance of the Freedmen's Bureau.

Arkansas

Arkansas' first school was the Dwight Mission, founded in 1822 for Cherokee Indians. In 1843, Arkansas established a statewide system of public schools, but private academies dominated education until a decade after the end of the Civil War.

Arkansas did not have many institutions of higher education prior to the Civil War. Public institutions of this sort founded soon after the war ended included Arkansas Industrial University (1871) in Fayetteville, a land-grant school that is now the University of Arkansas.

Private institutions founded soon after the war included Arkansas College (1872) in Batesville, a Presbyterian school now known as Lyon College; Central Institute (1876) in Altus, founded by the Methodist Episcopal Church and now known as Hendrix College; and Walden Seminary (1877), founded to educate freed blacks west of the Mississippi and now known as Philander Smith College.

Florida

In 1868, Florida adopted a new constitution that authorized voting rights for blacks and a state-wide system of public primary and secondary education, upon which the state was readmitted to the Union. The Florida Department of Education was established in 1870.

Public institutions of higher learning included West Florida Seminary (1851) in Tallahassee, now Florida State University, which was reclassified as the Florida Military and Collegiate Institute during the Civil War and whose cadets fought during the conflict; and East Florida Seminary (1853) in Ocala, now the University of Florida.

Private institutions of higher learning included Brown Theological Institute (1866), a historically black school founded by the African Methodist Episcopal Church and now known as Edward Waters College.

Georgia

Despite a promising start during the Colonial era, only limited primary and secondary educational opportunities existed in Georgia throughout the nineteenth century. During Reconstruction, the state legislature mandated a free public school system and, by 1872, a system of segregated schools was available, although often only for three or four months at a time.

Public institutions of higher learning included the University of Georgia (1785) in Athens, which was closed during the last two years of the Civil War.

Private institutions of higher learning included the coeducational Jefferson County Academy (1818), which eventually became the Martin Institute—the first privately-endowed educational institute in the country—and operated under that name until it closed in 1942.

Louisiana

Louisiana's first school is thought to have been the Ursuline Convent for girls in New Orleans, founded in 1727. There was little in the way of public education until 1841, when New Orleans established free public schools and supported them with poll taxes and property taxes.

Public institutions of higher learning in Louisiana during the era of the Civil War included the Louisiana State University Agricultural and Mechanical College (1860), which was founded with land grants from the U.S. government. Its first superintendent was William Tecumseh Sherman, who resigned this position and left to serve in the U.S. Army when Louisiana seceded from the Union in 1861. The school was closed during most of the ensuing war.

Private institutions of higher learning during the era of the Civil War included the Medical College of Louisiana (1834), known today as Tulane University, which was closed from 1861 to 1865 because of the conflict.

Mississippi

Primary and secondary education in antebellum Mississippi was provided by a limited number of private academies, nine of which had been established by 1817. Educational opportunities for blacks did not exist at all until 1862, when a school was established in an area occupied by Union military forces. In 1870, during Reconstruction, the mixed-race legislation of the state attempted to establish public education but resistance to taxation and a relatively poor economy retarded these efforts.

Public institutions of higher learning established prior to or soon after the war included the University of Mississippi (1848) in Oxford, whose School of Medicine was used as a hospital for both Confederate and Union troops during the war; Alcorn State University (1871), a historically black land-grant college founded on the site of the former Oakland College (see below); and Natchez Seminary (1877), now known as Jackson State University, also a historically black school founded to educate freed slaves and their offspring.

Private institutions included Oakland College (1830), a school started by Presbyterians that closed during the war because so many of its students joined the Confederate military forces; Rust College (1866), a historically black school founded by Northern missionaries from the Freedman's Aid Society of the Methodist Episcopal Church; and Blue Mountain Female Institute (1871), now Blue Mountain College, founded by Confederate Brig. Gen. Mark P. Lowrey.

North Carolina

North Carolina's first public primary and secondary schools began in 1840 but were, of course, open only to whites.

Institutions of higher learning included the University of North Carolina (1789) in Chapel Hill, the oldest public university in the country. Many of its students were given exemptions from the Confederate draft and it was one of the few colleges in the South to remain open during the war.

Private institutions of higher education included Trinity College (1838), originally known as Brown's Schoolhouse and now as Duke University; and Wake Forest College (1834), originally as Wake Forest Manual Labor Institute and now Wake Forest University, which closed during the war because most of its students and some of its faculty enlisted in the Confederate military forces.

South Carolina

Prior to the Civil War, private academies provided primary and secondary education in South Carolina. In 1868, a new state constitution called for public education for all children, but this did not actually occur in South Carolina until the 1890s.

Public institutions of higher learning established by or during the era of the war included the College of Charleston (1770), whose founders included three signers of the Declaration of Independence; South Carolina College (1801), now the University of South Carolina, whose students led the movement in the state to secede from the United States; and South Carolina Military Academy (1842), now known as the Citadel, a military college founded on the site of an arsenal in Charleston that claims two of its students participated in the first military action of the war, an attack on a steamer attempting to resupply Fort Sumter.

Private institutions included Wofford College (1854) in Spartanburg and Furman University (1826) in Greenville.

Tennessee

Education in Tennessee was provided largely by private schools and churches until well after the Civil War. Tennessee established a statewide public school system funded by taxes in 1873, during the era of Reconstruction, but it remained underfunded and largely ineffective until the early twentieth century.

Public institutions of higher education included East Tennessee University (1794), originally Blount College and now the University of Tennessee—Knoxville, which was perceived to be a bastion of Union sympathies during the war and which was used as a barracks and hospital and severely damaged during the conflict.

Private institutions included Bethel College (1842), originally Bethel Seminary and now Bethel University, a Presbyterian school in McKenzie; Christian Brothers University (1871), founded by a Roman Catholic religious order and the oldest college in the city of Memphis; and Cumberland University (1842), a Presbyterian institution in Lebanon that, by the 1850s, included schools of law and theology.

Texas

Significant moves toward public education began in 1839 when what was then the Republic of Texas set aside land for two state universities and designated land in each county for public use as primary and secondary schools. Tentative plans for public higher education date to twelve years before this, and are mentioned in the constitution for the Mexican state of Coahuila y Tejas, which the area was known as before the Texas Revolution.

Public institutions of higher education included the Agricultural and Mechanical College of Texas (1871) in College Station, a land-grant institution that is now better known as Texas A&M University. None others were established until the 1880s.

Private institutions of higher education included Baylor University (1845), established by Baptists in Independence (and subsequently moved to Waco and merged with Waco University); Baylor Female Institute (1851), a separate offshoot of Baylor University that merged with it in 1887; and St. Edward's Academy (1878), a Roman Catholic school in Austin that is now named St. Edward's University.

Virginia

Virginia had a long tradition of educational institutions, the Syms Free School being founded in 1634 and the College of William and Mary in 1693. However, the state made no provisions for public education until 1810, when the Literary Fund was established to assist poor children. The state constitution first provided for public primary and secondary schools for all in 1869.

Public institutions of higher education included the University of Virginia, founded by Thomas Jefferson in Charlottesville in 1819; the Medical College of Virginia

After the war, Northern reformers often came to the South to set up Freedman schools to educate freed slaves, both adult and children.

(1854) in Richmond; and Virginia Military Institute (1839) in Lexington, whose pre-war faculty included Thomas "Stonewall" Jackson and whose cadets distinguished themselves at the Battle of New Market in 1864.

Private institutions included Washington College (1749) in Lexington, which Robert E. Lee served as president from when the war ended in 1865 until his death in 1870 (the school is now Washington and Lee University); Hampden-Sydney College (1775), a men's-only school that is the oldest private college in the state; and Roanoke College (1842), the second-oldest Lutheran college in the country.

Education in U.S. Territories

In 1785, the Federal government passed a Land Ordinance that set aside a piece of every township in the unincorporated territories of the country for use by public schools and this helped to ensure the availability of education as the country expanded westward. Educational opportunities were, nonetheless, severely limited in the U.S. territories during and in the years following the Civil War. There were, however, a few exceptions to this.

The Arizona Territory, for example, opened its first public school in 1871, and, in 1879, the territory's legislature founded the office of the state superintendent of public instruction.

In the Utah Territory and the State of Deseret, public education began in 1850, when Mormon settlers founded the University of Deseret, the first public university west of the Mississippi River.

And primary and secondary education existed in the Washington Territory (1853-1889) since its earliest days.

Terms

BLUE-BACKED SPELLER: A colloquial name for Noah Webster's guide to reading, spelling, and pronunciation, initially published in 1783 and widely used in primary education during the era of the Civil War and in the decades following it. It was the first part of his three-part *A Grammatical Institute of the English Language*, which also included a grammar (1784) and a reader (1785).

COMMON SCHOOL: A term coined by educational reformer Horace Mann and used to refer to schools designed to educate people of all social levels and religions. Such schools typically taught reading, writing, arithmetic, history, and geography, and also sometimes geometry, algebra, Greek, and Latin.

FREEDMEN'S BUREAU (BUREAU OF REFUGEES, FREEDMEN, AND ABANDONED LANDS): A Federal government agency that assisted freed slaves from 1865-1872, generally with emergency food, medical care, and housing. It was very unpopular with Southern whites during the era of Reconstruction.

LAND-GRANT INSTITUTIONS (LAND-GRANT COLLEGES, LAND-GRANT UNIVERSITIES): State colleges and universities founded or expanded with the help of Federal land grants (under the provisions of the 1862 Morrill Land Grant Act), in exchange for establishing programs in agricultural, scientific, industrial, and military studies.

MCGUFFEY READERS: A series of progressively more challenging educational texts developed by educator William Holmes McGuffey and his brother in the 1830s and 1840s to teach reading. They were widely used during the Civil War and throughout the century following it.

NORMAL SCHOOL: Taken from the French term *école normale*, this was a type of school established to train high school graduates to be elementary school teachers. The first private institution of this sort in the United States was founded in 1823 and the first public one was founded in 1839.

SEMINARY: Traditionally, a sectarian school founded for training priests or ministers. During the 19th century in America, however, this term was also sometime applied to institutions, like normal schools, established for providing post-secondary education to teachers.

WHIG PARTY: An American political party that operated from 1833 until 1856 and was formed in opposition to the policies of President Andrew Jackson. Among other things, the party supported economic protectionism, modernization, and the supremacy of Congress over the presidency. It was destroyed by internal dissension over the question of whether or not to permit the expansion of slavery into U.S. territories.

SLANG AND IDIOM:
HOW PEOPLE AND EVENTS SHAPED LANGUAGE

"A national language is a very large matter. It reflects everything that happens to a people,
the cultural forces that create ideas and words, the content and form of regional and social expression."
— Mark Twain, "Concerning the American Language," 1880

When reading material written during the Civil War, modern readers are often surprised that the writing is so similar to that of today, on the one hand, while containing so many idiomatic terms and expressions on the other.

A lexicon of terms is created during the course of any great conflict or period of change. This is especially true in the case of the Civil War, and many of the terms and expressions we take for granted today have their origins in the conflict (while others that we continue to use today have their origins prior to the war, and would have been used during it, such as "bark up the wrong tree," which dates to 1832).

Contemporary idiom can also give modern readers some insight into what many people thought and felt during the Civil War. For example, Union soldiers referring to the U.S. flag as "God's flag" hints at the fervency felt by many of the combatants.

So, too, many words we use to describe the events of the Civil War have their origins in the years following the conflict. For example, Union Maj. Gen. William Tecumseh Sherman is widely known to have stated, "War is Hell." However, he did not say this until 1879, some fourteen years after the war had ended.

Likewise, some words were used widely during the war but have now fallen into disuse. In addition, the way even familiar words were used was sometimes quite different from the way they are used today. For example, today the word "supposed" is generally used to mean "should have," as in "He was supposed to have been promoted." During the Civil War, it was generally used to mean "thought," as in "His family supposed he had been promoted."

A Nation of Many Tongues

Since Colonial times, the American language diverged from the language spoken in England and began to acquire a variety of what are known as "Americanisms." Such Americanisms were often the products of local conditions and the influences of other languages, and, by the 1800s, America was a country of many distinct dialects. Not only did people in the North and South speak languages with different words, grammar, and forms, groups of people in geographical pockets or even entire regions also had their own ways of speaking the English language. Wilderness, lack of roads or means of communication, and no centralized education helped propagate this fragmentation of the national language. Such dialectical differences generally manifested themselves in speech rather than in the written word.

Beyond this, of course, were ethnic enclaves that did not speak English at all. Examples include the German-speaking Pennsylvania Dutch, immigrant populations in many large cities, communities of Spanish speakers in the far West, and American Indians throughout the country. These non-English-speaking populations also influenced the evolution of the American language.

In the decades following the Civil War, many factors combined to erode the clearly differentiated American dialects and homogenize the language. Regional differences were smoothed over by factors that allowed people from different regions to more effectively communicate with each other, such as improved roads, rail transportation, telegraphy, the rise of public education, and increased literacy because of more widespread newspapers and publications, such as Noah Webster's *The American Spelling Book* and William McGuffey's *Eclectic Readers*.

Language in the North

People in the North, including all the non-Confederate states of the West, spoke a wide variety of distinct dialects during the Civil War. These included dialects spoken by people in Appalachia (influenced by Scottish), the Hudson River Valley (influenced by Dutch), and Minnesota (influenced by various Scandinavian languages).

The two largest and most distinct dialects spoken in the North, however, were the New England dialect and what is often referred to today as Standard American English.

This New England dialect was—and to a great extent still is—spoken in Connecticut, Rhode Island, Massachusetts, Vermont, New Hampshire, and Maine. At the time of the Civil War, it was closer to the English spoken in England than any other major American dialect.

Most English-speaking people in the areas controlled by the Federal government spoke the standard American dialect of English. However, this dialect could still be divided into several other regional subdialects that featured their own idioms and accents.

Language in the South

A distinct Southern dialect was spoken by people in all of the Confederate states (except for western Arkansas and Texas), as well as Maryland, Kentucky, and southern Missouri.

This Southern dialect could be further divided into the modes of speech in the upper and Deep South, and even further into regional dialects, such as those spoken in the South Carolina Low Country, in the Virginia Tidewater region, and in the vicinity of major population centers, such as Atlanta, Charleston, or New Orleans. And beyond the Southern dialect, were other regional dialects, including those spoken in the Florida Keys and by Cajuns in the bayous of Louisiana, which often mixed other languages with English.

Ethnic Influences

African Influences

African slaves came from hundreds of different tribes and subtribes and spoke scores of different languages. Many of the words from these languages remained or worked their way into the everyday speech of slaves, and ultimately into the language as a whole. During the Civil War, these influences were greatest in the South, where the vast majority of blacks in America lived.

Many slaves were not formally taught English and, as a result, developed their own synthesis of English and African words, pronunciations, speech patterns, syntax, and tones. This spoken language was generically referred to as Nigger by 1825 and both influenced and was influenced by the dialect spoken by white Southerners. It also included numerous pidgin English words, altered pronunciations and forms, dropped auxiliary verbs, and simplified conjugations of many other verb forms or used them unconjugated (e.g., the verb "to be").

In some areas, this sort of black English was mixed with other languages, such as French in Louisiana and Spanish in Florida. One of these sublanguages, Gullah, was spoken by a black people of the same name who lived on the Sea Islands of South Carolina, Georgia, and Florida.

Direct introduction of African words into American English by enslaved blacks dropped off in the early decades of the nineteenth century, after the importation of new slaves was banned in 1808. Other African words entered English indirectly, however, from Dutch, Portuguese, and Spanish traders, from England, and from black slaves in the Caribbean. Several English words with African roots are included in the term list at the end of this chapter.

German Influences

As early immigrants to the Americas, Germans have influenced the language of the United States since its earliest years. It was in the decades immediately before and during the Civil War that they made their greatest contributions, however, as they arrived in even larger numbers having been driven from Germany by the failed German Revolution of 1848 and by the same European potato blight that caused so many Irish to abandon their homes.

The German influence was most palpably felt in the North and East and what was then known as the West (and today as the Midwest).

A great many terms Americans take for granted today entered the language during the nineteenth century or earlier, either in their original form, as translations or as modified German words or phrases. Other words that seem to have two meanings often derive one meaning from their German genesis and another from their British. Some words have also been influenced by German forms, prefixes, or suffixes.

The word "German" was also used during the nineteenth century to identify the origin of specific groups, as in "German Jew" or "German Lutheran," or other things, such as "German measles," a condition prevalent in Germany and sometimes brought to the United States by immigrants.

Irish Influences

Although the Irish have been present in America since early Colonial times, it was waves of immigrants fleeing the 1846 Irish Potato Famine that led to their greatest influence on the American language. At the time of the Civil War, this influence was felt most in the North and East, especially the great urban areas like Boston and New York City.

As with other ethnic groups, the Irish contributed a variety of words to the nineteenth-century American vocabulary. As recent immigrants at the time of the Civil War, the Irish also inspired a variety of unfortunate terms and disparaging nicknames. For example, a slang term for a bullfrog was "Irish nightingale," a play upon "Swedish Nightingale," nickname of the contemporary popular diva Jenny Lind.

However, beyond their influences upon the American vocabulary, the Irish's greatest influence was not so much upon what people said but rather how they said it, through grammar, pronunciation, and syntax.

One of the most noticeable contributions is in the addition of the definite article and pronoun, something not used in England.

Spanish and Mexican Influences

The influence of Spanish on the language of Americans is not surprising considering the Spanish had settlements in Florida and the Gulf states decades before English settlers ever landed in Massachusetts or Virginia. Also, Spain or Mexico controlled all of what became the states of Texas, California, Arizona, New Mexico, and Nevada. Because of this geographical influence, Spanish words and phrases were most common in the Southwest and on the West Coast.

During the 1800s, the words "Mexican" and "Spanish" also appeared in conjunction with other words and phrases, including "Mexican dollar," "Spanish America," "Spanish American," "Spanish Creole," "Spanish dance," "Spanish fly," "Spanish Mexican," and "Spanish moss."

Spanish terms and phrases would have been familiar to veterans of the Mexican War (1846–1848), of soldiers formerly stationed in California, or of those who took part in the Gold Rush of the late 1840s.

A War of Many Names

Few wars have been referred to in quite so many ways as the American Civil War, and its various names reflect a wide range of attitudes toward the conflict. The official name given to it by the victorious Federal government is, of course, the Civil War, a term that came into use in 1861. In the Southern states, however, the terms used in 1861 included the Revolution, the Second War for Independence, and the War of Secession.

A variety of other names came into use during the war and in the decades following it, most of which reveal partiality to one side or the other, a tone of reconciliation, humor, or an emphasis on some aspect of the conflict.

These include the Great Fratricide, the War of Northern Aggression, the War for Constitutional Liberty, the War Between the States, the War Between the North and the South, the War for Southern Independence, the Second American Revolution, the War for States' Rights, Mr. Lincoln's War, the Southern Rebellion, the War for Southern Rights, the War of the Southern Planters, the War of the Rebellion, the War to Suppress Yankee Arrogance, the Brothers' War, the Great Rebellion, the War for Nationality, the War for Southern Nationality, the War Against Slavery, the Civil War Between the States, the War of the Sixties, the War Against Northern Aggression, the Yankee Invasion, the War for Separation, the War for Abolition, the War for Union, the Confederate War, the War of the Southrons, the War for Southern Freedom, the War of the North and the South, the Lost Cause, the Late Unpleasantness, the Late Friction, the Late Ruction, the Schism, the Uncivil War and, especially in the South in the years since it ended, simply as the War.

Overseas, the conflict was given still other names. For example, contemporary German writers referred to it as the North American War.

An Enemy by Any Other Name

All sorts of nicknames for troops on the opposing armies were coined during the Civil War. These included both pejorative names that the men of one side applied to those of the other and terms that soldiers used to refer to certain classes of troops on their own sides.

Derogatory terms Northerners used for Southern troops included Rebel, Reb, and Johnny Reb; Butternut, from the light gray, almost tan uniforms colored with butternut dye worn by many Confederate troops; Grayback, inspired by the typical gray Confederate uniforms and co-opting the slang term for a louse; Graycoat, for the quintessential color of the Southern uniforms; and Secessionist and its shortened versions Secesh and Secesher, from the Confederate states' secession from the Union.

Derisive nicknames Southerners used for their Northern antagonists included Yankee, Yank, and Billy Yank; Blue Belly, from the characteristic color of the Union uniforms; and Hessian, which, taken from the mercenary German soldiers from Hesse who fought for the British during the American Revolution, was applied to Germans, any people of low character and, during the war, to Union soldiers by people in the South.

Soldiers often also had nicknames for their comrades from various states or regions. According to Confederate officer Bromfield L. Ridley, an aide-de-camp on Lt. General Alexander P. Stewart's staff, for example, nicknames given to soldiers from particular states included "Yaller Hammers" for those from Alabama, "Toothpicks" for those from Arkansas, "Gophers" for those from Florida, "Goober Grabbers" for those from Florida, "Corn Crackers" for those from Kentucky, "Tigers" for those from Louisiana, "Sandlappers" for those from Mississippi, "Border Ruffians" for those from Missouri, "Tarheels" for those from North Carolina, "Rice Birds" for those from South Carolina, "Hog Drivers" for those from Tennessee, "Cowboys" for those from Texas, and "Tobacco Worms" for those from Virginia. "Josh" was also a nickname sometimes applied to a person from Arkansas.

Military personnel also sometimes had nicknames for other members of their own forces, including those in certain specialties or those who engaged in certain sorts of behavior. "Paper collar," for example, was a derisive term used by western Federal soldiers to refer to eastern Federal soldiers, who they often thought looked like fancy dandies. "Bummer" was used to label a malingerer or someone who deliberately lagged behind the movement of their own forces in order to forage or steal. "Redleg" was a nickname for Union artillerymen inspired by the red stripes worn on such soldiers' trousers. And "lobsterback" was a derisive nickname used by sailors for shipboard marines.

SOLDIERS' NICKNAMES

Following are nicknames for soldiers by state:

Alabama	Yaller Hammers
Arkansas	Toothpicks or Josh
Florida	Gophers or Goober Grabbers
Kentucky	Corn Crackers
Louisiana	Tigers
Mississippi	Sandlappers
Missouri	Border Ruffians
North Carolina	Tarheels
South Carolina	Rice Birds
Tennessee	Hog Drivers
Texas	Cowboys
Virginia	Tobacco Worms

The Written Word

During the era of the Civil War, people often wrote in a manner that would seem melodramatic or even unnatural today. Examples of this are easy to find. One of the more striking is an article in the *Baltimore American* and *Commercial Advertiser* about Confederate Maj. Gen. Joseph Johnston's burning of Baltimore and Ohio property in June 1861, in which he is said to have performed an "act of diabolism" and performed a crime "effected by means worthy of the spirits tenanting the nether world."

Other idioms that turn up in contemporary writing include capitalization of many or most nouns, even non-proper nouns (e.g., Rail Road, instead of railroad). Also, many words that today would be contracted to one word were written as two, as in the previous example.

Terms

Following are some of the words and phrases that were in use, or originated, during the Civil War. Also, see the term lists at the end of many chapters, which contain specialized terms specific to the material in those sections. For example, in the chapter on the opposing armies there are many terms which refer specifically to soldiers.

Some of the words derived from African, Irish, German, and Spanish dialects are marked for ease of reference, with an "A," "I," "G," or "S," respectively. Many of these words were used predominantly by the ethnic group in question or in certain geographical areas. For example, most of the Spanish words would have been used only in areas once controlled by Spanish speakers.

Terms that were used predominantly by military personnel are marked with an "M."

ABSQUATULATE: To leave or disappear.

ACKNOWLEDGE THE CORN: To admit the truth, acknowledge a personal shortcoming, or confess a lie.

"ALL QUIET ALONG THE POTOMAC": A phrase used by Northern newspapers in the weeks after the Union defeat at Bull Run, making fun of General McClellan's interminable delay in attacking the Rebel forces. This phrase also became the name of a popular Union song.

ANTE-BELLUM: A Latin term that means "before the war," specifically before the Civil War. It first appeared in print in 1867 and eventually came to be written without a hyphen.

(S) ARROYO: A brook or gully.

(M) A.W.O.L.: An acronym for "Absent With Out Leave."

BAD EGG: A bad person, a good-for-nothing.

BALDERDASH: Nonsense.

BEAT THE DUTCH: If that don't beat all.

BEEN THROUGH THE MILL: Seen it all, been through a lot.

(I) BELAVE: A variant of "believe."

BELLYACHE: To complain.

BIG BUGS: Important people, bigwigs.

(M) BIG THING: A term used to describe any significant event, from a new shipment of shoes to a major battle.

(I) BILE: A variant pronunciation of "boil."

(M) BIVOUAC: To camp temporarily

and without formal shelter such as tents or barracks.

BLACK MARIA: From the 1840s, a wagon used to transport people arrested by the police.

BLOWHARD: A bully or braggart.

BLUFF: To deceive or trick.

(S) BODEGA: A wine shop or liquor store.

BOOK: From 1846, to enter charges against a suspect into a police registry.

(M) BRAGG'S BODY GUARD: Lice.

(M) BREAD BAG: A haversack.

(M) BREAD BASKET: One's stomach.

(A) BUCKRA, BUCCARA, BOCCRA:

A word used by slaves to address their masters that remained in use through the 1860s. In Colonial times, buckra was used to refer to any white, and eventually to a gentleman.

BULLY: An exclamation meaning "hurray," "terrific," or the like.

BULLY FOR YOU: An expression meaning "good for you."

(S) CAFETERIA: Since about 1830, a coffee house. Its usage for a self-service restaurant did not arise until the 1890s.

(S) CALABOOSE: From the Spanish calabozo, or dungeon, this colloquial word for a jail was popularized by American cowboys in the 1860s.

(M) CAMP CANARD: Gossip or a tall-tale

circulating around camp.

(M) CASHIER: To dishonorably dismiss from the military.

(S) CAY, KEY: A low island.

CHAIN GANG: This practice of using manacled prisoners to perform labor, and the term for it, came into use around 1835.

(I) CHAW: A variant of "chew."

(M) CHICKEN GUTS: Slang term for the gold braid used on officers' uniforms.

CHIEF COOK AND BOTTLE WASHER: Term for the person in charge or someone who can do anything.

CHIEF OF POLICE: A term from the 1840s that refers to the head of a police department.

"I'm afraid Smith is feeling poorly. He joined Company Q last night."

It was a long night. I was up every hour with the quick step.

(A) CHIGGER, CHEGO, CHIEGO: A chigger or a flea.

(S) CHINCH, CHINCH BUG: Used variously to describe an insect that destroyed wheat and corn or a bedbug.

(M) COMPANY Q: A fictitious unit designation for the sick list.

CONFEDERACY: Prior to 1829, this term referred to the confederation of all the United States. From 1829 to 1861, as secession of Southern states from the Union became more and more widely discussed, this term came to refer to the states of the South, and, ultimately, to the Confederate States of America.

CONFEDERATE: The use of this word as a modifier or qualifier began in 1861, as in the Confederate Capital, Confederate money, and Confederate stamps.

CONNIPTION FIT: Hysterics, temper tantrum.

CONSTABLE: A policeman. "Police" and "policeman" were also in wide usage.

CONTRABAND: Term for escaped slaves who sought refuge behind Union lines.

(A) COOTER: This word for a box turtle entered the Southern dialect of English from Gullah.

COP: To arrest.

COTTON BLACK, COTTON SLAVE: Terms that arose in the early 1860s for blacks who worked the cotton plantations.

(M) CRACKER LINE: Slang term for the supply line of troops on the move.

(A) CUFFY, CUFF: A common black male name, which, at the time of the war, was used to refer to any black man. From Kofi, a name often given on the Gold Coast of Africa to boys born on Friday.

(A) CUSH, CUSHIE: A sweet fried cornmeal cake. From the Gullah word kush or kushkush and ultimately derived from the Arabic kusha or couscous.

CUT OFF: A euphemism for being killed.

DEADBEAT: A useless person or malingerer.

DO TIME: A slang term for spending time in jail that came into use around 1860.

(S) DOBIE, DOBY: Informal term for a house made of adobe.

(M) DOG COLLAR: A cravat issued with uniforms and usually discarded by troops.

DOWER NEGRO: A slave owned by a woman at the time of her marriage or given as part of her dowry.

DRAFTEE: A citizen conscripted, or drafted, into military service.

DUDS: Clothing.

(S) EMBARCADERO: A landing place or wharf.

FIT AS A FIDDLE: In good shape.

FIT TO BE TIED: angry.

FLUX, QUICK STEP: diarrhea.

(M) FORAGE: To hunt for food or live off the land, but also to plunder enemy property for sustenance.

(M) FORTY DEAD MEN: A full cartridge box, which typically held forty rounds of ammunition.

FREE PAPERS: Papers, first used in 1838, issued to freed blacks as documentation of their status.

(M) FRENCH LEAVE: Slang term for going absent without leave.

(M) FRESH FISH: New recruits.

FUGITIVE SLAVE: A term originating in 1793 with the Fugitive Slave Act that became familiar in the 1840s, when conditions on large plantations became increasingly oppressive.

GERMAN CORN: Rye.

GERMAN COTILLION: A complex, round dance popular in the 1830s and 1840s.

GET ONE'S IRISH UP: To get angry.

GO BOIL YOUR SHIRT: Bug off, get lost, take a hike.

(M) GOD'S COUNTRY: Term used by Union troops to refer to the North, especially when suffering from heat, humidity, mosquitoes, and other unfamiliar conditions while campaigning in the South.

(M) GOD'S FLAG: Term used by Union troops to refer to the U.S. flag.

(A) GOOBER: A peanut.

GRAB A ROOT: To eat something, especially a potato.

THE GRAY: A term for the army of the Confederacy—or for the nation itself—taken from the official color of Confederate uniforms.

GRAFT: From about 1859, this meant to earn a living dishonestly as a con artist, robber, or thief.

GRIT: Bravery, toughness.

(A) GUMBO: A soup made from okra, shrimp, and powdered sassafras leaves.

HANKER: A strong wish or desire.

HARD CASE: A tough guy.

HARD KNOCKS: Rough treatment.

HIGH-FALUTIN': Fancy, highbrow.

(G) HOLD ON!: An expression meaning "wait" or "stop" that comes from the German halt am.

HOODLUM: Used from about 1871 to refer to a tough or rowdy person.

(S) HOOSEGOW: A cowboy slang term for a jail, taken from the Spanish juzgado, meaning sentenced or jailed.

HORSE SENSE: Common sense, good judgment.

(M) HOSPITAL RAT: A malingerer, someone who fakes illness to get out of duty.

HOUSE NEGRO: A term applied to slaves who worked in their masters' houses.

With all the chores I've done this morning,
I haven't had time to grab a root.

There's scarce a hen's teeth of lard left in the house.

HUFFY, IN A HUFF: Annoyed, angry, irritated.

HUMBUG: Nonsense, a sham, a hoax.

HUNKEY-DOREY: Very good.

IRISH HOIST: A kick in the pants.

(M) IRON CHEER: A celebratory discharge of artillery fire.

IRONCLAD: Warships armored with metal plate. While this term now refers to the USS *Monitor* and the CSS *Virginia* (*Merrimac*) and the armored ships that descended from them, it did not come into use until 1867.

JAIL FEVER: An informal term for typhus, contracted by many prisoners through lice infestation.

JAILBIRD: A term for a habitual criminal (although spelled "gaolbird" until about 1814).

JAILHOUSE: A common term for a jail since the early nineteenth century.

JAWING: Talking.

(I) JINE: A variant of join.

JONAH: Slang term for someone who has or brings bad luck.

(A) JUBA: A group dance of African origin popular with plantation slaves that included complex routines of clapping and knee- and thigh-slapping.

(S) JUG: A slang term for a jail used since the 1810s, probably taken from the Spanish juzgado.

(S) JUNTA: A Spanish or Italian legislative council. Its meaning of a military government did not arise until the end of the century.

(G) KATZEN-JAMMERS: A term that referred to the effects of a hangover.

KNOCK INTO A COCKED HAT: To knock someone senseless or completely shock them.

LET 'ER RIP: Bring it on, let it happen.

LET DRIVE: A term meaning "do it," "go ahead."

(G) LIEDERKRANZ: German American men's social groups that met to sing and drink beer.

LIGHT OUT: Leave quickly.

LIKELY: Able-bodied, serviceable.

(G) LOAFER: A lazy person.

LOCKUP: A term for a jail in use since the late 1830s.

(S) MOSEY: A word alternately used to mean both "to move quickly" and "to move slowly."

MUGGINS: A scoundrel.

(M) MUSTERED OUT: To be discharged from the military. Also, a sarcastic term meaning to be killed in action.

NO-ACCOUNT: Worthless.

NOT BY A JUG FULL: No way, not by any means.

(M) OLD SOLDIER, PLAY OLD SOLDIER: Although this term could simply mean a veteran, it could also be used sarcastically to refer to soldiers who had learned all the tricks of malingering and avoiding work and combat.

(M) ON HIS OWN HOOK: Of one's own volition, without orders.

(M) OPENING THE BALL: starting the battle.

OPINE: Be of the opinion.

(M) PARLOR SOLDIERS, SUNDAY SOLDIERS: Derogatory terms for unsuitable soldiers.

PATROLMAN: This term for a policeman originated in the 1860s.

PEACOCK ABOUT: Strut around.

PEAKED: Sickly or weak.

PEN: An informal abbreviation for "penitentiary" that came into use around 1870.

PIE-EATER: A country boy, a rustic.

(M) PIG-STICKER: A knife or bayonet.

PINCH: A slang term meaning "to arrest."

(A) PINDAL, PINDER: A peanut, from the Kongo word npinda.

PLAYED OUT: exhausted, worn out.

(S) PLACER, PLACER MINE: A deposit of gravel or sand or the means of mining it.

POLICE COMMISSIONER: From the 1850s onward, this term referred to the official at the head of a city's police force.

(A) POOR JO, POOR JOB: Name used, mainly in Georgia, to refer to the great blue heron.

(S) PRESIDIO: A fortress or garrison, the central feature of many early Spanish settlements.

PRISON PENS: The outdoor stockades used to house prisoners of war. Conditions within these were often horrible, and thousands of prisoners on both sides suffered and died from exposure, malnutrition, and disease. For example, more than thirteen thousand Union troops died at the Andersonville prison in Georgia, considered the worst such facility of the war.

(M) PUMPKIN RINDS: Gold lieutenant's bars.

(M) QUARTERMASTER HUNTER: Slang term for an artillery shot or shell that goes over the lines and far into the rear.

RAP: Since 1777, a term that meant blame or rebuke (i.e., "a rap on the knuckles").

(G) RATHSKELLER: This term for a beer hall or restaurant entered the American vocabulary during the Civil War but was not commonly used until several decades afterwards.

RED BADGE OF COURAGE: Slang term for a wound.

REFORMATORY: This term for a jail came into regular usage after 1807, when the reformatory in Elmira, New York, opened.

(M) ROBBER'S ROW: The area where sutlers set up to sell their wares.

ROW: A fight.

(A) SAMBO: A common black male name that, by the early nineteenth century, was loosely used to refer to any black man or boy. From a name given to a second son in northern Nigeria.

SANDWICH MAN: A person wearing two signboards, strapped together and hung over his shoulders, one in front and one behind, as a form of advertisement.

(M) SARDINE BOX: slang for a firing-cap box.

(I) SASS: A variant of sauce.

(M) SAWBONES: Slang term for a surgeon.

SCARCE AS HEN'S TEETH: Very rare or hard to obtain.

SCREW: A harsh disciplinarian, martinet (i.e., someone who applied thumbscrews).

(M) SEE THE ELEPHANT: To experience combat or other significant events.

THE SHAKES: Malaria.

SHANKS MARE: On foot.

SHERMAN'S NECKTIES, SHERMAN'S HAIRPINS: Railroad rails that had been heated in fires then wrapped around trees to make them useless.

From the practice employed by Sherman's troops during their rapacious march across Georgia.

SHERMAN'S SENTINELS: The still-standing chimneys of buildings burned down by Sherman's troops. Called "Sherman's monuments" after the war.

SHILLELAGH: A cudgel, especially one made from oak or blackthorn.

(I) SHODDY: A word for a type of cheap cloth that, in the 1860s, came to describe anything of low quality.

(M) SING OUT: yell, call out.

(M) SKEDADDLE: Although it had entered the U.S. lexicon in the 1820s, this word did not come into wide usage until 1861, when it became popular after Union troops used it to describe fleeing Confederate

soldiers. (Its origin is a bit obscure, and could be derived from some Scottish or northern English idiom or even from the Greek skedannunai, "to split up").

(G) SLIM: In its meaning bad, as in "slim chance," this term is derived from the German schlimm.

(G) SMEARCASE: A type of spreadable cheese, from the German Schmierkaese.

SNUG AS A BUG: Very comfortable.

SOLITARY CONFINEMENT: This punishment and the term for it, originally thought to be a humane alternative to flogging, came into use in the 1780s.

(M) SOMEBODY'S DARLING: Reference to a dead soldier.

SPARKING: to court a girl.

SPONDULIX: slang term for money.

SPANISH FEVER, TEXAS FEVER: A cattle disease transmitted by ticks.

SPANISH TRAIL: Name applied to various routes in the far West, including the one between Santa Fe, New Mexico, and Los Angeles, California, and the one between New Orleans, Louisiana, via El Paso, Texas, to Los Angeles.

STARS AND STRIPES: The primary nickname for the United States flag.

STATIONHOUSE: A police station.

(I) TAY: A variant of tea.

"10 ACRES AND A MULE," "40 ACRES AND A MULE": From about 1862 onward, Union propagandists spread the word among slaves that, after the war was won, their

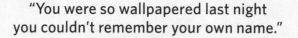

"You were so wallpapered last night you couldn't remember your own name."

masters' plantations would be parceled out to the former slaves. Union Major General Sherman exacerbated this idea on January 16, 1865, when he stated in a field order that "every family shall have a plot of not more than forty acres of tillable ground." When the war ended, the Federal government made no attempt to fulfill such promises, which it had not itself explicitly made.

TIGHT: Drunk.

(M) TOE THE MARK: To follow orders and do as told.

TOP RAIL: First class, top quality.

TRAFFIC POLICE: A term that dates to 1860, the year New York City's Broadway Squad was established to manage horse-drawn traffic and help people cross the streets.

(M) TRAPS: equipment, belongings.

TUCKERED OUT: Exhausted.

TUMBLED OVER: A Euphemism that meant to be killed.

UNCONDITIONAL SURRENDER: Although widely associated with the Allied ultimatum to Nazi Germany during World War II, this term traces its roots to the Civil War. When on February 16, 1862, Confederate Gen. Simon Bolivar Buckner, commander of Fort Donelson, Tennessee, requested terms for his surrender from Union Gen. Ulysses S. Grant, the Northern general responded with, "No terms except unconditional surrender." Because "unconditional sur render" also matched Grant's initials, it

became his wartime nickname.

UPPITY: Arrogant.

VIRGINIA QUICK-STEP, TENNESSEE QUICK-STEP: Slang terms for diarrhea.

WALLPAPERED: Drunk.

WAR CORRESPONDENT: Widespread accompaniment of armies by journalists took place during the Civil War. The most famous of these was Winslow Homer, a writer and artist for *Harper's Weekly*, who accompanied the Federal forces during the war. The term "army correspondent" came into use in 1863.

WAR WIDOW: A woman whose husband was away for military service (but not

necessarily dead, as the term might imply).

"THE WAR WILL BE OVER BY CHRISTMAS": A popular expression in 1861 that became progressively less popular (or believable) each year the war progressed.

WHIPPED: Beaten.

WRATHY: Angry.

YARD: A prison yard.

(M) ZU ZU: A slang terms for Zouaves, troops distinguished by their colorful, North African-style uniforms, which typically included fezes and baggy trousers.

RELIGION:
WHAT PEOPLE BELIEVED

"... Congress should not establish a religion, and enforce the legal observation of it by law, nor compel men to worship God in any manner contrary to their conscience ..." — James Madison, 1789

When the Civil War erupted at the start of the 1860s, America already had a well-established and diverse religious tradition that had developed over the previous two centuries and was an amalgamation of Old World and indigenous institutions. From the seventeenth century onward, successive waves of immigrants had brought their religious traditions to the shores of the New World and, over the years, these had evolved in their new home and been joined by new ideas, customs, and beliefs.

Freedom of religion was a fundamental tenet in America and, while the young nation's citizens were not always as sympathetic with or tolerant of the ideologies of others as they might have been, they nonetheless availed themselves of the liberty to practice their own beliefs.

Overall, Americans of the era had an ambivalent attitude toward religion; the overwhelming devotion of some was offset by the indifference of others. A great religious movement called the Third Great Awakening did commence in the years just prior to the Civil War. In that it was targeted at the unchurched, however, the movement may very well not have occurred if a need for widespread conversions and the improvement of society had not been perceived among the most fervent of the faithful.

President Abraham Lincoln himself exemplified this split mindset to a great extent. On the one hand, he was the first U.S. president to use the phrase "This nation under God," which, along with his thorough knowledge of the Bible and frequent reference to an almighty God, inspired his successors and is often taken as evidence of his piety. On the other hand, Lincoln was never baptized and was the only U.S. president to never join a church.

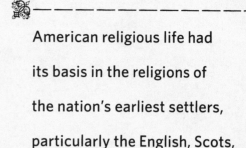

American religious life had its basis in the religions of the nation's earliest settlers, particularly the English, Scots, and Germans.

Another dichotomy existed among some of the most religious of the generals on either side who, while not averse to warfare in general, curtailed their pursuit of it to some extent on Sundays. Union Maj. Gen. William Rosecrans, for example, declined to pursue a retreating Rebel force on the Sabbath. Confederate Lt. Gen. Thomas J. "Stonewall" Jackson would only engage in "more ordinary battles" on Sundays, and others chalked up their defeats to the fact that they had fought on the day of rest.

In any event, religious leaders in both the North and the South generally took the stance that the side of which they were part represented "right and truth and justice" and that their enemies were engaged in "wrong and malice and outrage," in the words of one contemporary clergyman.

Religious Denominations

Initially, American religious life had its basis in the religions of the nation's earliest settlers, particularly the English, Scots, and Germans, who brought with them a variety of Protestant denominations and Catholicism. To these were added the religious beliefs of Irish, Scandinavians, southern and eastern Europeans, and others, who brought their own traditions, including various strains of Orthodoxy and Judaism. New denominations were established in America as well, and many of these went on to become mainstream religions in their own right.

Early in the history of the republic, various states had established churches that they supported with tax revenues, following a tradition that had been observed since the Colonial era. This was, however, deemed to violate the doctrine of separation of church and state called for by the First Amendment to the U.S. Constitution, and by 1833 all the states had discontinued this practice. ("Separation of church and state" does not actually appear in the Constitution itself and can instead be traced to an 1802 letter by Thomas Jefferson on the subject.)

Churches' structures throughout America differed greatly at the time of the Civil War, from small, austere structures in rural areas to much larger, more elaborate places of worship in the major cities of both North and South. Houses of worship also varied according to the tenets of the faiths practiced in them, the ethnicity of their primary worshippers, and the affluence of the religions to which they were dedicated.

Sects and denominations active in the United States beyond those described in detail in this chapter include the Congregationalist, Disciples of Christ/Christians, Dutch Reformed, Friends, German Reformed, Mennonite, Moravian, Shaker, Spiritualist, Swedenborgian, Unionist, Unitarian, and Universalist churches.

Overall, according to 1860 U.S. Census data, there were well over fifty-thousand churches of various denominations and sizes established throughout the United States at the time of the Civil War—about 60 percent of them in the North and the balance in the South—with estimated total property valued at $169,074,197. The number of churches and the value of property associated with individual denominations is provided in the listings that follow as an indicator of their relative size and influence.

About 25 percent of the combined population of the South, white and black, were members of various churches, and an estimated 64 percent of Southerners are believed to have attended religious services regularly.

Methodists

Methodism was the largest and most widespread religion in the United States at the time of the Civil War. Methodism expanded throughout the country, especially, the frontier, during the Second Great Awakening, when ministers called circuit riders traveled from community to community, spreading the word, establishing relationships with families, and converting the unchurched. There were nearly twenty thousand Methodist churches in the United States at the outbreak of the war, somewhat more than half of them in the North. Total value of Methodist church property in the country at that time was $32,888,421.

Although Northern and Southern Methodists had separated in 1845, bishops in the Confederate states were initially wary of secession.

Presbyterians

In 1860, Presbyterians were one of the major denominations in the United States and, beyond their main branch, could be further divided into three major sects, Cumberland Presbyterians, Reformed Presbyterians, and United Presbyterians. Many of these divisions had occurred or been reinforced during the First and Second Great Awakenings.

At the time of the Civil War, there were some 5,048 Presbyterian churches in the country, about two-thirds of them in Northern states, along with 820 Cumberland Presbyterian churches (more than 80 percent in the South), 136 Reformed Presbyterian churches (125 of them in the North), and 389 United Presbyterian churches (all but a couple of them in the North). Overall value of Presbyterian church property in 1860 was an estimated at $24,028,859 ($914,256 Cumberland Presbyterian, $386,635 Reformed Presbyterian, $1,312,275 United Presbyterian).

Presbyterian leaders in the South initially sought to prevent involving the church in secession or the politics associated with the war. In October 1861, however, the Southern members of the Presbyterian General Assembly met to establish the Presbyterian Church in the Confederate States.

Episcopalians

Essentially an Americanized form of Anglicanism, the Episcopal Church was formed in the wake of the American Revolution in order that a religion in communion with the Church of England might exist but not compel Americans to pledge loyalty to the English monarch. The root religion had, in any event, been well-established in America since the Colonial era, where it had been the official religion in Virginia since its earliest days and spread outward from there.

Episcopalian ministers in the South generally opposed support of secession and instead prayed for the preservation of the nation as a whole. There were notable exceptions to this, of course, as in the case of Bishop Leonidas Polk of Louisiana, who went on to become a Confederate lieutenant general. By the fall of 1861, Episcopalian clergy in seven Southern states had formed the Protestant Episcopal Church in the Confederate States and approved a new constitution for it (members from North Carolina, Tennessee, Texas, and Virginia abstained from these actions).

There were more than 2,100 Episcopalian churches established throughout America at the onset of the Civil War, about two-thirds of them in the North and one-third of them in the South. Value of Episcopal church property at that time was $21,481,498.

Baptists

On the eve of the Civil War, Baptists were one of the largest denominations in the country and among those that were considerably more widespread and influential in the South than in the North. At the time of the Civil War, there were some 11,219 Baptist churches in the country, with about two-thirds of them in Southern states (this is an especially telling proportion when one considers that the white population of the North was about three-and-a-half times larger than that of the South). Value of Baptist church property was an estimated $19,746,378.

In 1845, Northern and Southern Baptists split over the issue of slavery, and the latter formed a separate denomination under the Southern Baptist Convention (SBC); the leaders of this offshoot denomination strongly supported secession and were in favor of the South becoming its own nation. Then, in the years following the war, many blacks split off from the SBC and established their own congregations.

A number of smaller Baptist sects also existed throughout the country at the time of the war, and these sects included the Free Will Baptist (530 churches, property value $789,295), Seventh Day Baptist (fifty-three churches, property value $107,200), Six Principle Baptist (nine churches, property value $8,150), and Winnebrenner Baptist (sixty-five churches, property value $74,175). Approximately nine out of ten Winnebrenner Baptist sects were located in Northern states.

Lutherans

German and Scandinavian immigrants brought Lutheranism with them to America, with significant numbers of them arriving in the 1830s and 1840s. At the time of the Civil War, there were some 2,125 Lutheran churches in the country, about six out of seven of them in Northern states, especially Indiana, Ohio, Michigan, and Missouri (although a significant number of those in

Southern states were located in south Texas, were large numbers of German immigrants settled from about 1848 onward). Value of Lutheran church property was an estimated $5,352,679.

Roman Catholics

America was predominantly a Protestant country on the eve of the Civil War, which contributed to significant anti-Roman Catholic sentiment and the marginalization of Catholics. There were nonetheless a number of significant Catholic redoubts throughout the country, some of the most notable being Baltimore and southern Maryland, the latter of which had been settled by Jesuits starting in 1634. Large numbers of Irish immigrants that began to arrive in the United States beginning in the middle of the nineteenth century swelled the number of Catholics in the country and helped to bolster the strength of the religion.

By 1860, there were 2,117 Catholic churches active in Northern states and 539 in Southern ones. Roman Catholic property in America at the time of the Civil War was valued at $26,047,159.

African Methodist Episcopal Church

The Second Great Awakening was the defining event in the spread of Christianity among blacks in the United States when, during the revivals associated with it, Baptist and Methodist ministers converted large numbers of them. As slaves or, at best, second-class citizens, many blacks were disappointed with the way they were treated by whites with the same religious beliefs and at the lapsed promises from many of them to support abolition. As a result, from the late eighteenth century onward, the strongest black religious leaders began to form their own denominations, and a number of independent black Baptist congregations were among the most significant of these. Minister Richard Allen and his colleagues separated themselves from the Methodist Church and founded what would become one of the largest and most successful, the African Methodist Episcopal (AME) Church, in Philadelphia in 1815. This new denomination thrived and, by 1846, it had expanded to 296 churches with 176 clergymen and 17,375 members.

America was predominantly a Protestant country on the eve of the Civil War, which contributed to significant anti-Roman Catholic sentiment and the marginalization of Catholics.

Church of the Brethren

Colloquially known as Dunkers (as in the "Dunker Church" on the Antietam Battlefield), the Brethren were a type of Baptist that was established primarily in the Northern states. At the onset of the Civil War, there were some 163 Church of the Brethren churches in the United States with a total property valued at $162,956.

Like other religious groups that opposed the war on moral grounds, the Brethren were persecuted for being pacifists. While its members were ultimately exempted from military service upon payment of a $500 fee, some still paid heavy prices for their position. One Brethren leader, for example, became distrusted by the authorities for providing medical assistance to the wounded of both sides, and as a result was jailed without legal reason and, in the summer of 1864, attacked and killed.

Adventists

Adventism started as an interdenominational movement during the Second Great Awakening and was based on a belief in the imminent second coming of Jesus Christ. At the start of the Civil War, there were some seventy Adventist churches in the country, all of them located in Northern states. Total value of Adventist church property was $101,170.

Quakers

Members of the Society of Friends, better known as Quakers, were well established in America by the time of the Civil War and, in 1860, they had 663 churches established in Northern states—particularly Pennsylvania, which was home to nearly a quarter of them—and sixty-two churches in Southern states. Total value of church property was valued at $2,534,507.

As pacifists unwilling to serve in the military forces of either the Union or the Confederacy during the war, Quakers were treated with suspicion by the governments of both sides.

Jews

The first Jews, some twenty-three of them, arrived in what was to become New York City in 1654. Judaism thrived in the New World—although it did not expand as quickly or to extent that other denominations did in the early years of America—and was bolstered by the arrival of highly-educated German Jews who began to arrive in the mid-nineteenth century and establish themselves as merchants in cities and towns across the country. By 1860, there were some fifty-two synagogues established in Northern states and nineteen established in Southern ones (notably Charleston, South Carolina). Total value of Jewish ecclesiastic property was valued at $1,125,300.

Jewish troops served in both Confederate and Union regiments during the war. Prominent Jews included Judah P. Benjamin, the first Jewish U.S. senator and a member of Confederate President Jefferson Davis' cabinet.

Mormons

More properly known as the Church of Jesus Christ of Latter-day Saints, Mormonism was founded in western upstate New York by Joseph Smith Jr. in 1830 after he claimed to experience a series of visions, visitations from angels, and revelations from God. Mormon beliefs were atypical to say the least—and included a new written canon and practices like polygamy—and adherents of the new faith were savagely persecuted as a result and driven further and further westward. Smith himself was murdered in 1844 and his successor, Brigham Young, led the members of the church to the unregulated Utah Territory.

There were just two Mormon churches in the country in 1860, both of them in Northern states. The total estimated value of their property was $1,100.

The Great Awakenings

Three "Great Awakenings," widespread evangelical movements that transformed the religious landscape of America, took place in the 130 years or so leading up to the outbreak of the Civil War. Each of these events had significant and permanent effects on the institution of religion in the country and was based on forceful evangelism and large-scale events, such as revivals and camp meetings. They encouraged people to be passionately involved in their religion and, in addition to attending church, to also study the Bible at home on their own. Each followed, to a great extent, on the momentum of the one preceding it.

The **First Great Awakening** took place in the 1730s and 1740s, during the Colonial era, and was a wave of religious fervor that moved away from ceremony and ritual, challenged established authority and changed the way people worshipped. This event instilled churchgoing Protestants with a profound sense both of personal guilt and salvation through Christ; caused division among various denominations, notably the Congregational and Presbyterian churches; and was used by Baptist and Methodist ministers to bring Christianity to enslaved blacks in the South. It helped to consolidate the Presbyterian, Baptist, and Methodist denominations as the largest in the country by the early part of the nineteenth century. The Anglican, Quaker, and Congregationalist churches generally opposed the movement and were both divided by and left out of it.

The **Second Great Awakening** took place during the first three decades of the 1800s and focused largely on non-churchgoers and the idea that all people could be saved through revivals. It resulted in millions of unchurched people joining established churches and in the foundation of many of the new denominations that appeared in America during the nineteenth century. During this time, evangelism and camp meetings became hallmarks of American religious life. It also encouraged the creation of reform movements and benevolent societies designed to heal the ills of society ahead of the second coming of Jesus Christ. As with the movement that preceded it, Methodism in particular prospered during the Second Great Awakening and became the country's biggest and most widespread religious denomination. Presbyterians and Baptists, too, were very active in the movement—and the latter denomination in particular benefitted from it—but distanced themselves from the most fervent elements once they began to lose control of their roles in them.

The **Third Great Awakening** began in the late 1850s and continued on through the era of the Civil War and up to the end of the century. Its hallmark was a strong sense of social activism and, as with the previous movements, it affected primarily the pietistic Protestant denominations (that is, those that emphasized a vigorous Christian lifestyle and individual piety). It, too, drew strength from the idea of a second coming of Christ that would be precipitated by a general reformation of the world, and many of its adherents set about trying to eradicate social problems like alcohol abuse, bad hygiene, child labor, crime, inadequate education, inequality, pornography, prostitution, racism, slums, weak labor unions, and war. Its followers were, to a great extent in the North, at least, supporters of the Republican Party (the party of Lincoln) which, in that era, was characterized by social progressiveness.

While the Second Great Awakening occurred to a great extent on the frontier, the third was centered primarily in towns and cities. Various denominations sought to accomplish their goals through vigorous outreach to the unfaithful, worldwide missionary work, and establishment of colleges and universities. Revivals were also a major component of the movement, and some areas experienced so many of them that they acquired appellations like "the burned-over district." An estimated one million people in America—one in thirty, including blacks—converted during this movement and a like number are believed to have been reinvigorated in their faith.

In the North, the Third Great Awakening was, to a great extent, interrupted by the Civil War and lost momentum among the civilian populace until after the war's conclusion. In the South, however, it continued largely unabated, primarily within the Baptist church, which benefitted from it greatly. In any event, many clergymen on both sides, but especially in the North, believed that the war heralded the second coming of Christ.

The Third Great Awakening also extended into the camps of the opposing armies and, over the course of the war, huge revivals broke out within them and as many as 10 percent of Civil War soldiers may have been converted to Christianity during the war (an estimated 100,000 to 200,000 in the Northern forces and an estimated 150,000 in the Southern forces).

Benevolent Societies

Benevolent societies were a type of institution established throughout the United States in the early nineteenth century and several were active at the time of the Civil War. Such groups were a direct outgrowth of the evangelical movement as exemplified in the Second and Third Great Awakenings. They included the American Bible Society (1816), the American Board of Commissioners for Foreign Missions (1812), the American Baptist Home Missionary Society (1832), the American Sunday-School Union (1817), and the American Tract Society (1825).

Such groups were devoted to the salvation of souls through the extirpation of social ills and were used by the evangelical movement to Christianize America. Many of them were active in the military camps of both sides, where they sought to save the souls of soldiers and gain converts to Christianity from among the unchurched.

"The evidence of God's grace was a person's benevolence toward others," wrote Presbyterian evangelist Charles Grandison Finney, a major figure in the Second Great Awakening.

One of the means benevolent societies used for spreading their various messages was through tracts, and tens of millions of these were distributed throughout the course of the war (for example, the U.S. Christian Commission by itself distributed some thirty million tracts).

For many women volunteers, involvement with benevolent societies or the activities of groups like the **U.S. Sanitary Commission** was their first experience with work outside the home.

Chaplains

At least 3,694 clergymen are known to have served the opposing sides as military regimental or hospital chaplains, nearly two-thirds of them for Northern forces and the balance for Southern units. They came from every major religious denomination in the country, and the best of them shared the hardships with the men to whom they ministered and made a difference in their lives.

While there were many overtly pious men on both sides—including generals like Union William S. Rosecrans and Confederate Robert E. Lee, Thomas J. "Stonewall" Jackson, and Leonidas Polk, who was an Episcopal bishop—many commanders nonetheless viewed chaplains as extraneous, obstructive, or even a bit suspect. Such uniformed ministers ran the gamut from those with true ability, dedication, and a sense of ministry on the one hand, to those who were out of their depth, looking for an easy job, or seeking personal gain on the other.

The role of chaplains and their place in the unit chain of command was only poorly defined during the Civil War and those in the Army did not have any organization above the regimental level (this situation was, in fact, not significantly changed until after the conclusion World War I, in 1920). Their primary mission was, in any event, the spiritual well-being of the soldiers in their regiments (or ships for those in the opposing navies). And the best of those who served used the flexibility afforded them to make the most of their positions in their units.

Attitudes of troops toward chaplains varied widely, from those who welcomed uniformed ministers to those who, in the words of one Catholic chaplain, "could find their way to hell without the assistance of clergy."

Actual duties of chaplains varied widely and were an amalgam of those they undertook of their own initiative and those directed by their commanders. These duties included any and all of the responsibilities associated with conducting Sunday services, offering prayers at daily formations, serving as a friend to lonely and isolated troops, distributing tracts, tending to the sick, and retrieving wounded soldiers from the battlefield.

The average Union chaplain was a bit older than thirty-eight.

Union Chaplains

Some 2,398 clergy members served as Union hospital, navy, or regimental chaplains (2,154 in the latter capacity). They ranged in age from 19 to 76 years of age, the average chaplain being somewhat more than thirty-eight. Their terms of service ranged from less than a month to more than fifty-one months, with the mean being thirteen-and-a-half months.

Denominations they represented included Methodist (38 percent), Presbyterian (17 percent), Baptist (12 percent), Episcopal (10 percent), Congregational (9 percent), Unitarian/Universalist (4 percent), Roman Catholic (3 percent), and Lutheran (2 percent), with other denominations collectively representing 5 percent.

Early in the war, chaplaincy in the Union forces was open only to ordained Christian ministers; Jewish rabbis were prevented from serving in this capacity, which led to significant outcry and was reversed by the summer of 1862. And, just as they were not allowed to serve as Union soldiers until 1863, blacks were not allowed to serve as chaplains until then, after which as many as seventeen were commissioned as uniformed clergymen. In at least one case, however, the paymaster general paid black clergymen as laborers, rather than the commissioned officers that they were, and at a rate of only $10 a month. At least one woman also sought to become a regimental chaplain but, despite the blessing of Abraham Lincoln himself, was denied by the War Department; serving at her own expense, she was not officially recognized until after the end of war, not given any pay until eleven years after the conflict ended, and was denied disability benefits.

Initially, pay for Union military chaplains was $145.50 per month, with three daily rations and forage for one horse. On July 17, 1862, however, the War Department reduced compensation for chaplains to just $100 per month, two daily rations, and forage for one horse. Furthermore, the paymaster general of the Union armed forces interpreted the regulations to mean that chaplains should only receive pay while on active duty, and, unlike other soldiers, they were thus deprived of remuneration while on leave. This situation had to be rectified by an act of Congress, which was passed April 9, 1864, a full three years into the war.

Standards for Union chaplains were also tightened in July 1862 (for example, they were required to produce letters of reference from five other clergymen of the same denomination). The War Department ordered that chaplains already assigned to units to be retroactively held to such standards, but regimental commanders had a great deal of leeway with regard to those they wished to retain.

Very early in the war there was little specifying what chaplains should wear, and many commanders dictated that they should be attired in civilian garb appropriate to their role as clergymen. In November 1861, the war department dictated that the official uniform for chaplains should be a plain, black officer's frock coat with a single row of buttons, black trousers, and a black hat. There was much variation from regiment-to-regiment, however, and some chaplains even found it expedient to wear a regular captain's uniform, commensurate with their pay grade, in order to emphasize their position as commissioned officers, and many who did so also wore swords for the same reason. Many Union chaplains also augmented whatever ensemble they wore with a blue waist sash—inspired, in part, by the green sashes worn by surgeons—and with various other regalia, such as embroidered gold crosses on their epaulets. The regulations dictating the uniforms for chaplains were revised in 1864, but this had little impact on what was actually done in the field.

Throughout the course of the war, some eleven Union chaplains were killed in action, another four were mortally wounded, and seventy-three suffered non-combat deaths. The rigors of military life were evident in the post-war mortality rates of many of them, however, and about two hundred of them died either by 1871 or at inordinately young ages.

Ninety-seven Union chaplains received special commendations for their service, notably caring for the wounded and being incarcerated as prisoners of war. Four were awarded the Medal of

Honor, one for leading a counterattack after the leadership of his regiment had been annihilated. Of the roughly two thousand who served the Union, 112 of them did so for three years or longer.

Confederate Chaplains

More than 1,300 Southern clergymen and soldiers accepted commissions as chaplains with Confederate military units between 1861 and 1865. About half of them were thirty years or younger in 1861. Some 14 percent of eligible clergy in the South ultimately served as chaplains during the war.

Initially, there were no provisions for chaplains in Confederate military units, and Southern leaders focused on organizing and arming their forces without consideration for them. There were a number of reasons for this, and they included the lack of an existing military tradition that

About half of the Confederate

chaplains were under the age of thirty.

included chaplains—only one, who taught at U.S. Army Military Academy at West Point, was on the rolls in the years leading up the war—and a lack of their perceived value from Southern leaders who included C.S. President Jefferson Davis. Almost immediately, however, Southern clergymen hoping to serve as Confederate military chaplains began to protest this disregard and to petition the government to address it.

In late April 1861, the Virginia Convention for Secession directed the governor to appoint one chaplain for each of the state's brigades. Then, less than a week later, on May 2, the C.S. Congress passed a bill authorizing the president to commission chaplains and assign them to various units as appropriate.

Confederate chaplains served at the regimental, brigade, and even corps level, and in a variety of other posts as well, such as at hospitals, but all were considered to hold the same rank and none had command authority.

Pay for Confederate military chaplains was initially set at $85 a month, with no allowances for meals, forage, quarters, uniforms, or the like. Within two weeks, however, the C.S. Congress reduced the pay for chaplains to just $50 a month, an action that sparked outrage amongst the religious throughout the South. Ministers with families simply could not afford to serve in the military for any extended period of time.

Chaplains were eventually provide rations equal to those of privates and lobbying by religious organizations prompted the Confederate government to raise the pay for chaplains to $80 a month by the spring of 1862. In 1864, chaplains were also provided with forage if they owned a horse and an allowance for stationery. Individual commanders also sometimes provided nominal subsistence to chaplains, such as firewood in the winter or an issue of clothing.

No particular training, experience, or other qualifications were required for a chaplain to be commissioned into the Confederate military. Many of those chaplains who were ordained ministers had received their training through apprenticeships to older clergymen in their own churches rather than at seminaries, which were few and far between in the largely rural South. Most of the

The 50th New York Volunteer Engineer Regiment built this log church in Poplar Grove, Virginia.

rest had studied at universities in the South, while a handful had received their educations in the North or Europe.

Denominations for somewhat more than seven in ten Confederate chaplains are known, and these included Methodist (47 percent), Presbyterian (18 percent), Baptist (16 percent), Episcopal (10 percent), and Roman Catholic (3 percent), with Cumberland Presbyterian, Lutheran, Disciples of Christ, Missionary Baptist, and Congregational each representing less than 1 percent each. The Presbyterian and Missionary Baptist denominations each sent missionaries to the Confederate forces, and the former group also sent commissioners to recruit chaplains from the ranks to fill available openings. Missionaries were often better paid by their churches than they would have been by the military, something that allowed them to stay in the field with the armies. The Southern churches were, in any event, generally slow to provide chaplains early in the war.

Confederate chaplains had no authorized uniforms, rank, or insignia, and many simply wore the same attire they did in their role as civilian clergy. Some also wore uniforms based on those worn by other Confederate officers, especially surgeons, or modified or created their own outfits, insignia, and accessories. As the war dragged on and resources dwindled, however, many simply wore whatever was available, like most of the other personnel in the Southern ranks.

During the war, nine Confederate chaplains were killed in action or as the result of their wounds, thirty-two died from illness or other causes, and twenty were wounded but not killed as result of their injuries.

Terms

ARMINIANISM: A school of thought within Protestantism based on the ideas of Dutch Reformed theologian Jacobus Arminius that provided much of the theological basis for the Second Great Awakening.

BIBLE STUDENTS: A religious movement started in Pittsburgh, Pennsylvania, in 1870 by minister Charles Taze Russell that was one of the sects inspired by the spiritual fervor of the Third Great Awakening and which eventually became known as Jehovah's Witnesses.

CHAPLAIN MILITANT: A term used for Union chaplains who chose to wear the same uniforms as other officers rather than the regular black garb authorized for military clergymen.

CONFEDERATE MEMORIAL DAYS: Holidays that differed by state and which were

observed in the South in lieu of Decoration Day in the North.

DECORATION DAY: The predecessor to Memorial Day, this holiday was first observed on May 5, 1866, in Waterloo, New York, to honor those slain in the Civil War and included parades, placing flowers on graves, and flying flags at half-staff. It was celebrated on a national level for the first time on May 30, 1868, almost three

years to the day that the last Confederate army surrendered.

DUNKARD, TÄUFER, TUNKER: Variant names for the Dunker sect, more properly known as the Old German Baptist Brethren, a denomination that practiced adult baptism by immersion and appeared in America starting in 1719, after some of its adherents fled persecution in Germany.

HOLY JOE: A nickname for military chaplains used primarily by U.S. troops.

NEW LIGHTS: A term used for ministers who adopted an evangelical style of preaching during the Great Awakenings. Compare with old lights.

OLD LIGHTS: A term used for ministers who retained a traditional style of preaching during the Great Awakenings. Compare with new lights.

U.S. CHRISTIAN COMMISSION: A civilian agency founded by the Young Men's Christian Association during the war to offer religious support and other services to military personnel. It was very evangelical in nature and competed throughout the war with the "godless" U.S. Sanitary Commission.

U.S. SANITARY COMMISSION: A civilian commission, strongly supported by the Federal government, that looked after the well-being of troops by providing them with food, medicine, and clothing; helped to oversee their living conditions; and established field hospitals for them. The commission had more than four thousand local branches and held fundraisers, such as art exhibitions or teas, which they called Sanitary Fairs. It was strongly influenced by a Universalist leadership and was constantly at odds with the evangelical U.S. Christian Commission.

WOMAN'S CHRISTIAN TEMPERANCE UNION: A non-sectarian women's organization founded in 1874 at a national convention in Cleveland, Ohio, that spearheaded a national crusade for prohibition that various local groups had started in the preceding years. Members fought intemperance by going into saloons where they sang, prayed, and urged bartenders to stop selling alcohol.

YOUNG MEN'S CHRISTIAN ASSOCIATION: Better known as the YMCA, this evangelical group devoted to the idea of "muscular Christianity" was founded in 1844 and active during the Civil War, attempting to take over the operations of the military's chaplain corps in 1861–62. It founded U.S. Christian Commission.

FUN AND GAMES:
HOW PEOPLE ENTERTAINED THEMSELVES

"No human being is innocent, but there is a class of
innocent human actions called Games." —W. H. Auden

D uring the nineteenth century, people were less accustomed than modern Americans to constant sensory bombardment. Nonetheless, civilians and soldiers alike enjoyed games, music, spectator and participant sports, and other recreations as diversions from the problems and tedium of everyday life or a mental escape from the specter of combat and death.

Entertainment in the North

Society in the North was becoming increasingly urbanized and diverse, and many forms of entertainment evolved that were both tailored to large crowds and likely to suit a wide variety of tastes and backgrounds. Spectator sports like horse racing and boxing were popular.

Gambling was also popular, both on spectator sports and at the gaming table, and people often played casual card or board games with friends and family.

Theater, another largely urban form of entertainment, evolved during the nineteenth century, and vaudeville and burlesque emerged as unique forms of staged entertainment for the masses.

Circuses, in both cities and the country, also came into their own as a distinct form of entertainment, especially in the years following the Civil War.

Entertainment in the South

Being less urbanized than the North, people in the South tended toward smaller-scale kinds of entertainment, especially prior to the war. Balls held by the upper crust, activities shared by farm families, and festivals celebrated in towns, villages, or plantations predominated.

Venues for spectator activities, such as baseball parks or race tracks, were much less widespread than in the North. Participant sports, however, such as horse racing among the members of a club or village, were likely activities.

Travelling circuses and carnivals, especially in conjunction with county or state fairs, were also popular, and broke up the day-to-day routines of rural life.

Shortages imposed by the war changed the nature of many social activities, of course, but Southerners still enjoyed them. "Biscuit parties" were thrown by those able to obtain some wheat flour or by friends who might each bring what they had available. Later in the war, when for many there was not flour or anything else to be had, people held "starvation parties," where the only refreshment served was water.

Games

Card, board, and dice games were popular among civilians and soldiers alike. Because of the monotony of camp life, many soldiers in particular spent as much time as they could absorbed in games when other duties did not call.

Dice were generally small, a bit crude, and made out of wood (although some might be made from flattened musket balls, such as those of the Revolutionary War, among troops still using muskets). Craps was the dice game played most often, but others included one known variously as **birdcage**, **chuck-a-luck**, or **sweet cloth**. Skewed results or even cheating were easily facilitated by the fact that so many dice were imperfect, or even designed to produce certain results more often than others.

Board games included checkers, chess, and backgammon, more-or-less in that order of popularity. Checkers, in particular, were popular throughout the armies and navies of both sides. Boards used by soldiers in the field might be handmade and were small so as not to be an encumbrance. Checkerboard patterns in red and green or red and yellow were as common as today's more familiar red and black. Chess was played much less frequently, but was not unknown at the time.

> Later in the war, when for many there was not flour or anything else to be had, people held "starvation parties," where the only refreshment served was water.

Although soldiers enjoyed gambling, many considered gambling to be a mortal sin. As a result, soldiers would play cards or dice right up until marching off to battle, then destroy or discard their gaming implements so they would not be upon their persons if they were slain.

Soldiers—enlisted men and officers alike—played many different card games including draw poker, **cribbage**, euchre, faro, keno, seven-up, and twenty-one. Regiments tended to have games that they favored, poker being the most common. Such games were usually played for stakes, which, among less-than-friendly groups, could lead to sore feelings or even charges of cheating.

While dice and board-game components were frequently crude or homemade, many sorts of manufactured playing cards were available. During the Civil War, numerous varieties of decks were produced that replaced traditional playing-card symbols with military and patriotic imagery. The Union Playing Card Company, for example, replaced the traditional suits of spades, clubs, hearts, and diamonds with eagles, shields, stars, and flags. Similarly, a deck manufactured in the South depicted a different Confederate general or cabinet member on each card in the deck.

Although soldiers enjoyed gambling, a preponderance of men considered gambling, or "**throwing the papers**," to be a mortal sin. As a result, soldiers would play cards or dice right up until marching off to battle, then destroy or discard their gaming implements so they would not be upon their persons if they were slain. After the battle, survivors eager for a game would search the former campsite for their cards or dice or purchase new ones from sutlers, the traveling merchants who followed the armies during the war.

Other games, such as jackstraws, were also played by some civilians and soldiers, and games like **prisoner's base** were also popular with children.

Soldiers had little of their time occupied by battle, and found many ways to fill the lonely hours of camp life.

Music

Singing as a group activity was a common activity in the nineteenth century, whether hymns by the devout or bawdy drinking songs among comrades, and soldiers in the field often sang around the proverbial campfire (see Appendix E). Lyrics to popular songs tended to be widely-known, especially in the armies, where they were often disseminated rapidly.

Many people also owned and knew how to play a wide variety of instruments, banjos being among the most popular. While the banjo

Harper's Weekly and *Godey's Lady's Book* were popular and common publications during the Civil War.

is today associated with Appalachia and the South, it was as likely to be played in the camps of either side. Pianos might be found in middle-class or wealthy homes or saloons, while portable instruments—like harmonicas and mouth harps—were more likely to be found in the hands of the less affluent or those who had to carry their possessions or had less room to store them, such as soldiers or sailors.

Reading

Many sorts of reading materials were available to people during the Civil War, among them publications such as *Harper's Bazaar* and *Godey's Lady's Book*, classic and popular literature, and a wide variety of daily and weekly newspapers (newspapers are discussed in greater detail under Communications in chapter 10). Many families entertained themselves by listening to one member read aloud from a novel or periodical.

Popular novelists of the day included Louisa May Alcott and Augusta Jane Evans, and, in the years following the war, Mark Twain, whose *Innocents Abroad* was published in 1869, and former Gen. Lew Wallace, whose *Ben Hur: A Tale of the Christ*, was published in 1880. Popular among many readers were dime novels, which detailed the often exaggerated adventures of people like Buffalo Bill and other heroes of the far West.

An 1863 illustration of Union prisoners playing baseball at a Confederate prison in Salisbury, North Carolina. This image likely bears very little resemblance to the actual conditions found in a Southern prisoner-of-war camp.

Many sorts of magazines and newspapers were also readily available and covered a wide variety of themes, including agriculture, art, children's literature, education, etiquette, fashion, fiction, finance, gardening, home architecture, humor, labor reform, medicine, music, politics, religion, sports, and women's issues. And, with subscription rates as low as $2 to $4 per year, such publications could easily be obtained by most people interested in them. After the war ended, numbers of such publications increased markedly and, by 1870, almost six thousand different periodicals were being published in the United States.

Sports

Sports, both as participant and spectator events, were popular with people during the mid-nineteenth century. Prior to the Civil War, horse racing and boxing were among the most popular spectator sports with many Americans, especially in the North. Race tracks with open green space were especially popular in crowded urban areas.

After the war, baseball entered the scene as America's most popular pastime, a role it has continued to play to a lesser-or-greater extent. Other popular sports included football, cricket, heel-toe walking races, and horse trotting.

Theater

Prior to and during the nineteenth century, American theater was heavily influenced by trends in Europe. In Europe as well as America, the Industrial Revolution created a need for entertainments geared toward the tastes of working-class people, such as pantomimes, spectacles, melodrama, and the previously-mentioned vaudeville. And, on a somewhat higher plane, there were romantic dramas and revivals of classic operas and plays, including Shakespeare.

Several different sorts of variety shows arose during the nineteenth century as forms of entertainment for the great masses of working people, many of them immigrants living in the rapidly-growing urban areas. Music halls in England and minstrel shows and burlesque in America often employed coarse humor and were generally considered appropriate fare for saloons or male-only audiences. More wholesome variety shows and vaudeville arose in the years following the Civil War as a response to the growing demand for family entertainment.

Because the North was more urbanized, such forms of entertainment were better known there than in the South, but these would have been found in larger cities like New Orleans.

Music Halls

At the time of the Civil War, music halls were the most popular form of mass entertainment in England. These were theaters or taverns with stages where people could drink, hear and sing popular songs, and watch dance routines, comedy, magic, and other acts, all presided over by a master of ceremonies. Many of the professional music hall entertainers became famous throughout England and some of them even toured the United States.

Minstrel Shows

While music halls were largely a phenomenon peculiar to England, minstrel shows were indigenous to the United States. Together, they helped to influence the rise of the burlesque and vaudeville variety shows in America.

Also called blackface shows, minstrel shows had existed in America since Colonial times, mainly as short acts with travelling carnivals. In the 1820s, troupes like the Virginia Minstrels began to put on full-length variety shows and, before long, these spread throughout the United States and to England, where they joined other music hall acts. During the 1840s, the Virginia Minstrels were touring cities both in the United States and Europe.

Such blackface shows included comedy, dance, and popular music, typically performed by white men wearing black face paint and singing and speaking like stereotypical blacks. Indeed, the basis of such shows was the parodying of blacks, something that has made them anathema today. It also seems a bit strange today that such a widespread, popular form of entertainment could have at its heart such a narrow gimmick.

Minstrel shows typically consisted of three parts. In the first, the entire troupe sat on stage in a semicircle and sang popular songs such as "Camptown Races" or "Old Folks at Home," and engaged in riddles, puns, and comedic one-liners. The second part, called the olio, was a variety show in which entertainers appeared and performed individually. The third part was a farcical skit that combined comedy and music in what was often a parody of current fads or events. A master of ceremonies, or interlocutor, usually oversaw the events of the show.

Among the best known minstrel acts of the age were the Christy Minstrels. Formed by Edwin P. Christy, this troupe played in New York City from 1846 until 1854 and helped popularize the songs of Stephen Foster.

Burlesque and vaudeville replaced minstrel shows as a popular form of variety show during the nineteenth century.

Minstrel shows dominated the American entertainment scene until long after the end of the Civil War. They reflected a preoccupation with slavery and the role of the freed black in society, and highlighted how racist much of white society was. As a form of entertainment, however, their days were numbered.

Variety Shows

Some impresarios saw a market for "clean" variety shows that left behind saloon environment and were suitable for women and children as well as men. One of these was Tony Pastor, the "father of American vaudeville," who abandoned his career as a circus clown for the variety show business. In 1865, he opened his first variety theater in New York City, which specialized in wholesome acts and songs that poked fun at the upper crust, aspects that made his shows popular with working-class family people.

Burlesque

There was still a market for the off-color show, however. Burlesque shows began as comic parodies of well-known people or subjects, but steadily evolved into "girlie" shows that included provocative displays of the female form. One of the most famous of these was Lydia Thompson and her British Blondes, who brought their burlesques of classical drama to America in 1868. In this all-girl show, the women wore tights and short tunics when playing male roles, outfits that were considered very risqué at the time.

By the 1870s, American producers like M.B. Leavitt capitalized on the market for **"burleycue"** and "leg shows" by organizing female burlesque troupes who replaced parody with racy dance routines like the cancan. Before long, the buxom stars of these shows were being referred to as "burlesque queens." Increasingly, however, male comedians were also added to the acts and developed comedy routines designed to appeal to the sorts of crowds who came to such shows.

Vaudeville

Vaudeville shows combined a variety of unconnected musical, dancing, comedy, and specialty acts and developed in the decades following the Civil War. To a large extent, they evolved from the olio, or variety portion of the minstrel show (minus, of course, the blackface). First built in the 1880s, vaudeville houses were ornate, opulent theaters with uniformed attendants where people of any class could feel like honored guests for an entry fee of 25¢.

Vaudeville, predecessor of the modern variety show, emerged in the 1870s as a popular form of urban entertainment and eventually came to replace the minstrel show. In its early years, however, it was widely considered a lewd form of entertainment for men only, and it was not until the 1880s that it became a popular form of family entertainment.

Stars

Like celebrities today, the theatrical stars of the nineteenth century were well-known and loved. Stage divas were also popular during the Civil War and the years following it, and many were as well-known and popular as celebrities today.

Most beloved of all was "Swedish Nightingale" Jenny Lind (1820–1887), a singer who appeared in every major European opera house between 1838 and 1849 and toured throughout the United States in the early 1850s, where she was lauded in the press. Other European stars, like William Charles Macready, were also well-known on both sides of the Atlantic, and frequently toured American cities during the mid-nineteenth century.

The New World also produced its own stars during this period. Edwin Forrest (1806–1872) was perhaps the greatest, and certainly the most popular, American tragic actor of the nineteenth century. Known for his arrogance, short temper, booming voice, and fierce looks, Forrest was famous for his many Shakespearean roles, especially Othello. He also offered prizes to encourage the writing of American plays and, as a result, had many roles created for him.

Stage divas were also popular during the Civil War and the years following it, and many were as well-known and popular as celebrities today.

PHINEAS TAYLOR "P.T." BARNUM

JOHN WILKES BOOTH

CIVIL WAR *Celebrities*

Following are some of the most influential writers, entertainers, orators, and performers of the Civil War era, along with brief notations about their claims to fame. Many military leaders, politicians, and clergymen became well known during this era as well, and many of these are mentioned in their appropriate context elsewhere in this book.

CHARLOTTE SAUNDERS CUSHMAN

» **LOUISA MAY ALCOTT**, author of *Little Women*.

» **IRA FREDERICK ALDRIDGE**, a free black from New York City, who became the first famous black American actor (albeit in Europe).

» **PHINEAS TAYLOR "P.T." BARNUM**, an impresario and showman who ran the American Museum in New York City from 1841 to 1868 and who took his show on the road in the form of a huge travelling circus, museum, and menagerie in 1871.

» **EDWIN BOOTH**, a popular stage actor and the manager of a theater in New York City (and brother of presidential assassin John Wilkes Booth).

» **JOHN WILKES BOOTH**, a popular stage actor whose fervent Southern sympathies promoted him to assassinate President Abraham Lincoln.

» **EDWIN P. CHRISTY**, founder of the Christy Minstrels troupe of entertainers that played in New York City in the 1840s and 1850s.

» **WILLIAM FREDERICK "BUFFALO BILL" CODY**, who reflected his experiences as a soldier and bison hunter in his Wild West show starting in the 1870s.

» **CHARLOTTE SAUNDERS CUSHMAN**, a popular American stage actress from Boston.

JENNY LIND

MARK TWAIN

EDWIN FORREST

» **FREDERICK DOUGLASS**, a free black orator and writer.

» **AUGUSTA JANE EVANS**, a prominent Southern author of nine novels.

» **EDWIN FORREST**, the most popular American tragic stage actor of the nineteenth century.

» **STEPHEN FOSTER**, a popular American songwriter.

» **JOICE HETH**, an aged black slave who P.T. Barnum purchased in 1835 and then exhibited as the 161-year-old nurse of George Washington.

» **M.B. LEAVITT**, an impresario who specialized in burlesque shows.

» **JENNY LIND**, the "Swedish Nightingale," an opera singer.

» **WILLIAM CHARLES MACREADY**, an English stage actor who was popular in both Europe and America.

» **TONY PASTOR**, the "father of American vaudeville," opened his first variety theater in New York City in 1865.

» **JOHN BILL RICKETTS**, an American circus proprietor.

» **HARRIET BEECHER STOWE**, author of *Uncle Tom's Cabin*.

» **LYDIA THOMPSON**, leader of the British Blondes troupe of burlesque entertainers, which came to America in 1868.

» **MARK TWAIN**, author of *Innocents Abroad* (1869) and numerous other books.

» **JULES GABRIEL VERNE**, the French author of science fiction classics like *A Journey to the Centre of the Earth* (1864), *From the Earth to the Moon* (1865), *Twenty Thousand Leagues Under the Sea* (1870), *Around the World in Eighty Days* (1873), and *The Mysterious Island* (1875).

» **MAJ. GEN. LEW WALLACE**, author of *Ben Hur: A Tale of the Christ* (1880).

The British Blondes was a famous all-girl show in which women wore risqué costume of tights and short tunics.

Ira Frederick Aldridge (c. 1807–1867), a free black from New York City, became the first famous black American actor, albeit in Europe. In 1825, he debuted with an acting troupe in London as the African prince Oroonoko in *The Revolt of Surinam*. Nicknamed the "African Roscius," he was also lauded for his roles as Othello, King Lear, and Macbeth. Aldridge was popular throughout Europe, especially in Germany, and became a British citizen in 1863.

Other well-known American actors of the day included Charlotte Saunders Cushman; Edwin Booth, who also managed his own New York City theater; and his brother, John Wilkes Booth, most famous today as the assassin of Abraham Lincoln.

Directors and Playwrights

As stage productions became more complex, they increasingly required a director, a role which arose in its modern incarnation during this period. While he or she might still have a leading part in a play, the director was also responsible for overseeing every aspect of its production.

Playwrights also enjoyed improved status during the nineteenth century. They increasingly acted in or directed their own plays, benefited from new copyright laws that protected their work in both the United States and Europe, and began to receive royalties.

Scenery and Lighting

New technology allowed for a revolution in lighting and scenery during the nineteenth century. By the 1820s, candles and oil lamps had been replaced by gaslights in many theaters, and spotlighting effects through the use of limelight and the carbon arc were common by the 1850s. Many theaters were also fully trapped or even had hydraulic lifts, as did Edwin Booth's theater, allowing scenery to either be raised from below the stage or "flown in" from above.

Costumes, props, and settings also reached a high level of realism and historical accuracy during this period, especially in renditions of plays with historical underpinnings, such as those of Shakespeare. Scenery had traditionally been simply painted on flats, a practice that gave way to elaborate settings, such as sinking ships, falling trees, and erupting volcanoes. Such elaborate sets often required a long period between scenes to set up. Real animals— ncluding dogs, horses, and even elephants—joined human actors on stage. Other innovations of the era included completely enclosed, or "box" sets, often adopted for comedies, and moving panoramas to give the illusion of movement or travel.

Such elaborate production values meant that long-running plays also became increasingly common. As a result, the repertory system, in which theaters changed their performances almost nightly and under which a single theater might present dozens of plays in a single season, was largely supplanted.

Circuses and Carnivals

Circuses of all sizes, both travelling and stationary, were increasingly elaborate and popular forms of entertainment during the mid-nineteenth century.

Traveling circuses with three rings and a bigtop became increasingly popular during the nineteenth century, and largely replaced permanent, indoor circuses.

Travelling Circuses

Tent circuses started in America around 1830 and reached their peak in the early 1880s with the great traveling shows of Barnum and Bailey. Carnivals, smaller affairs that included games, rides, and sideshows, also existed and increasingly began to set up camp in conjunction with state and county fairs.

American circuses typically featured three rings, with individual acts playing simultaneously in each of them. In between the rings and to the sides of them were platforms for additional displays. Surrounding all of these staging areas was a large hippodrome track used for pageants, parades, and races.

Despite the familiar term "three-ring circus," American circuses could actually have anywhere from two to seven rings; many, few or no additional platforms; and lack the usual hippodrome track. In Europe, the multi-ring circus never really caught on, and most retained a single ring.

Indoor Circuses

During the nineteenth century, many circuses were housed within permanent, roofed buildings and did not travel from place-to-place. Among such indoor circuses were the amphitheaters of John Bill Ricketts in America, Astley's in England, and the Cirque Olympique in Paris.

In addition to the ring, many of these circuses had large scenic stages used for presenting spectacular theater dramas that included horses and other animals.

Circus Acts

Prior to and during the early part of the nineteenth century, circus programs consisted largely of trick horsemanship performed by costumed entertainers within large circles, or rings.

Horses in such acts were trained to gallop within a circle at a constant speed, allowing a standing rider to maintain his or her balance by leaning inward slightly and making use of centrifugal force. To this basic act many variations were added, such as standing astride a pair of running horses, riding with one foot on the horse's head and the other in the saddle, and balancing head-downward in the saddle while firing a pistol at a target.

More sophisticated acts included somersaults from one horse to another, human pyramids upon several galloping horses, pantomimes, and **pas de deux** between partners. Female trick riders were also extremely popular during this period, leaping over broadcloth banners and through paper-covered hoops.

In between such strenuous acts, a "clown to the ring" performed acrobatic feats and comedy to give the riders and their mounts a needed rest.

In the years prior to and following the Civil War, trick horsemanship began to decline and was increasingly replaced with **dressage** and routines in which several matched, unmounted horses executed various evolutions at the behest of a trainer, rather than a rider.

During this period, many sorts of new, non-equestrian acts were also added to the circus, such as the flying trapeze. Wild animal acts also began to appear in circuses, performed by "lion kings" and "lion queens" and caged animals.

One of the most popular features of traveling circuses in the years following the Civil War was the exotic spectacle of the street parade, performed by a circus as it came into town. Such parades included brass bands; elephants; brilliantly painted, carved, and gilded wagons; and costumed entertainers mounted on horses or in chariots, all to the sounds of a **calliope**.

America's most famous circus bears the name of and owes much of its success to Phineas Taylor Barnum (1810–1891), perhaps the most famous of all American showmen. In 1835, the self-proclaimed "Prince of Humbugs" launched his career as a showman with the purchase of slave Joice Heth, an aged black woman who he exhibited as the 161-year-old nurse of George Washington.

From 1841 to 1868, Barnum ran the American Museum, one of New York City's most popular attractions, a museum and menagerie that was home to thousands of curiosities, freaks, and wild animals. And in 1871, Barnum took his show on the road, in the form of a huge traveling circus, museum, and menagerie.

Fairs and Expositions

Some of the most popular events of the nineteenth century were great national or international exhibitions showcasing culture or technological advancements. Among the greatest of the century were those held in the United States in 1876 (in celebration of the Centennial) and 1893, in England in 1851, and in France in 1855, 1878, and 1889. Scientists, captains of industry, arms manufacturers and futurists like H.G. Wells and Jules Verne were among the luminaries at such events.

In the United States, such fairs included all the elements of carnivals. For example, entertainers formed a kind of midway outside of the 1876 Philadelphia Centennial, America's first exposition. Likewise, state and county fairs, originally intended to promote trade and agricultural education, gradually began to include carnival amusements.

Tobacco and Other Vices

Partaking of tobacco and liquor were two of the ways soldiers and sailors on both sides passed the time and distracted themselves from the rigors and anxieties of military life.

Smoking and chewing tobacco were widespread among the soldiery and beloved pastimes for many. In the late 1840s, U.S. Army soldiers had returned from the Mexican War with a taste for the richer, darker tobacco of South and Central America, leading to an increased demand for cigars and other tobacco products, which in turn stimulated a U.S. tobacco industry.

During the Civil War, tobacco rations were given to both Union and Confederate soldiers, and many Northerners were introduced to tobacco this way. During Sherman's 1864 march across Georgia, Union soldiers attracted to the mild, sweet "bright" tobacco of the South raided warehouses for chewing tobacco. Some of this bright tobacco made it back to the North, where it became extremely popular among tobacco users.

Shortages of tobacco constantly threatened to deprive soldiers of these pleasures, and a great many letters home include requests for tobacco. Tobacco was one of the few shortages to hit the North more profoundly than the South because it was produced primarily in Confederate, rather than Union, states. Union soldiers often compensated for this shortage by trading Confederate soldiers coffee or other items rare in the South for tobacco.

IN PRAISE OF THE PIPE

Contemporary diaries are replete with references to tobacco use, most of them positive, as is this example:

"Who can find words to tell the story of the soldier's affection for his faithful root-briar pipe! As the cloudy incense of the weed rises in circling wreaths about his head, as he hears the murmuring of the fire, and watches the glowing and fading of the hour pervading his mortal frame, what bliss! And yonder sits a man who scorns the pipe—and why? He is a chewer of the weed. To him, the sweetness of it seems not to be drawn out by the fiery test, but rather by the persuasion of moisture and pressure."

-John D. Billings, Union soldier

TRADING FOR TOBACCO

Following is an excerpt from the Civil War journal of Harry M. Kieffer—often referred to as *Recollections of a Drummer Boy* — who served for three years as a drummer boy with the Union forces. This entry was written during the summer of 1864 during the siege of Petersburg, Virginia, and describes one of the ways men on the opposing sides would obtain commodities from each other.

"It was no unusual thing to see a Johnny picket—who would be posted scarcely a hundred yards away, so near were the lines—lay down his gun, wave a piece of white paper as a signal of truce, walk out into the neutral ground between the picket-lines, and meet one of our own pickets, who, also dropping his gun, would go out to inquire what Johnny might want to-day.

'Well, Yank, I want some coffee, and I'll trade tobacco for it.'

'Has any of you fellows back there some coffee to trade for tobacco? Johnny Picket, here, wants some coffee.'

Or, may be he wanted to trade papers, a Richmond Enquirer for a New York Herald or Tribune, 'even up and no odds.' Or, he only wanted to talk about the news of the day—how 'we 'uns whipped you 'uns up the valley the other day;' or how, 'if we had Stonewall Jackson yet, we'd be in Washington before winter;' or may be he only wished to have a friendly game of cards!

There was a certain chivalrous etiquette developed through this social intercourse of deadly foe-men, and it was really admirable. Seldom was there breach of confidence on either side. It would have gone hard with the comrade who should have ventured to shoot down a man in gray who had left his gun and come out of his pit under the sacred protection of a piece of white paper. If disagreement ever occurred in bartering, or high words arose in discussion, shots were never fired until due notice had been given. And I find mentioned in one of my old army letters that a general fire along our entire front grew out of some disagreement on the picket-line about trading coffee for tobacco.

The two pickets couldn't agree, jumped into their pits, and began firing, the one calling out; 'Look out, Yank, here comes your tobacco.' Bang!"

The Tobacco Industry

In 1849, in the aftermath of the Mexican War (1846–1848), John Edmund Liggett established the J.E. Liggett and Brother tobacco company in St. Louis, Missouri, and others soon followed. In 1852, matches were introduced, making smoking immeasurably more convenient. By 1860, nearly 350 tobacco factories existed in Virginia and North Carolina alone, virtually all of them producing chewing tobacco. Only a half dozen of them produced smoking tobacco, manufactured as a side product from scraps left over from plugs.

Cigarettes, originally a Turkish innovation, had for some years been imported by English tobacconists. In 1854, however, London tobacconist Philip Morris began making his own cigarettes, and Old Bond Street soon became the center of the retail tobacco trade. Manufactured cigarettes appeared in America in 1860, a popular early brand being Bull Durham, and, in 1864, the first domestically-produced cigarettes were manufactured.

Tobacco was big business by the eve of the Civil War. An example of the industry's wealth is when Lorillard wrapped $100 bills at random in packages of Century cigarette tobacco to celebrate the hundredth anniversary of their firm in 1860.

In 1862, the U.S. government capitalized on the lucrative nature of tobacco and imposed a tax on it to help fund the war efforts, realizing about $3 million in revenue by the end of the conflict. In 1863, to help facilitate taxation, the U.S. Congress passed a law calling for manufacturers to create cigar boxes on which IRS agents could paste Civil War excise tax stamps, a law that inspired the beginning of cigar box art. In 1864, Congress levied the first cigarette tax.

Tobacco use continued unabated after the Civil War. From 1865 to 1870, for example, there was a growing demand in New York City for exotic Turkish cigarettes, which prompted tobacconists to seek skilled tobacco rollers from Europe. And, in 1873, Myers Brothers and Company marketed Love tobacco with a theme of North-South Civil War reconciliation.

In 1875, R.J. Reynolds founded R.J. Reynolds Tobacco Company and began producing chewing tobacco, including such brands as Brown's Mule, Golden Rain, Dixie's Delight, Yellow Rose, and Purity. Also in 1875, Allen and Ginter began including picture cards in their cigarette brands, Richmond Straight Cut No. 1 and Pet, to stiffen the packs and serve as premiums, something that was a big hit with smokers. Themes included "Fifty Scenes of Perilous Occupations" and "Flags of All Nations," as well as boxers, actresses, and famous battles. The cards were a huge hit with customers. The same year, the company also offered a reward of $75,000 for development of a functional cigarette-rolling machine.

Indeed, at the 1876 Centennial Celebration in Philadelphia, Allen and Ginter's cigarette displays were so impressive that some contemporary writers thought the exposition marked the birth of the cigarette.

Opponents of Tobacco

Tobacco use was not, however, universally enamored. In 1836, Samuel Green wrote in the *New England Almanack and Farmer's Friend* that tobacco was a poison lethal to men and insects alike (it was often used as an insecticide component), in addition to being filthy. And an 1859 tract by Rev. George Trask, called "Thoughts and Stories for American Lads: Uncle Toby's Anti-Tobacco Advice to His Nephew Billy Bruce," said that "physicians tell us that twenty thousand or more in our own land are killed" every year by tobacco.

Indeed, contemporary doctors widely recognized tobacco as a health threat, as evidenced by an 1845 letter of John Quincy Adams, who wrote that "in my early youth I was addicted to the use of tobacco in two of its mysteries, smoking and chewing. I was warned by a medical friend of the pernicious operation of this habit upon the stomach

> In the nineteenth century, contemporary doctors widely recognized tobacco as a health threat.

and the nerves." And in 1856 and 1857, there was a running debate among the readers of the British medical journal *Lancet* about the health effects of tobacco (which ran along moral as well as medical lines, with little substantiation on either side).

Some military diarists complained of how filthy camps became when a preponderance of men chewed tobacco and of the noxious quality of the smoke. There were also social movements, akin to the temperance movements, that decried the use of tobacco in pamphlets that were distributed to soldiers.

Ulysses S. Grant himself died of throat cancer, likely caused by his chronic cigar smoking, at age sixty-three in 1885.

Alcohol

"No one agent so much obstructs this army," wrote Maj. Gen. George McClellan, "as the degrading vice of drunkenness." Complete abstinence among the troops, he continued, "would be worth fifty thousand men to the armies of the United States."

Union and Confederate officers have a drink together before prisoners were exchanged, in this drawing by Arthur Lumley. Many artists sketched the battlefields of the war.

Indeed, a high number of insubordinations, camp brawls, sexual assaults, and other crimes involved alcohol, as indicated by letters, diaries, and official U.S. Army court marshal proceedings. Many other distasteful episodes from the war also involved drinking to excess. For example, on July 30, 1864, Union Brig. Gen. James H. Ledlie hid behind the lines in a bombproof shelter while the troops of his division were massacred in the "Crater" outside of Petersburg, Virginia. Desperately seeking orders, some of Ledlie's subordinate officers eventually found him, drunk in his hideaway. And Ulysses S. Grant, Lincoln's champion general in the final phase of the war, had himself been forced out of the Army in 1854 on account of his heavy drinking.

> An unfortunate result of the proliferation of prostitution is that at least one in ten Union soldiers suffered from some sort of venereal disease during the war.

Military personnel obtained alcohol at saloons when near towns and from sutlers when in the field, and were even issued it on occasion.

"Someone at headquarters got the idea that a quantity of whisky issued to each man in the evening would be beneficial to the general health of the men," wrote John M. King, a soldier with the 92nd Illinois Volunteer Infantry Regiment, in describing one such episode. "There was not enough given each man to make him drunk ... but there was just enough to make the men boisterous, excitable, talkative, and foolish. After the drinks there was a sort of pandemonium in nearly every tent."

When soldiers could not buy alcohol or did not receive it with their rations, they would make it, and gave names like "Bust-Head," "Nockum Stiff," "Oh! Be Joyful," "Pop Skull," and "Tanglefoot" to such bootleg liquor. Ingredients in one Northern recipe for bootleg liquor included "bark juice, tar-water, turpentine, brown sugar, lamp-oil, and alcohol." Southern recipes had similar ingredients and sometimes called for the addition of a piece of raw meat, which, after fermentation for a month, produced "an old and mellow taste," in the words of one veteran.

Prostitution

Despite the overt moral prudishness of the day, prostitution existed during the era of the Civil War and then blossomed with its outbreak. Soldiers and sailors, far from home and family, frequently engaged the services of prostitutes.

An unfortunate result of the proliferation of prostitution is that at least one in ten Union soldiers suffered from some sort of venereal disease during the war, and a similar proportion was likely among personnel in other services and in the Southern forces. And in an age before the introduction of antibiotics, the effects of such diseases could be terrible.

Brothels were available in urban areas and common in places with high concentrations of troops, especially in the national capitals. In Washington, DC, in 1863, there were more than 450 brothels employing more than seven thousand prostitutes. And in Richmond, Virginia, streetwalkers openly plied the streets, going so far as to solicit customers in the very shadow of the Capitol.

Prostitution was often considered an activity plied by theater actresses, although this perception was probably more widespread than whatever reality on which it was based. On the other hand, there are many documented cases of young women being forced into prostitution after finding they were unable to support themselves at low-paying jobs as clerks or factory workers. With so many prostitutes operating in heavily populated areas during the Civil War, prices tended to be competitive, and $3 or $4 for a session was not uncommon.

Terms

BIRDCAGE (CHUCK-A-LUCK, SWEET CLOTH): A game of chance in which players placed bets on what numbers would appear on a trio of dice rolled from a cup or contained within an hourglass-shaped container.

BURLEYCUE: A popular name for burlesque shows.

CALLIOPE: A set of steam-powered brass whistles operated by a keyboard or a pin-and-barrel mechanism that imitated the sounds of a train locomotive whistle. With sound that could carry up to twelve miles, the calliope was intended to attract attention rather than play music, and it was a familiar feature of circuses, fairs, and riverboats. It was invented by J.C. Stoddard in 1855 in Worcester, Massachusetts.

CRIBBAGE: A card game for two or more players that involves playing and grouping cards into specific combinations and which uses a special board, typically fitted with holes to accommodate pegs, for scorekeeping.

DRESSAGE: The execution of precision movements by a highly-trained horse in response to nearly imperceptible signals from its rider.

LEG SHOWS: One of the nicknames given to burlesque shows.

PAS DE DEUX: An intricate dance or other entertainment routine intended for two performers. Taken from the French and its original application to ballet.

PRISONER'S BASE, PRISON BASE: A game played by children since at least the 1840s. Each of two teams has a home base that players are sent to after being tagged or otherwise caught and from which they can be freed only in some specified way.

THROWING THE PAPERS: A slang term that meant to play cards.

VOLTIGE: A form of trick riding that involved a rider leaping on and off a moving horse.

WAGES AND CURRENCY:
COINS, GREENBACKS, AND POSTAL CURRENCY

"Americans speak of a man being worth so many thousands or millions. Nowhere is money sought so eagerly; nowhere is it so much valued; and in no civilized country does it bring so little to its possessor. The real work of America is to make money for the sake of making it. It is an end, and not a means."
— T.L. Nicols, *Forty Years of American Life*, 1864

During any period of national strife, the economy suffers from inflation and price increases, and both the North and the South suffered these effects during the Civil War. For a variety of reasons, including the lack of industrialization in the South and the Union blockade of its ports, these effects were more profound in the Confederacy than within the Union.

Examples of salaries and the values and appearance of United States and Confederate currency are all covered here.

Wages

While it is difficult to characterize an average American's wages during the Civil War—with factors like age, race, geographic location, occupation, inflation, demand, and gender all playing a role—it is nonetheless possible to get an idea of what many people earned by looking at a number of specific examples.

Once the war began, inflation caused wages to increase more in the Confederacy than in the Union states, but Southerners actually tended to have less buying power than people in the North (for example, in 1863, a Federal dollar was worth about seven Confederate dollars). Local conditions in some areas, such as labor shortages, also affected salaries.

In the North, buying power for wage earners stayed stable from 1860 through 1861, then declined 7 percent by 1862, 16 percent by 1863, 23 percent by 1864, and rose again to 18 percent below what it had been at the start of the war by 1865. In the South, real wages plummeted even more quickly and dramatically, going down 16 percent by 1861, 65 percent by 1862, 81 percent by 1863, and 89 percent by 1864.

Pay for soldiers, sailors, and other military personnel remained fairly static throughout the course of the war (for example, U.S. Army infantry, artillery, and cavalry privates earned $13 per month from 1861 through June 20, 1864, when it was raised to $16 per month). From their pay, Union privates had $2 per month withheld until expiration of their terms of enlistment, and another 12.5¢ per month withdrawn for support of the Soldiers' Home, a home for old or invalid military retirees.

All Union enlisted men, both privates and noncommissioned officers, earned an additional $2 per month for reenlisting, provided that they reenlisted within a month of the expiration of their terms, and an additional $1 per month for each five-year period after the first. States also offered reenlistment bonuses for veteran soldiers that could be quite substantial, typically $100 to $400 per reenlistment (other incentives were also offered, such as thirty days leave in between enlistments). Such bonuses were sometimes contingent upon many or most of the soldiers in the regiment reenlisting together.

Confederate privates were paid $11 a month until June 1864, when it was raised to $18. Confederate officers were generally paid a bit less than their Union counterparts throughout the course of the war.

Military rates of pay were often theoretical, however, as soldiers on both sides were frequently paid late. Both Union and Confederate troops in the field were supposed to be paid every two months, but there are documented cases of pay being given four, six, and even eight months late for Northern troops and even more sporadically and late for Southern troops. And, because of rampant inflation in the South, Confederate soldiers' pay in the latter part of the war was worth little, whether it was on time or not.

Pages 128–130 list examples of what some jobs paid in both the North and South. Wages for many unskilled civilian jobs from 1866–1877 are probably comparable to what they would have been in the North prior to the war; in the South, slaves would have performed much of this work.

Although salaries increased dramatically in the South during the war, sometimes they were still not enough to provide for the needs of a family. In many cases, men who were not in military service had to take second jobs, and women had to leave their homes and seek employment. In almost all cases, women were paid considerably less than men for comparable work, usually about half as much, a trend that continued after the war.

Military Wages (per month)

1861

U.S. ARMY	CONFEDERATE ARMY
infantry, cavalry, or artillery private: $13	marine private: c. $8
infantry or artillery 1st or 2nd lieutenant: $105.50	private: $11
infantry or artillery captain: $115.50	corporal: $13
infantry or artillery major: $169	sergeant: $17
infantry or artillery lieutenant colonel: $181	first sergeant: $20
infantry or artillery colonel: $212	engineer sergeant: $34
brigadier general: $315	infantry colonel: $195
major general: $457	artillery, cavalry, or engineer colonel: $210
lieutenant general: $758	brigadier general: $301

1864

U.S. NAVY	U.S. ARMY	CONFEDERATE ARMY
seaman: $14 to $18 per month	general: $209.50 to $720 per month	private: $18 per month ($20 by midyear)
rear admiral: $3,000 to $5,000 per year		marine private: c. $15 per month

1865

U.S. ARMY
infantry, cavalry, or artillery private: $16 per month
rear admiral: $3,000 to $5,000 per year

1866–1877

U.S. ARMY
infantry, cavalry, or artillery private: $13 per month (reverted from $16 per month in 1871)

Civilian Wages

1860

JOB	PAY
Carpenter	$1.60 per ten-hour day
Clerk in U.S. Government Printing Office	$16 per week for a ten-hour day
Southern workman	$3 per day
Streetcar driver in Washington, DC	$1.50 per day
Teacher	$2 per student per month (i.e., by subscription), plus room and board with local families

JOB	PAY
Clerk in War Department in Richmond, Virginia	$1,200 per year
Pressman in U.S. Government Treasury Department	$5 per week
Southern workman	$4 per day

JOB	PAY
Clerk in U.S. Government Printing Office	$18 per week for an eight-hour day
Confederate post office clerk	$700 to $800 per year
Female clerk in U.S. Patent Office in Washington, DC	$1,400 per year
Female spindle or loom operator in the South	$8 to $10 per week
Female worker in U.S. Government Treasury Department:	$50 per month
Nurse, North or South	$12 per month (from which she was expected to buy small items to help care for the soldiers in her charge)
Pressman in U.S. Government Treasury Department	$6 per week for a six-day week
Streetcar driver in Washington, DC	$2 per day
Southern clerk	$125 per month
Southern workman	$30 per day (in area with labor shortages)

A Confederate post office clerk would have earned between $700 and $800 per year in 1863. This photo shows the post office in Charleston, South Carolina, in 1865.

1864

JOB	PAY
Clerk in War Department in Richmond, Virginia	$3,000 per year
Female U.S. Army nurse	40¢ per day, plus one ration
Married woman working for Confederate States Laboratory, in Richmond, Virginia	$7 per day
Single woman working for Confederate States Laboratory	$5 per day

1865

JOB	PAY
Blacksmith, carpenter, or machinist in a Confederate government workshop	$10 per day

1866-1877

JOB	PAY
Blacksmith	$2.50 to $3 per day
Boilermaker	$2.50 per day
Cook in a home	$2 to $10 per week, plus room and board
Clerk, bookkeeper, etc.	$1,000 to $2,000 per year if male, $500 to $1,000 per year if female
Domestic worker/maid in a home	$2 per week, plus room and board
Fireman	$1,000 per year
Iron worker, skilled	c. $4.50 to $6 per ten-hour day (highest rate in any industry during this period)
Laborer, skilled (e.g., carpenter, mason, plumber)	$2.80 to $3.80 per day
Laborer, unskilled	$1.50 per twelve-hour day
Police officer	$1,200 per year
Street vendor (e.g., matches, pencils, shoelaces, newspapers)	a few cents a day
Scullery maid in a home	$1 to $2 per week, plus room and board
Teacher	$2 per student per month (i.e., by subscription), plus room and board, or $25 to $30 per month in state-supported schools
Teamster	$2 per day

From top to bottom: An example of postal currency issued by the Federal government during the war; a $5 bill printed in Philadelphia; and a $50 bill printed in Washington.

At left, United States $1 and $2 bills. Below, the obverse and reverse of an 1864 two-cent piece.

Currency

Both the Union and the Confederacy helped finance their war efforts by issuing paper currency, which led to inflation in both the North and the South. Inflation, however, was always far worse in the South and ultimately reached crisis level, which it never did in the North. In the North, the cost of most goods and services increased by about 75 percent from 1861 to 1865; in the South, goods cost sixty to seventy times as much in 1865 as they had at the start of the war.

Currency in the North

In the North, Congress used the war to establish a stronger centralized banking system. In February 1862, it authorized the first legal-tender paper banknotes and, throughout the war, issued nearly $500 million worth of them. By the war's end, inflation reduced the value of such bills to 39 percent of face value (i.e., a $1 bill was worth 39¢ in gold). Currency issues were not the only means of financing the war, however; they were used in conjunction with taxes, loans, and bond issues.

Union Notes and Coins

Some of the most common Union coins and notes in use during the Civil War are described next, along with the years they were issued. U.S. banknotes were green in color and, naturally, immediately acquired the nickname "**greenbacks**."

2-CENT PIECES (bronze, 1864–1865, although actually issued through 1873). These coins, the first to be minted bearing the motto "In God We Trust," depict images of a shield, an eagle, and a laurel sprig.

3-CENT PIECES (silver, 1860–1873, minted in a different form starting in 1851). Depict images of a star and shield.

HALF DIMES (silver, 1860–1873). Depict an image of **Liberty** seated on the **obverse** and the words "United States of America" and a wreath on the **reverse**. Originally minted in a different form in 1794.

DIMES (silver, 1860–1891). Depict an image of Liberty seated and the words "United States of America" on the obverse and a wreath on the reverse.

QUARTERS (silver, 1838–1865). Depict an image of Liberty seated on the obverse and of an eagle on the reverse.

HALF-DOLLARS (silver, 1839–1866). Depict an image of Liberty seated on the obverse and an eagle on the reverse.

DOLLARS (silver, 1840–1865). Depict an image of Liberty seated on the obverse and an eagle on the reverse. Minted both before 1840 and after 1865 in different forms.

DOLLARS (gold, 1856–1889). Depict a large Liberty head wearing a feathered headdress on the obverse. A **mint mark** appears below a **laurel wreath** on the reverse. Originally minted in a different form in 1849.

$2.50 "QUARTER EAGLES" (gold, 1840–1907). Depict a Liberty head wearing a **coronet** on the obverse and a mint mark beneath an eagle on the reverse. Minted both before 1840 and after 1907 in different forms.

In the North, the cost of most goods and services increased by about 75 percent from 1861 to 1865; in the South, goods cost sixty to seventy times as much in 1865 as they had at the start of the war.

Two examples of U.S. postal currency, a five-cent stamp and a thirty-cent stamp.

Because coins were in such short supply, the U.S. postal service issued un-gummed stamps that could be used as change.

$3 GOLD PIECES (gold, 1854–1889). Depict a Liberty head wearing a feathered headdress on the obverse. A mint mark appears below a wreath on the reverse.

$5 "HALF EAGLES" (gold, 1839–1908). Depict a Liberty head wearing a coronet on the obverse and an eagle (with no motto) on the reverse.

$10 EAGLES (gold, 1838–1907). Depict a Liberty head wearing a coronet and no motto on the obverse and an eagle with a mint mark below it on the reverse.

$20 DOUBLE EAGLES (gold, 1838–1907). Depict a Liberty head on the obverse and an eagle on the reverse.

Union Fractional and Postal Currency

Faced with early battlefield defeats and the prospect of funding a long, expensive war, and reluctant to levy new taxes, the Federal government, along with Northern banks, stopped issuing coinage soon after the Civil War began. This action shook public confidence in the government, prompting people to hoard coinage. Before long, coins had virtually disappeared from circulation.

Merchants responded to this dearth of coinage by issuing due bills, tickets, and other forms of private obligation in lieu of change and, soon after, the U.S. Congress authorized the use of postage stamps as change. Such glue-coated money proved very unpopular and inconvenient, however, and Congress finally approved glueless stamps that were referred to as "postal currency."

This stop-gap measure was supplanted in October 1863, when the government began issuing fractional paper currency in 3, 5, 10, 15, 25, and 50-cent denominations. Such fractional currency was flimsy, easily became torn and dirty, and was widely considered unattractive, gaining the derisive nickname "shinplasters."

Public outcry resulted when the 5-cent note was issued bearing the image of a Bureau of Engraving and Printing division chief (the image of U.S. Treasurer Francis E. Spinner appeared on the 50-cent note, something that apparently did not upset people). This public protest induced Congress to pass a law prohibiting the likeness of any living person from being used on U.S. Treasury notes.

Despite the problems with shinplasters, people eventually accepted them in place of metal coinage. By the time the government stopped issuing fractional currency in February 1876, more than $368 million worth of it had been put into circulation.

Confederate Currency

The Confederacy did not widely employ measures like taxes and loans to finance its war effort. Instead it financed its efforts almost entirely through seven different issues of paper currency between 1861 and 1864.

These issues had a total face value of more than $1 billion and as much as $1.5 billion, a total uncertain in part because of counterfeiting. In any case, none of this currency was backed by gold or silver, which, coupled with increasing shortages of consumer goods, led to some of the worst inflation ever seen in America.

Over the course of the war, the Confederate States Treasury Department issued seventy different notes with imagery that included day-to-day themes, such as laboring blacks, and classical themes, like Roman deities. Coins were far more rare in the Confederacy, the only ones struck by the Confederate States of America being experimental pennies and half-dollars.

Confederate currency always exchanged at a lower rate than did Federal money, and depreciated steadily throughout the war, even as shortages caused prices to increase.

When Confederate currency was first issued in 1861, it was valued at ninety-five U.S. cents on the dollar. By 1863, the notes were worth about one-third this amount and were trading at thirty-three U.S. cents to the dollar, prompting one resident of Richmond, Virginia, to remark in a letter that "Confederate money is not worth keeping."

On May 1, 1865, on the last known day that Confederate currency was actively traded, it was sold in bales of 1,200 notes for $1.

A wide variety of banknotes were issued by the Confederate states, including fractional currency. $10 notes were the most common in the Confederacy.

Indeed, Southerners had almost no confidence at all in Confederate currency in the last year or so of the war. Goods and services could be purchased only through barter or with U.S. greenbacks obtained on the black market; Union currency was even used to some extent for paying soldiers in the Confederate army.

After April 9, 1865, when Lee surrendered his army to the Union, the value of the Confederate dollar dropped in value to 1.6 cents against the Union dollar. Less than a month later, on May 1, 1865, on the last known day that Confederate currency was actively traded, it was sold in bales of 1,200 notes for $1.

C.S. paper currency, as well as the banknotes issued by many Southern states, was printed in all the denominations found in the United States, including fractional currency, which was needed as much in the South as the North.

Counterfeit Confederate Currency

Confederate currency was easy to counterfeit, and large amounts of it were printed in the North and circulated in the Confederacy in an attempt to debase its value, something that has contributed to uncertainty as to how much was legitimately issued.

One of the best-known of the Civil War counterfeiters was Samuel C. Upham, who printed fake Confederate currency and claimed to be selling it for novelty purposes, each note supposedly being labeled in its margin with the words "Fac-Simile Confederate notes sold, wholesale or retail, by S. C. Upham, 403 Chestnut Street, Phila." How much this impeded their circulation in the South is not clear; the words may not have been noticeable at a glance, might have been deliberately obscured by those who wished to spend the notes, and would have been meaningless to the illiterate.

"I sold the notes as curiosities—mementos of the rebellion—and advertised them as such in several of the most widely circulated papers in the Union," he said. "During the publication of those facsimile notes I was the 'best abused man' in the Union (by the Confederacy). Senator Foote, in a speech before the Rebel Congress, at Richmond, in 1862, said I had done more to injure the Confederate cause than Gen. McClellan and his army."

Confederate Notes and Coins

Some of the various banknotes issued by the Confederacy over the course of the war, along with the two Confederate coins, are described next, including years of issue. Most Confederate banknotes were blue-gray in color and as a result acquired the nicknames "**graybacks**" and "**bluebacks**."

1-CENT PIECES/PENNIES (copper or silver, 1861). Depict a Liberty head on the obverse and a laurel wreath on the reverse.

HALF-DOLLARS (silver, 1861). Depict Liberty seated on obverse, Liberty cap, stalk of sugar cane, cotton, and the words "Confederate States of America Half Dol." on the reverse.

$2 NOTES (1861). Show a personification of the South striking down the Union.

$5 NOTES (1861). Depict the legend "Confederate States of America" in blue on the reverse.

$10 NOTES (1861). Printed in black and red ink on red fiber paper, showing a pair of Indians in the center, **Thetis** at left, and a maiden with the numeral "X" at right.

$10 NOTES (1864). Show horses pulling cannon. More than nine million such notes were issued, more than any other denomination.

$20 NOTES (1861). Show **Ceres** seated between Commerce and Navigation in the center and Liberty on the left.

$50 NOTES (1861). Depict a bust of C.S. President Jefferson Davis.

$50 NOTES (1864). Depict a bust of C.S. President Jefferson Davis.

$100 NOTES (1861). Depict **Moneta** seated next to treasure chests in the center and a sailor in the lower left.

TERMS

BLUEBACKS: a nickname for some Confederate paper currency given for its blue-gray color.

CERES: A classical goddess of agriculture and abundance that was featured on some Confederate currency.

CORONET: A small crown.

GREENBACKS: A slang term for U.S. money.

GRAYBACKS: A slang term for Confederate paper currency.

LAUREL WREATH: A traditional symbol of victory that appeared on some Civil War-era coinage.

LIBERTY: A classical goddess who exemplified the concept of freedom.

MINT MARK: An inscription on a coin indicating where it was struck.

MONETA: In Roman mythology, a name applied to Juno, wife of Jupiter and queen of heaven, that emphasized her role as an advisor.

OBVERSE: The primary ("front" or "head") side of a coin, as opposed to its reverse.

REVERSE: The back ("tail") side of a coin, as opposed to its obverse.

SUTLER TOKEN: A type of currency often used for transactions between civilian merchants called sutlers and troops that developed because of the shortage in government-issued coinage.

THETIS: In classical mythology, a minor goddess who was the mother of the hero Achilles.

CLOTHING AND DRY GOODS:
WHAT ITEMS COST AND THE IMPACT OF SHORTAGES

"Next to the plough, this sewing machine is perhaps humanity's most blessed
instrument." — Louis Antoine Godey, 1856

During the mid-nineteenth century, Americans scrupulously imitated European fashions, which they modified little or not at all. This was in keeping with a trend established in Colonial times and adhered to until the 1910s. This rigidity of style was always greatest in the East, especially in urban areas, and became more and more diluted the farther West one went.

  This chapter describes period clothing, as well the costs of apparel, its components, and other dry goods. It also looks at some of the ways people, particularly those in the South, dealt with shortages and the sorts of substitutions they availed themselves of.

Clothing
While styles were rigid and conventional, they were not always austere, and men and women in the big cities, such as New York, Charleston, and New Orleans, were more likely to be concerned with elegance and ostentation. Local mores varied from region-to-region, of course, and would have affected attitudes toward fashion; the Puritan heritage of Boston's upper crust or the Quaker underpinnings of Philadelphia society, for example, would have made sobriety more acceptable than caprice, at least in the most conservative circles.

One of the most significant technological advances of this period was the introduction of the sewing machine, something that helped the industrialized North keep its troops in uniforms much more consistently that the South was able to do. Most clothing was still hand-sewn during this period, however, regardless of whether it was made at home or purchased from a tailor. The time it took to hand-sew a garment was indeed greater than it took to machine-sew it, but not by that much. A simple, one-layer gown, for example, could be completed by hand in a day or so (although home-sewers' stitches were longer and not as consistent as those produced by machines).

This period also marks the beginning of haute couture, exclusive custom-fitted clothing, starting with the opening of Charles Frederick Worth's Paris fashion house in 1857. Major American urban areas like Boston, New York, and Philadelphia had their own fashion houses, and these tended to scrupulously copy the latest fashions from London and Paris.

> Most clothing was still hand-sewn during this period. A simple, one-layer gown, for example, could be completed by hand in a day or so.

By 1860, the shoulder seams on both men's and women's clothing swept down toward the back of the shoulders, which forced people into a more restrictive posture that limited arm movement (posture was considered to be very important during this era, and was even taught in school as part of the subject of deportment).

Prior to the onset of the war, affluent Southerners obtained clothing that was imported from Europe or the Northern fashion houses. Many well-to-do families also escaped the worst of the sultry Southern climate by summering in various Northern states, in many cases in vacation homes along the New England coast, and they would typically incorporate shopping excursions through big cities into their travel plans. Some families even traveled to Europe every few years or so and acquired the latest fashions in conjunction with their "grand tours."

Men's Clothing

During the era of the Civil War and the years following it, the prevailing image in men's clothing was that of the lawyer-statesman, as exemplified by Abraham Lincoln himself. Men wanted to present a distinguished appearance, impress their peers, and appear substantial. An austere black suit, white linen shirt, black bow tie, and low-cut boots composed the quintessential outfit for the middle- or upper-class man. Some fashion-conscious men also wore corsets, more generally associated with women, in order to enhance their physiques.

An elegant appearance was important to men in certain circles, especially those in major urban centers like New York or New Orleans. While a certain sobriety accompanied the appearance of professional men in the smaller cities and towns, more ostentation could be found in the garb of big city dwellers (for example, fur-trimmed cuffs and collars).

Male fashion was designed to create the impression of distinction and substance. This self-portrait of Civil War photographer Mathew Brady typifies the style of the era.

This political poster shows the wide variety of fashions men would have worn in various occupations. It features a farmer, military officer, engineer, doctor or pharmacist, politician, lawyer, merchant, and clergyman.

Work clothing was less formal but not much less conventional, and typically included trousers, boots, and a double-breasted wool pullover shirt that buttoned up only from the waist to the collar: Depending on the sort of work they did, men's garb also frequently included a jacket or sack coat. Nonetheless, many farmers, clerks, and other lower-middle-class or working-class men were sensitive to their image and attempted to appear prosperous or ambitious through their apparel.

Foremost among men's accessories were hats, among which top hats and derbies predominated. Top hats, generally worn for business and formal occasions, came in a variety of shapes, brim widths, and crown heights, and included bell crowns and stovepipes. Derbies, including bowlers, were hard, round-crowned hats that originated in the 1850s. Such hats were less formal than top hats and popular with all classes of men. The most expensive men's hats were made from beaver

The prevailing

philosophy

toward garb

was to make

the body fit the

clothes, not

make clothes to

fit the body, so

waist training,

or tightlacing,

was a way of

life for women

of all classes.

There were also

special corsets

for pregnant

women and to

accommodate

breastfeeding.

fur felt (which contributed to the expansive North American fur trade). Other popular accessories included canes and suspenders.

Women's Clothing

Women had very little flexibility of dress in the years leading up to and including the Civil War, and slavishly imitated European fashions, drawing many of their rules of attire from the popular *Godey's Lady's Book*.

The prevailing philosophy toward garb was to make the body fit the clothes, not make clothes to fit the body, so waist training, or tightlacing, was a way of life for women of all classes (albeit to a lesser degree for women of the working classes). Young women were encouraged to make their waists as small as possible and might have started the practice of tightlacing even as young girls.

Victorian-era morality had a huge influence on clothing of the period and prudery was taken to the extreme in many circles and the look was generally demure, prim, and genteel. Respectable women wore several layers of clothing even in the hottest months.

Formal ball gowns and hoopskirts, of the sort worn by Vivien Leigh in *Gone With the Wind* or Deborah Kerr in *The King and I*, are the women's clothing most popularly associated with this era but were the exception more so than the rule. Many different variations came into style, and women would have been judged, or sensitive to judgment, for their fashion sense as much as anybody today. Generally, such dresses had a tightly fitting bodice that rode low on the shoulder and had a V-shaped neckline. Gowns were cinched tight around the waist, and then mushroomed out to several feet wide at the floor, stiffened, pushed outward, and given their characteristic shape by hoops and specialized undergarments called **crinolines**.

Other female undergarments, many worn for day-to-day use, included **petticoats**, **camisoles**, **chemises**, **corsets**, **corset covers**, pantaloon-like drawers, and stockings. Such garments could be made of cotton, wool, or silk, and were often patterned, in keeping with prevailing fashions.

Even working-class women wore corsets. Poor women used reed or cane for stays, stiffened material like canvas, or several layers of material quilted together. Whalebone stays were used by those who could afford it. There were also special corsets for pregnant women and to accommodate breastfeeding.

Naturally, working-class women and those whose activities took them near battlefields, did not wear cumbersome hoop dresses and lace on

This illustration from *Harper's Weekly* shows women's fashions in 1864.

a daily basis, if at all. Plain, long skirts, blouses, bonnets, and completely-hidden petticoats were standard garb. Aprons were also typical and appeared in many styles, from those that simply tied around the waist to ones worn like smocks.

Garibaldi shirts, reminiscent of the shirts worn by the followers of Italian revolutionary Giuseppe Garibaldi, were another popular style of women's garb, and featured dropped shoulders, bloused bodices, and puffed sleeves. A variation on this theme was the Garibaldi dress, which featured a bodice similar to the Garibaldi shirt.

Once the war began, military-style dresses came into fashion for informal or day-to-day wear.

Women's Accessories

Parasols were probably the most important women's accessory during the Civil War. Such small umbrellas came in all appearances and materials, and were imported from as far away as Europe or China.

Lavishly-trimmed bonnets were
fashionable throughout the period.

This illustration from *Godey's Lady's Book* shows women's fashion
from the 1850s.

Female undergarments (from top): a
chemise, drawers, and nightgowns.

Practically, the main function of a parasol was to help protect the delicate female complexion from the sun—a pale-to-fair skin being considered attractive and a sign of social standing (because upper-class women did not have to spend time in the sun working).

Other popular accessories included bonnets, fans, snoods, reticules, shawls, and cloaks, often with hoods large enough to accommodate a bonnet. Lavishly-trimmed bonnets were fashionable throughout the period, and an eye-catching accessory of this sort was another one of the means used to draw attention away from an otherwise drab ensemble.

These children's fashions were typical of the upper-class in the 1870s. Note the boy's military-style suit, which became fashionable during the war.

Women also wore detachable white collars and false sleeves called *engageantes* to emphasize the look of primness. These accessories were decorated with a type of embroidery called white-work (one of the ways women spent their time), which could enhance the appearance of an otherwise drab outfit.

In all classes of society, a certain modesty was expected of women. The limits of such strictures could be, and were, however, tastefully stretched. While the parasol, for example, did have a practical function, it was also used in rather elaborate flirting rituals. And, while the petticoat was an undergarment that was generally hidden, at times it was also fashionable to wear a decorative petticoat that was meant to be glimpsed.

Women also frequently carried fans in hot weather for cooling themselves. Like parasols, the use of fans went beyond their practical applications, however, and they too played an important role in flirting.

Hard times forced many women, especially in the South, to sell their jewelry or to donate it in support of the war effort. Nonetheless, women still wanted things with which to adorn themselves and made new jewelry from available items. In the absence of precious metals, broaches, bracelets, necklaces, and rings were fashioned from bone, wood, brightly-colored scraps of yarn and fabric, seeds, fruit pits, palmetto, **gutta-percha**, and even shiny fish scales.

Combs were another accessory that could be expensive to replace if lost or broken, and replacements were made from wood, horn, and bone. Hairpins could also be made from these materials, and even from large thorns.

Hair switches—pieces of hair used to augment women's own hair—were generally manufactured in Europe and became harder to obtain as a result of the blockade, forcing women to either make substitutes or make do without them.

Children's Clothing

Children's clothing was not quite so conventional as adult clothing, and imitated military uniforms increasingly after the onset of hostilities. Indeed, little soldier and sailor outfits were especially popular for both boys and girls during the Civil War. Photographs and other media exist depicting boys wearing military-style shirts, coats, and jackets, and girls wearing Garibaldi shirts and Zouave-style outfits.

Children—both boys and girls—were often placed in corsets because it was believed that these would improve their posture.

Cloth

Cotton, being a plentiful prewar crop, was a primary component in many clothes. Wool and silk were other important clothing materials, especially for imported goods.

Shortages for cloth and clothing seem to have been nearly as acute as for food and other commodities. In the South, some cloth was produced at a handful of textile mills, but the rest of it had to be imported. This made cloth and clothing more difficult to obtain for those with means, and out of the reach of the less affluent.

Once shortages began to take their toll on the Confederacy, many Southern women who could not afford to buy cloth or clothing, or simply balked at the inflated prices, learned to make their own cloth, thread, and yarn. Just as most people today consider such activities a thing of the past, so did many Civil War-era women, who had to pull old spinning wheels and looms from attics or storerooms and learn how to use them from people of their parents' or grandparents' generations.

Although many women turned to carding fibers, spinning thread and yarn, and weaving cloth themselves, these activities were impeded by many obstacles. For one, many farmers had stopped growing cotton in lieu of food—something many large plantations were not forced to do—and there were fewer sheep than before the war, so the raw materials needed for thread and cloth were often hard to obtain. Hair from cows, dogs, horses, rabbits, and raccoons was mixed with cotton or wool to make it go further, and fibers from nettles were used instead of flax to make a fabric akin to linen.

Buttons

Buttons were made from a wide variety of materials, especially brass, pewter, tin, bone, wood, and mother-of-pearl.

Brass buttons predominated for military uniform jackets and generally bore some national or state symbol, such as a Federal eagle, Texas star, or North Carolina sunburst. Confederate buttons might also bear a branch marking, such as an "E" or "M," as worn by the Confederate Army Engineers or the Confederate Marines, respectively. And, in ethnic units, such as an Irish regiment, they might bear a foreign phrase or slogan, such as the Gaellic "Erin Go Bragh" ("Ireland Forever"). Brass buttons were also used on some military equipment.

Pewter buttons were used on heavier garb, such as great coats, as well as other heavy-duty gear. As with brass buttons, pewter buttons were also often emblazoned with characteristic symbols, such as a Louisiana pelican or Scottish thistle.

Wood, bone, and mother-of-pearl were typically used for shirt, frock, trouser, or blouse buttons. Tin buttons were used for men's trousers or military equipment like shelter halves.

After the war began, machine-made buttons were no longer available in the South, and buttons had to be recycled from old garments or made by hand. Wood, bone, horn, peach pits and other large seeds, bark, pasteboard, balls made from stuffed squares of fabric, and pieces of dried gourd covered with cloth were all used for homemade buttons. Some of these would be ruined by immersion in water and had to be removed before laundering the garment to which they were attached.

> "There seemed to be no scarcity of dry-goods of ordinary kinds. Bombazines, silks, etc., are scarce and very high. Carpets are not to be found, since they are too large to run the blockade from Baltimore."
> –Judith McGuire, a Southerner, November 1863

Thread

Because yarn and thread became increasingly scarce during the war, Southern women often had to make their own. Such thread was adequate for hand-sewing, but was too coarse for sewing machines, which required much finer, machine-spun thread. Thus, Southern women who owned sewing machines were often unable to use them for want of proper thread.

Hair of various sorts was also sometimes used as substitute for regular woven thread.

Dye

One of the significant technological advances of the period was the introduction of aniline dyes—starting in 1856—which could produce more vibrant colors than those typically achieved with natural dyes.

Commercially-produced dyes became scarce during the war, particularly in the South, necessitating a return to the use of natural dyes. Butternut, for example, was used to create dye that could be used to give cloth a brownish-gray color that was widely used for Confederate Army uniforms.

Other Shortages and Substitutions

Shortages and inflation forced people in both the North and South, but especially the latter, to devise substitutes for many common items and the components of which they were comprised, including clothing, dye, cloth, and thread (discussed above); fans, jewelry, and other accessories; and toiletry items and medicines.

People also wanted to maintain the illusion or pretense that they were able to look as nice or live as well as they always had, despite the effects of the war (recall the episode in *Gone with the Wind* where Scarlet O'Hara has a dress made from draperies). Often, however, conditions conspired to make this impossible.

As it became more difficult in some parts of the country to obtain new clothing and accessories, people made much more of an effort than they had before to take care of the things they had and make them last as long as possible; even the affluent in the South were considerably less likely or able to discard items from previous years for the latest fashions from London or Paris.

In addition to the ways people dealt with clothing shortages, they devised substitutes and replacements for most other types of dry goods that became difficult or expensive to obtain. Some examples follow.

Toiletries

Hygiene remained as important during the war as it ever had been (perhaps even more so, as cleanliness helped impede the diseases that claimed so many, although most people in the mid-nineteenth century, even physicians, did not understand this).

Bed linens, cannibalized for bandages and clothing, often could not be replaced in the South, and many families had none at all by the end of the war.

Soap in its simplest form could be produced from water, lye, and grease (rosin and salt were other possible components) and had long been made at home by women in the country. When lye became hard to obtain, it could be produced at home by filtering water through a tray filled with wood ash. As meat became less common, so did grease, and chinaberry and cottonseed oil could be used instead. Soap root and yucca root could also be used as satisfactory substitutes for soap itself.

Tooth powder—rather than paste—was made from mixtures of many different items, including arrowroot, chalk, charcoal, cuttlefish bone, honey, myrrh, orris root, salt, and soda. Toothbrushes could be made from hog bristles or from twigs or licorice roots, the ends of which had been frayed like brushes by chewing them.

Substitutes for many sorts of cosmetics were devised. These included face powder, which could be replaced with rice flour, and hair oil, which was made from lard that had been left to melt in the sun and then scented with rose petals.

Furnishings and Housewares

Refugees and other people who had been driven from their homes or had them destroyed often had trouble replacing their furniture, tableware, and other items. Soldiers in winter quarters might also have employed many of the following to make their lives more comfortable.

Bed frames were fitted with poles or ropes pulled taut. When down or feathers were unavailable for pillows and mattresses, they were instead stuffed with things like corn shucks, leaves, moss, palmetto, and cotton (which was considered the best substitute). Blankets were replaced with rugs and carpeting. Bed linens, cannibalized for bandages and clothing, often could not be replaced in the South, and many families had none at all by the end of the war.

China and glassware were replaced with clayware, which was cheaper and sturdier. Tin cups were often unavailable, so emptied tin cans were used instead, and tumblers were made from bottles that had been cut off at the necks. Broken, lost, or stolen silverware was replaced with knives, forks, and spoons made of wood. Bowls, cups, dippers, and ladles were made from gourds. Boxes and other containers were replaced with handwoven baskets.

Heat and Lighting

Sources of lighting, such as whale oil, kerosene, and candles, were in short supply in the Confederacy, all of them having been imported from the North. Firelight was one substitute, but was not always practical or available, especially as coal and wood became more expensive—notably in urban areas—necessitating fuel substitutes like "**fireballs**."

Candles were made at home, ideally from beeswax, but more often from **tallow** (which produced more smoke than other candle components) or a combination of both. Wax could also be extracted from myrtle berries, blackberries, and prickly-pear pads by boiling them, although very large quantities were needed to obtain a reasonable quantity of wax.

"Confederate candles" were one method of stretching limited quantities of wax. These were made by impregnating strands of twine with a mixture of tallow and beeswax or beeswax and rosin or fresh turpentine. A strand would then be wrapped tightly around a bottle and a few inches of it pulled above the mouth of the bottle, which could be lit and pulled upward as it burned down (six inches would typically burn for about twenty minutes).

Kerosene for lamps was replaced with a mixture of cottonseed oil, peanut oil, and melted lard. Other means of producing light included burning knots from pine branches and stalks of candlewick plants that had been soaked in grease or tallow, and "**fairy lights**," makeshift lamps made by floating sweet, burning balls of gum in saucers of melted lard.

Pen, Paper, and the Like

Paper, ink, pens, and pencils were often unavailable during the war, especially in the South.

Once the conflict began, much of the paper produced in both the North and South tended to be lower in quality than people were accustomed to using for correspondence or journals. It was often

Letter writers conserved paper by turning a page 90 degrees once it was covered with words and then writing across them until it was full again, a method called "cross-hatching."

brown, coarse, or very soft. Old business forms, wallpaper, and other scrap papers were folded into envelopes. Blackboards or slates and chalk were used for temporary work.

Letter writers conserved paper by turning a page 90 degrees once it was covered with words and then writing across them until it was full again, a method called "cross-hatching." This technique made letters a bit harder to read, but they were still generally legible and allowed someone to get twice the words onto a single sheet of paper. People also wrote letters in pencil so the recipient could erase the writing and use the paper again. Subsequent writing was, however, harder to read, the paper eventually wore out, and this method did not allow letters to be kept.

Ink could be made from logwood extract or berry juice, especially from elderberries. Pencils could be made using coal or even lead rather than graphite, although the latter did not leave much more than a faint gray streak on paper.

Newspapers dealt with shortages by printing smaller issues or by using paper other than newsprint (for example, some wartime newspapers were printed on wallpaper). Nonetheless, many Southern newspapers went out of business during the Civil War.

Glue was made from cherry, peach, or plum tree gum, or from egg whites mixed with lime. Paste was made from a mixture of water and flour, and a type of putty was made by mixing flour with a warm, mashed, sweet potato.

Other Items

People had to devise substitutes for many other items, especially in the unindustrialized South. Metal goods especially, including pins, needles, scissors, fishhooks, screws, nails, and locks, could not be replaced easily or at all, and this impeded seamstresses and other people attempting to manufacture their own clothing or other items.

Thorns or splinters of wood were sometimes used instead of pins, and needles made of porcupine quills or bone were used when necessary.

Starch was made by soaking grated green corn, potatoes, or wheat bran until it fermented, skimming the surface and straining the remaining solution. It could then be used to starch clothes or other cloth items.

Wooden pegs and joints were used whenever possible instead of screws or nails.

Tobacco pipes, ideally made from briarwood or meerschaum, could instead be made from clay or carved by hand from other woods, such as dogwood, hickory, mahogany, or walnut.

	1849	1860	1862	1863	1864	1864	1870
gold, per ounce	$21	$21				$30	$23

Costs of Goods and Services

As with food, the cost of other goods and services also increased dramatically during the course of the war. Cost for dental services in 1863 were: $120 for a gold filling and $1,800 to $4,000 for an upper set of dentures on a gold or vulcanite base.

As the value of goods increased and the value of money decreased, many people—especially women—tried to sell or trade homemade items, like soap, for food and other necessities. Soldiers often acquired items that were in short supply in some areas (such as pins and needles from house-wives or buttons from uniforms) and then used them to trade with the locals, whether friendly or enemy, for food, money, or other items.

Prices were affected throughout the country. In the North, this was due to the costs of support-ing the war effort, and, in the case of some goods, because of shortages of goods that had normally come from the South (cotton and indigo, for example). In the South, however, which produced almost nothing other than cash crops that it had previously been able to export, such price increases were the worst.

Following are examples of costs of goods and services in the South year-to-year during the war, along with some from years following it for comparison purposes (those from 1872 are from the first Montgomery Ward catalog). Prices in the North for most items would not have changed much after the start of the war, probably not even quite doubling over a four-year period, with the exception of cotton goods, which would have been even more expensive or completely unavailable. The cost of living for a family of five in a major Union city was $1,333 per month in 1863.

	1849	1861	1862	1863	1864	1865	1870
bed, bureau, and commode							$15
beeswax (per pound)		21¢ to 26¢					
blanket	$25 to $80						$3
buggy							$75
cartridges (per box)							50¢
chair							$1.25
coal (per bushel)					$1.75		
coal (per year)							c. $80
Colt .45 Peacemaker revolver							$17
Colt .45 Peacemakers, matched set of pearl-handled with holsters							$100
cookstove							$25

Household Goods

	1849	1861	1862	1863	1864	1865	1870
firewood (per cord)		$2.50	$20	$40	$100	$100 to $150	
harness							$50
kerosene (per gallon)							15¢
lantern							$1
laundry (per dozen pieces)			$3				
quinine (per ounce)			$60				
rifle, seven-shot Sharps repeater							$50
rifle, single-shot muzzle-loader (army surplus)							$8
saddle							$30
saddle, cowboy							$60
shotgun, breach-loading							$60
soap (per cake)			$1.25				
soap, common (per pound)		3.5¢ to 10¢		$1 to $1.10			
tallow (per pound)		4¢					
tea set	$24						
toothbrush				$2.50			
wagon							$65

Clothing

	1849	1861	1862	1863	1864	1865	1870
bonnet, new				$25 to $60		$200	
bonnet, used						$70	
boots (four pairs)	$96						
boots (per pair)			$30	$50			
boots, Balmoral						$250	
boots, women's Morocco (pair)					$110		
cloaks						$1,000 to $5,000	

A period illustration showing children's fashion typical of the very rich.

More examples of ladies' fashion from the 1850s.

	1849	1861	1862	1863	1864	1865	1870
dress		$9 to $30		$50 to $195	$150 or more		
dress, fine wool						$800	
dress, merino				$150			
gloves, French kid (per pair)						$125 to $175	
handkerchiefs (each)	c. 92¢	50¢		$5			
hat, men's					$75		
hat, women's						$600 to $1,500	
flannel shirts (24)	$192						
pants (six pairs)	$108						
shoes, men's (per pair)			$18	$25 to $50	$125 to $800		
shoes, resole (per pair)				$10	$50		
shoes, women's (per pair)			$15	$25 to $50	$125 to $800		
stockings, fine cotton				$6			
uniform jackets (four)	$128						
uniforms, officers' (each)					$2,000		

These period trade cards advertise home sewing machines.

This 1850s daguerreotype shows a seamstress at work. The cost of clothing skyrocketed during the war.

Chapter Eight

Fabric & Sewing

	1849	1861	1862	1863	1864	1865	1870
calico (per yard)			75¢ to $2	$2.50 to $4		$25 to $35	10¢
cloth				$2.25 to $5.50	$15 to $45		
cloth, blue (three yards)	$36						
fabric, alpaca dress (per yard)						$60	
fabric, bleached cotton (per yard)		12.5¢		$3.50		$15 to $50	15¢
fabric, muslin dress (per yard)			$6 to $8				
gingham, black-and-white (per yard)				$4.50			
ginghams, domestic							15¢
homespun, plain (per yard)			$1				
linen (per yard)					$22		
linen, Irish						$50 to $100	
ribbon (per yard)						$25	
sewing pins (per pack)					$5		
thread (five pounds)	$5						
thread, cotton (per spool)				50¢	$5 to $10		
toweling (per yard)				$1.25			
wool (per pound)		23¢ to 33¢					

Terms

BAREGE: A sheer, woven fabric generally made from cotton, but also sometimes from silk or wool, used for women's clothing.

BOMBAZINE: A fine, twilled fabric made of silk and cotton or wool that was often dyed black and used for women's mourning clothes.

CALICO: A coarse cotton cloth often printed with bright designs.

CAMISOLE: A women's undershirt, typically sleeveless and made of cotton or silk.

CASSIMERE: A contemporary variant of cashmere.

CHEMISE: A women's undergarment that typically rode low on the shoulders and fell to just below the knee.

CORD: A unit used for measuring cut fuel wood equivalent to 128 cubic feet (i.e., a stack four feet wide by eight feet long by four feet high).

CORSET, CORSET COVER: Undergarments that emphasized the feminine form by constricting the waist and accentuating the bust. Corsets, which were often noted for their discomfort, were typically worn over a chemise, fastened in the front, with a clasp and then tightened with laces in back or one of the sides.

CRINOLINE: A women's undergarment, cinched around the waist and extending to just a few inches above the floor, that was worn under a dress to give it body. Such devices could be made simply of padded material, such as cotton, but more often consisted of about two-dozen connected hoops, held together like a beehive-shaped cage.

EBONITE: See vulcanite.

ENGAGEANTE: A false sleeve that was a popular feature of women's garments in the nineteenth century.

FAIRY LIGHT: A lamp made by floating sweet, burning balls of gum in a saucer of melted lard. Used mostly in the South.

FIREBALL: A substitute for coal and wood used in the South. Made from a mixture of sawdust, small pieces of coal, water, clay, and sand, which was rolled into small balls and allowed to dry and harden.

FLOUNCE: A strip of gathered or pleated material attached to the hem of a dress, gown, or crinoline to help protect it from contact with the ground.

GODEY'S LADY'S BOOK (a.k.a., *Godey's Magazine and Lady's Book*): A magazine founded in 1830 and published in Philadelphia that was a popular guide to fashion in the era of the Civil War and contained articles, poetry, patterns, and engravings. In 1860, it had 150,000 subscribers who paid $3 a year for the monthly publication. Its publishers deliberately made no reference to the war, however, and this ultimately cost the magazine about a third of its subscribers.

GUTTA-PERCHA: A rubbery material derived from raw latex and used to make containers waterproof (e.g., collar boxes) or to fashion small items.

HOUSEWIFE: A sewing kit often owned by soldiers, containing needles, thread, pins, buttons, and other items for repairing clothing and uniforms.

LUCIFERS: a term for matches, particularly the non-safety type tipped with potassium chlorate and antimony sulphide.

MERINO: The fine wool taken from merino sheep, used especially for knitting hosiery, undergarments, and other items of clothing.

PARASOL: A small umbrella carried by women made of cloth or paper and with a frame of cane or wire. Such accessories could be plain or decorated with ruffles or fringe, and varieties for many different occasions existed (e.g., the plain paper parasol used for a stroll in the country would be replaced by a more frilly cloth one for a more formal occasion).

PETTICOAT: A women's underskirt.

RETICULE: A drawstring purse or handbag, often of netlike fabric.

SNOOD: A cloth net covering for women's hair.

TALLOW: The tasteless, solid white fat rendered from cattle, horses or sheep and used as a component in food, candles, leather dressings, lubricants, and soap.

TOWELING: A cotton fabric used for making towels.

VULCANITE: A period term for hard rubber, which was used for items like buttons, pocket combs, cups, denture bases, flasks, pipes, soap boxes, and syringes.

FOOD AND DIET:
HOW PEOPLE ATE AT HOME AND ON THE WAR FRONT

"The science and art of cooking may be divided into ten principal parts; the rest is all fancy. These ten parts are: Baking, Boiling, Broiling, Frying, Mixing, Roasting, Sautéting, Seasoning, Simmering, and Stewing. Tasting is an adjunct to all." — Pierre Blot, *Hand-Book of Practical Cookery*, 1868

F ood for people during the Civil War was important as a source of both life and enjoyment, just as it has been for people throughout history and even today. Many contemporary accounts and records describe the diets of soldiers and civilians, the impact of the war upon their eating habits, and the financial and health effects of shortages.

A variety of measurements for food quantities, including larger ones like **bushels** and **barrels**, appear in the following section, but people would have generally been able to purchase smaller amounts of food. Also, terms such as "barrel" sometimes reflected merely a measurement of amount, not a type of packaging, as barrels were often completely unavailable later in the war.

Food in the North

Food and recipes in the North were influenced greatly by the North's prevailing ethnic groups, predominantly the English, Irish, and Germans. Diet and the availability of food in the North were rarely affected by the war, except in areas subject to enemy invasion or raids. In such areas, most items would have been more expensive or even unavailable if the local inhabitants were hoarding or enemy troops had been pillaging.

Ironically, many people in the industrialized North went hungry or were malnourished as a matter of course, and their suffering was neither intensified nor alleviated by the Civil War. These were the inhabitants of the great urban slums who accounted for half the population of some cities. Most of them continued to suffer from the effects of a poor diet, even as the owners of the factories where many of them labored grew rich from wartime contracts.

Food in the South

As in the North, Southerners' diets were based on the traditional fare of their English, Irish, and German predecessors, and influenced by the large African-American population and crops that flourished in the region, such as rice and okra.

Largely because of the Union blockade and eventually because U.S. troops were marching through the Confederacy and occupying parts of it, food shortages began to affect Southerners early in the war, and grew acute as it progressed. A reduced ability to produce food because so many men and animals had been sent to the armies, along with wastage caused by raids and invasion, exacerbated these shortages.

Shortages tended to be the very worst in urban areas, which produced little food on their own and had relatively large, concentrated populations—populations that were often swelled by the influx of refugees from areas directly affected by the war. As the Confederacy's infrastructure deteriorated, the ability to transport food into the cities eroded. In rural areas, shortages were also felt, especially in areas touched directly by the war. However, shortages tended to be less devastating to people already accustomed to foraging, hunting, and growing their own food.

Southern blacks had a traditional diet rather different from their masters, and had long become accustomed to making the most of lesser cuts of meat and second-rate produce. As shortages took their toll on the Confederacy, the diet of whites shifted more and more toward the sorts of dishes blacks had traditionally eaten (for example, Hopping John, see recipe at right).

Civilian Diet

Wartime conditions led to shortages of food more acutely in the South than in the North, and far more Southerners suffered the effects of malnutrition and starvation than did their Northern counterparts.

HOPPING JOHN

1 lb. dried black-eyed peas
3 pints cold water
½ lb. sliced salt pork or bacon
1 tsp. Tabasco sauce
½ tsp. salt
2 tbsp. bacon fat or lard
2 medium onions, chopped
1 cup uncooked long-grain rice
1½ cups boiling water

Cover the peas with cold water in a large kettle. Soak overnight. Add salt pork, Tabasco sauce, and salt. Cover and cook over low heat about 30 minutes. Meanwhile, cook onions in bacon fat until yellow, then add to peas along with rice and boiling water. Cook this mixture until rice is tender and water is absorbed, about 20 to 25 minutes, stirring occasionally. Yield: About eight servings.
— McIlhenny Company, 1868

People did not have modern chemical preservatives or refrigeration, and foods were either eaten fresh or preserved through canning, pickling, smoking, salting, drying, or storing in cool areas such as root cellars. Alcohol, salt, sugar, and vinegar were all important elements in preserving and canning foods. Some manufactured foods familiar to people today were also eaten by people during the era of the Civil War, including Underwood Deviled Ham (since 1822), Lea and Perrins Worcestershire Sauce (since 1835), Borden's Condensed Milk (since 1856), Van Camp's Pork and Beans (since 1861), and McIlhenny Company's Tabasco Sauce (since 1868).

CAPILLAIRE

"Take one pound of loaf sugar, quarter of a pound of moist sugar, one egg well beaten, one pint of water. Simmer it one hour, skim it while boiling, let it get cold, then boil again and skim, add one ounce of orange-flower water and two tablespoonfuls of brandy. Strain through a jelly-bag, and bottle for use. A spoonful in a tumbler of water makes a pleasant beverage."

—*Godey's Lady's Book*, 1866

Typical food items of the day included a wide variety of soups and stews, many types of fried meats and vegetables, many sorts of breads and biscuits, and fruit pies. People also ate many sorts of regional specialties, such as seafood in coastal areas. Southern specialties included fried ham with **red-eye gravy** and biscuits, and Hopping John, a stew made from bacon, peas or beans, and red pepper. These were favorites of slaves before the war and with just about everyone after it.

Beverages included milk, hot coffee and tea, cold tea, water (which people tended to drink a lot more frequently than they do today), and some commercially-produced soft drinks, most notably sarsaparilla, which was similar to ginger ale. People also made a variety of refreshing homemade soft drinks, including lemonade, **shrubs**, **switchels**, and capillaire.

Fruits and Vegetables

Many of the varieties of fruits and vegetables eaten by people during the Civil War are today very rare or no longer exist at all (or are available only from dealers of heirloom plant seeds). This is not due to any inferiority amongst such produce; indeed, many varieties of vintage produce are better-tasting or have a unique flavor, are more versatile, or are better adapted to local conditions than those available today. However, considerations of shelf life and resilience for transportation are more important for our modern society than they were during the Civil War, when many people grew fruits and vegetables for their own consumption and many others bought what they needed from local markets.

In an age that predated supermarkets, many people had gardens and fruit-bearing trees and grew their own fruits and vegetables. This was much more common in the country than in the city, but even urban people might have small garden plots. As the South was more rural than the North, and because food shortages there were much more acute, people in the Confederacy depended much more upon their personal gardens. In both areas, especially the South, women often supplemented their family incomes by selling fresh or canned produce from their gardens.

Following are descriptions of many of the sorts of produce people were likely to grow themselves or purchase at the market or from farmers during the Civil War.

TOMATOES were probably the most common home garden produce, but did not become widely popular until just a generation or so before the Civil War. New England Puritans considered tomatoes to be an aphrodisiac and shunned them. The French introduced it into their cooking in New Orleans. Thomas Jefferson grew them as ornamental plants at his Monticello estate, and various gardeners praised their virtues. It was not until 1820, however, when a Col. Robert Johnson publicly ate an entire basketful of tomatoes in front of a crowd on the steps of the courthouse in Salem, New Jersey, that the tomato became an element in the evolving American cuisine (Johnson's personal physician predicted frothing at the mouth and appendicitis, a prophecy that was not fulfilled). Within a few decades, recipes containing tomatoes became commonplace.

Prior to the Civil War, tomato varieties tended to have fairly generic names, like Large Round Red and Yellow Pear-Shaped. By the time of the Civil War, however, more than a thousand varieties had been introduced. Names became more inventive and included varieties like Abraham Lincoln, Brandywine, Great White Beefsteak, Cherokee Purple, and Ruffled Yellow. As these names suggest, a variety of colors besides the familiar red, such as pink, purple, yellow, and white, also existed. Some of these can still be found today.

Most Civil War-era tomatoes were not as smooth and round as modern varieties. For example, many were beefsteak varieties, which tend to be flattened; others, like the Ruffled Yellow, had a pleated texture.

LETTUCE, including head, leaf, and romaine types, was also a familiar item in Civil War-era gardens (although there were not nearly as many varieties as tomatoes). Leaf varieties included Early Curly Simpson, introduced in 1864, and Grandpa Admire's, which had green leaves tinged with

 ——————————————————————————————

Tomatoes did not become part of mainstream American cuisine until 1820, when a Col. Robert Johnson publicly ate an entire basketful of tomatoes in front of a crowd on the steps of the courthouse in Salem, New Jersey. Johnson's personal physician predicted frothing at the mouth and appendicitis, a prophecy that was not fulfilled.

 ——————————————————————————————

bronze and was developed by Civil War veteran George Admire. Head varieties included Tennis Ball, a Boston type—meaning that the heads are loose—that Jefferson also grew at Monticello; it was developed in Kentucky in the early 1800s and is still popular today.

BEANS were another common garden item during the Civil War, and many different types were grown throughout the country. Bean varieties included Navy, Great Northern, Yellow Eye, Jacob's Cattle, and Cranberry, all of which were used primarily for baking and in soups. Varieties of snap beans included Yellow Pencil Pod, Hickman's Snap, and Cherokee.

SWEET CORN, intended to be eaten by humans rather than used as fodder, was introduced in the late 1820s but did not really catch on until the 1850s. Corn varieties available during the Civil War included Black Aztec (also called Mexican), Hooker's, and Luther Hill. Black Aztec is unusual in that, during the milk stage, the kernels are white but, as the corn matures and dries, the kernels become black and can be ground to make blue-purple cornmeal. Two yellow varieties especially well-suited for making cornmeal included Northstine Dent and Garland Flint, the former reputed to make some of the sweetest cornmeal.

The Ponderosa lemon was a popular Civil War houseplant that produced lemons weighing up to five pounds each. The fruit's thick rinds allowed them to hang for months without spoiling. For this reason, the fruit was usually left on the tree as a decoration, but could also be eaten if needed.

CABBAGE was a popular item, especially among people of German and Irish descent. Two common varieties included Early Jersey Wakefield and Winnigstadt, the latter a German variety that had yellowish green leaves and firm, pointed heads.

Several sorts of **POTATO** were also grown in areas suited to them (such as Texas and Idaho), including the Early Rose, a variety described as having "light pink skin with deep-set eyes and white flesh," and **Irish potatoes**.

Other plants likely to appear in Civil War gardens included cucumbers, pumpkins, melons, and beets.

Houseplants were very popular during the Civil War, especially among middle-class families. Some of these plants could also provide edibles, given bright daylight, moderate water, and cool evenings. Fruit-bearing citrus trees were among the most prevalent of such plants, and one of the most popular was the Ponderosa lemon. This sturdy four- to five-foot tree bore huge lemons that could weigh up to five pounds each, and which had thick rinds that allowed them to hang for months without spoiling. For this reason, the fruit was usually left on the tree as a decoration, but could also be eaten if needed.

Meat prices rose everywhere during the war, but mostly in the South, which was hardiest hit by the conflict. By 1864, dressed rats hung in the butcher shops of many Confederate cities and many Southerners were reduced to supplementing their diets with vermin.

Produce prices stayed fairly steady in the North during the Civil War. In the South, like everything else, they rose and varied widely from region to region, and from city to country.

A few examples include dried apples for 4.5¢ a pound, plums for 7¢ a pound and walnuts for 12¢ a pound in 1861; corn for $15 per barrel and wheat for $4.50 per barrel in 1862; cabbage for $1 per head, onions for $3 a dozen, sweet potatoes for $21 to $250 per bushel, watermelons for $10 each, cornmeal for $16 to $300 per bushel, and wheat for $20 per barrel in 1863; cherries for $1.50 a quart, peas for $48 per bushel, squash for 50¢ each, cornmeal for $104 per bushel, and turnip greens for $16 per bushel in 1864; and beans for $15 per quart, peas for $80 per bushel, and cornmeal for $400 per bushel in 1865.

Meat

People in the nineteenth century ate most of the same sorts of meat we do today, including beef and veal, pork and bacon, chicken, turkey, and lamb. Civil War-era Americans also tended to eat much more game than is common today, along with less-familiar fowl, such as pigeon and partridge.

Shortages in the South made meat very expensive and difficult to find as the war progressed. Beef, for example, could be purchased for 12¢ a pound in 1862, $1 or more in 1863, at least $2 in 1864, and $8 per pound in 1865, if it could be found at all. Fowl was similarly expensive. In 1862, a chicken cost 20¢; in 1863, a partridge 75¢; in 1864, a single turkey from $50 to $100; and in 1865, a simple hen cost $50. Other examples include hams, which were being sold in 1864 for $350 each; veal, which cost $6 per pound in 1864; and fish, which cost $25 each in 1865.

By 1864, people in cities hardest hit by the war (for example, by siege) were sometimes reduced to eating animals that a few years earlier would have been considered little better than vermin, including cats and dogs, crows, frogs, locusts, rats, snails, snakes, and worms. In some cities, including Richmond, Virginia, and Vicksburg, Mississippi, dressed rats were sold in butcher shops for $2.50 apiece and dog was passed off as lamb. According to Mary Elizabeth Massey, author of *Ersatz in the Confederacy*, conditions like this presaged the South's defeat more than any loss on the battlefield.

Beverages

Coffee was by far the most popular hot beverage in either the North or the South. In the North, coffee rarely ran short for civilians, and the U.S. Army went to great efforts to ensure soldiers always had coffee beans. In the South, however, coffee became nearly nonexistent early into the war.

Southerners experimented with a wide variety of coffee substitutes, none of which was widely satisfactory. Chicory, acorns, beans, beets, bran, corn, cornmeal, cotton seeds, dandelion root, okra seeds, peanuts, peas, sugarcane seeds, and wheat berries were variously parched, dried, browned, or roasted and used to make ersatz coffee. Other versions used tubers like carrots or yams, which were cut into small pieces, dried, toasted, and then ground up.

Tea was another popular drink, but was also imported. Tea prices in the South rose dramatically year after year, from an inflated 1862 low of $10 per pound to an 1864 high of $40 per pound, prices that applied only if it was available at all, which near the end of the war, it often was not. Decent substitutes for tea were much easier to devise than for coffee, however, as many domesticated and wild herbs, as well as leaves from fruit-bearing plants, could be made into an infusion. Leaves of blackberry, dittany, holly, huckleberry, spice berry, and the many varieties of mint could all be used to make "tea," as could saw palmetto berries, sassafras roots, sumac berries, and yapon shrub twigs.

When the weather was hot, beverages like cider and lemonade were popular, as were **shrubs** and **switchels**, drinks made from cool water, juice, vinegar, and a sweetener like **loaf sugar**, **moist sugar**, or **treacle**.

Wine, champagne, and distilled spirits were generally import items and became almost completely unavailable in the South as a result of the Federal blockade. Simpler, domestic beverages like apple cider and beer had always been popular among the lower classes and, because of shortages, frequently had to suffice for the affluent. At times, however, even they were not available, and substitutes had to be devised. One type of homemade alcoholic beverage used as a substitute for champagne that became popular in the South was made by mixing one part corn syrup and/or molasses with three parts water and then fermenting it in a barrel.

INSTANT COFFEE

"To every ¼ pound of ground coffee, add one teaspoonful of powdered chicory and one pint of water. Freshly roast and grind the coffee; put into a percolator or filter with the chicory and pour slowly over it the above amount of boiling water. When it has all filtered through, warm the coffee to bring it to the simmering point, but do not allow it to boil; then filter it a second time, put it into a clean, dry bottle, cork it well, and it will remain fresh for several days. Two tablespoons of this essence are quite sufficient for a breakfast-cupful of hot milk."

— *Book of Household Management*, Isabella Beeton, 1861

> When salt was unavailable to use as a seasoning, things with a salty flavor could be used, such as a pinch of wood ashes or a wild plant called coltsfoot, and soldiers sometimes used a dash of gunpowder.

Food Preservation

Salt was widely used for preserving meat in the nineteenth century, but was often in short supply or completely unavailable in the South during the Civil War. There were centers of salt production in the South, notably in Louisiana and Virginia, but transporting it to where it was needed became impossible as the war dragged on, the Confederate infrastructure collapsed, and hoarding and speculation increased. Such shortages limited the amount of food that could be preserved for the C.S. Army, not to mention civilians, and contributed to the failure of the Southern war effort.

Small quantities of salt, as for household use, could be extracted from the dirt in smokehouses. When this dirt was mixed with water and boiled, a scum would rise to the top that could be skimmed off and dropped into cold water, the salt sinking to the bottom. Salt could also be obtained in coastal areas by evaporating seawater. When salt was unavailable to use as a seasoning, things with a salty flavor could be used, such as a pinch of wood ashes or a wild plant called coltsfoot, and soldiers sometimes used a dash of gunpowder. Such substitutes did not, however, really help much with food preservation.

Meat was sometimes preserved by cutting it into very thin pieces and smoking it without the benefit of salt, and fish was preserved by pounding it flat and drying it in the sun, but these expedients were, presumably, not completely satisfactory. Meat could also be preserved in a briny solution of salt, water, sugar, or another sweetener, and a small amount of potassium nitrate (saltpeter), an expedient that used less salt than usual.

Other Food Substitutes

People in the areas hardest hit by the war, especially in the Confederacy, learned how to make substitute food items beyond those mentioned previously. An excellent source of information about how the rigors of war affected the Southern diet was *The Confederate Receipt Book,* published in 1863. It contained many suggestions for substitutes that could be employed in place of traditional food items or recipe ingredients. Such information was also spread via word of mouth, correspondence, and newspaper articles.

Cider vinegar was unavailable when apples were in short supply in the country or when it could not be bought in the city. Vinegar substitutes were instead made from beets, figs, honey, **Indian apples**, molasses, **persimmons**, and sorghum.

Leavening for baking was often unavailable, and an ersatz version could be made by slowly burning red corncobs in a pan over a bed of coals until they were reduced to a fine white ash. Sometimes this ash was subsequently added to water, left to stand until clear, then strained; the remaining liquid was mixed with sour milk in a one-to-two ratio.

Traditional jellies, jams, and syrups were often impossible to make because sugar was unavailable. Cider, however, could be boiled until thick and, when cooled, would gel. Also, water would thicken if boiled with red corncobs and could be used as a type of syrup.

Wild fruits like persimmons or **pawpaws**, while not as popular as dates or figs, made decent substitutes when more preferred items were not available, and often became more palatable when dried, which concentrated their natural sugar and made them taste sweeter.

Shortages and Inflation

Shortages made food items more expensive throughout the country. In the South, however, shortages caused prices to soar out of control, inflicting untold hardships on the Confederate home front. For example, a typical Southern family's food bill was $6.65 per month at the time of secession, $68 per month in 1863, and $400 per month in 1864. Indeed, by the spring of 1863, prices for food and dry goods were going up about 10 percent a month in the Confederacy. Ultimately, Confederate currency was so devalued that it quite often could not be used to buy food at all, necessitating barter.

Part of the supply crisis in the South could be attributed to the Union blockade. Beyond that, however, prices for civilians were also affected by the fact that so much food was diverted to the military. According to Southerner Judith McGuire, for example, "butter and milk are scarce because cattle had to go to the armies."

The chart on the next page is a year-to-year comparison of price increases for basic food items in the South, drawn from a variety of contemporary sources including diaries, letters, and

INFLATED FOOD PRICES					
	1861	**1862**	**1863**	**1864**	**1865**
bacon (per pound)	12.5¢	75¢	$1.25 to $6	$8 to $9	$11 to $13
beef (per pound)		12.5¢	$1 to $3.33	$2	$8
butter (per pound)	20¢	75¢ to $2	$2 to $4	$15 to $25	$15 to $20
coffee (per pound)	35¢	$1.50 to $4	$5 to $30	$12 to $60	
cornmeal (per bushel)		$3.50	$16 to $300	$20 to $104	$400
flour (per barrel)	$6	$16 to $40	$30 to $75	$125 to $500	$325 to $1,000
potatoes (per bushel)	75¢		$12 to $15	$25	
tea (per pound)		$10 to $20	$7 to $32	$22 to $40	

publications. Prices would not have been uniform throughout the Confederacy and would have been subject to local conditions and availability, but these examples should give some sense of the kinds of price changes. Ranges reflect prices earlier in the year vs. those later in the year. Quality of goods might be a factor as well. For example, in 1863 tea was running $32 a pound in some parts of the Confederacy, and only $7 a pound in others; however, the more expensive was imported green tea, while the less expensive may have been made from local herbs, rather than true tea.

Food prices were often higher in densely-populated areas, where resources were spread more thinly. For example, prices in urban Richmond, among the very highest, were considerably greater than in rural Halifax County, North Carolina (for example, sugar cost $1.25 per pound in Halifax in March 1863 and $10 per pound in Richmond in September 1863; even accounting for the six-month gap between these figures, the Richmond prices were much higher). In some cases, certain items were not to be had at any price. For example, by 1865 coffee, tea, milk, and sugar were completely unavailable in many Confederate communities.

Finally, items that did not need to be imported were likely to have less dramatic price increases.

Prices were also driven upward by speculators—in the North as well as the South—who were increasingly hated for growing rich upon other people's suffering. In December 1864, for example, a Baptist preacher in Richmond was attacked for selling flour and meal at inflated prices.

Goods were also much more scarce, or altogether unavailable, in areas invaded or occupied by Union troops, causing prices in such places to be much higher.

Military Diet

Soldiers were not very well fed during the Civil War, and malnutrition contributed greatly to illness, disease, and death. Officers tended to eat better than their men, as they could generally afford to purchase better rations from sutlers (subject to availability, of course). The most fortunate soldiers were also able to supplement their diets with the contents of packages from home, which could go a long ways toward making up for the deficiencies of a military diet.

Southern soldiers in particular suffered the effects of malnutrition and even starvation, especially toward the end of the war, when food shortages became acute as a combined result of the tightening Union blockade, the loss or destruction of agricultural land, and the disruption of Southern rail and supply lines.

In the field, Union soldiers subsisted mostly on **hardtack**, a thick, hard cracker three-and-a-half inches square made from flour, water, and salt that had been a staple army food item since the Mexican War (1846–1848). Such "teeth dullers" were typically issued to soldiers in one-pound packages.

Hardtack was designed for longevity rather than palatability. The high salt content of hardtack made it unattractive to mice and cockroaches but attracted weevils, who lived in and laid their larvae in the crackers, inspiring descriptive nicknames like "worm castles" and making this staple item even more unappealing to soldiers. While it could be eaten with no preparation, soldiers found ways to make this dreary staple slightly more palatable, including dunking, soaking, or crumbling it into coffee, or soaking it in water until soft and then frying it in fat from pork or bacon. **Bully soup**, **hellfire stew**, **lobcourse**, and skillygalee were among the names soldiers gave to the various dishes they made from hardtack.

Confederate soldiers were much less likely to be issued hardtack, unless some of it had been taken in captured or raided Union stores. They were generally provided with coarse, unsifted cornmeal that they baked into cornbread (which attracted vermin as well as, or better than, the Union hardtack).

Other staple food items included coffee, salt pork, and bacon. Fruits, vegetables, and fresh meat were considerably more rare.

Coffee was an important beverage for troops on both sides, and the Union army in particular went out of its way to ensure that coffee was one thing soldiers would not be deprived of. In the South, the Union blockade meant that coffee was perpetually in short supply, and soldiers and civilians alike had to make substitute hot beverages brewed from chicory, roasted corn, peanuts, peas, potatoes, and rye.

In the absence of modern preservation techniques, meat was preserved by smoking, drying, or salting. Despite the best efforts, however, meat frequently went rancid, and the meat provided to soldiers has been described as "black as a shoe" on the outside and "yellow with putrefaction" on the inside. Soldiers preferred salt pork, or **sowbelly**, to bacon, which in hot weather would sweat, saturating their haversacks with grease and possibly ruining other contents or staining uniforms. Pork was usually in short supply, although when it was available, soldiers often had so much of it to eat for a time that they became sick of it.

The lack of fresh fruits and vegetables contributed to all sorts of health problems, especially scurvy. To reduce the chance of malnutrition and its effects, the Union military provided troops with what it described as "desiccated and compressed mixed vegetables," dehydrated cakes of beans, beets, carrots, onions, turnips, and other vegetables. True to form, troops referred to these items as "baled hay" or "**desecrated vegetables**." In the Confederate military, some soldiers—notably Lt. Gen. Stonewall Jackson—sucked on lemons, a good antidote for scurvy. Of course, these were not always available, especially during the later years of the war, and commissary officers advised soldiers to forage for wild onions.

When fresh vegetables were available, potatoes and onions were the most common. Union soldiers were served a thin soup fortified with sliced potatoes in the mistaken belief that it would help ward off scurvy. It was described in one account as looking like "a dirty brook with leaves floating around" in it. When cooking for themselves, soldiers were more likely to quarter or thinly slice the potatoes, then fry them in bacon grease, a delicacy sometimes referred to as "camp potatoes."

UNION MILITARY RATIONS

Following are food items typically issued to U.S. Army troops.

» Beans or Peas
» Beef, fresh
» Beef, salted
» Coffee beans (green or roasted)
» Fruit, dried
» **Hardtack**
» Milk, condensed
» Pork, salted
» Potatoes, dried
» Rice or Hominy
» Salt
» Sugar
» Vegetables, mixed, dried
» Vegetables, fresh (e.g., carrots, onions, potatoes, or turnips in season)
» Vinegar

Preparing Military Food

Fresh food, typically beef or vegetables, were provided only infrequently and, when such fare was provided, soldiers had to prepare it themselves the best they could. This as much as anything contributed to poor diet and malnutrition, as many soldiers simply had no idea how to make edible food out of raw components like bags of meal.

Indeed, the concept of a mess hall was unknown during the Civil War, and soldiers generally cooked all their own meals in the field. In

Soldiers in many units pooled their rations and had them prepared by hired cooks or troops tasked with this responsibility.

camp, companies frequently designated cooks to prepare their rations and would often take up a collection of money so fresh ingredients could be purchased from sutlers. Quite often, these cooks had no particular culinary skill and, far from adding any quality during preparation, often produced food that was largely unpalatable.

Officers, particularly affluent ones, were sometimes accompanied by servants who cooked for them and thus avoided the difficulties of preparing their own food.

CAMP POTATOES

"Cut the vegetable into thin slices and throw them into cold water for half an hour; then put them into fat hissing hot and fry them until they acquire a golden hue. Some persons cut them only into quarters, but they are not near so crisp and nice."

— *Camp Fires and Camp Cooking, or Culinary Hints for the Soldier,* Capt. James M. Sanderson, 1862

Because they had to cook their own food, soldiers carried with them a variety of cooking implements and utensils. Utensils included traditional implements like knives, forks (usually three- but sometimes four-tined), and spoons, many made entirely of metal or fitted with bone or wood handles. Some officers, or even common soldiers in well-to-do volunteer regiments, may have also had silver-plated utensils, at least early in the war.

Larger implements were constructed of tin or cast iron and included plates (which could double as pans), cooking pots in a wide variety of sizes, skillets, coffeepots, and cups (some with wire handles as well as regular mug handles). Many sorts of makeshift items would have been used as well (e.g., bayonets, which could be used as skewers for roasting meat, or tin cans fitted with wire handles and used for campfire cooking).

In addition to cooking over open fires and coals, soldiers sometimes used manufactured camp stoves, many patents for which were filed after the war broke out. Some of these were quite elaborate and typically included a central firebox, as well as any or all of a double boiler, a baking oven, a broiler, and a flat surface for coffeepots, skillets, or pots. One stove inventor, George A. Higgins of New York City, said of his 1861 patent camp stove that "the object of this invention is to obtain a stove of the simplest construction, which, with its necessary fixtures ... may, when not required for use, be packed within a small compass, and the several parts when in use be capable of being so arranged that a large amount of cooking may be done." Even with such fancy implements invented as the war progressed, most soldiers simply did their cooking over coals or campfires.

CONFEDERATE MILITARY RATIONS

Following are food items typically issued to C.S. Army troops. Note that, under the best of conditions, such troops might also have had anything issued to Union troops if it was available or if they captured it. Under the worst of conditions, especially late in the war, they might have had little or nothing at all.

» bacon
» chicory
» cornmeal
» molasses
» peanuts
» sugar
» tea
» vegetables, fresh
   (rarely and in season)

Terms

BARK JUICE: A slang term for liquor.

BARREL: Used as a unit of measurement, from thirty-one to forty-two gallons.

BULLY SOUP, PANADA: A cooked mixture of crushed hardtack, cornmeal, ginger, and wine.

BUSHEL: A unit of dry measurement equivalent to four pecks (i.e., thirty-two quarts or eight gallons).

BUST HEAD: A slang term for cheap whiskey.

CONFEDERATE BEEF: Early in the war, a term used by Union soldiers to refer to the Confederate cows and horses that they took for food. After the summer

1863 Siege of Vicksburg, however, this term was more often used to refer to the mules eaten by the Southern defenders of the city.

CREEPER: A term used by New England soldiers for a small iron skillet.

DESECRATED VEGETABLES: A disparaging term for the dehydrated, or desiccated, vegetables

formed into yellowish squares that were issued to Union troops.

EMBALMED BEEF: A slang term for canned meat.

ESSENCE OF COFFEE: A type of instant coffee available in paste form.

HARD BREAD: A term sometimes used in

military documents for hardtack.

HARDTACK: Unleavened bread in the form of quarter-inch-thick crackers issued by the Union military.

HELLFIRE STEW: Hardtack crushed into pieces, soaked in water to make softer, then fried in bacon fat.

INDIAN APPLE: A perennial American herb and its yellowish, egg-shaped fruit. Also called May apple.

IRISH POTATO: The white potato brought to the United States by Irish immigrants.

JOHN BARLEYCORN: A slang term for beer.

JUNK: A slang term used by sailors for salt beef.

LOAF SUGAR: Granulated sugar.

LOBCOURSE: A soup made from hardtack,

salt pork, and whatever else was on hand.

LONG SWEETENING: Molasses.

MOIST SUGAR: Brown sugar.

MUCKET: A large tin mug or kettle with a hinged top that soldiers used for cooking and eating their food. Such implements either had a handle like a traditional mug, a wire handle like a bucket, or both.

MUD LARK: Humorous term used by soldiers to refer to domestic pigs they killed and ate. Presumably, the farmers who owned these pigs were not as amused as the soldiers.

MULE: A slang term for any meat of dubious quality.

O BE JOYFUL: A slang term for liquor.

PAPAW, PAWPAW: A bush or small tree and its compact, fleshy

fruit, found in temperate regions of North America.

PECK: A unit of dry measurement equal to eight quarts. Also used colloquially to mean "a lot."

PERSIMMON: An astringent, plum-like fruit found in the South that is sweet and edible when ripe.

POP SKULL: A slang term for cheap whiskey.

RECEIPT: A period term for a recipe.

RED EYE: A slang term for liquor.

RED-EYE GRAVY: A reddish gravy made from ham drippings and hot water, typically served with ham and biscuits.

SALT HORSE: An informal term for any salted meat.

SHEET-IRON CRACKERS: a slang term for hardtack.

SHRUB: A drink made from vinegar and fruit juice that was given to sick people as a remedy but also widely enjoyed during hot weather.

SKILLYGALEE: An informal name for hardtack softened by soaking in water then frying in bacon grease.

SLOW BEAR: One of the many lighthearted terms used by foraging troops to refer to the farmers' pigs that they killed and ate.

SOWBELLY: A term used by soldiers for pork.

SWITCHEL: A type of drink popular in hot weather that was made from a mixture of vinegar, a sweetener, and chilled water.

TEETH DULLERS: A slang term for hardtack crackers.

TREACLE: A largely Southern term for molasses.

TECHNOLOGY:
INVENTIONS THAT CHANGED LIFE AND WARFARE

"Technology is a gift of God. After the gift of life it is perhaps the greatest of God's gifts.
It is the mother of civilizations, of arts, and of sciences." — Freeman J. Dyson

One of the great ironies of history is that the greatest advances in technology, thought, and the arts often occur during times of warfare and strife. America's Civil War is certainly no exception to this rule. It saw the introduction or improvement of weapons, inventions, and industrial processes. Technological advances, such as telegraphy, railways, and mass production made it possible to raise, transport, and supply the huge armies that fought the Civil War.

In the 1860s, America was in the midst of its Industrial Revolution, being transformed by advancing technology into an industrialized rather than an agrarian society. When war broke out, each side was driven to bring to bear whatever advantages it could. Ultimately, the North, a more industrialized region and the beneficiary of more and greater modern technology, prevailed and won the war. And, as horrible as the Civil War was, the technology advanced and produced during the conflict subsequently helped the United States become the world power it is today.

Like so many other conflicts, the Civil War proved that technological superiority alone is usually not enough to win a war; if it had been, the war would have ended in 1861 and not dragged on for four long, bloody years. Northern technological superiority, however, meant that the war was an uphill battle for the South from the beginning, and a fight that the South eventually was unable to continue.

Many inventions associated with later ages saw their earliest incarnations during the Civil War. Military advances included the introduction of many new types of weapons and equipment, among them land mines, repeating rifles, automatic weapons, revolving gun turrets, armored warships, long-range sniper rifles, railroad artillery, double-barreled cannon, and the first naval mines (many of these weapons are discussed in chapter 13).

The military also made great advances in the usage of existing types of weapons and equipment, including observation balloons, hand grenades, submarine and semisubmersible vessels, mobile siege artillery, and rockets.

 Technological advances such as telegraphy, railways, and mass production made it possible to raise, transport, and supply the huge armies that fought the Civil War.

Medical advances included vast improvements in medical care, improved prosthetic limbs, the first orthopedic hospital, improvements in pharmacology, techniques for handling infection and the spread of disease, and anesthetics.

Other technological advances included the first fire extinguishers, periscopes, the first railroad signal system, the first oil pipeline, great advances in photography (see appendix A), improved telegraphy, mobile field communications, canned food, improvements to the factory system, instant coffee, and rudimentary refrigeration.

Technology in the North

In the North, on the eve of the Civil War, more than one million people worked in some 100,000 factories of varying sorts and sizes, which included virtually all of the nation's weapons manufacturers and shipyards. Several parts of the North, especially the New England states and New Jersey, were also noted as being sites of particular innovation and inventiveness.

Northern ability to produce whatever it needed, rather than import it from other countries, simply eclipsed that of the South. A striking example of this is that, in 1860, the textile factories of a single Northern city, Lowell, Massachusetts, had more spindles turning thread than did the entire South.

Technology in the South

At the outbreak of the Civil War, the South had about 100,000 workers employed in a mere 20,000 factories and workshops. Some of these were very technologically advanced, such as Augusta Powder Works, which produced some of the best gunpowder used on either side. Overall, however, the

INVENTIONS OF THE 1860s

This time line shows some of the top inventions from the decade of the Civil War. Many of them were at least peripherally military in nature.

18 60

Light Bulb (Joseph Wilson Swan)
Linoleum (Frederick Walton)

Repeating Rifle (Christopher Spencer, Oliver F. Winchester)
Self-Propelled Torpedo (Giovanni Luppis)

61

Siemens Regenerative Furnace (Carl Wilhelm Siemens)

Pantelegraph (Giovanni Caselli)

62

Gatling Gun (Richard J. Gatling)
Combustion Engine-Driven Submarine (Narcís Monturiol i Estarriol)

Pasteurization (Louis Pasteur, Claude Bernard)

63

Player Piano (Henri Fourneaux)

Underground Railway/Subway (John Fowler)

64

Metal-Hulled Icebreaker (Mikhail Britnev)

18 65

Barbed Wire (Louis Jannin)

66

Dynamite (Alfred Nobel)

67

68

Typewriter (Christopher Sholes, Carlos Glidden, Samuel W. Soule, James Densmore)

Margarine (Mege Mouries)

69

Railway Air Brake (George Westinghouse)
Periodic Table (Dmitri Mendeleev)

Vacuum Cleaner (Ives W. McGaffey)

18 70

South probably had about a tenth the industrial capability of the North. This capacity diminished as the war progressed, too, as the South was unable to furnish the raw materials it needed to produce goods in its factories, and Southerners had to become adept at improvisation and devising substitutes as needed.

At the beginning of the war, for example, the Confederacy had only two major metal foundries, Leeds Company in New Orleans and Tredegar Ironworks in Richmond, Virginia. It lost Leeds when Union forces captured New Orleans in April 1862 and, less than a year later, Union forces occupied Tennessee, depriving the Confederacy of its primary source of iron. This left Tredegar, as well as many smaller factories, at a standstill for months at a time for want of raw materials to work with. Nonetheless, throughout the course of the war, Tredegar produced thousands of artillery pieces, as well as armor plating for ironclad warships.

In 1860, the textile factories in Lowell, Massachusetts, had more spindles turning thread than did the entire South.

Southern ironworks produced only a quarter as many cannon as did factories in the North, but this still represented a high level of ingenuity and dedication. A side effect of this was that even the limited numbers of consumer goods that had been produced prior to the war were no longer manufactured in the Confederacy.

Prior to the war, of course, the South was able to import whatever products of technology and industrialization it needed. Indeed, it was technology that had made the institution of slavery profitable by the time of the Civil War. By the early 1800s, slaves could not pick or process enough cotton to make them highly profitable. The invention of the **cotton gin**, however, allowed far more cotton to be grown and processed by fewer slaves, ensuring the economic viability of the slave-based plantation system, which otherwise would have likely died a natural death within a few generations. Cotton became the world's cheapest and most widespread textile fabric.

Military Technology

Military technology is very reactive and tends to improve only in response to specific threats, conditions, or needs, and technological advances in some areas prompt corresponding advances in others. The heavy rifled artillery pieces of the Civil War, for example—which could blow apart existing masonry fortresses—necessitated improvements in fortification. And the war's deadly weapons in general prompted improvements in many areas, from battlefield medical care to prosthetic limbs for soldiers who had been horribly maimed.

Military tactics, too, had to change in the face of improved technology. Battlefield tactics at the beginning of the war were based on principles little modified since the Napoleonic Wars (1793–1815). Commanders studied the strategies, techniques, and maxims of those wars, and soldiers on both sides were taught corresponding drill and maneuver from a variety of training manuals.

One of the foremost of these was *Rifle and Light Infantry Tactics* (subtitled *For the Exercise and Manoeuvres of Troops When Acting as Light Infantry or Riflemen*), written in 1855 by William J. Hardee, a veteran of the Mexican War who served as a Confederate general during the Civil War. It was better known among soldiers as "Hardee's Tactics" or the "Hardee Manual." Other contemporary texts included *Scott's Tactics*, "Casey's Manual" (*Infantry Tactics for the Instruction, Exercise, and Maneuvres of the Soldier, a Company, Line of Skirmishers, Battalion, Brigade or Corps D'Armee*), "Gilliam's Manual," and a manual on bayonet fighting that had been translated from the French by Union Gen. George B. McClellan.

Unfortunately, these strategies and tactics assumed an antiquated level of technology in which soldiers bearing smoothbore muskets with limited accuracy and range had to line up on open ground in tight formations within a few hundred yards of the enemy and blaze away at each other in volleys, eventually following up with a spirited bayonet charge. Rifled muskets, however, allowed defenders to shoot apart tightly-packed enemy formations while still hundreds of yards away. Many commanders, nonetheless, persisted in employing the tactics of a previous age right through until the end of the conflict, something that contributed to it being the United States' costliest war ever.

Tactics did evolve, of course, in response to the new technology. Referred to as "skirmisher tactics" or "Zouave tactics," they emphasized fighting in small groups and loose formations, making good use of cover and charging for short distances before dropping behind cover.

Improvements in Artillery

Industrialization allowed for the manufacture of more powerful, accurate artillery pieces than had ever before existed, and for vast improvements to explosive shells and other types of artillery ammunition. Such improvements included breech-loading mechanisms, rifled barrels, smokeless gunpowder, systems for absorbing recoil, and vastly superior metallurgy.

Many commanders persisted in employing the tactics of a previous age right through until the end of the conflict, something that contributed to it being the United States' costliest war ever.

Cannon makers also developed new ways to construct guns so that they could withstand heavier powder charges, firing heavier projectiles further and with greater velocity. Thomas J. Rodman, for example, developed a process for producing incredibly strong gun barrels by casting successive layers of the tube around a removable metal core that was cooled by water. As each layer cooled, it shrank and further compressed the layer beneath it. Robert Parker Parrott created artillery barrels by wrapping wrought iron or steel hoops around a central tube made of cast iron or steel.

Redoubts, trenchworks, and other forms of modern fortification were used extensively during the Civil War for the first time.

Fortifications and Siege

In addition to modern tactics, soldiers who survived their first experiences in battle learned to take cover behind trees, fences, walls, and anything else available, and to make use of **firing pits**, **trenches**, and other means of defense. Although it had existed in a much simpler form since the seventeenth century, trench warfare was adopted and refined throughout the course of the Civil War, foreshadowing the way conflicts of the future would be fought. And, just as the trenchworks were a reaction to highly-lethal small arms, weapons were developed during the Civil War to harry or kill soldiers within such defensive works, including hand grenades and relatively light mortars.

Just as infantrymen had to react to the power of modern small arms, so too did engineers have to react to the power of the newest artillery pieces. Most of the forts in existence when the Civil War began were "Third System" fortifications, planned in the decades following the War of 1812 and constructed according to the canons of the early nineteenth century. These polygonal brick forts were designed to withstand the weapons of an earlier age and not heavy, rifled artillery pieces firing explosive shells; such guns, especially when used in mass, wreaked havoc on the outdated fortifications. Fortifications built during or after the war utilized low, earthen walls that could absorb the force of artillery projectiles, rather than try to resist or deflect them with high stone walls.

After making history as the flash point for the Civil War in 1861, Fort Sumter came under fire again in 1863, this time from Union siege artillery. For twenty-two months, the fort withstood bombardment and was almost completely reduced to rubble. Pounded into small pieces, however, Sumter became even more defensible, and Southern defenders burrowed into the rubble, living in subterranean bombproofs and firing their guns from behind berms of smashed masonry.

Many sorts of obstacles were used on Civil War battlefields, including *chevaux de frise*, sharpened stakes affixed to logs that were especially effective at impeding cavalry.

More soldiers actually perished from disease than from any other causes during the Civil War. In general, for every man who died from wounds, there were two who succumbed to disease.

Medical Technology

When the Civil War broke out, contemporary medical technology proved unable to adequately cope with the widespread diseases and horrific wounds it would be faced with over the ensuing four years. Blood transfusions, penicillin and other antibiotics, antiseptics, hypodermic needles, X-ray machines, and innumerable other innovations that could have helped save innumerable lives did not yet exist.

In 1861, the U.S. Army Medical Corps consisted of a mere ninety-eight surgeons and assistant surgeons (in the mid-nineteenth century, doctors were usually referred to as surgeons). Its equipment consisted of a few dozen thermometers, no microscopes (not until 1863), and no working knowledge of devices like the laryngoscope, stethoscope, or ophthalmoscope.

Hypodermic syringes did not exist either. When painkilling drugs had to be administered, they were generally rubbed or dusted into open wounds, or administered in pill or solution form. Morphine and other opiates were the most common sorts of painkillers, and many soldiers became addicts as a side effect of their widespread usage; after the war ended, they could easily obtain such drugs at local drugstores.

By the end of the war, surgeons had learned much about wounds, diseases and drug addiction—much more than they ever could have learned spared the horrors of the war—and medical technology advanced as a result of their knowledge.

Patients, doctors, and volunteer nurses at Carver Hospital in Washington, DC.

Hospital design was one area of improvement. During the era of the war, new hospitals were designed as a series of pavilions connected by covered or enclosed walkways. Soldiers were separated based on their particular wounds or afflictions, reducing the spread of disease. Modern hospitals are based on this model today.

Advances were also made in areas peripheral to the treatment of wounds and illness. Improvements in photography, for example, allowed for wounds and their treatments to be studied by doctors after the war.

Because many families wanted their dead loved ones shipped home, great strides were also made in the science of embalming during the Civil War. A whole new profession concerned with embalming developed during this period, and families who could afford it could hire an "embalming surgeon" to preserve the body of a dead soldier and bring it back home for burial.

The role of medical personnel on the battlefield changed, too, and one important concept advanced during the war was the idea that doctors, nurses, and orderlies were neutrals who should not be shot at or taken prisoner.

Medical Training

Medical schools were common during the Civil War but, unfortunately, many of them provided little practical training. In the nineteenth century, training for surgeons typically consisted of three thirteen-week semesters of medical school. Some fairly good medical schools did exist, mainly at established colleges and universities, such as Princeton and Yale. Programs at such schools lasted one or two years and consisted almost entirely of classroom instruction, with just a few weeks of medical residency. Training during each year was identical and, consequently, some students did not bother to study a second year, although this was generally recommended.

No sort of medical licensing boards existed, however, so little could be done to regulate doctors. In fact, no training or certification of any sort was required for someone to call themselves a surgeon or doctor, and quacks and incompetents were not uncommon.

Causes of Death and Injury

Although battlefield injuries were among the most dramatic and horrible ways soldiers were killed, more actually perished from disease than from any other causes during the Civil War. In general, for every man who died from wounds, there were two who succumbed to disease. In camps and prisons alike, soldiers suffered the effects of overcrowding, inadequate waste disposal, malnutrition or even outright starvation, and parasitic infestation, all factors that caused diseases like influenza and cholera to spread almost unchecked.

Wounds, of course, were not to be underestimated. Because no sorts of antibiotics or antiseptics were available, even a minor wound could easily become septic or gangrenous, killing a soldier within days or requiring the amputation of an infected limb.

Nearly nineteen out of every twenty wounds were inflicted by small-arms fire and the worst of these were caused by cone-shaped, soft lead rifle slugs called minié balls. Minié balls could be fired at much higher velocity than the round musket balls of a generation before and were far more destructive to internal organs. Such projectiles would also flatten out upon impact with the long bones of the legs and arms, blowing them into splinters and requiring them to be amputated. Even wounds that did not require amputation or were not immediately fatal often became infected and ultimately proved mortal.

Amputation

During the Civil War, three out of four operations performed on soldiers by surgeons were amputations. It might seem to a casual observer that surgeons were taking the easy way out with amputation, that they were indifferent or incompetent, or that limited resources forced them to simply remove limbs rather than perform more delicate surgery. Unfortunately, while some contemporary doctors were truly incompetent, even the best doctors simply had no choice but to remove limbs irreparably mangled by minié balls, explosive shells, and other weapons of the age. Bones shattered by bullets had no chance of regenerating.

Paddlewheel steamers were used extensively for commerce along America's rivers and inland waterways. During the war, such vessels were used for ferrying troops, as hospital boats, and were sometimes armed and used as warships (although they were not generally considered sturdy enough for this role).

This famous Civil War image shows Union doctors performing an open-air amputation at a hospital tent at Gettysburg. Although amputation was common, this scene is likely posed and not taken during actual surgery.

Surgery in the field was usually performed in makeshift field hospitals, sometimes on operating tables consisting of a few boards laid across a pair of barrels. Chloroform was often available (more so in Union hospitals than those of the Confederacy), and a rag or sponge soaked with it would be held over the face of the soldier being operated on. This was in itself a dangerous procedure, and could result in chloroform poisoning if not removed often enough. In the absence of chloroform, a few shots of whisky might do; in any case, some sort of anesthesia was usually administered, and it was uncommon that nothing was available but a bullet or stick to bite down on. When no anesthetic was available, the risk of a soldier dying from shock was much greater.

Amputation usually consisted of the following steps. First, the surgeon would cut off blood flow to the afflicted limb with a tourniquet. Then, after selecting the place where he would have to cut through the limb, he would slice through the surrounding flesh and connective

The entire amputation process generally took about fifteen minutes, although some doctors were noted for performing amputations even more quickly.

tissue with a scalpel. He would then use a "capital saw"—a tool with replaceable blades that looked much like a hacksaw—to saw through the bone. Once the limb was completely removed, the surgeon would toss it onto a pile of other arms and legs and sew up the major veins and arteries with sutures (silk thread in the North, cotton thread in the South). The soldier would immediately be removed so another could take his place. The entire process generally took about fifteen minutes, although some doctors were noted for performing amputations even more quickly.

Amputation was most effective if performed immediately after a wound occurred. Mortality rate for soldiers who received an amputation within twenty-four hours of being wounded was 25 percent, a rate that doubled to 50 percent for soldiers who received an amputation more than a day after being wounded. Nonetheless, and as horrible a solution as it was, amputation saved the lives of many soldiers for whom there otherwise would have been no hope at all.

Medical Transportation

Medical personnel had to deal with greater numbers of wounded soldiers than they ever had before, and, as a result, numerous means of transporting the injured were developed.

Ambulances were among the most common. Two-wheeled varieties provided a very bumpy ride, and many severely wounded soldiers died after being transported in them. Four-wheeled ambulances were also used, and these provided a more comfortable ride. Horses were preferred to mules for ambulances, as they provided steadier service.

Steamboats, train cars, and barges were also modified as conveyances for the wounded. Converted passenger cars could carry up to three-dozen wounded soldiers, the least seriously wounded in stretchers hung from the ceilings and the most severely injured on wooden slats inserted across the seats.

Farm Technology

Agriculture in the United States had been transformed in the late eighteenth and nineteenth centuries. Improved understanding of chemistry helped fertilization and livestock feeding practices; productivity was increased through improvements in plant and animal breeding; inventions like steam-powered grain-threshing machines, sugar mills, and the **cotton gin** radically improved the yield of crops that had once been highly labor-intensive. Canals, railroads, and steamboats allowed surplus produce to be shipped into the growing urban areas, encouraging farmers to increase their production for profit.

Horse-powered farm machinery dominated American agriculture throughout the nineteenth century and reached the height of its effectiveness during this period. Elaborate horse-powered agricultural equipment increased labor productivity immensely and allowed new land to be brought under cultivation. Teams of horses pulled cultivators, harrows, mowers, plows, hay rakes, and reapers; activated combines and threshing machines; and performed many other useful tasks.

Rail Transportation

In 1861, most of the country's railroad tracks and rolling stock, along with the workshops needed to manufacture and repair them, existed in the North. As a result, the Union was able to use the railways as a significant tactical, strategic, and logistical tool.

The South had fewer miles of rail line, much less rolling stock, an inability to replace either, and handicaps in maintaining them. But, the Confederacy used the railways to accomplish a handful of impressive results, including their victory at the first Battle of Bull Run and the transfer of Lt. Gen. James Longstreet's corps in time for the Battle of Chickamauga, widely considered a master stroke. As Jeffrey N. Lash explains in *Destroyer of the Iron Horse*, however, a differing philosophies between Northern and Southern generals led the latter to not fully consider railways to the extent that their adversaries did, nullifying even the limited resources at their disposal.

Indeed, many otherwise exemplary Southern generals (notably Joseph Johnston, who had a strong background in railway construction, technology, and design) had a blind spot when it came to the possibilities offered by the railways. Some Confederate generals did try to make the most of railway resources, and Leonidas Polk was their most proficient rail general. Overall, however, this inability to exploit such an important resource tarnishes to a great extent the popular notion that Confederate generals were vastly superior to their Union counterparts.

This deficiency was, however, not limited to the Confederacy. Several high-ranking Union generals also failed to use rail to its fullest advantage, among them Maj. Gen. Henry Halleck, Maj. Gen. George McClellan, and Maj. Gen. William Rosecrans.

When used properly, railways could be used to quickly transport fresh troops to a new theater, evacuate worn units, or supply garrisoned areas. As a result, rail lines were often military targets. Quick ways to disrupt rail transit—employed especially by raiding troops—included tearing up railway tracks and ties, tipping over locomotives and cars, and blowing up railway bridges. Possible disadvantages to these methods were that they could make a section of line unusable to the side doing the destruction (which was not an issue if they would not have opportunity to use it anyway), and that their effects could be undone with relative ease once the vandals had retreated back to their own lines. Indeed, some Union army engineers made prefabricated bridge components and reached the point where they could replace demolished bridges within twenty-four hours.

More lasting methods of disrupting rail traffic included pushing rolling stock off bridges or into ravines; packing wood or coal in or around rolling stock and igniting it; and pulling up rail-

Some Union army engineers made prefabricated railroad bridge components and reached the point where they could replace demolished bridges within twenty-four hours.

The "General Haupt" was an engine built for the a U.S. Military Railroad in 1863. Railroads were a quick way to transport troops and supplies.

road ties, heating them in a fire, then wrapping them around trees to make the ties permanently unusable (a method employed by Sherman's troops when marching through Georgia in 1864).

Railroad equipment was expensive and its destruction could prove costly. In 1861, a heavy locomotive cost $9,000 and a passenger or freight car cost $2,200. As the war progressed, prewar costs became moot, and a new locomotive could not be had in the South at any price in the latter half of the war.

Communications

Many new forms of communications were developed prior to and during the Civil War, most notably the telegraph, while other innovations of the period were not widely used. For example, in 1843, Scottish physicist Alexander Bain invented a facsimile machine that could send a copy of image or printed material over telegraph lines. A working version of the system called the Pantelegraph was built in 1861 in Paris by Italian physicist Giovanni Caselli, and four years later he launched the world's first commercial telefax service between Paris and Lyon.

Telephones were invented eleven years later and came into limited use in 1877, during the last year of Reconstruction.

Mail

The amount of mail being sent increased dramatically during the war, as thousands of soldiers and their families tried to stay in touch

A wide array of daily and weekly newspapers were available during the Civil War, providing citizens detailed coverage of the war that had previously been unavailable.

with each other. One measure the Federal postal service employed to cope with this increased demand was to divide posted materials into first-class, second-class, and third-class mail. During this period, the postal service also began to provide free delivery in cities.

The famed but short-lived Pony Express reached its peak during the Civil War. Established on April 3, 1860, in hopes of winning a mail contract, the courier service strove to deliver mail from St. Joseph, Missouri, to Sacramento, California, about two thousand miles, in a mere ten days.

Pony Express employed some eighty riders during its brief tenure, including the famous "Buffalo Bill" Cody. Each rider rode seventy to eighty miles at a time, stopping to change horses at stations along the route, which were built at intervals of about ten miles. Despite its success, the Pony Express lasted little more than a year-and-a-half—until October 24, 1861—and was rendered obsolete by the linking of the East and West Coasts by telegraph, a considerably faster and cheaper means of communication.

Telegraphy

Message transmission during the nineteenth century was fairly simple. An **operator** used a key or switch to send short pulses of electricity to the telegraph line from a battery. Messages were sent by dispatching these pulses in patterns that formed codes representing letters and numbers.

Inventors Samuel Morse and Alfred Vail made great improvements to this early sort of receiver and modified it to print dot and dash symbols corresponding to electric pulses of short and long duration, creating what became known as Morse code. In 1844, Samuel Morse sent his first famous message, "What hath God wrought," from Baltimore to Washington, DC. His receiver was widely adopted, and telegraphy soon achieved a central role in communications. Western Union was founded shortly thereafter to provide telegraphy services and had extended its lines to California by 1861.

Telegraphic transmission was facilitated by relays, electromagnet receivers that operated switches and allowed power from a local battery to key a further length of telegraph line. At the time of the Civil War, relays were the only form of amplifier available to telegraph engineers.

Because telegraphers could easily distinguish and transcribe Morse's dot-and-dash signals onto paper by hand, devices for recording signals directly onto paper, used earlier in the century, were largely abandoned. New methods, however, were devised by other inventors.

Publications and Print Media

People learned about the major events of the war through a wide variety of publications. In many cases, newspaper stories were sensationalized, inaccurate, or even outright fabrications, and soldiers often commented that what was going on around them bore little resemblance to what the newspapers and newsweeklies were reporting. Nonetheless, people on the home front were better informed about what was happening on the battlefields than in previous conflicts.

Contemporary news publications tended to be much smaller than their modern counterparts in both length and dimensions. "Tabloid"-size publications were more common for mainstream daily publications than today, and many dailies were eight pages long (that is, two folded broadsheets, each comprising four pages) or shorter. Southern papers, in particular, shrunk in size along with available resources in general, and were often printed on less-than-ideal materials. Because of a shortage of newsprint, for example, one 1863 edition of the *Opelousas Courier* was printed on wallpaper.

Civil War-era news publications were also text-heavy, and frequently the front pages included no illustrations. There were exceptions to this, most notably *Frank Leslie's Weekly* (a.k.a., *Leslie's Illustrated Newspaper*), and when such publications did include artwork, the most common sorts were engravings and lithographs of scenes from the war, maps, and political cartoons.

During the war, reporters near the front would file their stories with their newspapers via telegraph. Because telegraphy was subject to so many vicissitudes, such as lines being cut by enemy raiders, reporters developed an "inverted pyramid" style of story writing, in which the lead paragraph of a story included its most critical information, and each subsequent paragraph contained information of decreasing importance. Thus, even if only the first paragraph went through, a newspaper might still have the basis for a story. This is the basic format used in most print news stories to this day.

CIVIL WAR PERIODICALS

Following are some of the periodicals available to people during the Civil War or the period of Reconstruction that followed it. A number of these publications are still read today and some have historic copies available online or on microfiche at libraries, particularly in the areas where they were originally published. There are many others that existed only briefly, in some cases after being founded during the war but unable to prevail during it.

A publication's affiliation with a particular city is noted (unless such information is obvious from the name or is not relevant), as are the dates publications were founded and, if applicable, when they ceased publication.

Names given are those in use during the era of the war and, in some cases, their names changed at some point before or after the conflict, often due to mergers with other publications (for example, the *Baltimore American and Commercial Advertiser* was part of the *Baltimore News-American* when it folded).

Northern News Publications

» *Baltimore American and Commercial Advertiser* (1773–1986)
» *The Detroit News* (1873–Present)
» *Harper's Weekly* (1857–1916)
» *Hartford Evening Press* (Connecticut, 1856–1868)
» *Hickman Daily Courier* (Kentucky, 1859–Present)
» *Frank Leslie's Weekly* (1852–1922)
» *National Police Gazette* (1845–Present)
» *Newark Daily Advertiser* (1832–1904)
» *New-York Daily Tribune* (1842–1866)
» *The New York Herald* (1840–1920)
» *New York Tribune* (1866–1924)
» *New York Semi-Weekly Tribune* (1853–1866)
» *The New York Times* (1851–Present)
» *Philadelphia Inquirer* (1829–Present)
» *Oregonian Weekly* (1850–Present)
» *Rochester Daily Union and Advertiser* (1860–1885)
» *Rochester Evening Express* (1859–1882)
» *Rutland Herald* (1794–Present)
» *The True Union* (Baltimore, 1849–1861)

Southern News Publications

» *Alexandria Gazette* (Virginia, 1834–1974)
» *Arkansas Gazette* (1819–1991)
» *Army & Navy Messenger* (Petersburg, Virginia, 1863–186?)
» *Charleston Daily Courier* (1852–1873)
» *The Charleston Mercury* (1825–1868)
» *The Chattanooga Gazette* (1839–1866)
» *The Weekly Southern Guardian* (Columbia, South Carolina, 1857–1865)
» *The Nashville Daily Press* (1864–1865)
» *Nashville Daily Times and True Union* (1864–1865)
» *The Galveston News* (1842–1861)
» *The Galveston Daily News* (1865–Present)
» *Galveston Tri-Weekly News* (1863–1873)
» *Galveston Weekly News* (1845–1893)
» *The Houston Daily Telegraph* (1864–1866)
» *The* (Houston) *Tri-Weekly Telegraph* (1855–1870)
» *The Louisville Daily Journal* (1830–Present)
» *The Mobile Daily Register* (1849–1861)
» *The Sunday Delta* (New Orleans, 1855–1863)
» *Opelousas Courier* (Louisiana, 1852–1910)
» *The Post and Courier* (Charleston, South Carolina, 1803–Present)
» *Republican Banner* (Nashville, 1837–1875)
» *Richmond Enquirer* (1815–1867)
» *The Southern Enterprise* (Greenville, South Carolina, 1854–1870)

Mathew Brady, arguably the best-known Civil War photographer, took this portrait of Confederate Gen. Robert E. Lee days after Lee surrendered to U.S. Lt. Gen. Ulysses S. Grant in Virginia in April 1865.

Photography

Photography emerged as a significant new medium during the Civil War. Photographers followed in the wake of the armies and provided a visual record of units in the field, troops in camp, and the aftermath of battles. Photographers provided coverage of the war, its participants, and its effects that had not previously been possible.

Indeed, after the Battle of Antietam in September 1862, the Army of the Potomac held the field, allowing Northern cameramen to thoroughly photograph the aftermath of the encounter. And, in the days following the battle, photographers recorded Lincoln's visit to McClellan's headquarters and then followed the Union army across the Potomac and into recaptured Harpers Ferry, Virginia.

Notable Civil War-era photographers included William R. Pywell, Alexander Gardner (who photographed Richmond after it was destroyed by Federal troops), Timothy H. O'Sullivan (who accompanied the Union army in the western theater and recorded the course of its operations), and, perhaps most famous of all, Mathew Brady (who had employed both Gardner and O'Sullivan until 1863).

Beginning in 1845, Brady had made **daguerreotypes** of several famous Americans and published them in 1850 as *The Gallery of Illustrious Americans*. By 1860, he was making a good living through his three daguerreotype studios, two in New York City and one in Washington, DC.

War offered Brady new opportunities. At the expense of nearly his entire fortune, he outfitted a score of photographers with camera equipment and mobile darkrooms and sent them off to cover all fronts of the war. Contemporary equipment was too primitive to take action shots but the thousands of photographs they took depicted the war in a shocking, brutal way. Brady's name appeared on all of the photographs, in keeping with the convention of the day, something that has helped identify the work of his studios (for example, more than a third of the one hundred known photographs of Abraham Lincoln bear Brady's name).

George N. Barnard served as official photographer of the Chief Engineer's Office. This photograph, taken outside of Atlanta in 1864, shows his equipment.

Official military photographers, too, added to the pictorial archive of the war. For example, George N. Barnard, official photographer of the Chief Engineer's Office, created the best photographic record of the war in the West and made many pictures of Atlanta, Georgia, just prior to its destruction by fire upon Sherman's departure from the city.

Terms

ABATIS: An obstacle made from sharpened stakes or timbers, especially for blocking roads and impeding cavalry.

AMBROTYPE: An underexposed, negative photograph on a glass plate that appeared positive when set against a black background. Used primarily for portraits, glass photo plates had been invented in 1851 by Englishman Frederick Scott Archer.

BANQUETTE: A small mound of earth below the crest of a parapet that allowed shorter soldiers to fire over it more easily.

BARTON, CLARA: This "Angel of the Battlefield" played a significant role in providing medical care throughout the course of the Civil War. Her wartime activities included collecting and distributing supplies to soldiers, caring for the wounded, and gathering identification records for soldiers who were missing or dead. In 1881, she founded the American Red Cross, basing it to some extent on the Swiss-based International Red Cross.

BLUE MASS: A widely-used sort of medicine during the war that typically took the form of a blue or gray tablet and was used to treat disorders as diverse as tuberculosis, constipation, toothache, parasitic infestations, and birthing pains. Ingredients for one formulation included thirty-four parts rose honey, thirty-three parts mercury, twenty-five parts althaea, five parts licorice, and three parts glycerol, and most included the blue chalk or dye that gave it its namesake color. This term was also used, after the name of the medication, for the mass of men who would turn out for sick call.

CABLEGRAM: A telegram sent via undersea cable, a service that began to appear reliably in the late 1860s.

COTTON GIN: A device for removing seeds from cotton fiber. Devices for removing the seeds from long-staple cotton had long existed but were ineffective at removing seeds from the short-staple cotton of the Americas, a task that had traditionally been performed by slaves. In 1793, Eli Whitney invented a machine for removing the seeds from short-staple cotton. This device consisted of a boxed, revolving cylinder set with spiked teeth that could be turned by a crank, pulling the raw cotton through small slots and thereby separating the seeds from it. At the same time, a rotating brush operated pulleys, and a belt removed the cotton lint from the spikes. Many variations on Whitney's design appeared over the following years, including horse-drawn and water-powered gins, which radically speeded up the ginning process and lowered production costs.

DAGUERREOTYPE: Invented by Frenchman Louis Daguerre in 1837, this first practical means of photographic reproduction created detailed images on silver-plated copper sheets. Although popular, this process was also expensive and time-consuming, and was soon replaced.

DIPLEX: An innovation that allowed two telegraph signals to be transmitted simultaneously in the same direction.

DUPLEX: An improvement in telegraphy that allowed signals to be simultaneously transmitted from opposite directions over the same line.

FASCINES: Bundles of branches or saplings used to line earthworks or trenches.

FERROTYPE: See tintype.

FIRESTEP: See banquette.

FIRING PIT: A shallow pit dug out by hand and used to protect one or more infantrymen in combat. Veteran soldiers learned to begin digging such defense works whenever they stopped for an extended period of time and then continued to improve upon them as time and resources allowed.

"LAUDABLE PUS": A term used by nineteenth-century doctors to describe the pus that formed in a wound after surgery or amputation and thought to be a beneficial sign of healing. In actuality, of course, it was a sign of massive bacterial infection, which often proved fatal.

OPERATOR: Since the 1840s, a telegraph operator.

PLANK ROAD: A road wide enough for two wagons, one side of which was dirt and the other side of which was covered with thick wooden planks. Conventions of the day dictated that heavily-laden wagons had right-of-way on the plank-covered side and that less full wagons should move on to the dirt side. As with other dirt roads, the parts not covered with timbers often became mud tracks in wet weather.

QUADRUPLEX: A combination of diplex and duplex technology that allowed a total of four messages, two coming from each direction, to be sent simultaneously along a single telegraph line and invented by Thomas Edison in 1874.

SWITCHBOARD: An term used in the 1860s to describe telegraphy routing equipment.

TAKE AN IMAGE: A period term that meant to have a photograph taken.

TELEGRAM: A term that came into use about 1850 to describe a message sent by telegraph. Prior to this, such messages had been variously called telegraphic dispatches, telegraphic communications, and telegraph messages.

TELEPHONE: Until being applied to Alexander Graham Bell's invention in the 1870s, this referred to a kind of non-electronic megaphone used for carrying music or voices over a distance.

TINTYPE: A photograph made by exposing a thin, black-enameled metal plate coated with a chemical compound called collodion. Small tintypes were the most common and inexpensive form of portraiture prior to the Civil War.

TRENCHES: Narrow, deep holes excavated to protect infantrymen. Ideally, a trench would be deep enough so a man could stand erect within it and still not be exposed to enemy fire. To fire from within a trench, a soldier would step up onto a one- to two-foot high parapet called a firestep. Civil War trenchworks, especially around besieged cities, often stretched for several miles, anticipating the style of warfare now most often associated with World War I.

THE WAR ON THE HOME FRONT:
THE DRAFT AND CIVIL UNREST

"Conscription was neither equitable nor popular in either the North or the South. Both systems favored the rich. In the North, draft liability could be commuted for a $300 fee, while in the South owners of slaves were exempted ... The governors of Confederate states exempted tens of thousands of men from draft liability."
— David R. Segal, *Recruiting for Uncle Sam*

Tensions between the North and South had been building for nearly fifty years prior to the outbreak of war, yet when armed conflict did erupt, it came as a surprise to many people. While the question had been raised several times in the past whether an individual state had the right to withdraw from the nation, or whether several states could form a new confederacy, it had never so dramatically demanded an answer.

When civil war erupted in early 1861, it was in response to states rights, and not directly due to the issue of slavery. Nonetheless, almost all the rifts of the preceding decades could be attributed to differences between abolitionists and radical Republicans in the North and proslavery Democrats in the South.

In the years immediately preceding the war, three historic events that set the stage for Southern secession were all concerned with the issue of slavery. In early 1857, the U.S. Supreme Court declared that Congress had no power to prohibit slavery in the various U.S. territories, but Republicans and even many Northern Democrats refused to accept this opinion. Soon after, newly elected Democratic President James Buchanan (1857–1861) asked Congress to admit Kansas to the Union as a slave state, an act that enraged many Northern politicians and voters and contributed to the election of abolitionist Republican Abraham Lincoln in 1860. Tensions continued to smolder throughout Buchanan's unpopular presidency and, in 1859, fanatical abolitionist John Brown attacked the Federal arsenal at Harpers Ferry, Virginia (now West Virginia), hoping to ignite a general slave uprising.

After Lincoln was elected in November 1860, Southern states began to secede. Seven left the Union and formed the Confederate States of America by the time the new U.S. president was inaugurated in March 1861. Despite a conciliatory inaugural speech, the seceding states remained recalcitrant, seizing Federal forts and arsenals in the South, raising troops, and granting commissions in their own forces to Southern officers who had or were willing to resign their commissions in the U.S. Army, Navy, Marine Corps, and Revenue Cutter Service.

U.S. President Abraham Lincoln assumed broad powers in order to see the country through the crisis of civil war, and was regarded by some as a dictator. His unwavering resolve, however, helped move the United States toward reunification and reconciliation.

On April 12, 1861, Confederate forces commanded by Gen. P.G.T. Beauregard opened fire on the Union garrison at Fort Sumter, South Carolina, igniting war between the followers of the two opposing governments and flinging the country into turmoil. (An overview of the war can be found in Appendix B. Thousands of books contain descriptions of the various battles of the war, and several of the best resources can be found in Appendix C and Appendix D.)

The Northern View

Cries of "On to Richmond" resounded throughout the Northern states as war hysteria spread and the Union began to implement the **Anaconda Plan**. Thousands of ninety-day volunteers rushed to join state regiments, and the country moved to put down the rebellion and restore the Union. This goal marked the Northern struggle from beginning to end, as exemplified by Abraham Lincoln.

Unfortunately, many of the Union's other leaders were not so steadfast in their resolve. Maj. Gen. George McClellan, commander of the Army of the Potomac, the main Union army in the East, demonstrated great organizational talents in training troops and organizing military units. However, he consistently refused to engage the enemy in battle, and after he botched the 1862 Peninsula Campaign—a plodding attempt to capture Richmond—and refused to pursue and destroy the Confederate army after the September 1862 Battle of Antietam, Lincoln finally removed him from command in November 1862. Generals who immediately followed McClellan were, unfortunately, not much more satisfactory.

As the death toll from the conflict mounted, Lincoln feared that preserving the Union alone might not be enough to maintain public support for the war, and he announced a preliminary Emancipation Proclamation in the wake of Antietam and followed it with a formal proclamation on January 1, 1863. From that point onward, the war was no longer simply a pragmatic one of national unity, but also a moral one of abolition.

Some Northerners, however, resented the idea that they might be forced to fight for the rights of blacks. When a draft was initiated in 1863, riots broke out in many Northern cities. The worst was in New York City, where the riots were led by Irish immigrants, who, being at the bottom of the social ladder, disliked the idea that blacks might advance socially and feared having to compete with them for jobs. Irish volunteer firemen attacked the officials drawing the names of those being drafted, battled with the police, and assaulted blacks on the streets, hanging many from lampposts and even burning an orphanage for black children. In the course of the violence, stores and warehouses were looted and burned. Finally, heavy rains, the police, and troops ordered in from the battlefield at Gettysburg were able to subdue the violence, which lasted for three days.

In the last years of the war, hard-edged generals like Ulysses S. Grant inexorably led the Union to victory against the Confederacy.

> Some Northerners, however, resented the idea that they might be forced to fight for the rights of blacks. When a draft was initiated in 1863, riots broke out in many Northern cities.

Various pro-Southern and antiwar organizations also worked against the Union cause or on behalf of the Confederacy during the war, mostly in the slave-holding border states and in the Midwest. Such groups included the **Copperheads** and the Knights of the Golden Circle.

For more than a year, Lincoln dealt with a series of senior generals, among them Maj. Gen. Joseph Hooker, Maj. Gen. George G. Meade, and Maj. Gen. Ambrose E. Burnside, who he considered inadequate in terms of competence, aggressiveness, or a desire to preserve the Union. But by March 1864, he had found an able general whose attitudes about the war matched his own, and placed Gen. Ulysses S. Grant at the head of all the armies of the United States. Grant, along with Maj. Gen. William T. Sherman in the West, was concerned not with capturing Richmond, but rather with a strategy of total war, annihilating the Confederate military forces, and destroying the South's infrastructure and ability to fight.

Early in the election of 1864, there was some notion that Union soldiers would rally around Democratic peace candidate George McClellan. The Democratic platform, however, was confused and at odds with itself, and many soldiers preferred to see the war to its conclusion, rather than acknowledge defeat and see all they had fought and suffered for thrown away. Lincoln went on to win an undisputed victory in the North.

War ended within months of Lincoln's second inauguration. When he was assassinated, just five days after Gen. Robert E. Lee surrendered the Army of Northern Virginia to Grant, he was elevated to the status of a martyr in the minds of many contemporary Americans.

Robert E. Lee, the Confederacy's greatest general, led the Army of Northern Virginia and drove it to perform almost superhuman feats.

The Southern View

In 1861, Southerners at all levels of society had a variety of reasons for linking their fates to the Confederacy. Loyalty to individual states, a burgeoning quasi-nationalism, and a sense of states' rights all played a part in the decision of Southerners to secede from the Union and form their own independent government.

Just as important, however, was that a relatively small, rich, very powerful landed aristocracy saw their wealth, lifestyle, and other interests threatened. This landholding upper class, along with most other whites in the South, feared that antislavery forces in the North would eventually have slavery abolished, destroying the South's plantation-based economy.

Such feelings were by no means universal. Indeed, there were pro-Union elements in every Southern state, and in some—notably Kentucky, Tennessee, and Virginia—large segments of the population were opposed to secession, mostly yeoman farmers who did not own slaves and ultimately had nothing to gain from rebellion.

Morale of soldiers and civilians was as important in the South as in the North. Shortages of staple food items and consumer goods caused by federal blockades of Southern ports contributed to sagging Southern morale and bread riots erupted in Richmond and a few other Confederate cities in 1863. Soldiers increasingly received letters from home telling of the hardships their loved ones were suffering, something that led to higher rates of desertion amongst Confederate forces than in the North.

After the twin defeats of Gettysburg and Vicksburg in the summer of 1863, the Confederacy lost all hope of European support and much of its ability to take the war onto Northern soil. From that point onward, the war became a slow, bloody struggle for survival that the South realized it was less and less able to win.

Confederate Gen. Robert E. Lee surrendered his forces to Union Lt. Gen. Ulysses S. Grant at Appomattox Courthouse, Virginia, on April 9, 1865. Influenced by Lincoln, Grant went out of his way to keep from humiliating the defeated Rebels.

Union forces intensified their operations in the South in 1864, destroying farms, cities, railroads, and anything else the Confederacy needed to continue fighting. Desertions soared as soldiers abandoned the army and returned to their homes and families. On April 9, 1865, with his army starving and undermanned, Gen. Lee surrendered to Lt. Gen. Grant at Appomattox Courthouse, Virginia.

Other Confederate commands continued their increasingly hopeless struggle for several months but, before long, war ended for the South and Reconstruction loomed ahead of it.

Who Fought?

It is easy to think of the Civil War as simply being a conflict between two great armies of white men, along with some African Americans near the end of the war. Northerners and Southerners, however, could further be divided into men and women; officers and enlisted soldiers; whites and blacks; and many ethnic groups, including English, American Indians, Irish, Germans, Italians, and Jews. And, while a great many people came from families who had lived in America for several generations, there were also many people whose parents, or themselves, were immigrants. Consequently, many different sorts of people fought in or were otherwise directly affected by the Civil War.

Every state loyal to the Union provided regiments of soldiers to the U.S. military, every state that joined the Confederacy provided regiments of troops for the defense of the South—especially Georgia, North Carolina, and Virginia—and some states, notably the Northern slave states, provided regiments of troops to each side. And, within each state, there were individuals who chose to throw in their lot with one side or the other, based on a variety of personal reasons and circumstances. While both sides struggled to keep their ranks full throughout the war, the Confederacy in particular suffered from a continual shortage of manpower.

Union soldiers and sailors were mainly white, but significant numbers of blacks and American Indians also served. Confederate soldiers were also mainly white and included some American Indians (policies preventing blacks from fighting in the Southern forces were not repealed until near the end of the war, too late for any to be put into uniform). In many cases, the Confederacy was so undermanned that it had to make do with anyone it could attract into the service. In the C.S. Navy, for example, many sailors were not Americans at all, but rather sailors and adventurers from a variety of nations, notably Great Britain.

Beyond simply being "white," many of the soldiers on both sides came from ethnic groups that, if anything, were more distinct during the Civil War than they are today. Soldiers often formed into regiments made up wholly or largely of troops from the same ethnic background.

Regional nicknames became common during the Civil War, as units from around the country came into contact with each other. For example, "Dutchman" was used for anyone of German origin, and "Mick" was a disparaging term for an Irishman. That such terms are listed in this chapter should not be taken as a sanctioning of their usage.

Germans

About a million Germans lived in the United States when the Civil War broke out, about half of them having arrived since the German Revolution of 1848. These immigrants made their homes mostly in the large urban areas of Cincinnati, Milwaukee, Minneapolis, and St. Louis (although significant numbers also settled in southern Texas). By 1860, the country had twenty-eight German-language daily newspapers in fifteen cities. Because of the areas they occupied, Germans were widely represented in the Union military forces and much less so in the Confederate forces.

Several all-German regiments served in the Union forces, many in the XI Corps, and there were also a number of German artillery units. Germans who fought for the Union included generals Franz Sigel, August von Kautz, Godfrey Weitzel, and Carl Schurz, whose career as a professor at the University of Bonn was dashed by his role in the German Revolution. Among the most famous Germans to fight for the South were Capt. Justus Scheibert and Maj. Johann August Heinrich Heros von Borcke, both of whom served as Confederate staff officers (neither of them were Americans, however, and both ultimately returned to Germany).

Nicknames applied to Germans in the mid-nineteenth century included "cabbagehead," "sauerkraut" and "sausage." "Prussian," from the northern German region, had long been applied to Germans in general, but during the nineteenth century was also applied to arrogant or militaristic Germans. Similarly, "Junker," a word for a German nobleman, was used increasingly during the 1800s to mean an overbearing or militaristic German. "Dutch," from the German Deutsche, or "German," was also used in nicknames (e.g., a German bartender or neighbor might be referred to as "the Dutchman").

In the C.S. Navy, many sailors were not Americans, but rather

sailors and adventurers from other nations, notably Great Britain.

By 1860, the country had twenty-eight German-language daily newspapers in fifteen cities. Because of the areas they occupied, Germans were widely represented in the Union military forces and much less so in the Confederate forces.

Hispanics

About ten thousand Americans of Spanish descent fought on both sides of the Civil War. In the Southwest, many Tejanos, Hispanic natives of Texas, fought in most of the ninety-or-so actions fought in Texas. It is uncertain if there were any non-Tejano all-Hispanic regiments, but there probably were not. A number of individual Hispanic soldiers became prominent during the war, among them Union generals Don Carlos Buell and Edward Ferrero.

In the 1800s, the most common derogatory term for a Hispanic was "Dago," from the common Spanish name Diego (it was not until the late 1880s that it was applied mainly to Italians). "Greaser" was a common epithet for Mexicans that originated in Texas during the 1830s prior to the Mexican War.

Irish

In 1846, the Irish Potato Famine caused a mass exodus of people from Ireland and, by 1860, more than 1.5 million Irish immigrants lived in America, as well as many people of Irish descent. Large numbers of Irish fought on both sides during the war, more than 150,000 of them for the North, which fielded a number of Irish regiments and an entire Irish brigade. An uncertain number of Irishmen fought for the South, which was home to fewer Irish immigrants, and, as a result, colorful all-Irish units are a phenomenon associated with the Union armies.

After the war, some Irish soldiers were drawn to the Fenians, a quasi-military organization equipped with surplus Civil War weapons that made a number of abortive military attacks into British-controlled Canada.

Common terms used to refer to the Irish in mid-nineteenth century America included "Paddy," "Pat," "Irisher," "Irish American," and the disparaging "Mick."

Italians

Italians were one of the smaller European minorities in America at the time of the Civil War (although millions immigrated to the United States in the decades following the war). Nonetheless, Italians—many of them former followers of Italian revolutionary Giuseppe Garibaldi—fought on both sides during the war, especially for the North.

Many of these former republican revolutionaries identified with the Union cause, and some of them joined the 39th New York Volunteer Infantry Regiment. It was known as the Garibaldi Guard for its large number of Italian soldiers and was distinguished by red shirts similar to the ones they had worn when fighting tyranny in Italy.

Prominent Italians during the Civil War included Brig. Gen. Luigi Palma di Cesnola, whose military academy in New York City trained many young Italians for Union military service; Luigi Tinelli, a militia commander; and Francesco Spinola, who raised four regiments of Italian-Americans and led them as their general.

Women

Although women were not generally allowed to join the military at the time of the Civil War, a number found ways to serve the armed forces on both sides, some of them in uniform. Most of these were vivandieres or cantinieres (see chapter 12)—a European concept American military observers brought back from the 1853–1856 Crimean War—women or girls attached mostly to Union armies who carried water and ammunition to soldiers in combat, helped the wounded, and carried messages between commanders and their troops.

Notable women in uniform included Sally Tompkins, who ran a hospital in Richmond and was rewarded with the rank and pay of a captain, and Bridget Divers, who served as a trooper in her husband's unit, the First Michigan Cavalry. Quite a number of other women also served, almost always posing as men. When discovered, most were either honorably discharged or simply dismissed from service.

African Americans

In 1860, about 344,000 free blacks lived in the North, while nearly nine times as many, about three million, were enslaved in the South (which was also home to about 133,000 free blacks).

After the Emancipation Proclamation, African Americans were allowed to enlist in the U.S. Army and about 179,000 of them did, many of them former slaves from areas occupied by Federal forces. Such black soldiers, however, were not treated particularly well. Pay for their first year in service was about half that of white troops, something that caused many morale and pay problems; casualty rates in combat were about 35 percent higher than average white units, in part because Confederate troops were less likely to take black prisoners; twice as many succumbed to disease, largely because they were poorly clothed; and fewer than one hundred were made officers, none of them greater than the rank of captain. About 37,300 of those who served were killed.

The 39th New York Volunteer Infantry Regiment was known as the Garibaldi Guard for its large number of Italian soldiers, some of whom were former republican revolutionaries.

In the South, legislation was passed in March 1865 allowing blacks to enlist in the Confederate army, although it is not likely that many would have willingly joined. Before this effort could be organized, however, the war was over.

African Americans were referred to as "negroes," "blacks" or "niggers," a term which, while never benign, did not acquire its most hateful connotations until the years following the Civil War.

Slavery

Slaves were a part of American society from its earliest days and, by the time the Civil War broke out, at least three million slaves lived in the Southern states.

Slavery as an institution had become unprofitable by the end of the eighteenth century and was waning. The introduction of revolutionary new agricultural equipment like the cotton gin, however, once again turned large-scale plantation slavery into a paying proposition. Prices of

In 1860, about 344,000 free blacks lived in the North and about three million slaves lived in the South (which was also home to about 133,000 free blacks).

slaves rose throughout the nineteenth century, increasingly as slavery was curtailed in the North and the territories. A healthy, young black male slave, who cost $500 in the 1830s, cost $1,800 by the late 1850s. Even as antislavery sentiment strengthened in the North, a Southern aristocracy grew increasingly rich from the fruits of slavery and became increasingly determined to ensure its continued survival.

Because of the vested interest the South had in the plantation system, slavery remained viable in America well after it had been abolished by other nations. Britain outlawed the slave trade in 1807, authorizing the search and seizure of ships suspected of carrying slaves and payment for their liberation, and completely outlawed slavery in 1833. By 1840, Spain and Portugal had also officially outlawed the slave trade, but Portuguese ships remained a major source of smuggled slaves throughout the century. And throughout much of Africa and the Middle East slavery remained an institution for many years (even up to the present day in some areas).

Abolitionist sentiment had acquired momentum in America by 1831, with publication of the antislavery newspaper *The Liberator*. In 1833, the American Anti-Slavery Society was founded in Philadelphia, and by 1840 the Underground Railroad was actively helping slaves escape into the North and Canada.

TYPICAL UNION AND CONFEDERATE SOLDIERS

Following are descriptions adapted from some created by the Gettysburg National Military Park of the typical combatants who served in the ranks of the opposing armies.

The typical Union soldier had been a farmer before the war who volunteered to defend his home and put down the rebellion of the Southern states. Like his Confederate enemies, he probably enlisted for the excitement of leaving the farm for a war that most believed would last only three months, but he also had patriotic reasons. Most Northern soldiers believed very strongly in the Federal government and despised the unjust accusations of southern politicians and secessionists. The departure of the southern states was a rebellion, and the Confederacy had to be brought back into the Union, whether they liked it or not! Most of the first volunteers were at least twenty years old, although there were others who were considerably younger. Most northern states required a man to be eighteen years old to stand in the ranks with a musket but some teenagers lied about their ages and got into the ranks anyway. As the need for manpower grew, teenage boys were accepted as musicians and older men were enrolled as quartermaster assistants, surgeons, and officers. By the time of the Battle of Gettysburg, the average age of a Union soldier in the rank-and-file was twenty-four though there were also quite a number of older soldiers, including many in their mid-forties.

With war on the horizon, in early 1861 the newly-formed Confederate government appealed to the Southern states to raise regiments of infantry, artillery, and cavalry. Many southerners responded to this appeal and enlisted for three or six months of service in state organizations known as volunteer regiments. As in the Union forces, the Confederacy soon found that it needed these regiments much longer than it had predicted and the length of service was changed to three years. The typical Confederate soldier had been a farmer prior to the outbreak of the war and by the time the Battle of Gettysburg was a lean veteran of many hard-fought battles. Southern volunteers enlisted for what they considered to be patriotic reasons—to protect their homes, state borders, and laws, and abandon a Federal government that was not representing their interests. A typical one-hundred-man company of soldiers was raised in the county where they lived. Once they were organized and offered to the state, the company went to a training camp usually located near the state capitol. They were then organized into regiments, elected officers, received clothing and arms, and began the process of becoming soldiers.

While abolitionist sentiment continued to grow, spurred in large part by books like Harriet Beecher Stowe's *Uncle Tom's Cabin*, few people in the North actively opposed slavery until it became the major issue in the 1860 presidential campaign (for example, in the 1857 Dred Scott decision, the U.S. Supreme Court ruled that neither slaves nor their dependents could be citizens of the nation or any state within it). In his speech accepting the Republican nomination, Lincoln summed up the political dilemma of slavery by stating that a country could not survive half-free and half-slave.

Thus, on the eve of the war, slavery existed largely in the South. Only about a quarter of Southern whites actually owned slaves and, of those who did, nearly nine out of ten owned fewer than twenty. In the Deep South, the majority of slaves lived and labored on cotton plantations, most of which had fifty or fewer slaves but some of which had several hundred. About half of all slaves in the South lived on plantations, working either as "field slaves" or in the homes of their masters as "house servants." Enslaved blacks were also referred to as "slaves," "negroes," "blacks," "niggers" or, by those squeamish about slavery, as "servants."

Only about a quarter of Southern whites actually owned slaves and, of those who did, nearly nine out of ten owned fewer than twenty.

Slaves made up nearly a quarter of the population of many Southern cities and, in some, such as Charleston, South Carolina, actually outnumbered whites. Many of these slaves worked as house servants, but many others worked at trades, such as baking, blacksmithing, carpentry, and cobbling. Skilled slaves were often hired out by their masters, and slaves were sometimes allowed to hire themselves out.

Sale was a constant threat to most slaves, and even those owned by relatively benign masters might be sold if they had to pay off debts. Fathers, mothers, and children, not to mention grandparents, cousins, aunts, and uncles, might be sold off individually and separated forever, without any recourse. Being sold to a more undesirable location was also used as a punishment.

Discipline on the plantation was maintained by the slave masters and their overseers through physical punishment or the threat of it. Even slave owners who were considered kind or lenient were likely to resort to whippings at times, and the harshest masters employed mutilation, torture, and killing to enforce their rules. Offenses that could lead to a slave being beaten included talking back, working slowly, being late to the fields, or trying to run away.

Nonetheless, thousands of slaves did run away. Many were subsequently caught and brought back to face punishment, while some grew fearful and returned on their own. Some escaped for good, to the North, Canada, or the territories, or lived in small communities in the wilderness.

Lincoln's Emancipation Proclamation laid the groundwork for ending slavery throughout the United States and, two years later in 1865, passage of the **Thirteenth Amendment** made slavery illegal under the Constitution.

Filling the Ranks

Early in the war, volunteers flocked to join state regiments in great numbers, responding to the calls from presidents Abraham Lincoln in the North and Jefferson Davis in the South and from their own local leaders.

Unfortunately, recruiters were not very selective, and many men with disqualifying factors, including physical disabilities, were nonetheless enlisted. Once units were formed, however, regimental surgeons tended to be fairly discriminating in removing unsuitable enlistees prior to combat. As the war dragged on and stories of its horrors drifted home in letters and from soldiers maimed and discharged, enthusiasm waned among enlistees, and it became more and more difficult for states to form new regiments. Eventually, the personnel needs of the opposing armed forces could not be met by volunteers alone and they had to seek other methods.

The Draft

Troop shortages were felt first in the Confederacy and then in the Union. This need for additional troops resulted in the passage of the Confederate Conscription Act of April 16, 1862, in the South and the Enrollment Act of March 3, 1863, in the North.

The Confederate law required troops already in the army to serve an additional two years and subjected white males aged eighteen to thirty-five to three-year enlistments (later, in 1863, the upper age was raised to forty-five and by 1864, the range was widened to ages seventeen to fifty). Initially, there were various exemptions, notably for slave owners. By 1863, however, slave owners had to pay a $500 "commutation fee" to be exempted, and substitutions were prohibited.

The Union conscription law made men aged twenty to forty-five subject to conscription. While no exemptions were allowed, Northern men could hire substitutes or pay a $300 commutation fee each time their names were drawn in the draft lotteries.

Whether or not the intent of substitutions, exemptions, or commutation fees were to allow the more affluent to avoid military service, this was their practical effect, a fact that did not escape the attention of those who could not afford these options.

Questions also arose on both sides as to the legality of draft laws. Southern governors, particularly Joseph Brown of Georgia, vehemently objected to conscription, and insisted that a central government did not have the power to enforce such laws over a confederacy of independent states. In the North, citizens reacted to the draft laws in many cases by rioting.

Ultimately, only about 2 percent of the troops in Union armies were draftees, while about 20 percent of Confederate soldiers were drafted.

Bounties

In the North, soldiers were not drafted from districts that could fill their troop quotas with volunteers. Thus, local citizens, politicians, and draft boards sought ways to entice enough people to join the military so that no one who did not wish to go would be forced. Bounties were one of the most widespread methods.

> Ultimately, only about 2 percent of the troops in Union armies were draftees, while about 20 percent of Confederate soldiers were drafted.

Cities offered "volunteers" as much as $1,000 cash to enlist in their districts and often filled all of their troop requirements in this way. Unfortunately, the caliber of such men was almost uniformly bad. While many were family men trying to take advantage of a financial windfall, a disproportionate number were rogues or petty criminals who became **bounty jumpers**, taking bounties, enlisting, deserting, and then moving on to new areas and enlisting again in return for other bounties. Penalties for desertion could be as severe as execution, but bounty jumpers were actually caught so rarely that threat of death did not markedly curb the practice.

When bounty jumpers did end up in units, they were almost always worthless as soldiers. They dragged down unit morale, caused excessive punishments to be instituted, and often had to be assigned to noncombat duties by commanders (for example as hospital orderlies, where they routinely robbed the sick and wounded of their own armies).

Criminals

While most Civil War soldiers were decent men, a substantial number of criminals ended up in the ranks of both sides, particularly the Union army, which attracted an unsavory element with its bounty system. And, just as a criminal element found ways to profit from the war, so too, was a brand of violent criminal created by the war. Men from both sides acquired a taste for killing and adventure during the Civil War, tastes that they sought to fulfill even after the end of hostilities.

Jesse James was one of the most famous of such outlaws. Born in Clay County, Missouri, in 1847, James was only fourteen when the war began. His family's farm was twice ravaged by pro-Union militia raids and, at the age of fifteen, he joined William Quantrill's band of Confederate mounted guerrilla "bushwhackers." Quantrill's Raiders—a name that caught on in postwar reunions—were among the most savage irregular cavalry units of the war and were, debatably, little more than heavily-armed outlaws who took advantage of the chaos of war to ply their trade.

After the war, many of the men from units like Quantrill's continued to use the skills they had honed during the war to further criminal careers, among them James, who after the war was an outlaw until his death in 1882.

Reconstruction

As early as 1863, leaders in the North began to discuss how to "reconstruct" the South after the final shots of the war were fired. The Reconstruction period lasted for twelve years, from 1865 to 1877, during which Union troops occupied the secessionist Southern states and the Federal government strove to change the region's political and social institutions. It was the U.S. government's first major attempt at what would a century later be known as "nation building"—and, like those that would follow, it was marked by animosity and only limited success.

Many of the measures imposed under Reconstruction were intended to be retributive, and thousands of **carpetbaggers** flooded the devastated South seeking personal gain. These factors made Reconstruction a difficult, painful time for the South, and created many long-term resentments in its residents.

Lincoln and his closest generals had favored a plan for Reconstruction that would have helped mend the rifts of the war; had Lincoln survived, the country might have been less painfully reunified. Andrew Johnson, however, a Southerner himself, did not have the popularity or political force to see Lincoln's plan through, and his attempts led to his impeachment (although his opponents failed to remove him from office).

Three amendments to the U.S. Constitution were ratified during this period, the Thirteenth, **Fourteenth**, and **Fifteenth**, and these "Reconstruction Amendments" were intended to guarantee equality under the law to the entire adult male population of the country, regardless of race.

All of the seceding states were readmitted to the Union by early 1870, but violence, civil unrest, and military occupation continued throughout various parts of the South as late as 1877.

> All of the seceding states were readmitted to the Union by early 1870, but violence, civil unrest, and military occupation continued throughout various parts of the South as late as 1877.

American Terrorism

During this period, many white Southerners resented the ability of newly enfranchised black voters to vote into office hated Republican politicians, black and white alike, and some of them reacted by forming white supremacy groups. Likewise, some former Rebel soldiers were not willing to surrender at the conclusion of the conflict and carried on a clandestine war in the guise of night riders, attacking freed blacks, Union military forces, and Republican politicians.

Many domestic terrorist organizations grew out of such activities during the era of Reconstruction, especially in North Carolina, South Carolina, and Tennessee. One of the best-known and most successful of such groups was the Ku Klux Klan (KKK), a secret society of white Southerners opposed to blacks, the Republican party, and the Federal government, which conducted terrorist activities during the period 1866–1872. It eventually absorbed many of the smaller groups that were active immediately after the conclusion of the war. For a time, the KKK was led by former Confederate Lt. Gen. Nathan Bedford Forrest, who so hated blacks that he had ordered the slaughter of those serving as Union soldiers when they attempted to surrender during the war.

KKK members were sworn to secrecy and hid their identities behind white robes and hooded masks. Groups of them, using the flaming cross as their symbol, were especially active during election campaigns, when they used violence, rape, murder, and intimidation to help sway votes and prevent Republican political victories in their states. Favorite targets were local Republican leaders—both white and black—and blacks who no longer conformed to the antebellum standards of conduct.

In areas under Republican control, authorities were hard-pressed to quell the violence and were loathe to send their mostly black state militias against the KKK for fear of provoking a full-blown race war. In areas under Democratic control, the authorities themselves were frequently KKK members or sympathizers. Even when local law enforcement authorities did take action, KKK members often sat on juries or the judge's bench and saw that little or no justice would be meted out.

By the 1870s, most Americans—Northern and Southern alike—agreed that the KKK was out of control and even Forrest renounced their activities. In 1871, the Republican-led Congress authorized President Ulysses S. Grant to use Federal troops to restore order in the worst areas, where they had the power to arrest suspects and hold them indefinitely without trial (under the provisions of posse comitatus, it is normally illegal for government troops to be used as police against U.S. citizens, a fact as true today as it was in the 1870s).

By 1872, the KKK was dead as an organization, although there was a resurgence of violence as a political tool by smaller Southern groups, including the Red Shirts and the White League, from 1874 to 1877. It was not until 1915, however, that the name and iconography of the KKK was once again readopted.

Terms

ANACONDA PLAN:
A plan for subduing the South formulated under Union General-in-Chief Winfield Scott in early 1861. It called for a naval blockade of Southern ports, military control of the Mississippi River Valley so as to split the South in two, and placement of Federal armies to contain the movement of Confederate forces. Scott estimated a year of such treatment would force the South to capitulate. Lincoln initiated the first two components of the plan, but believed the third would be ineffective and called for a massive military buildup. The aging and infirm Scott resigned and was replaced by his field commander, Maj. Gen. George McClellan, a man forty years his junior.

BOUNTY JUMPER:
Volunteers who joined the Union Army in exchange for sizable cash bounties offered in the latter half of the war but then deserted and reenlisted under different names for additional bounties. This process could be repeated almost limitlessly and generally with little fear of consequences. When bounty jumpers were caught, however, they were often shot.

CARPETBAGGERS:
A Southern term for unscrupulous adventurers from the North who swarmed into the South during Reconstruction in search of political offices and financial gain. This name derived from a popular form of cheap luggage, the carpetbag, which many of them carried.

COPPERHEAD: A derogatory term used during the war to refer to Northerners with Southern sympathies who were considered capable of striking without warning—like the snake of the same name—against the Union war effort. People with such sympathies were strongest in the Midwest, which was home to many people of Southern descent. The most well-known Copperhead was Ohio politician Clement L. Vallandigham. Copperheads tended to be anti-black, conservative "peace Democrats" who sensed that the war was forever changing the ideal of an egalitarian, rural America. They favored state's rights over a stronger central government and believed that Lincoln's policies were destroying constitutional government. While they did win some local elections and exerted some influence within the Democratic party, the Copperheads were not ultimately very influential. Nonetheless, for years after the war the Democratic party suffered from charges of "Copperheadism."

FIFTEENTH AMENDMENT: An amendment to the U.S. Constitution that prohibited the Federal or state governments from infringing on a citizen's right to vote on account of "race, color, or previous condition of servitude" (that is, having been enslaved). It was ratified February 3, 1870.

FOURTEENTH AMENDMENT: An amendment to the U.S. Constitution adopted July 9, 1865, which provides a broad definition of citizenship; prohibits state and local governments from depriving persons of life, liberty, or property without first taking certain steps; and requires each state to provide equal protection under the law to all people within its jurisdiction.

KNIGHTS OF THE GOLDEN CIRCLE: A secret pro-Southern organization that flourished in the Midwest during the 1850s. During the war, this organization was thought to have been active on behalf of the Confederacy and may have had connections with the Copperheads.

SLAVE CODES: Legal codes established in Southern states that defined slaves as property rather than people. The codes prevented them from testifying in court against whites, learning to read or write, making contracts, leaving a plantation without permission, striking a white, buying or selling goods, owning firearms, gathering without white supervision, possessing antislavery literature, or visiting the homes of whites or free blacks. Slave patrols—similar to local militias—enforced the codes and arrested slaves who had left plantations, broke up unauthorized gatherings, and searched slave quarters for contraband. When slave insurrections were rumored or actually occurred, local slave codes were more strictly enforced and vigilance committees were often formed, beating, killing, and terrorizing blacks.

THIRTEENTH AMENDMENT: An amendment to the U.S. Constitution adopted December 6, 1865, abolishing and prohibiting the institution of slavery. It states that "Neither slavery nor involuntary servitude, except as a punishment for crime whereof the party shall have been duly convicted, shall exist within the United States, or any place subject to their jurisdiction" and that "Congress shall have power to enforce this article by appropriate legislation."

BROTHERS AT WAR:
BILLY YANK, JOHNNY REB

"Our Southern brethren have done grievously, they have rebelled and have attacked their father's house and their loyal brothers. They must be punished and brought back, but this necessity breaks my heart." —Union Major Robert Anderson, after the April 1861 Confederate attack on Fort Sumter

N orth America has never seen battles, before or since, greater or more terrible than those fought by **soldiers** during the Civil War, nor has it seen larger armies **mustered** and sent against each other. During the four full years of warfare, more than ten thousand skirmishes or battles took place throughout the continent, an average of seven per day.

It is difficult to say precisely how many men fought and died during the Civil War, and historians debate the specifics to this day. Because of a lack of records, this is particularly difficult to determine with regard to the Confederacy. Most historians accept, however, that from a relatively small combined population of about thirty-one million people, from two million to 2.25 million men served throughout the course of the war in the Northern military forces and that some 750,000 to one million served in the Southern military forces.

Not all of these men served at the same time, of course. When war broke out in 1861, the Union forces consisted of a mere sixteen thousand men, little more than a national defense force. The Union military reached a peak strength of about one million men under arms in 1863. Most of these men were very young, about two-thirds of them twenty-one or younger. The Confederate armed forces, which consisted almost entirely of its **army**, its navy and **marine** forces being fairly negligible, reached a peak of about 500,000 men in 1863. As with the Union armed forces, the majority of its personnel were less than twenty-two years of age. On either side, about half the total men in uniform were present for duty at any given time (the rest being ill, wounded, or on furlough).

Of the total number of combatants who served on both sides, an estimated 625,000 were killed, about one in every five men who served, a horrifically high proportion (and hundreds of thousands more wounded and maimed). This is more than all the American military personnel killed in World War I, World War II, the Korean War, and the Vietnam War combined. Total deaths were equal to nearly 2 percent of the population in 1860, significantly higher than for any other American war (as compared to the Revolutionary War, in which soldiers' deaths were about 0.9 percent of the population, and World War II, for which they were 0.3 percent of the population).

The Armed Services

Both the Northern and Southern military forces were composed of two major branches, an army and a navy. Smaller military or quasi-military organizations on each side included a Marine Corps and a Revenue Cutter Service. The latter two services were much more significant in the Federal forces and played smaller roles for the South.

The Army

Most of the military actions of the Civil War were fought between units of the U.S. Army and the C.S. Army. It was in these two opposing services that most combatants served.

Army Units

During the Civil War, the basic tactical and recruitment unit was the regiment, a unit that was supposed to number 1,046 men and be under the command of a lieutenant colonel or colonel. In practice, regiments were perpetually understrength and usually consisted of three to five hundred men. After Northern states had raised regiments of troops, they made no effort to reconstitute them once they were depleted, instead forming new regiments when required to provide additional troops. One exception is the state of Wisconsin, which recruited soldiers for service in existing regiments. For this reason, many generals liked to have a few Wisconsin regiments in their commands.

In descending order, regiments were further divided into companies, platoons, and sections. In ascending order, regiments were grouped into brigades, divisions, corps, and armies. The term battalion described a unit with only six companies, created when it proved impossible to raise a full-strength, ten-company regiment of a specific type.

COMPANIES consisted of about one hundred men—two platoons—plus company **officers**. A company's ranking officer, the company commander, was typically a captain, who was assisted by a 1st lieutenant and a 2nd lieutenant; its ranking **noncommissioned officer (NCO)** was generally a first sergeant. A full-strength regiment consisted of ten companies.

PLATOONS consisted of up to fifty men, or half a company. In battle, the captain in charge of the company would take command of the first platoon and his 1st lieutenant would take command of the second platoon. If the captain was absent or a **casualty**, the 2nd lieutenant would also take charge of one of the platoons.

SECTIONS consisted of up to two-dozen men, or half a platoon.

BRIGADES were supposed to consist of three or four regiments and number from about 3,138 to 4,184 men and **officers** at full strength. However, because regiments were perpetually under-strength, brigades often included additional regiments to function effectively.

Union veteran John D. Billings summed up the situation in his book *Hardtack and Coffee*.

"As a brigade became depleted by sickness, capture and the bullet, new regiments were added, until, as the work of addition and depletion went on, I have known a brigade to have within it the skeletons of ten regiments, and even then its strength [was] not half that of the original body," Billings wrote. "My camp was located at one time near a regiment which had only thirty-eight men present for duty."

A brigade was usually under the command of a brigadier general ("one star"); the ranking NCO in a brigade was usually a sergeant major.

DIVISIONS typically consisted of three or four brigades and included, at full strength, ten thousand to twenty thousand soldiers. In addition to infantrymen, a division had attached to it anywhere from a company to two regiments of cavalry and from one to four artillery batteries, as well as any necessary support troops.

A division was usually under the command of a major general ("two star").

CORPS consisted of three or four divisions and, at full strength, were supposed to contain about fifty thousand men. Because none of its generals had the skills needed to command a corps, the Union army did not have units within its armies larger than divisions until March 1862. The Confederacy did not organize its divisions into corps until September 1862.

The term "corps" also referred to all the cavalry, artillery, and signal troops in the army as a whole. Throughout the course of the war, the Union had twenty-five infantry corps in service at various times, each designated by an appropriate Roman numeral, in addition to the cavalry, engineer, and signal corps. Corps were subject to attrition just like brigades and divisions, and some of them consolidated after becoming too reduced. In early 1864, for example, the decimated I (First) and III (Third) Corps were deactivated and merged into the II (Second), V (Fifth), and VI (Sixth) Corps. A corps was generally under the command of a lieutenant general ("three star").

ARMIES on either side consisted of up to five or more army corps, or some 100,000 to 200,000 men, and each were responsible for military operations in a specific area or region. In general, Union armies were named for the major rivers in their areas of operation or origin. Confederate armies tended to be named for geographical regions. Examples of several major Union and Confederate armies appear next. An **army** was typically under the command of a lieutenant general ("three star") or a full general ("four star").

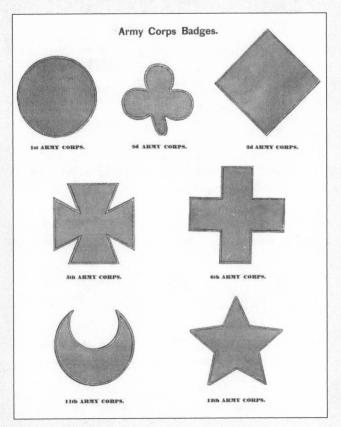

Army Corps Badges.

1st ARMY CORPS.   2d ARMY CORPS.   3d ARMY CORPS.

5th ARMY CORPS.   6th ARMY CORPS.

11th ARMY CORPS.   12th ARMY CORPS.

Distinctively shaped badges were worn in most Union Army corps by the end of the war. Color of the badge was determined by division within the corps, and was usually red for the 1st Division, white for the 2nd Division, and blue for the 3rd Division (in the case of a 4th Division the color varied, but was often yellow.

ARMY UNITS	SIZE	COMMANDING OFFICER
Section	up to 25 men	
Platoon	up to 50 men (two sections)	Captain and 1st and 2nd lieutenant
Company	up to 100 men (two platoons)	Captain
Regiment	1,000 men (ten companies)	Lieutenant Colonel or Colonel
Brigade	3,000–4,000 men (3 or 4 regiments)	Brigadier General ("one star")
Division	9,000–12,000 men (3 or 4 brigades)	Major General ("two star")
Corps	about 50,000 men (3 or 4 divisions)	Lieutenant General ("three star")
Army	100,000–200,000 men (five or more corps)	Lieutenant General ("three star") or full General ("four star")

Combat and Noncombat Troops

Each side's army was divided into three major combat arms: infantry, cavalry, and artillery. Ultimately, the Union army included at least thirty-four combat corps during the course of the war. There were also several noncombat arms, including the hospital and quartermaster **departments**. Detachments of troops from these branches would be assigned to the various field armies and their subordinate units as needed.

The Infantry

Of all the branches of the army, the infantry was the oldest. Infantrymen, foot soldiers, represented the largest arm of the ground forces. They played a major role in nearly every battle and skirmish, and consequently inflicted and received the highest numbers of casualties throughout the war. Because of the role they served, infantrymen on both sides bore the brunt of the fighting, suffering, and casualties, and often resented what appeared to be the easy lots of cavalry or artillerymen (particularly garrison troops, like the heavy artillerymen who guarded Washington, DC).

Most of the infantrymen on either side marched into battle as raw recruits and, if they survived, learned quickly and became veterans. New infantry regiments were often derided as green troops by their more experienced comrades, only to be hailed as veterans a day later following some particularly grueling engagement.

While the competence of commanders who ordered masses of infantry into attacks that turned into slaughters can be questioned, the courage and esprit de corps of the men who took part in those attacks cannot. The widespread dedication and steadfastness of the Civil War infantry, ironically, contributed to the heavy toll of many battles. In some cases, advancing infantry from both sides fought each other at point-blank range, firing rifles and wielding mounted bayonets and clubbed muskets, stumbling forward across mounds of their own dead into ranks of enemy soldiers who were doing the same.

Naturally, the best infantrymen were those trained and experienced in the use of infantry weapons and tactics. In the absence of proper equipment or an appropriate mission, however,

ARMIES OF THE CIVIL WAR	
UNION	CONFEDERATE
Army of the Cumberland	Army of Northern Virginia
Army of the James	Army of the Shenandoah
Army of the Ohio	Army of Tennessee
Army of the Potomac	Army of the Trans-Mississippi
Army of the Tennessee	
Army of Virginia	

other types of troops were utilized as infantry. For example, cavalrymen sometimes fought on foot as **skirmishers**, and cavalrymen for whom remounts were unavailable were sometimes used as infantrymen when expedient.

One of the better-known Union infantry units was the 54th Massachusetts, a black regiment that has gained recognition in large part because of the movie *Glory*. Formed a month after the Emancipation Proclamation in 1863, the 54th consisted of 650 free blacks from Northern states. Later the same year during an assault on Battery Wagner, a Confederate fortification in South Carolina, nearly half of the 54th were slain in combat, including its commander, Col. Robert Shaw. Nonetheless, its valiant performance laid the way for some 179,000 black troops to take the field as Union soldiers.

One of the most colorful Confederate infantry units was the 1st Special Battalion, Louisiana Infantry, a **Zouave** unit under the command of Maj. Roberdeau Wheat. Better known as "Wheat's Tigers" for its lack of discipline, this unit of mercenaries, New Orleans riffraff, and second sons of plantation owners was, according to one officer, "so villainous that every commander desired to be rid of it." It fought well, however, suffered extremely heavy casualties, and had to be disbanded in August 1862, shortly after its commander was slain at the Battle of Gaines's Mill.

Some 179,000 black troops served as Union soldiers.

The Cavalry

Cavalrymen on both sides were used as scouts, raiders, and, to a lesser extent early in the war, as mounted soldiers on the battlefield. The mobility of cavalry allowed it to range far ahead of an army to serve as its eyes; to attack into the rear of an enemy army, destroying or plundering its supplies; and to serve as a highly versatile arm on the battlefield, either charging in to support a collapsing **flank**, fall upon an enemy's flank, or pursue a retreating enemy.

While they could fight from the saddle, most Civil War cavalrymen were nonetheless used as mounted infantry, soldiers who would ride to battle and then, especially when a good defensive position was available, dismount, leave their horses behind the line of battle, and fight as skirmishers or as a loose screen of foot soldiers in front of massed formations of infantry. Cavalrymen used in this manner could be deployed more quickly than foot soldiers but still gain some of the advantages unavailable to mounted soldiers, such as being able to take cover behind **breastworks**.

At the start of the war, the Confederate cavalry was notably superior to that of the Union. This was due partly to an innate superiority of Southern horsemen, but was also a function of leadership and the ways that cavalry were utilized by the Northern leadership. As the war progressed, however, the gap between the Northern and Southern cavalry narrowed and, by the end of the war, Union horse soldiers faced and beat the best the Confederacy could field.

As a result of
a limited role
in combat,
Union
infantrymen
often
jeered at
cavalrymen
as they rode
by, heading
away from
battlefields
they had just
scouted even
as the foot
soldiers were
marching
toward them.

Union cavalry were also used ineffectively from early in the war onward. At the Battle of Bull Run, the first major engagement of the war, they were used merely as flank guards for infantry and artillery formations. Southern cavalry under the leadership of J.E.B. Stuart, on the other hand, was used adeptly at Bull Run, first defending the Confederate left flank, then sweeping in upon the retreating Union forces (Stuart was promoted to brigadier general as a result). This disparity, along with many others, contributed to a prolonged war, rather than one that might have otherwise been ended quickly.

Less experienced as horsemen, many Union soldiers entered cavalry service because they believed it would be easier duty than serving in the infantry (it probably also seemed more dashing to many). To their chagrin, they learned otherwise. For one thing, cavalry tactics and fighting from the saddle are difficult enough to learn and employ, all the more so for soldiers learning to ride at the same time.

In the first years of the war, primary duties for Union cavalrymen included constant picket duty and service as mounted escorts and orderlies for **general officers**. Later, after Maj. Gen. Philip H. Sheridan took over the Federal cavalry corps, horse soldiers were largely relieved of such duties, and an effort was made to transform the corps into a powerful combat arm (as the Confederate cavalry corps had always been).

As a result of this limited role in combat, Union infantrymen often jeered at cavalrymen as they rode by, heading away from battlefields they had just scouted even as the foot soldiers were marching toward them. "Who ever saw a dead cavalryman?" was one quip employed by Union soldiers about their own horse soldiers, and became so widespread that Abraham Lincoln even once posed it to General Sheridan, whose response reportedly evinced no humor. However, by the time the Battle of Gettysburg had been fought (July 1-3, 1863), the Union cavalry had improved greatly and this reputation had been eclipsed.

As the war progressed and Northern cavalrymen gained combat experience, the disparity between the Union and Southern cavalry shrank. Eventually, too, the Union army produced able cavalry commanders like Maj. Gen. John Buford, the hot-blooded Sheridan, and George Armstrong Custer (who in June 1863 at age twenty-three became the Union's youngest general; he was killed in the Battle of Little Big Horn in 1876).

Sheridan was ultimately the most important of these, after being appointed commander of the cavalry for the Army of the Potomac in April 1864. Pulling many of his cavalrymen from duty as sentries and orderlies, Sheridan formed them into a consolidated, heavy-hitting arm of the army that could provide a palpable presence on the battlefield or be used for raids in force, the likes of which only Confederate Maj. Gen. J.E.B. Stuart had ever led in the Eastern theater of war (although there were several large-scale cavalry raids in the West, as well).

An improved procurement process also led to improved Union cavalry. This process became more efficient as the Union cavalry acquired more conscientious officers with an eye for horseflesh. For example, Union Col. James H. Wilson, one of Sheridan's cavalry commanders, personally oversaw the acquisition of good horses at fair prices for Sheridan's troopers.

Overall, cavalry could play an important or even pivotal role in combat, and if used effectively, helped determine the results of major battles. Nonetheless, there were very few "cavalry battles" per se, but those that did occur were stirring in the extreme.

One such battle was fought on June 9, 1863, at Brandy Station, Virginia, an epic cavalry engagement that ranks among the greatest ever fought between mounted forces and the largest ever fought in North America. Union Maj. Gen. Alfred Pleasanton, at that time leader of the Army of the Potomac's cavalry corps, led his eleven thousand mounted soldiers against the Army of Northern Virginia's ten thousand man cavalry corps under J.E.B. Stuart. For more than two hours, the twenty-one thousand men charged and countercharged each other, fighting stirrup to stirrup with pistols, sabers, and rifles. Bugle calls and artillery fire added to the cacophony caused by neighing horses,

The Confederacy's 1st Virginia Cavalry Regiment acquired the nickname "Black Horse Cavalry," at the first Battle of Bull Run. Its uniforms included broad-brimmed, plumed black hats and gray or butternut trousers and short jackets.

barked orders, and wounded men. Some 936 Northern and 523 Southern soldiers were killed or wounded in the battle. The field was held by the Confederates; therefore, tactically, Brandy Station was a minor Confederate victory. Strategically, however, it demonstrated that Union cavalrymen could effectively challenge their Confederate counterparts.

One of the most distinctive Union cavalry regiments was the 6th Pennsylvania Cavalry, a unit of the Army of the Potomac, known for both its commander and weaponry as "Rush's Lancers." Initially, Col. Richard Rush's command was equipped like any other cavalry unit, but eventually adopted a nine-foot lance as a primary weapon. Unfortunately, this somewhat archaic weapon did not see distinguished service.

Like many cavalry regiments in the North and South, the Confederacy's 1st Virginia Cavalry Regiment was originally a handful of independent cavalry companies that the commonwealth of Virginia formed into a regiment under J.E.B. Stuart. At the first Battle of Bull Run, the unit acquired the nickname "Black Horse Cavalry," and for the rest of the war gave exemplary service to the Army of Northern Virginia. Its uniforms included broad-brimmed, plumed black hats and gray or butternut trousers and short jackets, the latter with black facings early in the war.

The Artillery

Of all the combat arms, artillery was the smallest in both armies. When war broke out, the U.S. Army had only four artillery regiments, which suffered the same levels of desertion to the Southern cause as the rest of the military. In early 1861, the government added the 5th U.S. Artillery Regiment.

Light or "field" artillery soldiers provided support on the battlefield and were especially effective against tightly-packed formations of infantrymen. Such troops typically used smoothbore artillery pieces that fired twelve-pound solid shot. Light artillerists could fire two rounds per minute or up to three if re-aiming the piece was unimportant.

Horse or "flying" artillery, trained to move and deploy quickly, was intended to accompany cavalry units and used the lightest sorts of artillery available. Such troops would fly into a firing position, unlimber and set up their guns, fire as many shots as would be effective, then limber up again and move forward to a better position or retreat in the face of an advancing enemy. Horse artillerists could maintain the same rate of fire as light artillerists.

> Because Washington, DC, was never attacked in force, the troops stationed there enjoyed a much better lifestyle than did field troops.

Heavy artillerymen used massive, unwieldy artillery pieces to defend fortified areas or to conduct sieges against them. These soldiers typically used rifled artillery pieces that could fire projectiles weighing 100 pounds or more. They were also armed with muskets and were expected to man ramparts as infantrymen when necessary.

Lincoln and his cabinet were determined that Washington, DC, should be safe from attack. They did this by ringing the capital with an interlocked chain of fortifications manned by a garrison of up to forty thousand troops, particularly heavy artillerists. Because the capital was never attacked in force, these troops enjoyed a much better lifestyle than did field troops, a fact that led to them being much resented. After taking command of the Army of the Potomac, however, Union Lt. Gen. Ulysses S. Grant pulled many of the heavy artillerymen from guard duty around the city and used them as infantrymen during the final year of the war.

The 1st U.S. Artillery, one of the heavy artillery units that guarded Washington, DC, was typical of such units. Like other heavy artillery units, it retained its prewar uniform, the dark blue frock coat and light blue pants of the infantry, along with a black Hardee hat and black leather accoutrements.

One of the most famous Southern artillery units was the Washington Artillery, a private or "fraternal" unit raised in 1838 and active in the Mexican War. It consisted of five light artillery companies, four of which deployed to Virginia early in the war and remained there for the duration, and one of which fought in the Army of Tennessee. Early in the war, its troops wore fancy blue uniforms and carried pistols and sabers, all of which were eventually abandoned.

Other Troops

Various sorts of troops were also attached to combat formations, or designated from within them, and tasked with performing specific functions (e.g., pioneers).

In addition to the soldiers of the combat arms (infantry, artillery, cavalry), there were also many noncombat soldiers, including chaplains, commissary sergeants, wagon drivers, engineers, signalmen, and the Union's Invalid Corps. Many of these noncombat support troops were organized into **departments**, in contrast to field troops, which tended to be organized into corps. Army departments at the time of the Civil War included the Quartermaster Department (responsible for supplying the army), a Medical Department, the Inspector General's Department, a Pay Department, and the Adjutant General's Department.

PIONEER EQUIPMENT

Soldiers designated as pioneers carried this equipment:

» axe
» spade
» shovel or pickaxe
» rifle or musket

By the midpoint of the war, the Union army included great numbers of such troops, more than some commanders thought necessary. Lt. Gen. Ulysses S. Grant reacted to this imbalance by pulling many soldiers from their noncombat duties and assigning them to infantry units.

PIONEERS were soldiers tasked with assisting a brigade or regiment by clearing obstructions in its path, building earthworks for light artillery pieces, and similar tasks. A dozen men, chosen from the ranks, usually served as pioneers for a regiment; most worked in this capacity temporarily, but the sergeant or corporal who led a detachment was usually permanently designated a pioneer and wore a small pair of cloth axes above his chevrons. Each pioneer carried an axe, a spade, a shovel, or a pickaxe, along with a sling that allowed the tool to be carried over the shoulder. Like other infantrymen, pioneer's weapons included a rifle or musket, which was sometimes replaced, if possible, with a more manageable cavalry carbine fitted with a standard rifle sling.

ENGINEERS were a military corps trained in building or demolishing bridges, dams, fortifications, and other structures. Engineer officers were attached to the staffs of unit commanders where they acted as advisors. During the Civil War, the engineer corps was very conservative and generally derided or refused to support engineering ideas that seemed radical or were not their own. Commanders with engineering backgrounds on both sides of the war were noted for their ability to dig in and fight defensively (e.g., Confederate Gen. Robert E. Lee, who was also exemplary on the offensive) and often for an inability to take the field and move decisively (e.g., Union Maj. Gen. George B. McClellan).

There was also a Corps of Topographical Engineers, charged with surveying and making maps.

SIGNALMEN were troops that helped the various elements of an army communicate with each other in the field through the use of colored signal flags. Signalmen increasingly used telegraphy as a means of communication and could even tap into an enemy's telegraph wires to intercept messages or send false information. This threat led to the creation of various ciphers, which required electronically-transmitted information to be decoded.

Congress acted to make the Signal Corps a separate branch of the U.S. Army on March 3, 1863.

CAMP FOLLOWERS: In addition to the soldiers, many civilians accompanied the army or followed in its wake, including photographers, **vivandieres**, **sutlers**, preachers, and relatives of soldiers. Seedier folk often followed the army as well, among them gamblers, criminals, and prostitutes, seeking opportunities for illicit profit among the soldiers. The term "camp followers" was sometimes used pejoratively, particularly with regard to women.

Many officers, particularly those in the Union army, developed scandalous reputations for the company they kept in camp. For example, Union Maj. Gen. Judson Kilpatrick, a cavalry officer, reputedly kept a succession of mistresses with him while in the field, even going so far as to dress them in uniforms so at a distance they could pass as young officers.

The Navy

Strategically, the most important role of the Union navy was to enforce the blockade of Southern ports, preventing goods from coming in or going out and attempting to slowly strangle the Confederate economy. Likewise, the most important role of the relatively small Confederate navy was to reduce the effects of this blockade.

Beyond such vital but rather mundane duties, however, the opposing navies fought each other everywhere their ships and gunboats were able to go—in coastal waters, inland waterways, rivers, and on the ocean, where Union ships hunted Confederate commerce raiders. Often, navy operations were conducted in cooperation with ground forces (e.g., navy gunboats provided artillery support for troops camping, fighting, or marching along the banks of major rivers).

At the beginning of the war, the Union navy consisted of some ninety warships, little more than a defensive force, but a framework that could be built upon. By mid-1864, the U.S. Navy had been built up to a peak strength of 670 ships and fifty thousand **sailors**, a level that allowed it to operate without significant opposition by Confederate naval forces.

When compared to the Union's military forces, it is in its navy that the Confederacy was most lacking. Throughout the course of the hostilities, the Southern navy never exceeded a strength of 130 warships and four thousand men, a force far too small to break the Union blockade or face its ships in a head-to-head contest. Indeed, it was civilian or foreign blockade runners, typically coming from Bermuda or up from the Caribbean with holds full of **contraband**, that were the biggest nuisance to the U.S. Navy.

Because of this relative weakness, the Southern navy developed different naval tactics than that of the North. A major component of the Confederate naval strategy was commerce raiding,

Armored vessels like the CSS *Virginia* (formerly USS *Merrimac*), used for some years by European powers, saw their first real action during the Civil War. This image of the ship in drydock shows how much of the ironclad vessel rode below the waterline.

attacking and looting U.S. merchant ships in international waters. This campaign was pursued globally and involved altercations literally on the other side of the world, as far away as Australia.

Nonetheless, the lack of telling Confederate strength limited the fruits of these efforts, and by the final year of the war, the South had only three effective commerce raiders. These were the *Alabama*, sunk in June 1864; the *Florida*, which surrendered at Bahia, Brazil, in October 1864; and the *Shenandoah*, which survived the Civil War and surrendered to British authorities at Liverpool, England, in November 1865.

Most of the seafaring warships used by either side were steam-driven wooden craft, many of which could also function under sail. Most of the river-going vessels were gunboats, paddle- or screw-driven boats of relatively shallow draft that were well suited for riverine operations but less reliable at sea.

Armored vessels debuted during the Civil War, going into action against each other in the famous duel between the USS *Monitor* and the CSS *Virginia* (a.k.a. *Merrimac*) on March 9, 1862. Although these ships were the first and most famous of the American ironclad warships, they were by no means the only ones to be launched into action during the war. By the end of the war, the U.S. Navy had dozens of armored warships and used them both as part of the blockade and to patrol rivers and coastlines. The South, hamstrung by its lack of heavy industry, was unable to construct nearly as many armored gunboats, but did manage to send a few into action, especially along the rivers flowing into the valley of the Mississippi.

Ships in Action

While the duel between the *Monitor* and the *Virginia* is the one most remembered from the Civil War, it was by no means the only high-profile naval battle of the war. One naval battle widely covered by the press—coverage that was marked in many cases by sensationalism and inaccuracy—was the one fought between the USS *Kearsarge* and the CSS *Alabama*.

As an indicator of how effective Southern commerce raiders could be, in a period of not quite two years, the *Alabama* had captured, burned, or sunk more than sixty Union ships, mostly merchant vessels. Nonetheless, the *Alabama* met its match off the coast of France on June 19, 1864, when the two ships sallied forth from the port of Cherbourg and fought a battle that caused very little damage to the *Kearsarge* but crippled and sunk the Confederate vessel.

Dramatic events, such as battles against other ships or bombardment of enemy positions ashore, were the exception to the rule. Sailors spent the majority of their time performing routine duties or combating the effects of tedium.

Cannon made ship-to-ship combat brutal, lethal, and often very quick. Maneuverability was paramount, as ships endeavored to align themselves to inflict the most telling damage against enemy vessels. Because warships' cannon face outward from the sides of the ship, the general goal was to maneuver into a position reminiscent of the letter "T," with the side of one's own ship, and half its major guns, facing the front or back of the enemy ship, and none of its major guns. Once so aligned, a warship could fire a "broadside," inflicting maximum damage with minimum risk. Solid iron shot and explosive shells, particularly those fired from the rifled cannon available in the latter half of the war, could blow the wooden ships to bits.

Once a ship was disabled from cannon fire, the victor would often send a boarding party to capture it, and hand-to-hand combat might ensue on the deck of the crippled ship (or, in rare cases, sailors and marines aboard the crippled ship might overcome the boarding party and fight their way onto the attacking ship). In shipboard combat, marines were armed with rifles or pistols, while sailors were typically armed with boarding axes, cutlasses, rifles, and pistols.

Dramatic events, such as battles against other ships or bombardment of enemy positions ashore, were the exception to the rule. Sailors spent the majority of their time performing routine duties or combating the effects of tedium. Running a ship required constant if monotonous activity; unlike soldiers, seamen tended not to have as much idle time on their hands. An exception to this was, of course, Union sailors on board blockading ships, who often complained of boredom in journals and letters. Like soldiers, sailors spent their free time playing cards or board games, mending clothing, singing, and writing letters.

In addition to their shipboard duties, sailors sometimes took part in armed landing parties. Or, even more rarely than shipboard combat, sailors could actually be sent into battle on shore. On January 15, 1865, for example, Rear Adm. David Dixon Porter ordered sixteen hundred sailors and four hundred marines into a frontal attack on Fort Fisher, North Carolina. In this rather cynical diversionary action, which was staged to allow an attack on the rear of the fort by U.S. Army infantrymen, the sailors were sent into combat before the marines arrived and suffered heavy casualties. Porter was widely criticized for his role in the operation, which nonetheless resulted in the taking of the strongly-held Confederate fort.

The primary role of marines was to serve in security detachments aboard navy ships.

The Marines

While marines played only a minor role during the Civil War, they were involved in military actions throughout the war—and on its eve, as well. In October 1859, eighty-six marines under U.S. Army Col. Robert E. Lee (future general-in-chief of the Confederate forces) stormed the engine house of the Federal arsenal in Harpers Ferry, Virginia, dislodging fanatic abolitionist John Brown and his followers.

When Southern states began to secede from the Union, the U.S. Marine Corps lost many of its **company grade officers**—about half of its captains, almost two-thirds of its first lieutenants, and half of its second lieutenants. Only one field grade officer, a major, resigned his commission from the corps.

After the U.S. Marine Corps appointed three-dozen officers to replace those who had resigned, its strength was about 2,200 men total. In July 1861, Congress approved the addition of twenty-eight officers and 750 enlisted men to the corps, raising its strength to about three thousand. Peak strength for the U.S. Marine Corps reached 3,900 men later in 1861, after Lincoln authorized two increases of five hundred men each. The Confederate Marine Corps played an even more marginal role and was never more than six hundred men strong.

For the most part, the primary role of marines was to serve in security detachments aboard navy ships. Beyond shipboard duty, small bodies of marines sometimes formed part of a ship's landing force, and in the Northern forces others were assigned directly to the U.S. Army.

Early in the war, the Union marines' role was as inglorious as that of the rest of the Northern military's. At the Battle of Bull Run (July 21, 1861), the first major battle of the war, a small unit of marines broke and ran—along with the rest of the Union forces—after sustaining repeated attacks from Confederate infantry and cavalry.

Such troops were better suited for coastal operations. In August 1861, marines assigned to four Union ships (the *Cumberland*, *Minnesota*, *Susquehanna*, and *Wabash*), took part in amphibious operations along the North Carolina coast, assisting in the capture of forts Clark and Hatteras.

The Union marines' last major operation of the war was also an amphibious assault on an important Confederate fortification. On January 15, 1865, Rear Adm. David D. Porter ordered four hundred marines to support a large body of sailors in a frontal assault on Fort Fisher, North Carolina. The marines arrived too late to help the sailors, suffered heavy casualties, and were criticized—probably unjustly—for their performance in the action.

Throughout the course of the Civil War, some 460 Union marines died from all causes (about 150 of them in combat). Casualty figures are harder to figure for the Confederate marines but were probably proportionate. Overall, by the end of the war, both the reputation and the morale of the marines were at a low point.

The Revenue Cutter Service

In addition to the navy, the Federal government enforced its will on the seas through the Revenue Cutter Service, the forerunner of the Coast Guard (which today is an amalgamation of the Revenue Cutter Service, the Lighthouse Service, the Steamboat Inspection Service, the Bureau of Navigation, and the Lifesaving Service, all of which were originally independent).

In its role as a law-enforcement agency, the service enforced tariffs, protected against pirates, and intercepted contraband. In 1794, the service was charged with keeping new slaves from being shipped in from Africa and, by 1861, had captured numerous slavers and freed almost five hundred slaves. Revenue cutters also performed rescue operations; from 1830 through 1870, immigrant packets proved to be the most vulnerable to disaster and received the most aid from the service.

During the Civil War, the service assumed quasi-military functions and was charged with augmenting the Navy with men and cutters and with undertaking special missions in keeping with its peacetime experiences and unique skills.

As with the other military services, the sympathies of the cutter force were divided between North and South. Principal wartime duties of cutters serving the Union were patrolling for commerce raiders and providing fire support for troops ashore. Those serving the Confederacy operated primarily as commerce raiders.

In 1860, the U.S. Revenue Cutter Service consisted of twenty-four vessels, twenty-two schooner-rigged sailing ships, one **brig**, and a single steamship. In early 1861, six of its vessels defected to the Confederacy. Four years later, at the end of the war, service strength had increased to twenty-seven ships (with eight more under construction), two-thirds of which were steamers.

A typical schooner-rigged cutter was crewed by twelve or thirteen men plus three officers; a larger steamer or brig would have had a crew four or five times as large. Some 219 officers served in the U.S. Revenue Cutter Service during the war; total numbers of seamen and noncommissioned officers are unclear, but were probably about eight to nine hundred. Of these, one was killed and an unknown number were wounded. It is uncertain how many served in the equivalent Confederate

An engraving of the USS *Harriet Lane*, which fired the war's first naval shots.

service or how many vessels it included, but both would have been considerably less than in the North.

USS *Harriet Lane*, the service's only prewar steamer, under command of Capt. John Faunce, had the distinction of firing the first naval shot of the Civil War on April 11, 1861, when it challenged the steamer *Nashville* by firing a shot across its bow. Four months later, in August 1861, it participated in the first joint Federal amphibious operation, an assault on the strategic Confederate forts at Hatteras Inlet, North Carolina, a vital opening for Rebel privateers and blockade runners.

One of the service's most interesting Civil War cutters was the *Naugatuck*, an ironclad semisubmersible that could be ballasted to sink almost three feet. Once semisubmerged and thus less vulnerable to enemy fire, it could still fire a single Parrott gun mounted above the water in its armored turret. In May 1862, the *Naugatuck* led a naval assault up the James River in hopes of shelling into submission the Confederate capital, during which it fought a four-hour duel with a Confederate **battery** on Drewry's Bluff.

Revenue cutters took part in a variety of other operations. In December 1862, the *Hercules* battled Confederate forces on the Rappahannock River; the *Miami* carried President Abraham Lincoln and his party to Fort Monroe in May 1862, preparatory to the Peninsular Campaign; the *Reliance* engaged Confederate forces on Great Wicomico River in Virginia in 1864; and on April 21, 1865, cutters were ordered to search outbound ships for President Lincoln's assassins.

Terms

A.W.O.L.: An abbreviation for "absent without leave." Apprehended deserters, particularly those from the Confederate forces, were frequently forced to wear placards emblazoned with the term. Pronouncing the initials as a word, rather than as individual letters, did not come into usage until eight decades later, during World War II.

ADMIRAL: Although a familiar naval term, the United States did not have any officers of this rank prior to or during the Civil War. After his victory at Mobile Bay, David Farragut was promoted to the rank of vice admiral in 1864 and further promoted to full admiral in 1866 after the conclusion of the war.

ARMY: A term that referred to the organizations known as the U.S. Army and the C.S. Army. Also, a major military organization of either side that operated at the strategic level and consisted of about five Army Corps, or a total of about 100,000 to 200,000 men. At least sixteen Union and twenty-three Confederate organizations were referred to, officially or unofficially, as armies.

BATTERY: A basic unit of artillery, typically consisting of six guns and 155 men (55 drivers, 70 gunners and 30 officers, and NCOs, and other men). An artillery battery was the equivalent of an infantry company.

Typically, about a quarter of battlefield casualties were actual deaths.

BIG THING: A term used by soldiers to describe any significant event, from a new shipment of shoes to a major battle.

BLUE JACKETS: Informal nickname for Union sailors, taken from their uniform coats.

BOYS IN GRAY: Confederate soldiers.

BREASTWORKS: Field fortifications that, ideally, consisted of stacked timbers reinforced with earth. Time or availability of supplies sometimes resulted in less robust defenses of the same name. As their name implies, they were often chest high, so a rifleman could obtain maximum cover and still fire unimpeded. Soldiers might also rest their rifles on the breastworks when shooting for more stability or when they grew weary.

BREVET RANK: An honorary title conferred for meritorious action in wartime. During the Civil War, this system was done away with because of widespread abuse (e.g., in 1863 a single act breveted some 1,700 soldiers to the ranks of brigadier general or major general).

BRIG: A sailing ship with two masts, each equipped with a square-rigged sail. Most were also outfitted with two or more headsails and various other smaller sails.

BUMMER, SHERMAN'S BUMMERS: Used from about 1850 to refer to an army deserter, and from 1861 to refer to soldiers who would slip out of ranks prior to combat to loot or simply avoid fighting. Sherman's bummers were the rapacious bodies of foragers from the Union Army of the Tennessee that helped the army to live off the land as it marched eastward across Georgia.

CANTINIERE: See *vivandiere.*

CASUALTY: A soldier who could no longer be counted as a combatant, because of either injury, illness, or death. Typically, about a quarter of battlefield casualties were actual deaths (although this typical three-to-one ratio could vary widely by battle).

CHIEF: This term originated during the Civil War, but usually referred to the ship's cook with the most rank or authority rather than to a chief petty officer, a naval rank that was not introduced until the 1890s.

COFFEE COOLERS: Soldiers who hid behind the battle lines during combat, brewing and drinking coffee until the danger was passed.

COMPANY GRADE OFFICERS: Second

lieutenants, first lieutenants, and captains (i.e., those officers most likely to command a company or serve at the company level).

CONFEDERATE CRUISERS: The warships built by Britain and France for the Confederacy during the first two years of the war. By 1863, the Union looked like it was sure to win the war and pressured the European nations to stop providing such vessels to the South.

CONTRABANDS, CONTRABAND OF WAR: Term applied in areas under some Union generals (e.g., Maj. Gen. Benjamin F. Butler) to escaped slaves who made it into Union lines. Such slaves were considered to be "contraband of war" that could not be returned to their masters.

COUTER UP: An informal command to put on one's equipment and get ready to fall into ranks, derived from the word "accoutrements."

CUTTER: A vessel sixty-five feet or more in length that could accommodate a crew for extended deployment.

DEPARTMENT: A basic geographical organization that typically gave its name to the friendly army operating within its boundaries (e.g., the Army of the Potomac, the Army of Northern Virginia). This term was also used to refer to a noncombat army function, such as the Pay Department.

DOUGHBOY: Although widely associated with World War I, this term for a soldier was used during the Civil War, albeit not widely.

DRAFTEE: A citizen conscripted, or drafted, into military service.

DRAGOON, MOUNTED RIFLEMAN: Soldiers who travelled on horseback and fought on foot. In 1861, the designations of dragoon and mounted rifleman were done away with, all such troops being redesignated as cavalry. In general, cavalry was used as mounted infantry during the Civil War.

ENSIGN: The lowest commissioned rank in the U.S. Navy, established in 1862. In the British army, the term had been used to refer to various navy or army ranks for about three hundred years. Also, a flag, especially on a ship.

FIELD GRADE OFFICERS: Officers bearing rank higher than captain (i.e., majors, lieutenant-colonels, and colonels). The naval equivalents were lieutenant commander, commander, and captain, respectively.

FLANK: The side of a military unit and where, other than its rear, it was most vulnerable to attack. This term could also be used as verb, as in "to flank," meaning to attack a unit along an unprotected side.

FOUGASSE(S): A type of land mine, usually placed by engineers, made by packing explosives at the bottom of a sloping pit then covering them with boards followed by rocks or other debris. During an enemy attack, the explosives could be detonated, showering a large area with chunks of heavy shrapnel. Such devices generally used a ratio of 16 pounds of powder to one ton of rocks and affected a maximum area of about 150 yards in length and 100 yards in width.

GENERAL OFFICERS: The highest level of army rank, which included, in ascending order, brigadier general ("one star"), major general ("two star"), lieutenant general ("three star"), and general, or full general ("four star").

GUNBOAT: A type of shallow-draft warship, used largely by the U.S. Navy and on inland waterways and rivers. Early in the war, such vessels might be little more than armed steamers. After 1862, however, gunboats were more likely to be purpose-built warcraft after the models of the USS *Monitor* or CSS *Virginia*, riding low in the water; covered to just below the waterline with armored plate four or more inches thick; and equipped with a low, flat deck and a round pillbox that held a pair of guns or with sloping sides that housed a dozen or so guns in armored ports.

HAYFOOT: See *strawfoot*.

HOMEGUARD: A term used from 1861 onward to refer to militia and other local soldiers on either side who would only be used against invading forces or for local military duties.

IRONCLAD: Warships armored with metal plate. While "ironclad" is now used to refer to the USS *Monitor* and the CSS *Virginia* (*Merrimac*) and the armored ships that descended from them, this term did not appear in print for the first time until 1867; during the Civil War, Northern warships of this sort were often referred to as "monitors." See *gunboat*.

KENTUCKY WINDAGE: A technique of compensating for range, wind, or other conditions by aiming slightly high or just to one side of a target.

MARINE: A naval soldier trained to fight on ship and take part in boarding and amphibious operations (although the role of marines went beyond shipboard activities; e.g., the troops that battled John Brown at Harpers Ferry were U.S. Marines).

MEDAL OF HONOR: A decoration awarded to military personnel for valor, established by Congress for Union heroes in 1862. Sometimes incorrectly referred to as the Congressional Medal of Honor.

MILITIA: Civilians who formed military units and trained as local defense units that would fight in cases of enemy invasion or raids.

MUSTER IN, MUSTER OUT: Terms that meant, respectively, to enter military service and to leave it. During the Civil War "mustered out" was also a euphemism that meant to be killed in action.

NONCOMMIS-SIONED OFFICER, NCO: An enlisted man elevated to a leadership position but given no commission from the government. Sergeants and corporals are noncommissioned officers.

OFFICER: A soldier who is given a commission to serve on behalf of the issuing government. In ascending order, army officer ranks are second lieutenant, first lieutenant, captain, major, lieutenant colonel, colonel, and general officer.

PICKETS: Soldiers tasked with guarding and patrolling an army's lines when it was encamped.

POWDER MONKEY: A young sailor, often a boy, who helped serve shipboard cannon.

PROVOST, PROVOST GUARD: Military police. A provost marshal would be the chief military policeman for a military command, and his office would be called the Provost

Marshal's Office (PMO).

SAILOR: The military or civilian crewman of a ship, as well as the general term for any member of the U.S. or C.S. navies.

SKIRMISHERS: Troops who deployed in loose formation to the front and flanks of an army and were thus the first to come into contact with the enemy. Such troops were used to keep an army in the field from being surprised, and usually withdrew once the big formations moved into battle or they were driven away during the course of the battle.

SLOOP, SLOOP-OF-WAR: A single-masted warship somewhat larger and more seaworthy than a gunboat that, because of its small size, carried all of its guns on a single deck.

SOLDIER: A member of the Union or

Confederate armies. This term cannot be accurately applied to all the combatants of the Civil War (i.e., navy personnel are sailors and Marine Corps personnel are marines).

SPIKE, SPIKING: If gunners had to abandon their guns, the last thing they would do—if they were able to—was hammer a metal spike into the touch-hole near the breech of the gun, thus making it temporarily unusable. Soldiers would also do this to captured enemy guns if they were unable to use them for themselves.

STRAWFOOT: A term applied to a raw recruit or levy who had trouble learning to step off with his left foot. Training instructors dealt with this by having the soldier put a piece of straw in his left shoe or in his left hand, and possibly a bit of hay in his right shoe or hand, as reminders. They would then drill

such troops by calling a cadence of "strawfoot, hayfoot," rather than the regulation "left, right." This term might also be used pejoratively to refer to any backwoods soldiers.

SUTLER: A civilian merchant who followed military units and sold food and other goods and services to troops (e.g., gambling, liquor, prostitutes). Such merchants tried to establish stores near or within camps and generally required permission from military commanders to do so and were thereby subject to their regulations. They were often the only suppliers of non-military goods and frequently obtained influential monopolies on commodities like coffee, sugar, and tobacco.

VEDETTE: A mounted sentry (i.e., a cavalryman assigned to guard duty).

VICTUALER: See *sutler.*

VIVANDIERE, CANTINIERE: A woman or girl who accompanied an army for purposes of helping out with chores in camp, providing company for the troops or maintaining morale. Some accounts describe such women carrying water to the troops of their regiment, even while under fire from the enemy. Such camp followers often wore feminized versions of the regimental uniform.

ZOUAVE: A member of one of the war's volunteer regiments that adopted the North African-style uniforms and precision drill reminiscent of the French Algerian Zouaves. Costume typically included baggy pants, vest, and fez.

ARMS, EQUIPMENT, AND UNIFORMS:
SUPPLYING THE SERVICEMEN

"The main foundations of every state … are good laws and good arms. You cannot have good laws without good arms and, where there are good arms, good laws inevitably follow." — Niccolo Machiavelli

A mind-boggling variety of weapons, equipment, and uniforms were used during the four years of the Civil War. While the military forces of either side would have preferred equipment and weapons to be standardized for logistical reasons, this was not always possible, especially when war materiel was being produced by scores of domestic manufacturers and being imported from abroad.

Equipment and uniforms, and weapons to a lesser extent, were often cheaply made by profit-hungry government contractors and of substandard quality, something that contributed even more to the suffering of soldiers in the field.

Arms, equipment, and uniforms—those prescribed by regulation and those actually worn and used by troops—are covered thoroughly but not exhaustively in the following section. For most readers, this information will be more than enough, but those who require extensive detail should check with more specialized sources, several of which are listed in Appendix C.

Nomenclatures

Military equipment differed from civilian equipment in that it often had both a name and a nomenclature, an identifying combination of letters and numbers.

Often, the nomenclature identified the year a particular weapon or piece of equipment was produced, or its place in a sequence. For example, the sword carried by Union light artillerymen was labeled as the "M1840 light artillery saber" and, because the original pattern was first produced in 1840, all swords of that pattern are identified as an M1840, regardless of the year they were actually manufactured. A piece of military equipment might also be described in terms of its pattern, or model, as in an "1858-pattern hat." Nomenclatures were not generally used in everyday speech and not all items were assigned one.

Small Arms

Small arms are those firearms used by individuals—as opposed to artillery pieces or other crew-served weapons—and include rifles, muskets, carbines, pistols, and shotguns. Such weapons, notably rifles firing **minié balls**, inflicted 94 percent of all fatal battlefield injuries during Civil War battles.

For many logistical and practical reasons, military systems prefer to have their small arms be as standardized as possible (for example, the rifles used by almost all modern U.S. military personnel are part of the M16 series of weapons, including the M16A4 and the M4 carbine). During the Civil War, however, at least eighty-five different sorts of small arms were used in all of the Union military services, and an uncertain but similarly unwieldy number was employed by the Confederacy. These ranged from Revolutionary War-era flintlock muskets to the most modern repeating, metallic-cartridge rifles, and included both domestic and European weapons.

Despite the great variety of weapons in use, however, the primary rifles used on both sides were the M1842 .69-**caliber** Harpers Ferry Rifle and the M1861 .58-caliber Springfield rifle, both **muzzle-loaders**. Most other rifles made in either part of the country were little different than these two basic types. One of the most notable foreign rifles was the English Enfield, some 700,000 of which were purchased by the Confederacy (many were also purchased by the U.S. government).

Pistols of many sorts were used during the war, but the most common were Colt revolvers, notably the M1851 .32-caliber navy model and the M1860 .44-caliber army model.

Carbines were generally **breach-loaders** that accepted either metallic or combustible linen cartridges. These included the M1865 .56-caliber Spencer carbine (which held seven metallic rounds in an internal magazine), the .44-caliber lever-action Henry repeating rifle (which held fifteen rounds and was released in 1860), and the M1855 .577-caliber Sharps carbine, which was a single-shot breach loader that accepted a linen cartridge. Such weapons had much better rates of fire than single-shot muzzle loaders. However, because ammunition was perpetually in short supply during the war, many commanders disliked such modern weapons, believing that they were overly expensive, unreliable, and would induce soldiers to squander ammunition.

Hand grenades were also used during the Civil War. Hanes' Excelsior was a metal sphere about the size of a softball that was armed by opening it, attaching **percussion caps** to several nipples on an inner core filled with gunpowder, then reassembling it. Thus armed, the grenade could then be thrown and it was expected that upon impact at least one of the caps would bang against the inside

Pistols like this Colt revolver, typically in .32 or .44 caliber, were used in the various military services of each side. Beyond the war, such reliable, powerful sidearms found a place in the frontier culture of the Far West.

of the outer shell, causing it to explode. Because it was hazardous even to its user, however, this weapon did not see wide use. Ketcham's grenade, a percussion explosive that consisted of a fin-stabilized body armed with an egg-shaped explosive head, was used more extensively, especially in siege and trench warfare.

Costs of small arms varied widely but represented a large expenditure for both governments. Sharps carbines, when purchased in bulk, cost the government $30 each. Colt revolvers cost around $10 each, with the price varying by model (in the 1850s on the West Coast, however, when such weapons were considerably newer and had to be shipped, Colt revolvers sold for $250 to $500 apiece).

Small-Arms Ammunition

Ammunition in a wide variety of types and calibers was used during the Civil War, reflecting the many sorts of weapons in use on both sides. Logistically, this presented all kinds of difficulties to commanders on both sides, who often had to ensure their troops were supplied with many different sorts of ammunition.

Minié balls were the most common sort of ammunition for rifles, and ranged in size from .44 to .69 caliber. Smoothbore weapons could fire either a round musket ball or the somewhat more lethal **buck-and-ball**. **Pistols**, whether single-shot or revolvers, generally fired simple round balls.

Both rifle and pistol ammunition was usually issued to soldiers in cartridge form, a lead slug and the amount of powder needed to fire it wrapped in paper. Cartridges were usually issued in paper packages and transferred into tins that would hold twenty rounds each. In combat, a rifleman would tear open the cartridge, pour the powder down the muzzle of the weapon, put the slug into the rifle muzzle and discard the paper, and ram the slug down to the bottom of the barrel. To fire the weapon, he would place a percussion cap on the hollow nipple of the weapon's lock, cock it, point it at what he wanted to shoot, and then squeeze the trigger.

Cartridges were often unavailable to Confederate soldiers early in the war. When this was the case, they would carry their musket or minié balls loose in a pouch or pocket and their powder in a flask or horn.

Powerful, rifled longarms like this .57 caliber Enfield, firing bone-shattering, high-velocity minié balls, were carried by most soldiers during the Civil War. Elevated sights like those shown here were disliked by many troops and, when provided, they were often removed.

Smoothbore muskets, little different from those used during the Revolutionary War, were carried by some regiments at the beginning of the war. Most of these had the antiquated flintlock (shown above) replaced by a modern percussion lock.

Ammunition was usually stored and shipped in pinewood boxes. A standard box had a wooden handle on each end, was sixteen inches wide, eleven inches long, and eight inches deep, and was packed with one thousand rounds (cartridges) of ammunition. Boxes were sometimes color-coded to indicate the kind of ammunition within; the specific type of ammunition, its caliber, and its quantity were usually marked on the side of the box; and the date and place of manufacture was generally stenciled on the lid.

Melee Weapons

Swords, bayonets, knives, daggers, pikes, axes, and other hand-to-hand combat weapons inflicted a relatively small—some might even say negligible—number of fatal injuries during the Civil War. However, it is impossible to say how many soldiers were wounded by such weaponry, or how many enemy positions were routed by the spirited charge of infantrymen wielding bayonet-mounted rifles.

Civil War bayonets came in many shapes and sizes. The most common were more spike-like than knife-like and were typically triangular in cross section, inflicting wounds that would not heal properly. Other types included sword bayonets and saber bayonets. Curved sword bayonets were often issued to Zouave regiments.

Prices for hand-to-hand combat weapons increased dramatically after the outbreak of the war. Ames cutlasses, for example, cost $2.25 each in 1860 and doubled to $4.50 apiece in 1861. Sword or saber bayonets cost the Union government from $5 to $7 each in 1864.

Curved slashing swords like this M1860 U.S. Cavalry saber were favored by cavalry soldiers on both sides. Infantry officers and NCOs typically carried straight swords, while Union heavy artillery troops carried heavy, leaf-shaped short swords.

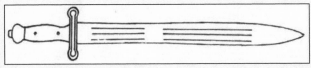

M1833 Heavy artillery sword.

Heavy Weapons and Ammunition

Almost as large a variety of heavy weapons as of small arms were used during the Civil War by the armies and navies of each side. These could be broadly divided into **cannons**, **mortars**, and **howitzers**, and further divided into weapons that were either smoothbore or rifled.

Cannons and howitzers, with their long bronze, iron, or steel barrels, looked very much alike, although howitzers tended to be somewhat shorter. Lighter ones were mounted on wheeled carriages drawn by teams of horses. Heavier ones were mounted upon large, stationary frames that could be rotated within an arc of fire; such guns were set up either within fortifications for defense, outside of them for siege and even on the battlefield. Heavy cannons and howitzers could also be mounted on ships, barges, and gunboats and used for shelling coastal positions, such as fortifications.

Mortars had thick, stubby barrels and were aimed upward at a steep angle. Such weapons were almost always mounted on flat, sturdy wooden platforms and used against fortified areas or cities. Like other artillery pieces, mortars were also mounted on watercraft, notably mortar boats, and were also sometimes mounted on railroad flatcars, allowing them to be used as mobile artillery.

Especially large or powerful siege guns were sometimes given proper names. For example, a large Union mortar mounted on a railway car and used during the siege of Petersburg, Virginia, was dubbed "The Dictator," while a 180-pounder, 8-inch **Parrott gun** that had to be transported over marsh to bombard Charleston, South Carolina, was nicknamed the "Swamp Angel" (this weapon is traditionally misidentified as a 200-pounder).

Even light artillery pieces required six or more men to operate optimally, and the larger siege or seacoast weapons needed even larger crews as well as special equipment, such as small cranes, to help move and load their shot and shells.

Regardless of caliber, light smoothbore artillery pieces had a range of about 1,500 yards (that is, about a mile), while light rifled artillery pieces had a range of about 2,500 yards (which is well over a mile-and-a-half), depending on the type of ammunition being fired. Heavy and seacoast artillery pieces, which fired much heavier ammunition, had a range of about 2,000 yards.

The most basic type of ammunition for artillery pieces was solid shot, or cannon balls. Various other forms of ammunition were also used, including explosive shells, **canister** or **case shot**, bar shot, **chain shot**, and **grapeshot**.

Beyond the standard types of artillery weapons used during the war, more exotic and deadly weapons were also sometimes used, generally on an experimental basis. Such weapons included the Gatling gun, a forerunner of the machine gun, a six-barreled .45-, .50-, or 1.0-caliber weapon that was fired by turning a crank. More amazing than such weapons existed during the Civil War is that they were used on such a limited basis, despite their evident lethality.

During the war, bronze cannon typically cost 46¢ per pound; for example, a 1,000-pound barrel for a 6-pounder bronze gun generally cost $460 each. **Rifling** cost an additional $50 and sighting an additional $20. Iron weapons cost 8¢ to 10¢ per pound; additional cost for rifling and sighting varied with the size of the gun in question.

Cost of ammunition was based on the size of the gun for which it was manufactured. In 1861, the Ames Manufacturing Company charged $2.25 each for solid shot, explosive shells, and canister shot for a 6-pounder gun, and $32.12 each for solid shot or explosive shells for a 400-pounder gun (in quantities of 580 rounds). Powder charges for shot more than six pounds cost extra.

Infantry Weapons and Equipment

Infantrymen had to be able to carry all of the weapons, ammunition, and equipment they would need, which frequently amounted to more than fifty pounds of gear. As a result, experienced soldiers threw away whatever was not absolutely essential. Often, however, something that was a hindrance at one point could be deeply desired at another; overcoats tossed away in the heat of the summer, for example, had to be replaced when the weather cooled.

An enlisted infantryman or noncommissioned officer was generally armed with a single-shot, muzzle-loading rifled musket (typically of .58 caliber), forty rounds of ammunition, and a bayonet. Officers and sometimes noncommissioned officers typically carried six-shot revolvers and swords.

Other infantry equipment included a canteen and tin cup, a **knapsack** or blanket roll, a cartridge box, a **haversack**, a **cap box**, and possibly a rubber blanket. Some of the Union equipment was shoddily made by

Even light artillery pieces required six or more men to operate optimally, and the larger siege or seacoast weapons needed even larger crews, as well as special equipment, such as small cranes, to help move and load their shot and shells.

government contractors and fell apart quickly. Confederate troops, on the other hand, especially later in the war, often carried copies of the equipment used by Northern troops, captured Union equipment, or simply lacked certain types of gear.

Bulky equipment that soldiers tended to leave behind the lines when going into battle, such as knapsacks, was sometimes marked with their regiment, company, and state (for example, Co. A, 54th Massachusetts Regiment, or, if light artillery, 5th Rhode Island Battery). Occasionally, haversacks, canteens, and other equipment were also marked in this way.

Many period photographs and etchings also that show private soldiers posing with pistols and bowie knives or other sorts of large daggers, and there are numerous references in letters from soldiers requesting their families send them items like pistols, derringers, and fighting knives. There is also evidence that soldiers carried various other weapons to augment their rifles or muskets, such as knuckledusters. In the Confederate army, such non-regulation weapons would have been more common. As indicated by court martial proceedings, however, such weapons were far more likely to be used while on furlough or against fellow soldiers in camp than in combat.

Some soldiers also purchased armored vests for about $12 each. Owners of these bullet-resistant vests, however, were generally ridiculed by their comrades, and, as such items were also heavy and bulky, they were usually abandoned before long. Greaves—armored shin guards—were also purchased by some soldiers, although less frequently than vests.

Cavalry Weapons and Equipment

Cavalrymen on both sides were among the best-equipped soldiers of the war. Typical cavalry weapons included breech-loading **carbines**, six-shooter revolvers, and sabers. Some Southern cavalrymen also carried shotguns.

Equipment included saddles, spurs, bits and bridles, blanket rolls, and saddle bags (used instead of the infantryman's haversack and knapsack).

The most important piece of equipment for a cavalryman was his horse. Union troops had their mounts issued to them by the government. Unfortunately, early in the war these were acquired through an inefficient and sometimes corrupt procurement system that often secured substandard mounts for the Union cavalrymen.

Confederate soldiers, on the other hand, personally owned their horses and, as a result, their mounts tended to be much higher in quality than those of Union cavalrymen. A Southern cavalryman who lost his horse in combat, however, had to replace it at personal expense. If he was unable to purchase or otherwise procure a remount within thirty days, he became a foot soldier and was sent to the ranks of an infantry regiment.

When the war ended, these soldiers were generally allowed to keep their horses, which were treated by the victors as personal property rather than public Confederate war materiel subject to confiscation. This was a veritable lifesaver in many cases, as it provided the deactivated soldiers with the means for plowing their fields when they returned to their farms.

Artillery Weapons and Equipment

Light, horse, and heavy artillery units on either side used markedly different equipment, in keeping with their different missions and responsibilities. While the weapons used by Northern and Southern gunners varied to some extent, for the most part they were the same, and new artillery weapons developed by the Union were often copied by the Confederacy.

Light artillery batteries on both sides fired about 90 percent of their rounds from about ten basic sorts of cannon, including a 3-inch rifled cannon; 6- and 12-pound cannons; 12-, 24-, and 32-pound howitzers; a mobile 12-pound mountain howitzer; and 10- and 20-pound Parrott rifles. In all cases, "pound" referred to the weight of a piece of solid shot, or ball, fired by the weapon, not to the weight of the gun itself, and "inch" referred to the caliber, or width of shell, not to the weapon's barrel length.

The quintessential model 1857 smoothbore **Napoleon 12-pound howitzer** fired more projectiles than all other types of artillery piece combined. Virtually all of the Union's Napoleons were of bronze, but Confederate knockoffs were made of bronze, brass, or even cast iron.

Horse artillery tended to use the lightest, most mobile guns available to the light artillery, such as 6- and 12-pound cannons, 12-pound howitzers, the 12-pound mountain howitzer, and the 10-pound Parrott rifle.

Heavy artillery batteries manned the heaviest, most unwieldy, and destructive artillery pieces. These included huge cannon mounted on wooden barbette carriages, which allowed them to be rotated in a semicircle and cover an arc of fire in front of a fortification; 13-inch seacoast mortars; 24-pound guns mounted on heavy siege carriages; and the largest sorts of heavy-rifled cannon, such as 100- and 300-pound Parrott guns.

CLOTHING, WEAPONS, AND EQUIPMENT OF CIVIL WAR SOLDIERS

The clothing, weapons, and equipment used by combatants during the Civil War varied to a great extent by whether they were from the North or South, their branch of service (for example, Army, Navy) or corps within it (for example, infantry, artillery, cavalry), their rank, and even what theater of the war in which they served. There were many common items used by soldiers of both sides, and following is a list of some of the equipment that might have been carried by an Army infantryman of either side.

» frock coat
» rifle or pistol (some NCOs)
» haversack
» trousers
» cartridge box and cartridges
» dnapsack
» forage cap/**slouch cap**
» cap box and percussion caps
» canteen
» bayonet
» blanket roll ("**mule collar**")
» brogans (Union)/shoes
» rubber blanket
» tent half
» personal items (razor, shaving brush, soap, towel, other toiletries, pocket knife, eating utensils, pipe, tobacco pouch, writing kit, sewing kit, musical instrument, playing cards or dice, carte de visite, fighting knife, pistol/derringer)

Additional Artillery Equipment

Ideally, a single 12-pound light artillery piece was supplemented by a limber and a caisson, drawn by a total of twelve horses and serviced by a crew of eight gunners and six drivers. Artillerymen were, however, trained to work with smaller crews in the case of casualties, and limbers and caissons could be drawn at a slower rate of speed by fewer horses. Heavier guns required proportionately more horses for transportation and larger crews to operate them. As with their cavalrymen, Confederate artillerymen typically owned the horses they used.

Accessories included the thumbstall, a leather guard used to protect the thumb from a hot gun barrel while ramming powder and shot down the **bore**; a quadrant, used to measure a gun barrel's angle of elevation; a rammer, for shoving a bag of powder and shot into the bore of the cannon; a sponge mounted on the end of a haft, used to swab out the bore in between shots and extinguish sparks that could prematurely ignite the powder; and the worm, a double corkscrew mounted on a haft and used to remove obstacles from the bore (such as damp powder bags that would not ignite).

Light artillerymen were also equipped with brass shoulder boards, which theoretically helped protect against downward-cutting saber blows from enemy cavalrymen. It is not likely, however, that these **accoutrements** ever served the desired effect, as veteran soldiers usually lost or discarded them early on and new recruits threw them away so as to look less green.

Twenty-pound Parrott rifle—a heavy artillery cannon.

Navy Weapons and Equipment

Sailors did not generally carry weapons (marines were responsible for security on board ships), but when it was necessary, they were issued revolvers (if available), cutlasses, sabers, pikes, and axes. In boarding actions, sailors might also wield makeshift weapons, such as **belaying pins** or **gaffs**.

Marine Corps Weapons and Equipment

Marines on both sides tended to use the same weapons, equipment, and accoutrements as did army infantrymen. When on board ship, weapons and equipment were generally stored in an arms room and issued when needed.

Revenue Cutter Service Weapons and Equipment

In the decade prior to the Civil War, weapons issued to Revenue Cutter crews were typically requested from the War Department. Most of these were armaments none of the other services wanted, and a great many of them were substandard.

In 1853, for example, the service purchased single-shot, muzzle-loading pistols and carbines from the Perry Arms Company of Newark, New Jersey, the primary criteria apparently being that the muskets were short enough to fit within a cutter's four-and-a-half foot long arms chest. One Revenue Cutter officer, 1st Lt. Edgar O. Murden of the USS *Washington*, proclaimed the weapons "unfit for sea use." Requests by cutter officers for Jenks or Sharps carbines, Colt revolvers, and law enforcement equipment like handcuffs and leg irons were nonetheless repeatedly denied. Heavy weapons tended to be similarly antiquated or substandard and included 9-pounder cannons dating to the War of 1812.

By 1861, some cutters had been equipped with more modern weapons, including Sharps rifles, Maynard carbines, Colt 1858 revolvers (in the hands of officers) and new 12-pounder cannons. Most of these were cutters stationed at Southern ports and many of their crews defected to the Confederacy and took the vessels with them at the outbreak of war.

Other equipment included bayonets for the muskets, rifles, and carbines; pikes, cutlasses, and axes; and belts designed to hold a cutlass or a cutlass and pistol.

Other Items

Soldiers, sailors, and marines lived in the field or on shipboard for extended periods of time and were often away from home for a year or more. Thus, in addition to their weapons, equipment, uniforms, and other items prescribed by regulation, military personnel often had other things, subject to the limitations of what they had room for in their knapsacks or sea chests.

Such personal items included razors, shaving brushes, soap, towels, and other toiletry items; pocket knives; eating utensils or folding knife-fork-and-spoon combinations; pipes and tobacco pouches; writing kits; sewing kits, called "housewives"; musical instruments, such as banjos or harmonicas; dice or decks of cards; and **cartes de visite**.

Uniforms

At the beginning of the war, troops wore a staggering array of different uniforms, from the Algerian-style outfits of the Zouaves, to tartan kilts in the largely-Scottish 79th New York Volunteer Infantry Regiment, to the regulation blue of the North and gray of the South. But some blue uniforms did appear in the Confederate ranks, and gray

A 3-inch Ordnance Rifle—a light artillery cannon.

The 1857 model Napoleon, a brass, smoothbore, muzzle-loading howitzer that fired 12-pound solid shot, was the basic artillery piece used by both the Union and the Confederacy. An experienced crew could fire three rounds a minute with this gun.

Coastal artillery piece, mounted on a wooden barbette.

Mortar

uniforms among some regiments of the Union, and soldiers on both sides were dressed in uniforms that included many other colors.

One reason for this startling variety of uniforms is that most of the units that fought were volunteer or state regiments that were initially uniformed and equipped locally, rather than by the Federal or Confederate governments. As the war progressed, however, uniforms became more and more standardized and alike, and, ideally, were issued by the appropriate quartermaster department. By the end of hostilities, a preponderance of men in the North were wearing regulation blue, while those in the South were wearing gray, butternut (a yellowish-gray made from a readily available dye), or anything they could obtain, from civilian clothes to Union uniforms.

A forage cap, often called a kepi, was the regulation headgear for soldiers on both sides. Even in the North, however, some other sort of headgear was substituted, either because a regiment desired a distinctive look, because regulation caps were not available, or because individual soldiers preferred different sorts of hats.

Footwear included a low-heeled black shoe called a brogan for infantrymen and knee-high black boots for cavalrymen. In Southern units especially, soldiers were often poorly equipped with shoes and boots and wore whatever they could find, going barefoot if necessary. This was also sometimes true of Northern units.

In the border regions of the West and Midwest, a preponderance of troops in any given locally-raised unit might have no uniforms at all, and at times troops of either side in any theater of the war might be wearing only what their families were able to send them. Captured stores of enemy uniforms were typically distributed to—or looted by—victorious soldiers. When Union Maj. Gen. Sherman's men marched into Atlanta, for example, many of them were wearing captured Rebel uniforms. Understandably, commanders did not want their men wearing uniforms that looked like those of the enemy and usually put out an order stating that uniforms had to be dyed and that they would be confiscated if they were not.

Uniforms, shoes, belts, and other equipment, especially those mass-produced in Northern workshops by war profiteers, were frequently cheaply made and of substandard quality.

Union Uniforms

Army officers were to wear, according to regulation, "a frock coat of dark blue cloth, the skirt to extend from two-thirds to three-fourths of the distance from the top of the hip to the bend of the knee; single-breasted for captains and lieutenants; double-breasted for all other grades." The number and placement of buttons was dictated by rank. Trousers were to be dark blue (except for light artillerymen, who were supposed to wear light blue trousers), with a gold cord along the outer seam for staff officers, a colored cord along the outer seam for regimental officers, and plain for general officers.

Enlisted foot soldiers in the U.S. Army were to wear "a single-breasted frock, of dark blue cloth, made without plaits, with a skirt extending one-half the distance from the top of the hip to the bend of the knee; one row of nine buttons on the breast, placed at equal distances; stand-up collar, to rise no higher than to permit the chin to turn freely over it, to hook in front at the bottom, and then to slope up and backward at an angle of 30 degrees on each side; cuffs pointed according to the pattern, and to button with two small buttons at the under seam; collar and cuffs edged with a cord or welt of cloth" in a color appropriate to the corps.

Infantrymen also wore a four-button fatigue jacket designed for field wear (worn in every branch of the service, this jacket was possibly the most frequently seen garment worn by Federal troops).

Enlisted cavalry soldiers were to wear a jacket rather than a coat, with twelve buttons in a single row. Musicians were to wear a coat or jacket the same as that of the other soldiers in their corps, with the addition of lace in line with each button, forming a herring-bone pattern on the chest, in appropriate colors, as above.

Regulations called for trousers to be of plain dark blue cloth for all except light artillerymen, who were to wear sky blue, with the addition of a stripe of a color appropriate to the corps for sergeants and corporals. In practice, however, light blue trousers predominated in all branches of the army.

Cuff edgings, musician's lace, and trouser stripes and cords were colored according to the corps of their wearer—sky blue for infantry, yellow for cavalry, and red for artillery.

Regulation headgear for all ranks included broad-brimmed black felt hats and smaller, dark blue forage caps ("kepi"). Union soldiers generally embellished their caps with their regimental numbers and/or company letters and the emblems appropriate to their combat arm—a bugle for the infantry, two crossed cannons for the artillery, and two crossed sabers for the cavalry.

Navy uniforms included navy blue, double-breasted frock coats for officers' dress or undress uniform, and jackets. Officers also wore **epaulets**, cocked hats, and sword knots in full dress, but dispensed with them otherwise. Petty officers, seamen, and other enlisted sailors wore navy blue jackets or blue wool frocks and blue trousers in cold weather (substituting white frocks and trousers in warm weather), dark blue hats, black silk neckerchiefs, and black shoes or boots.

Marine Corps officers and enlisted men wore uniforms similar to those worn by soldiers in the army, distinguished by scarlet stripes and edging appropriate to the rank of the wearer and U.S.M.C. buttons and insignia.

Revenue Cutter Service uniforms were similar to those of the navy. Officers wore a double-breasted blue frock coat; a buff, blue, or white vest; white or blue pantaloons; a black silk cravat; and a regulation blue Navy cap emblazoned with a gold Treasury shield. Officers wore gold epaulets in full dress and blue shoulder straps embroidered with gold in undress (a pair of **foul anchors** for a cutter's captain, a single foul anchor and two bars for its first lieutenant, a single foul anchor and one bar for its second lieutenant, and a single foul anchor alone for its third lieutenant). Captains were distinguished by two strips of gold lace around their cuffs, first lieutenants by a single strip of gold lace.

Revenue Cutter Service petty officers wore blue jackets and white or blue pantaloons. Seamen, firemen, coal-passers, stewards, cooks, and boys wore either a white frock with blue facings and collar or an all-blue frock, white or blue trousers, and a blue mustering cap or **sennet hat**. The season determined whether white or blue pantaloons or other items were appropriate.

Confederate Uniforms

At the outbreak of the war, many Confederate troops and officers wore civilian clothes or U.S. military uniforms until C.S.A. uniforms could be issued to them by the quartermaster. In early 1861, the Confederate Congress did issue descriptions of what the uniforms in the various services were supposed to look like. Infantrymen, for example, were supposed to wear a "Cadet Gray" double-breasted frock coat with sky-blue facings, sky-blue pants, and a sky-blue kepi with a dark blue band. It is unlikely, however, that any such uniform was actually issued to or worn by very many Confederate troops.

In practice, Confederate soldiers were issued uniforms similar to those worn by their Union counterparts, the main difference being the color, which was usually gray or butternut. Regulations prescribed a mid-length frock coat, but these were always in short supply and infantry and cavalry soldiers alike tended to wear a shell jacket.

As in the North, regulation headgear for soldiers was the kepi, or forage cap. Naturally, however, the shortage of regulation equipment in the South meant the forage caps were often the exception to the rule, which was toward a broad assortment of military and civilian headgear.

C.S. Navy regulation uniform consisted of either a gray jacket, similar to that worn in the U.S. Navy, or a gray wool shirt with white duck cuffs and collar, along with the traditional wide-bottomed trousers. Accessories, such as shoes, boots, silk neckerchiefs, and hats, were all supposed to be black. Early in the war, Confederate sailors tended to wear their old U.S. Navy uniforms, but regulations eventually called for all of their items to be gray, a measure that proved to be quite unpopular. It was a difficult order to fulfill in any case and, throughout the war, sailors and officers alike wore blue, gray, and even black uniforms and, regulations notwithstanding, Confederate seamen often adopted a casual attitude toward their garb. There were some notable exceptions to this rule, however, among them the case of Capt. Raphael Simmes of the CSS *Alabama*, who was adamant that his sailors be in proper, Confederate gray uniforms.

Confederate marines usually dressed like their army infantry counterparts, and revenue service personnel generally looked much like any other Southern sailors.

> Although forage caps were regulation headgear substitutions were frequently made if a regiment desired a distinctive look, if regulation caps were not available, or if individual soldiers preferred different sorts of hats.

Rank and Insignia

The following descriptions of rank and insignia apply mostly to field uniforms. The color and appearance of some accessories varied for dress uniforms.

Branch Insignia

Each branch of the opposing armies had its own distinctive insignia. Some also had distinctive colors associated with them that might be incorporated into uniform components, such as jacket facings or trouser stripes. Branch symbols are described below.

ARTILLERY CORPS	Two crossed field guns, of gold-colored metal. In continuous use since 1834, when they were placed on regimental colors, knapsacks, and as part of the cap insignia for artillery officers. Color: Scarlet.
CAVALRY CORPS	Two crossed sabers in scabbards, cutting edge up, of gold-colored metal. Color: Yellow.

INFANTRY CORPS	A bugle. Color: Sky or light blue.
ENGINEER CORPS	A gold-colored, triple-turreted castle. Selection of the turreted castle as the engineer insignia followed the first major construction undertaken by the Corps of Engineers, the building of a system of castle-like fortifications for the protection of harbors along the Atlantic Coast. These fortifications, many of which are still standing, were called "castles."
MEDICAL DEPARTMENT	A caduceus embroidered in yellow silk on a half chevron of emerald-green silk (worn by hospital stewards).
ORDNANCE CORPS	Flaming bomb, of gold-colored metal. The use of the "shell and flame" by the Ordnance Corps dates back to 1832. It is considered to be the oldest branch insignia of the army. Color: Crimson.

Union Rank and Insignia

Union army and marine rank for both enlisted men and officers was similar in appearance to that worn in the U.S. Army today.

Enlisted men's rank was designated by chevrons—devices shaped like the letter V—and worn on their coat sleeves. Color of U.S. Army chevrons, as for other uniform embellishments, was appropriate to the corps of the wearer: sky blue for infantry, yellow for cavalry, and red for artillery. U.S. Marine Corps chevrons were of yellow silk on a scarlet background.

Union army and marine enlisted men wore the following rank insignia:

PRIVATE	none
CORPORAL	two chevrons
SERGEANT	three chevrons
1ST SERGEANT	a hollow diamond above three chevrons
ORDNANCE SERGEANT	a hollow star above three chevrons
QUARTERMASTER SERGEANT	three stripes above and connecting three chevrons
SERGEANT-MAJOR	three rainbow-shaped stripes above and connecting three chevrons

In addition to rank insignia, enlisted men wore service stripes, diagonal bands just above their jacket cuffs, and were entitled to one stripe for every enlistment or three years of service. Such insignia, however, were not frequently seen in state regiments.

Officers wore rank insignia on their epaulets. Union officers wore the following rank insignia:

SECOND LIEUTENANT	none (that is, empty rectangular shoulder boards)
FIRST LIEUTENANT	one bar on each shoulder

CAPTAIN	two bars on each shoulder
MAJOR	a gold oak leaf on each shoulder
LIEUTENANT COLONEL	a silver oak leaf on each shoulder
COLONEL	a silver eagle on each shoulder
BRIGADIER GENERAL	one silver star on each shoulder
MAJOR GENERAL	two silver stars on each shoulder
LIEUTENANT GENERAL	three silver stars on each shoulder
GENERAL	four silver stars on each shoulder

Union Army Corps Badges

From 1863 onward, Union soldiers wore badges designating their army corps membership, following a tradition begun in the First Corps by Gen. Philip Kearney in 1862. The intent was to build esprit de corps and make soldiers, whether straggling or on the battlefield, recognizable to officers.

These badges were generally of cloth, but soldiers could purchase and wear ones made of colored metal. Corps badges were typically 1½- to 2-inches wide and were generally worn on the front or top of the cap, or on the breast. Eventually, the corps insignias appeared in other places, such as on wagons and ambulances. Officers were sometimes expected to wear the badges in conjunction with colored ribbon or other backgrounds, something that varied widely by corps, which were designated with Roman numerals.

Each corps was generally divided into three divisions, and the color of the badges was in most cases determined accordingly, red for the first division, white for the second division, and blue for the third division. For example, soldiers in the Third Division, V (Fifth Army) Corps, would have worn a blue Maltese cross. If a corps contained a Fourth division, an additional color was selected, yellow or green being typical.

Union army corps wore the following badges. Contemporary terms used to describe them are defined as needed. Most badges were adopted in 1863 but if an exact date for the order of issue is available it is listed. In some cases, part of the order is quoted.

I CORPS	a sphere (circle; March 21, 1863)
II CORPS	a trefoil (three-leaf clover; March 21, 1863)
III CORPS	a lozenge (equilateral diamond; March 21, 1863)
IV CORPS	an equilateral triangle (March 26, 1864)
V CORPS	a Maltese cross (March 21, 1863)
VI CORPS	a Greek cross (cross with equal arms; March 21, 1863)
VII CORPS	a crescent nearly encircling a star (June 1, 1865)
VIII CORPS	a six-pointed star (date uncertain)

IX CORPS	"a shield with the figure nine in the center crossed with a foul anchor and cannon" (April 10, 1864)
X CORPS	no badge
XI CORPS	a crescent (March 21, 1863)
XII CORPS	a five-pointed star (March 21, 1863)
XIII CORPS	no badge
XIV CORPS	an acorn (April 26, 1864)
XV CORPS	a miniature cartridge box with the words "Forty Rounds" above it (February 14, 1865)
XVI CORPS	"a circle with four minié balls, the points toward the center, cut out of it" (no orders issued)
XVII CORPS	an arrow (March 25, 1865)
XVIII CORPS	a cross, worn on the left breast (June 7, 1864)
XIX CORPS	"a fan-leaved cross, with an octagonal center" (November 17, 1864)
XX CORPS	"a star, as heretofore worn by the Twelfth Corps," which, along with the Eleventh, was absorbed into the Twentieth (April 26, 1964)
XXI CORPS	no badge
XXII CORPS	"quinquefarious in form, that is, opening into five parts, and having a circle in the center" (no orders)
XXIII ARMY CORPS	a plain shield (no orders)
XXIV CORPS	a heart (March 18, 1865)
XXV CORPS	a square (February 20, 1865)

Confederate Rank and Insignia

Rank worn by Confederate enlisted men was very similar to that worn by Union soldiers (that is, none for privates, chevrons for corporals and sergeants, chevrons and a diamond for first sergeants, etc.). Color for Confederate army chevrons was supposed to be appropriate to the corps, as in the U.S. Army, but when colored cloth was unavailable chevrons were typically just black.

Rank worn by Confederate officers deviated to a great extent from that worn by their Union counterparts, the most immediately noticeable difference being that it was worn on the collars and sleeves, rather than on shoulder boards. Such rank would have been more important for ceremonial occasions rather than for day-to-day wear and, in practice, company-level Confederate officers—second and first lieutenants and captains—were often indistinguishable from their enlisted men. Confederate officers wore the following rank insignia:

Corporal	Sergeant	First Sergeant
Ordnance Sergeant	Quartermaster Sergeant	Sergeant Major

SECOND LIEUTENANT	one bar on each collar
FIRST LIEUTENANT	two bars on each collar
CAPTAIN	three bars on each collar
MAJOR	one star on each collar
LIEUTENANT COLONEL	two stars on each collar
COLONEL	three stars on each collar
GENERAL OFFICERS	a cluster of three stars inside a wreath on each collar

Flags

Soldiers and civilians of the opposing sides rallied around many different sorts of flags during the war. In addition to the types of flags described on the following pages regiments carried regimental flags and state units carried state flags.

United States Flags

In 1860, on the eve of the rebellion, the U.S. national flag looked much the same as it does today, the only exception being that it had thirty-four, rather than fifty stars (that is, one for each state).

With the formation of the Confederacy in early 1861, the number of states loyal to the Union had been depleted by eleven. Nonetheless, to remove that many stars from the flag would have been a flagrant admission that the Union had failed and could not be restored (indeed, had this been done there might not have been a war at all, nor a United States as we know it today). So, not only were thirty-four stars retained for the nation's flag, additional stars were added in 1863 and 1864, when West Virginia and Nevada, respectively, were admitted to the Union as states.

Confederate Flags

The flag most generally associated with the Rebel cause—a square red field bearing two crossed diagonal blue bands bordered with white, inside of which were thirteen white stars—was not a Confeder-

A Union soldier holds the United States flag on the cover of contemporary sheet music. Stars were not removed from the flag after Southern states seceded. Two stars were added to the flag during the war when West Virginia and Nevada joined the Union.

ate national flag at all. Designed by Gen. P. G. T. Beauregard mainly as battle **colors** for cavalry, infantry, and artillery units, this flag was often given a blue, yellow, orange, or white border. Eventually, the battle flag did become the canton (upper inside corner) of the second and third Confederate national flags.

In March 1861, the Confederate States of America adopted its first national flag, the "Stars and Bars," which consisted of a blue canton holding seven stars and a broad white bar in between two broad red bars. Each of the seven stars represents one of the original Confederate states. This flag, however, was often hard to distinguish from the United States flag, especially during battle, something that led to unintended fratricides and the accidental capture of prisoners-of-war by both sides.

In March 1863, the Confederacy adopted its second national flag, which was intended to bear no resemblance either to the first national flag or the Union's **Stars and Stripes**. It was a solid white field that used for its canton the familiar Rebel battle flag. Unfortunately, in the haze of combat this flag's long white field often made it appear to be a surrender flag. It was this flag that draped Lt. Gen. Stonewall Jackson's casket in 1864 and flew over Fort Sumter until the Confederate evacuation of Charleston in February 1865.

On March 4, 1865, the Confederacy adopted its third national flag, but did not have the opportunity to use it much. It was essentially a modification of the second national flag, with a red stripe added to its fly (outer) end to reduce the chances of it being mistaken for a surrender flag.

To Genl. P. G. T. BEAUREGARD, C. S. A.

BEAUREGARD'S MARCH.

COMPOSED FOR THE PIANO
BY
CHAS. LENSCHOW.

PUBLISHED BY MILLER & BEACHAM, BALTIMORE.

Entered according to Act of Congress, A. D. 1861, by Miller & Beacham, in Clerk's Office of the Dist. Court of Md.

The first national flag of the Confederate States of America, the "Stars and Bars" was difficult to distinguish from the United States flag in battle. In March 1863, a second national flag that looked nothing like the Stars and Bars or the Stars and Stripes was adopted. Unfortunately this flag's long white field often made it appear to be a surrender flag in battle.

Looting

Looting was an inevitable event in the aftermath of battle. In its most innocuous form, it involved the victors helping themselves to needed stores of enemy food, clothing, and equipment. Beyond this, however, looting was extended to dead and wounded soldiers, civilian farmsteads—both occupied and abandoned—and other easy targets. In the aftermath of a battle, poorly-equipped troops, particularly Rebels, would often strip bodies for shoes, uniforms, and anything else of use. Sometimes the looting took on an even more

As in all other wars, soldiers of both sides took part in looting. This ranged from seizing food at farms in enemy territory to taking clothes, money, and other goods from dead or wounded soldiers.

brutal aspect, as in the looting of dead or wounded soldiers for valuables rather than necessities. This phenomenon is most characteristic of the second half of the war, when people were becoming increasingly brutalized by the conflict.

One of the most striking examples of this was the case of Col. Ulric Dahlgren, a Union cavalry officer who led a raid against Richmond, deep into enemy territory, on March 2, 1864. Killed in an ambush by Confederate militia, Dahlgren was stripped of his personal papers, gauntlets, sash, and even his wooden leg, and his mutilated body was publicly displayed in Richmond (while this is sometimes explained by referring to rumors that Dahlgren was intending to assassinate Confederate President Jefferson Davis, it really points to how desensitized many people on both sides had become by 1864).

More disturbing than the pillaging of dead enemy soldiers was the looting of friendly soldiers. Many accounts exist of this being done by hospital orderlies, who were often assigned to such duty because they had shown themselves to be otherwise useless to their regiments. Observers of field hospitals have noted that every dead man and almost every wounded man had his pockets cut open and his personal possessions looted by such ruffians.

Terms

ACCOUTREMENTS, ACCOUTERMENTS: Equipment other than clothes or weapons carried by a soldier, including his belt, blanket roll, cap, cartridge box, canteen, mess kit (i.e., cup, plate, knife, fork, and spoon), haversack, and knapsack or backpack.

AIGUILLETTE: An ornamental tasseled cord worn on dress uniforms after the war. Different colors were often used to distinguish various army corps (e.g., red for Union light infantry, scarlet for artillery, yellow for cavalry, etc.).

ARKANSAS TOOTHPICK: A long, heavy fighting knife with a blade as much as 20 inches in length that was originally carried by sailors in the late eighteenth and early nineteenth centuries and was carried by some soldiers during the war as a personal weapon.

ARMES BLANCHE: A French term that literally means "white weapons" and traditionally referred to swords. In the American armies of the Civil War, its meaning was also extended to the bayonet.

BAR SHOT: A type of artillery shot used primarily against enemy ships. Bar shot consisted of two oval-shaped iron pieces, connected like a pair of paper clips. When fired, the two pieces would extend and whirl through the air like a dull blade that could effectively tear through sails and rigging.

BEECHER'S BIBLES: Term used for the 1848 model .50-caliber Sharps' hunting rifles that Rev. Henry Ward Beecher purchased and sent to antislavery forces in Kansas, using money he had raised to buy Bibles.

BELAYING PIN: A short, club-like wooden pin designed to fit into a hole on the rail of a ship to secure running gear.

BOOTEE: An ankle-high boot or shoe.

BORE: The open part of a cannon barrel into which powder and shot were rammed.

BREACH-LOADER: A weapon that was loaded from the rear, with a cartridge, rather than through the barrel as in the case of a muzzle-loader. Only a small minority of the small arms used during the war were of this type.

BRICOLE: A leather harness, about 18 feet in length, used by artillerymen for dragging guns when horses were unavailable.

BROGANS: Ankle-high black boots that laced in front. Standard for Union soldiers.

BUCK-AND-BALL: One large and three smaller balls used as ammunition for smoothbore muskets, producing an effect similar to that of a shotgun. Such ammunition had terrible range but, when fired in volley, could be devastating at close ranges.

BULL'S-EYE CANTEEN: The M-1858 canteen, which sometimes had nine concentric rings stamped into each side to give it extra strength.

BUMMER'S CAP: A slang term for the regulation army forage cap, so called because its deep crown could be filled with gathered foodstuffs.

CALIBER: The width of a round of small-arms ammunition or artillery ammunition. For weapons during the Civil War, this was generally in inches (e.g., a .60-caliber musket ball was six-tenths of an inch across, and a 10-inch howitzer fired a shell that was 10 inches wide).

CALTROPS (CROW'S FEET): Jack-like metal obstacles with four or more points forged from pieces of iron or nails. Caltrops were scattered across an area to impede enemy cavalry.

CAMP COLORS: Flags 18-inches square, white for infantry and red for artillery, with the number of a regiment on them. Mounted on 8-foot-long poles, they were used to identify the occupants of a camp.

CAMP GEAR: Equipment that armies took to the field with them, including camp cots, field desks, tents, and the like.

CANISTER, CANISTER SHOT, CASE SHOT: Tin containers or bags of shot that could be fired up to two hundred yards, turning a cannon or howitzer into a giant shotgun that was extremely lethal at close ranges. Canister was usually the last thing artillerymen fired at infantry advancing on their positions, generally either crippling the assault or being overrun immediately thereafter.

CANNON: An artillery piece that fired a projectile in a straight line toward its target (compare with howitzer and mortar).

CAP BOX: A small belt pouch intended to hold rifle percussion caps. Cap boxes were manufactured in both the North and South and imported from England by the Confederacy.

CARBINE: A short rifle that was easier for cavalry troops to use than a full-length rifle would have been.

CARTE DE VISITE: Used since the end of the eighteenth century, a small card displaying the name and sometimes the address of the bearer and presented when visiting. During the Civil War, this term was applied to the pornographic cards imported from Europe depicting photographs of nude or scantily clad women.

CARTRIDGE BOX: A rectangular leather box closed with a wide flap and sometimes equipped with a shoulder strap. It could carry up to forty cartridges (usually in a pair of twenty-round tin containers) with a small pocket near the front to hold cleaning supplies. The black, .69-caliber and .58-caliber models were standard on either side. Confederate troops sometimes carried copies made from un-dyed leather.

CHAIN SHOT: A type of artillery projectile used primarily at sea and consisting of two balls connected by a short length of chain. When fired, chain shot would open up in flight and was much more likely to cut through the rigging of enemy ships than regular solid shot. Other versions consisted of a hollow sphere that would break into four pieces when fired, each piece connected by a chain to a round metal plate inside the sphere.

CHAPEAU DE BRAS: A type of hat.

COEHORN MORTAR: A relatively light, 24-pound mortar, used for indirect fire especially against troops hiding in trenches.

COLORS: A battle flag carried by an infantry or other unmounted unit.

CROOKED SHOES: Term used by rustic soldiers to refer to shoes made for left and right feet, as opposed to the straight shoes that could be worn on either feet that were more familiar to them.

DAHLGREN GUN: A large artillery piece used mainly by the Union navy that was invented by U.S. Naval officer John A. Dahlgren.

DITTY-BOX: Originally intended as a collar box but used during the war to carry all sorts of small items. Typically made of sandalwood with hinged gutta-percha covers.

EPAULETS: A shoulder decoration made of stiff gold braid worn on officers' uniforms, with a strap that displayed the regimental number and rank insignia of the wearer.

FEZ: A cap of Turkish or North African design, usually red with a round, flat-topped, brimless crown from which hung a tassel. Such headgear was worn in action by Zouave units and around camp by some other soldiers.

FOUL ANCHOR: An anchor that has become entwined with its own line.

FROG: A leather accessory used to attach a sword or bayonet scabbard to a belt.

GAFF: A piece of shipboard equipment consisting of a metal hook at the end of a pole.

GAITERS: Shin-high leather or cloth leg coverings worn in conjunction with low boots or shoes.

GARRISON FLAG: A national flag flown in a military fort, 36 feet in fly (length) by 20 feet in hoist (height).

GRAPESHOT: Cannon ammunition that consisted of about a dozen small balls of perhaps a pound each, sandwiched together between round pieces of wood.

GUIDON: A small silk flag carried by military units that was often used to signal the execution of commands in battle (when vocal commands alone might go unheard).

HAVELOCK: A cap cover made of white linen that included a short "cape" that covered the wearer's neck. Named for a British general who had designed this item for use in India during the 1850s, this accessory was worn by some regiments early in the war.

HAVERSACK: A leather, cloth, or canvas duck bag about one foot square with a shoulder strap that soldiers used to carry their food and eating utensils. Early in the war, some soldiers purchased non-regulation patent-leather haversacks but were often subsequently ordered to discard them. U.S. Army haversacks tended to be coated with tar, making them more impervious to water than most Confederate models. Regardless of construction, haversacks quickly became soiled from use. "By the time one of these haversacks had been in use for a few weeks as a receptacle for chunks of bacon fat and fresh meat, damp sugar tied up in a rag, potatoes and other vegetables that might be picked up along the route, it took on the color of a printing-office towel," one soldier wrote.

HOT SHOT: Solid artillery shot that was heated red-hot so as to set fire to buildings or ships.

HOWITZER: An artillery piece that fired a projectile in a low arc toward its target (compare with cannon and mortar).

IDENTIFICATION DISKS: Such devices were not issued to troops, but many individuals carried handmade metal or wood disks, or even scraps of paper, that could be used to identify them should they die in battle. Some were stamped with slogans like "Against Slavery" or "War of 1861." The widespread carnage of the Civil War, in which an entire company might be wiped out in one battle, made such identification a new necessity of war.

JEFFERSON BOOTS: A type of ankle-high boot or shoe.

KIT, KIT BAG: Informal term for a soldier's knapsack and its contents.

KNAPSACK: A leather or waterproof canvas backpack, sometimes mounted on a wooden frame, with a single pocket that was intended to carry a wool blanket, rubber blanket, or tent half. Most soldiers discarded the previous contents to make room for extra food, clothing, ammunition, and personal possessions; for a variety of reasons, many soldiers on both sides carried blanket rolls, or mule collars, rather than knapsacks. Most knapsacks were 14 or 15 inches wide, 15 to 17 inches high, and 4 or 5 inches deep.

MINIÉ BALL, MINNIE BALL: A conical lead ball that was standard ammunition for Civil War-era rifles and took its name from French army officer Claude Etienne Minié, who invented it in 1848. The minié ball was designed to be rammed down the bore of a weapon quickly and easily (although this was not always the case). It would expand when fired, catching the rifling of the weapon and spinning out of the barrel with much greater velocity than a standard musket ball. A preponderance of wounds during the war, especially those that required amputation, were inflicted by minié balls.

MORTAR: An artillery piece that fired a projectile in a high, indirect arc toward its target, which was often unseen by the gunners. Such weapons were not nearly as accurate as other artillery pieces and were generally fired into large areas rather

than at specific targets (compare with cannon and howitzer).

MULE COLLAR, HORSE COLLAR: The rolled blanket or quilt worn diagonally over one shoulder by soldiers and used to carry their belongings. Confederate troops often used this arrangement because of a lack of backpacks, while toward the end of the war, many Union troops adopted it instead of their own heavy backpacks. Regulations called for it to be worn over the left shoulder, but photographs of the period indicate soldiers often wore it over the right shoulder as well.

MUZZLE-LOADER: A firearm loaded through the front-end or barrel of the weapon, rather than through the breach or rear-end. Most small arms used during the war were of this type.

NAPOLEON 12-POUNDER: The 1857-model Napoleon,

a brass, smoothbore, muzzle-loading howitzer that was the basic artillery piece manufactured and used by both the Union and the Confederacy. Its name derived from the fact that it was the gun France adopted in 1856 while under Napoleon III. An experienced crew could fire three rounds a minute with this gun, which was also referred to as "the gun howitzer" and "the light 12-pounder."

OSTRICH FEATHERS, BLACK: Often used by cavalrymen to adorn the left side of their hats–one feather for enlisted men, two for company-grade officers and three for field-grade officers.

PARROTT GUN, PARROTT RIFLE: Introduced in 1862, this was America's first rifled cannon; its name derived from that of its inventor, Robert Parker Parrott, a West Point physics instructor who spent a decade developing the gun after learning that a German artillery firm had manufactured a similar weapon. This weapon played a significant role in the Union victory.

PERCUSSION CAPS: A small brass or copper cap filled with mercury fulminate that fit over a nipple on the lock of a rifle or musket. When the hammer of a cocked weapon snapped down and hit the cap, it would explode, sending a spark into the breach of the weapon, igniting the powder and discharging the ball.

PISTOL: Either a single-shot handgun or a revolver. Single-shot pistols were used mostly by the navy and Revenue Cutter Service or as civilian weapons. They could be either muzzle-loaded with powder and ball, like a musket (as with most regulation weapons), or, more rarely, breach-loaded with a metallic cartridge (as with several civilian models). Revolvers

included a metal cylinder that had five or six chambers into which could be loaded either black powder and lead balls or paper cartridges containing powder and a lead bullet. Percussion caps placed on hollow nipples at the rear of each chamber would discharge the ammunition. A revolver's metal cylinder would rotate when the weapon was cocked. Such weapons had greater rates of fire than single-shot weapons (but also took five or six times longer to reload).

PUP TENT: A slang term used from about 1863 to refer to the army's two-man tents. See shelter tent.

RIFLING: Spiral grooves cut into the inside of a weapon barrel that cause the ammunition being fired to spin, imparting upon it greater velocity and more stability in flight. Smoothbore muskets were inaccurate at ranges of greater than

100 yards, whereas rifled weapons could be lethal at 250 yards or more.

ROUND SHOT: The round iron balls that made up the majority of ammunition fired from artillery pieces. The weight of each piece of ammunition was identified by the sort of gun it was fired from; for example, a 12-pound Napoleon fired 12-pound iron round shot.

SENNET HAT: A type of white straw hat used by seamen during the war and officially authorized by the U.S. Navy starting in 1866.

SHELTER TENT: From about 1863, this term referred to a small, two-man tent that hung from a ridge rope supported by two poles.

SLOUCH HAT: A British style of soft, brimmed hat introduced to Americans in the 1830s and worn widely by soldiers of both sides,

especially Southerners, during the Civil War.

STARS AND STRIPES: The primary nickname for the United States flag.

SWORD BAYONET: A bayonet, usually with a single-edged blade, long enough to be either mounted on a rifle or used as a short sword. Such weapons were typically 18 to 24 inches in length.

WELLINGTONS: Ankle-high boots without laces in the front.

CIVIL WAR PHOTOGRAPHY
BY MAUREEN A. TAYLOR

Photography in the 1860s exposed American families to the reality of war. It's not that cameras weren't present at earlier conflicts. Portraits and some miscellaneous views exist from the Mexican American War, 1846-1848, and Roger Fenton, considered the first wartime photographer, documented the Crimean War between May and June 1855.

The Civil War was different. Battlefield images in crisp, clear photographic detail brought death into our ancestral homes while portraits of Presidents and generals created iconic figures. Never before had the American public seen such striking photographs. The war changed the way a generation interacted with the medium. Families treasured the pictures loved ones sent back from the war front and hoped not to see dead relatives in battlefield views. The photographs taken during the war—portraits of soldiers in uniform, battlefield scenes, home front images and even images taken for propaganda—all fueled the patriotism on both sides of the conflict and made photography part of the fabric of the Civil War.

On the Brink

In 1839, Americans gazed upon shiny reflective metal daguerreotype portraits for the first time. Constant improvements in photographic technology in the 1850s had made new formats, including glass ambrotypes, iron tintypes, and paper prints, extremely popular. On the eve of the Civil War, theoretically, an individual walking into a photo studio could choose from this wide variety of image types. Inexpensive card photographs or tintypes could be carried in a small pocket or

Union Sergeant Amos Humiston died on the battlefield of Gettysburg clutching this ambrotype of his children. The story captivated the nation and copies of the photo were sold to raise funds for a National War Orphans Homestead.

enclosed in a letter. Most cities and towns had at least one photo studio and rural folks could obtain a likeness from an itinerant photographer. The 1860 United States Census enumerated more than 3,154 individuals who claimed photography to be their sole occupation.[1] These numbers may not include businesses that offered photography as a side pursuit.

While landscape photography was available, the vast majority of images taken during the pre-Civil War period depicted individuals—men, women and children seeking original portraits or copy prints of earlier portraits. By 1861, thousands of Americans owned portraits of themselves and relatives. Millions more would be taken during the conflict itself with soldiers seeking to send portraits home and relatives posing for mementos to send to the men in the military.

On the battlefield, it was not uncommon to find a deceased soldier clutching a photo of a loved one. The most famous account of this is the story of Union Sergeant Amos Humiston, who was killed at Gettysburg. Humiston was found clutching an ambrotype of three children. His identity, and that of the children in the photo, was unknown to those who found him. The photo ended up in the possession of Dr. John C. Bournes, who had tended troops at Gettysburg. Bournes was moved by the dead man's final moments and wrote about them in a local newspaper. After the story was retold in numerous newspapers across the country, Bournes paid for thousands of copies of the ambrotype to be sent throughout New England and the Mid-Atlantic in the hopes that someone could identify the children and give a name to the soldier. Months after Humiston's death, his wife read the story, sought out a copy of the ambrotype and identified the children as her own. With the identification, the three fatherless children served as a catalyst for a national movement to care for children orphaned by the war. Additional pictures of them were sold to raise funds for a National War Orphans Homestead.[2]

1. Keith F. Davis, *The Origins of American Photography, 1839-1885 From Daguerreotype to Dry-Plate* (Kansas City, Missouri: Nelson-Atkins, 2007) 174.

2. William C. Darrah, *Cartes de Visite in Nineteenth Century Photographs* (Gettysburg, Penn.: W. C. Darrah, 1981) 84-85.

Union troops stand in formation in front of the Capitol building. Although some photos were taken during the Mexican War and the Crimean War, the Civil War was the first war captured in great detail through photography.

Documenting the War

As early as 1860–1861, prominent Washington and New York photographer Mathew Brady recognized the importance of photographically documenting the coming war. He met with Abraham Lincoln and received handwritten permission from the President to freely photograph the conflict. Although he is the best-known war-time photographer, he was not the only one engaged in this pursuit. In 1862 Alexander Gardner left Brady's employ to work as General George McClellan's Official Photographer for the Army of the Potomac.[3] As many as three hundred photographers in the Union received passes to photograph the action, but some estimates run as high as 1,000 to 1,500 other photographers that followed the troops without passes.

These military photographers took pictures of maps and wartime engineering. Their job was to document the war, including photographing bridges, buildings, and field fortifications. The U.S. Army Military Medical Department photographed the casualties of war. After the conflict, they were published in the *Medical and Surgical History of the War of the Rebellion* (6 vols).[4]

By the end of the war, Timothy O'Sullivan, an employee of Brady, was only one officially sanctioned photographer traveling with the U.S. Army on its last campaign. From 1864–65, O'Sullivan followed general Ulysses S. Grant as he led his troops from the siege at Petersburg to the Appomattox courthouse in Virginia where Grant accepted surrender from Confederate general Robert E. Lee.[5]

3. Keith, *Origins of American Photography*, 178.

4. Darrah, *Cartes de Visite in the Nineteenth Century*, 78.

In the South, only about one hundred photographers were sanctioned to work with the Confederate Army. At the onset of the war, photographer George S. Cook supplied portraits of significant individuals in the Confederate government for commercial reproduction. J.D. Edwards and the studio of Osborn and Durbec took photographs early in the conflict. However, by 1862, the Union blockade of Southern ports prevented the influx of supplies, drove up the cost of goods and very few images were taken by Confederate photographers. Cook was able to continue his work until 1863. While the first photographs of the war were taken by Confederates, few photographs of the South still exist.[6]

Many photographers set up mobile studios that followed to armies to fill the large demand for portraits of individual soldiers. The Bergstresser Brothers spent two years following troops, and it's estimated that they took 160 portraits a day, charging a dollar each.[7]

This unidentified soldier wears a Confederate uniform of Co. E, "Lynchburg Rifles," 11th Virginia Infantry Volunteers. He holds an 1841 "Mississippi" rifle and is equipped with a Sheffield-type Bowie knife, canteen, box knapsack, blanket roll, and cartridge box. Few photographs from the South survived the war and its aftermath.

Mathew Brady

Mathew Brady first established himself as a studio photographer in 1844 in New York City. He was well known for his portraits of famous individuals. Brady saw photography as a way to preserve history. In 1860, he created a composite portrait in two panels of the 250 members of the House and Senate and sold them to the public.

---

5. Richard F. Selcer, *Civil War America, 1850 to 1875* (New York: Facts on File, 2006).

6. Martha A. Sandweiss, ed., *Photography in Nineteenth-Century America* (New York: Amon Carter Museum, 1991) 135.

7. Sandweiss, *Photography in Nineteenth-Century America*, 144.

Photographers most often sought out scenes that would appeal to families at home, such as soldiers playing games or relaxing during encampment.

Timothy O'Sullivan, an employee of Mathew Brady, captured this image of dead Union soldiers at Gettysburg in July 1863. Titled "A Harvest of Death," it was probably the most iconic battlefield image from the Civil War.

While the images by Mathew Brady's studio are synonymous with the war, few were actually taken by Brady himself. He was at the First Battle of Bull Run attempting to capture the action, but lost all of his equipment in the stampede away from the field. Brady's poor eyesight prevented him from actively photographing scenes; instead he coordinated the action—commissioning, gathering, and selling pictures. He hired men for the field or used studio employees such as Gardner, a Scottish immigrant who worked as his studio manager. Brady's team of photographers, which included Gardner and Timothy O'Sullivan (who would later become famous for views of the West), traveled to the battlefields in photographic wagons and took images on 7 × 9-inch glass plates. There were plenty of obstacles to obtaining a print. Photographers had to coat each negative with light sensitive chemicals and then use them almost immediately. This wet-plate process was cumbersome and time consuming and fragile. Any dirt, bug, or fingerprint that found its way onto the glass during preparation, exposure, or development could ruin the image. The long exposure time (from ten to thirty seconds) and the timeliness of the process precluded any real action scenes. However, once a negative was obtained, an unlimited number of prints could be produced from it.[8]

Battlefield images show primarily dead Confederate soldiers because in many cases, Union soldier were already buried by the time photographers arrived on the scene. In fact, in many of Gardner's Gettysburg shots, the same body was re-posed in different images.[9]

8. Keith, *Origins of American Photography*, 173-205; David S. Heidler and Jeanne T. Heidler, ed., *Encyclopedia of the American Civil War* (Santa Barbara, Calif. : ABC-CLIO, 2000) 1514

9. Davis, *Origins of American Photography*, 186.

Brady's photographers, and others, weren't concerned with capturing only the carnage. They were on the lookout for scenes that would appeal at home, such as soldiers playing cards or relaxing during encampment. Everyday life in the military included military bands, prisons, and hospitals. These photographers also captured family and town life, along with destroyed buildings and landscapes.

In 1862, the *New York Times* reviewed an exhibit of Antietam battlefield photos at the Brady studio and remarked that he'd "done something to bring home to us the terrible reality and earnestness of war. If he has not brought bodies and laid them in our door-yards and along the streets he has done something very like it."[10] Gardner and James Gibson shot these images for Brady. The exhibit brought emotional crowds to see the dramatic images. It coincided with engravings of the images appearing in *Harper's Weekly* in late 1862. While newspaper publishing didn't include the reproduction of actual photographs, a detailed engraving could be made of the scene and then printed.

Francis E. Brownell, ("Ellsworth's Avenger"), posed here in his Zouave uniform, became a national hero for avenging the death of his commanding officer. This image was sold as part of a popular set of stereographs.

Death was omnipresent during the war. Friends, relatives, and neighbors all enlisted for the cause and a high death toll meant that nearly everyone knew a soldier who perished. It is no wonder that probably the most famous photograph of the war is Timothy O'Sullivan's "Harvest of Death" which shows the bodies of Union soldiers scattered over the Gettysburg field. In the summer of 1862, the first "spirit" photographs appeared. They usually depicted families or individuals with a "ghostly image" behind them or near them. The public loved these images, which use a double exposure to lead the viewer to believe that a ghostly apparition had been captured by the camera.[11]

War Photo Profits

In 1861, the *Boston Transcript* wrote that, "any photographer who would follow the army ... and be fortunate enough to obtain views of battles, or even skirmishes, would make a fortune by sale of copies."[12] Edward Anthony proved this statement to be accurate.

He began his career as a daguerreotypist in late 1840 or early 1841. By 1847, he focused his energy on manufacturing photographic equipment and on publishing images. His brother Henry joined him in 1852 creating E & HT Anthony & Co.

10. New York Times (October 20, 1862) 5.

11. Sandweiss, *Photography in Nineteeth-Century America*, 148.

12. "Photographic Views of the Army" *Boston Transcript*, June 10, 1861, 2.

Stereographs consisted of identical images mounted side-by-side on card stock. When viewed through a stereopticon viewer, the image appeared three-dimensional. This stereograph set shows the bridge at Hampton, Virginia, after it was burned by Confederate forces.

After the war broke out, Anthony's company struck a deal with Brady's studio manager, Alexander Gardner, and purchased publishing rights to Brady's images, from which they produced stereo cards and carte des visite (small paper prints about 2.5 × 4 inches). Anthony distributed these collectable images in sets or single prints both direct to consumers through catalogs and also through booksellers across America. Newspaper ads announced new photographic offerings.

He sold pictures the public wanted, starting with an image of Fort Sumter's Major Robert Anderson taken by George S. Cook. Anthony's company printed a thousand copies of Anderson's portrait daily, at the height of public interest in the opening battle of the war.

Anthony again capitalized on war events using Brady's images to create a photographic memorial of the first Union casualty of the war, Colonel Elmore Ellsworth, a close friend and former law clerk of President Lincoln. The memorial included a portrait of Ellsworth (taken by Brady at his Washington studio at the start of the war), a photo of the Marshall House (the Alexandria, Virginia, inn where Ellsworth was killed while taking down a flag), and a portrait of Francis Brownell (the soldier who slay the man who killed Ellsworth). The memorial was a runaway best seller.[13]

Anthony's business was so successful he couldn't keep up with the daily demand for thousands of card photographs. The technology needed to mass-produce and enlarge photographs had not been developed yet, so each card required development, which slowed down the production

13. Davis, *Origins of American Photography*, 176.

14. Davis, *Origins of American Photography*, 175.

This print was part of a series of sympathetic images sold by the American Missionary Association and the National Freedman's Relief Association in 1864 to raise money for the education of former slaves.

OUR PROTECTION.

ROSA, CHARLEY, REBECCA.

Slave Children from New Orleans.

process. The size of the print corresponded to the negative. For 25 cents each, a customer could own images of encampments at Bull Run, or portraits of Lincoln and his generals. These images fueled Union patriotism. An even cheaper, but more time-consuming, alternative was for a company to produce lithographs or engravings of popular photographs. Twenty of these prints could be sold for a dollar.[14]

In addition to card photographs or oversize views, Anthony and other studios sold stereographs of the war. These three-dimensional images were comprised of identical images mounted side by side on card stock and then viewed through a special device called a stereopticon viewer. Sets usually cost around four dollars a dozen; hand-colored ones were a dollar more.[15]

Alexander Gardener shot stereo-size negatives at Gettysburg. These negatives could be printed as a stereograph or a single side could become a carte de visite.

During the war, customers left photography studios with patriotic-themed images, such as cased ambrotypes surrounded by a mat of flags and stars. Carte des visite and tintypes also often featured national symbols of patriotism on the back or paper mat.

The backs of these card photographs bear witness to the Federal government's attempts to finance the conflict in the form of revenue stamps. Legislation that took effect August 1, 1864, required photographers to initial, date, and place tax stamps on the backs of images they sold. Few

15. Selcer, *Civil War America*, 1850 to 1875, 375.

16. Darrah, *Cartes de Visite in the Nineteenth Century*, 87.

Startling pictures of war wounds brought to public attention the realities of surviving battles. This one-legged veteran was photographed by Bell & Brother of Washington, DC.

fully complied with the initialing and dating, but the stamps themselves provide details about the cost of these card portraits. Two-cent stamps were applied to photographs costing less than 25 cents, and images worth 25 to 50 cents bore 3-cent stamps. Photographs that cost from 50 cents to a dollar bore 5-cent stamps. Tax stamps could be combined for added value. A modification to the law in March 1865 lowered the tax on images that cost less than 10 cents to 1 cent each. Congress repealed the law on August 1, 1866.[16]

There were also photographs that could be projected. The Langenheim Brothers of Philadelphia made glass transparencies of engravings of war scenes and projected them using a magic lantern.[17] A series of paper prints could be mounted in a circular device known as a zoetrope, which moved to project a moving image, much like a flip-book.

Photos and Fundraising

In the Union, one of the ways Sanitary commissions raised money to provide services for the troops was by selling images of the war. Other photographers followed this example. Photographer Frederick Gutekunst of Philadelphia sold copies of his images of Gettysburg with all monies benefiting injured or sick soldiers.[18]

17. Sandweiss, *Photography in Nineteenth-Century America*, 147.

18. Sandweiss, *Photography in Nineteenth-Century America*, 142.

19. Keith, *Origins of American Photography*, 196.

After the war, other groups commissioned specific images to sell as fundraisers. The American Missionary Association and the National Freedman's Relief Association raised money for free public education of former slaves by selling a series of photographs featuring eight students. The students' light colored skin and slave heritage brought home the message that these children could be your own. Abolitionist Sojourner Truth copyrighted her own photo so that she could profit from its sale rather than another group or agency. She sought employment for the emancipated and printed on her cards, "I Sell the Shadow to Support the Substance."[19]

Aftermath

Photographs kept the war memories alive and were just as popular after the conflict as during. Stereograph sets such as "Anthony's War for the Union" (1865) were in-demand as were numerous compilations of images by well-known photographers, among them *Gardner's Photographic Sketchbook of the War* (1866) and George N. Barnard's *Photographic Views of Sherman's Campaign* (1866). Gardner's *Sketchbook* contained seventy-five to one hundred battlefields and landscapes, ten portraits, and fifteen of camp life. This was nineteenth century print-on-demand technology as the number of printed copies equaled the number of orders.

Photographer's capitalized on the end of the war with sentimental staged card photographs showing simulated skirmishes between soldiers or warm homecomings. Startling pictures of war wounds brought to public attention the realities of surviving battles, while images documenting emaciated Union prisoners of war held in Confederate camps bear a haunting resemblance to twentieth century concentration camp survivors.

The reality of Civil War photography is that few battlefields were actually represented in photographs. It took time and money to travel to far-flung battlefields. Unfortunately, despite estimates that one million images were taken during the war, many sites were never or barely photographed. For instance, only one image of Fort Sumter exists. Several hundred thousand of those one million images are now thought to be lost.

While it appears that there are many photographs of deceased soldiers, those images come from primarily seven instances. Photographs were also used for war-time propaganda. An often photographed armament, the Dictator mortar, was rarely used, but photographs provide evidence of the massive gun.

In the 1880s, the Massachusetts group, Military Order of the Loyal Legion of the United States, set out to collect images of the war. In the 1970s, these images became part of the United States Army Heritage and Education Center (USAHEC) at Carlisle Barracks. Frances Trevelyan Miller's 1911/1912 Photographic History of the Civil War pictures, as well as those borrowed and copied for the publication, were donated to USAHEC as well.

The fact that photographs were taken during the war, changed the nature of war reportage. For the first time, photographic as well as journalist depictions of events could be used to tell the story of an event. Never again would the public have to imagine the horrors of war based on verbal descriptions; images would confront them with the gory reality.

CIVIL WAR TIMELINE

Major events of the Civil War and the period preceding and following it are listed on the following timeline.

While the Civil War was the result of decades of increasing tensions, the timeline begins in 1859 with abolitionist John Brown's raid on Harpers Ferry, Virginia, an event that portended the violence that was soon to sweep the nation. The timeline continues through 1877 and the end of Reconstruction. As with the years leading up to the Civil War, the legacy of the war continued long past Reconstruction, but the timeline concludes with the official reunification of the country.

The 1861 dates that the various Southern states seceded from the Union are listed. Note that seceding from the Union and joining the Confederacy were not, technically, synonymous acts. However, all states that seceded did join the Confederacy shortly thereafter.

Battles were sometimes known by different names in the North and South (for example, Northerners referred to the Battle of Antietam, while Southerners knew it as the Battle of Sharpsburg). Thus, in many cases the Southern name for the battle is given in parentheses. This difference in the names of battles can be attributed the fact that the Union tended to name battles for nearby streams, while the Confederacy generally named them for towns.

Initially, the Confederacy bested the Union on the battlefield. These early victories ultimately prolonged the war and, had the Federal government been able to deliver enough crushing defeats to the rebellion early on, the conflict might have ended in its first year. Three battles—Antietam in September 1862 and Gettysburg and Vicksburg in July 1863—heralded the shifting of the war in favor of the Union and represented major setbacks for the Confederacy.

In the casualty listings for major battles, numbers are given for troops missing; soldiers might be so classified because of desertion, capture, or death from which their bodies were not recovered (for example, from drowning, crawling into a ravine to die, etc.).

Events for which a specific date is not important (for example, the invention of some item or creation of a work of art) are simply listed under the year they occurred.

Note that leaders, such as generals, are listed with the ranks they held during a particular event and that they may have subsequently held different titles.

To help make it easier to follow the major events of the timeline, many are labeled with symbols. This key is for ease of reference and is not intended to make value judgments (that is, by labeling an event military rather than political).

E = military events in the eastern theater

W = military events in the western theater (that is., the Mississippi River valley)

P = political, rather than military, events (such as secessions)

C = civil unrest

1859

Alexandre Edmond Becquerel invents the fluorescent lightbulb (which is not perfected for another eighty years). The Great Atlantic and Pacific Tea Company (A&P) is founded. A "bellows-and-box" hand-powered vacuum cleaner is patented. Edwin Drake discovers and begins drilling for oil in Titusville, Pennsylvania. The first paper clothing patterns are sold under the name "Mme. Domoreset's Mirror of Fashions." Darwin's *Origin of Species* is published.

(C) OCT. 16, 1859: Fanatical abolitionist John Brown leads a force of eighteen armed men into Harpers Ferry, Virginia (now West Virginia), seizing the town and the Federal arsenal. A unit of marines commanded by U.S. Army Col. Robert E. Lee arrives the next day and battles Brown's followers, killing ten of them; Brown himself is wounded. Charged with treason, Brown arouses sympathy amongst Northerners, many of whom consider him a martyr, and outrage amongst Southern whites, who consider him a dangerous fanatic.

(P) DEC. 2, 1859: John Brown is hanged. His death eventually comes to symbolize the coming violence of the Civil War.

1860

Louis Pasteur demonstrates the process of killing germs with heat (i.e., pasteurization). Hamilton Smith patents an early washing machine (by 1873, more than two thousand additional patents for washing machines are issued). English inventor and industrialist Sir Henry Bessemer patents the tilting converter for steel manufacture.

(P) NOVEMBER 6, 1860: Abraham Lincoln is elected president of the United States.

(P) DEC. 20, 1860: South Carolina's legislature, perceiving a threat to the state's autonomy from the presidential election of Abraham Lincoln, a known opponent of slavery, votes to secede from the United States of America. It is the first Southern state to secede.

1861

Kansas is admitted to the Union as the thirty-fourth state. Van Camp introduces canned pork and beans. Julius Sturgis begins commercially baking pretzels in Lititz, Pennsylvania. Linus Yale patents the pin-tumbler lock. An early form of the bicycle dubbed a "bone shaker" is developed.

(P) JANUARY–FEBRUARY 1861: Six more Southern states (Mississippi, Florida, Alabama, Georgia, Louisiana, and Texas), driven by a perception of Abraham Lincoln as an especially strong opponent of slavery, declare their secession from the Union and form the Confederate States of America. Lame duck U.S. President James Buchanan (Lincoln's predecessor) refuses to surrender Federal forts in the South to the seceding states and Confederate troops respond by seizing them.

(P) JANUARY 9, 1861: Mississippi secedes from the Union, the second state to do so. In South Carolina, the first shots of the war are fired when military cadets from the Citadel fire upon Star of the West, a supply ship attempting to resupply Union-held Fort Sumter in Charleston Harbor.

(P) JANUARY10, 1861: Florida secedes from the Union.

(P) JANUARY 11, 1861: Alabama secedes from the Union.

(P) JANUARY 19, 1861: Georgia secedes from the Union.

(P) JANUARY 26, 1861: Louisiana secedes from the Union.

(P) FEBRUARY 1, 1861: Texas secedes from the Union (approved by Texas voters February 23).

(P) FEBRUARY 4, 1861: Delegates from the six seceding Southern states convene in Montgomery, Alabama. They begin to draft a constitution for the Confederate States of America, similar to the U.S. Constitution but with greater emphasis on the autonomy of each state and protection of the institution of slavery.

(P) FEBRUARY 8, 1861: The seceding Southern states form the Confederate States of America.

(P) FEBRUARY 9, 1861: Pending elections, the delegates select Jefferson Davis as provisional president of the Confederacy.

(P) FEBRUARY 18, 1861: Jefferson Davis is inaugurated provisional president of the Confederate States of America.

(P) MARCH 4, 1861: Lincoln is inaugurated president of the United States of America. At the ceremony, the new president says he has no plans to end slavery in states where it already exists. He also declares that secession is unacceptable and expresses hope that the national crisis can be resolved without warfare.

(P) MARCH 6, 1861: Jefferson Davis, with the authorization of the C.S. Congress, calls for 100,000 one-year volunteers for the Confederate military forces.

(P) MARCH 1861: About equally divided between secessionists and Unionists, an Arkansas state convention votes against secession.

(E) APRIL 1861: President Lincoln informs South Carolina that he is planning to send supplies to Fort Sumter. Although the president's goal is to avoid conflict, South Carolina fears trickery and demands the immediate surrender of the fort. Maj. Robert Anderson offers to surrender once his supplies are exhausted but Confederate authorities reject this offer.

(E) APRIL 12-13, 1861: Confederate artillery batteries under Gen. P.G.T. Beauregard fire on Union-held Fort Sumter in the harbor of Charleston, South Carolina. After a heavy bombardment, Fort Sumter surrenders to South Carolina. Armed rebellion has begun.

APRIL 15, 1861: Abraham Lincoln calls for 75,000 volunteers for the Federal forces.

(P) APRIL–JUNE 1861: Encouraged by the attack on Fort Sumter, four more states—Virginia, Arkansas, Tennessee, and North Carolina—join the Confederacy.

(P) APRIL 17, 1861: Virginia secedes from the Union and joins the Confederacy. Soon after, in May, the capital of the Confederacy is moved from Montgomery, Alabama, to Richmond, Virginia.

(C) APRIL 19, 1861: A mob of Southern sympathizers attacks the Sixth Massachusetts Regiment as it marches through the streets of Baltimore, Maryland, on its way to Washington, DC. Four soldiers and twenty rioters are killed.

(P) MAY 6, 1861: Reversing a vote of just two months earlier, an Arkansas state convention votes to secede from the Union and join the Confederate States of America. The Confederacy recognizes a state of war with the United States.

(P) MAY 20, 1861: North Carolina opts to secede and join the Confederacy.

(E) MAY 1861: Forces under Union Maj. Gen. George B. McClellan drive rebel forces out of western Virginia as far as the Alleghenies, bringing this anti-secessionist portion of the state under U.S. control. For his success, McClellan earns the nickname "Young Napoleon."

(P) JUNE 8, 1861: Tennessee votes to secede from the Union, the last Southern state to do so. The state is torn between almost unanimous support for the Union in its eastern third and equally strong support of the Confederacy in the middle and west.

(P) JUNE 1861: Although they are slave states and have divided loyalties, Delaware, Kentucky, Maryland, and Missouri remain within the Union, largely through a combination of military pressure from the Federal government and political maneuvering by Lincoln and other politicians.

(E) JULY 21, 1861: FIRST BATTLE OF BULL RUN (FIRST BATTLE OF MANASSAS). Bowing to public demand, Union General-in-Chief Winfield Scott orders Brig. Gen. Irvin McDowell to advance on Confederate troops stationed at Manassas Junction, Virginia, even though the Union troops are inadequately trained and untried. McDowell's attack is initially successful but the arrival of Confederate reinforcements results in a Southern victory and the rout of the Federal forces back to Washington. Fearing a protracted war and mindful of the army's need for training and organization, Lincoln replaces McDowell with McClellan, the "Young Napoleon."

Casualties of the battle include 460 killed, 1,124 wounded, and 1,312 missing Union soldiers and 387 killed, 1,582 wounded, and 13 missing Confederate soldiers.

(P) JULY 1861: Federal naval blockade of Southern ports begins to take effect, largely because of improvements in the U.S. Navy. The Confederacy responds by building small, fast ships that can outmaneuver the heavier Union vessels and be used to run their blockade, carrying cotton and spies out of southern ports and weapons and other goods into them.

(E) NOVEMBER 7, 1861: A naval bombardment by warships under Union Capt. Samuel F. Dupont drives the defenders from Confederate-held forts Walker and Beauregard, in South Carolina. This allows soldiers under Union Brig. Gen. Thomas W. Sherman to occupy Port Royal, Beaufort, and all the Sea Islands of South Carolina.

(P) NOVEMBER 8, 1861: THE TRENT AFFAIR. USS *San Jacinto*, under Capt. Charles Wilkes, stops the British ship *Trent* in international waters and seizes Confederate Commissioner to England J.M. Mason and Confederate Commissioner to France John Slidell (because the Confederacy was not recognized as a sovereign state, it had to send commissioners, rather than ambassadors, to appeal for aid and recognition). The two are transported to Boston, where they are imprisoned. Britain reacts strongly, and President Lincoln and Secretary of State William H. Seward disavow the action and release the two commissioners.

1862

Ebenezer Butterick creates the pattern for the Garibaldi blouse. The Federal navy launches its first ironclad warship, USS *Monitor*. Julia Ward Howe's *Battle Hymn of the Republic* is published in the *Atlantic Monthly*. The Internal Revenue Service is created.

(E) JANUARY 27, 1862: Lincoln issues General War Order No. 1, authorizing Union forces to launch a unified assault against the Confederacy. Union Maj. Gen. McClellan, overall commander of the Federal armies, ignores this order.

(W) FEBRUARY 6, 1862: U.S. Army Brig. Gen. Ulysses S. Grant captures Fort Henry, Tennessee.

(W) FEBRUARY 16, 1862: Confederate Gen. Simon Bolivar Buckner surrenders Fort Donelson, Tennessee, to Union Brig. Gen. Grant. This was the Union's first major victory of the war, and it destroyed the Rebel base of power in Tennessee and Kentucky.

(W) FEBRUARY 21, 1862: BATTLE OF VALVERDE. This first battle of the New Mexico campaign, fought near Fort Craig in the New Mexico Territory, was a significant Confederate victory. Casualties included 111 killed, 160 wounded, and 204 missing or captured Union soldiers (along with the loss of six artillery piece) and 150 to 230 killed or wounded Confederate soldiers.

(P) FEBRUARY 22, 1862: After officially being elected to a six-year term as president of the Confederate States of America, Jefferson Davis is inaugurated in Richmond, Virginia.

(P) FEBRUARY 25, 1862: For the first time, the U.S. Congress authorizes the issue of legal tender banknotes. Union forces occupy Nashville, Tennessee.

(E) MARCH 1862: Confederate Lt. Gen. Thomas J. "Stonewall" Jackson, commanding troops in the Shenandoah Valley, attacks Union forces and causes them to retreat across the Potomac River. This results in Union troops being rushed to protect Washington, DC, from possible Confederate attack.

(W) MARCH 7–8, 1862: BATTLE OF PEA RIDGE (BATTLE OF ELKHORN TAVERN). Union forces defeat Confederate troops in a bloody battle at Pea Ridge, Arkansas. Over a two-day period, Confederate Maj. Gen. Earl Van Dorn sends his 16,000-man force, which includes some Texas cavalrymen and two regiments of Cherokee Indians, against a dug-in force of 10,250 Union soldiers under Maj. Gen. Samuel R. Curtis. Union casualties include 203 killed, 980 wounded, and 201 missing. Confederate casualties include about a thousand killed or wounded and three hundred captured.

(E) MARCH 9, 1862: CSS *Virginia*, an ironclad warship, attacks and destroys two wooden Union warships off of Norfolk, Virginia. Steaming down the coast from New York, USS *Monitor* arrives on the scene before the Confederate ship can wreak any more havoc. The two ironclad warships engage in a five-hour battle in Hampton Roads, Virginia, the first such battle between armored vessels. The Confederate vessel had originally been the scuttled Union frigate USS *Merrimac*, which the Confederacy retrieved, renovated, and outfitted with iron plate and a ram.

(W) APRIL 6–7, 1862: BATTLE OF SHILOH. In the first great bloodbath of the war, some forty thousand Confederate troops under Gen. Albert Sydney Johnston launch an attack against Federal forces under Maj. Gen. Ulysses S. Grant at Shiloh, Tennessee. Nearly defeated, the Union forces receive reinforcements during the night, bringing their total strength up to about sixty-three thousand. Grant regains control of the battlefield by morning but the Union troops are too exhausted to pursue the retreating rebels.

Casualties of the battle include 1,754 killed, 8,408 wounded, and 2,885 missing Union soldiers and 1,723 killed, 8,012 wounded, and 959 missing Confederate soldiers.

(E) APRIL 10–11, 1862: Union Maj. Gen. Quincy A. Gillmore batters into submission Fort Pulaski, which guards entry to the Savannah River. This action highlights the vulnerability of even such an imposing masonry fortification when faced with modern rifled artillery.

(W) APRIL 25, 1862: U.S. Navy Flag Officer David Farragut leads an assault up the Mississippi River and captures New Orleans.

(E-P) APRIL 1862: Union troops of Maj. General McClellan's Army of the Potomac leave northern Virginia and begin to march toward Richmond, initiating the Peninsular Campaign.

(E) MAY 4, 1862: Union troops under McClellan occupy Yorktown, Virginia.

(E) MAY–AUGUST 1862: THE PENINSULAR CAMPAIGN. McClellan's army manages to advance as far as Fair Oaks, a mere five miles from Richmond. At this point, however, his advance is checked by Confederate Gen. Robert E. Lee, and he orders a retreat to Harrison's Landing on the James River.

(E) MAY 25, 1862: FIRST BATTLE OF WINCHESTER. Lt. Gen. "Stonewall" Jackson's sixteen thousand Confederate troops defeat the eight thousand men under Union Maj. Gen. Nathaniel Prentiss Banks, forcing the Federal troops to withdraw toward Harpers Ferry, Virginia. Casualties include 1,227 killed, wounded, missing, and captured Union soldiers and 400 killed, wounded, missing, and captured Confederate soldiers.

(E) MAY 31–JUNE 1, 1862: BATTLE OF FAIR OAKS (BATTLE OF SEVEN PINES). Confederate troops attack Union forces at Seven Pines, Virginia, and nearly defeat them. Union reinforcements, however, arrive at the last minute and prevent the victory from being complete. Gen. Joseph E. Johnston, commander of the Confederate army, is severely wounded, and leadership of the Army of Northern Virginia passes to Gen. Robert E. Lee.

Casualties of the battle include 790 killed, 3,594 wounded, and 647 captured or missing Union soldiers and 980 killed, 4,749 wounded, and 405 captured or missing Confederate soldiers.

(E) JUNE 25–JULY 1, 1862: SEVEN DAYS' BATTLES. Over a period of a week, Union and Confederate forces fight a series of especially savage battles (June 26–27, Mechanicsville; June 27, Gaines's Mill; June 29, Savage Station; June 30, Frayser's Farm; and July 1, Malvern Hill). The Confederate forces withdraw to Richmond on July 2, ending the Peninsular Campaign. Casualties incurred during the course of the battles include 1,734 dead, 8,062 wounded, and 6,075 missing Union soldiers, and 3,478 dead, 16,261 wounded, and 875 missing Confederate soldiers. With more than 36,000 casualties, the Seven Days are second only to Gettysburg in terms of total bloodshed.

(E) JULY 11, 1862: Annoyed by Maj. Gen. George B. McClellan's failure in Virginia and his plodding pace, Lincoln issues an order relieving him as general-in-chief of the Union armies, naming Maj. Gen. Henry Halleck general-in-chief of the Union army and Maj. Gen. John Pope commander of all the armies north and west of Virginia. McClellan is given command of a single army, the Army of the Potomac, under Pope.

(E) AUGUST–SEPTEMBER 1862: Northern Virginia Campaign.

(E) AUGUST 28–30, 1862: SECOND BATTLE OF BULL RUN (BATTLE OF SECOND MANASSAS). Confederate forces under Maj. Gen. James Longstreet and Lt. Gen. Stonewall Jackson decisively defeat Union troops under Maj. Gen. John Pope near Manassas, Virginia. Union Maj. Gen. Fitz-John Porter, who allegedly failed to send his troops into the battle quickly enough, is held responsible for the defeat and is forced out of the army by the beginning of the next year.

More than twenty-six thousand soldiers are among the casualties of the battle (1,724 killed, 8,372 wounded, and 5,958 missing/captured Union soldiers and 1,481 killed, 7,627 wounded, and 89 missing/captured Confederate soldiers).

Following this defeat, Lincoln replaces Pope with Maj. Gen. George B. McClellan.

(E) SEPTEMBER 1862: Union Maj. Gen. McClellan defeats Confederate Gen. Robert E. Lee at the battles of South Mountain and Crampton's Gap.

(E) SEPTEMBER 15, 1862: Confederate Lt. Gen. Stonewall Jackson captures Harpers Ferry, Virginia, along with thousands of Union prisoners and a great quantity of supplies. Despite his proximity to Harpers Ferry, plodding Maj. Gen. McClellan does not move quickly enough to prevent its capture.

(E) SEPTEMBER 17, 1862: BATTLE OF ANTIETAM (BATTLE OF SHARPSBURG). Maj. Gen. McClellan intercepts a Confederate force on the banks of Antietam Creek, near Sharpsburg, Maryland, leading to the single bloodiest day of the entire war. Casualties include 9,549 wounded and 2,108 killed Union soldiers and 9,029 wounded and 2,700 killed Confederate soldiers (more soldiers are slain in the combined three days of the Battle of Gettysburg, but never so many perish in a single day).

Tactically, the battle is a draw, but strategically it is a decided loss for the Confederacy. Gen. Lee is forced to retreat back to Virginia and McClellan claims a victory. In light of the Confederate defeat, Britain and France, both of which had been contemplating official recognition of the Confederacy, decide against it.

(P) SEPTEMBER 22, 1862. Lincoln announces in his preliminary Emancipation Proclamation that all slaves in rebelling areas will be free as of January 1, 1863. Slaves in Union and "neutral" states, however, are not covered by this proclamation.

OCTOBER 8, 1862: BATTLE OF PERRYVILLE. Kentucky's only major battle of the war is fought because of a chance encounter between Union foragers and Confederate troops. Union Maj. Gen. Don Carlos Buell's army defeats Confederate Gen. Braxton Bragg's force, despite being deployed piecemeal. In the aftermath of the battle, Lincoln relieves Buell of command for failing to destroy the Confederate army. Casualties of the battle include 894 killed, 2,911 wounded, and 471 captured or missing Union soldiers and 532 killed, 2,641 wounded, and 228 captured or missing Confederate soldiers.

(E) NOVEMBER 7, 1862: Annoyed by the escape of the Confederate forces from Antietam, continuous raiding by Rebel cavalry, and inactivity of McClellan's armies for more than a month, Lincoln relieves the "Young Napoleon" of all command for the last time and replaces him with Maj. Gen. Ambrose E. Burnside.

(E) DECEMBER 13, 1862: BATTLE OF FREDERICKSBURG. Maj. Gen. Burnside's forces are defeated in a series of attacks against entrenched Confederate forces at Fredericksburg, Virginia. As a result, Lincoln replaces Burnside with Maj. Gen. Joseph Hooker. Among the casualties are 1,284 killed, 9,600 wounded, and 1,769 missing or captured Union soldiers and 595 killed, 4,061 wounded, and 653 missing or captured Confederate soldiers.

(W) DECEMBER 31, 1862, TO JANUARY 2, 1863: BATTLE OF STONES RIVER (BATTLE OF MURFREESBORO). A sporadic, bloody, and pointless battle is fought between Union and Confederate forces struggling for control of Tennessee, resulting in 12,906 Union soldiers killed, wounded, captured, or missing and 11,795 Confederate killed, wounded, captured, or missing. After three days of fighting, Confederate Gen. Braxton Bragg inexplicably withdraws from the field, leaving Murfreesboro in control of Union forces under Maj. Gen. William S. Rosecrans.

1863

West Virginia is admitted to the Union as the thirty-fifth state. Ebenezer and Eleanor Butterick sell their dress patterns throughout the world. James Plimpton invents steerable roller skates.

(P) JANUARY 1, 1863: Lincoln issues the Emancipation Proclamation, declaring free all slaves in areas under Confederate control. This act comes amid growing public sentiment in favor of abolition, favored by radical Republicans but resisted by Lincoln, who wishes to placate slave-holding border states and keep them loyal to the Union.

This proclamation follows a series of measures that had been moving in the direction of abolition. Some Union generals had decreed that in areas under their control, slaves belonging to men bearing arms against the Union were to be considered free. Congress had also taken steps toward abolition, in 1861 passing an act stating all slaves being used against the Union were to be considered free, and in 1862 passing an act stating that slaves owned by men supporting the Confederacy were to be considered free.

(P) MARCH 1863: The Federal government responds to recruiting difficulties by passing the First Conscription Act. This makes all men between ages twenty and forty-five liable for military service, which can nonetheless be avoided by providing a substitute or by paying a fine. Because of this, the act is seen as unfair to the poor and leads to riots in some cities. Facing similar recruitment problems, the Confederacy also passes a conscription act, which provokes similar reactions.

(E) APRIL 27, 1863: Union Maj. Gen. John Hooker crosses the Rappahannock River in Virginia, intending to attack Gen. Lee's army.

(E) MAY 1–4, 1863: BATTLE OF CHANCELLORSVILLE. Confederate Gen. Lee responds to Maj. Gen. Hooker's foray across the Rappahannock by splitting his forces and attacking the Union army in three places. He defeats it nearly completely and forces Hooker to withdraw back across the river. Although a clear Southern victory, it is the Confederacy's most costly in terms of casualties, with 1,665 killed, 9,081 wounded, and 2,018 missing or captured; Gen. Thomas J. "Stonewall" Jackson is among the dead. Union casualties are 1,575 dead, 9,594 wounded, and 5,676 missing or captured.

(W) MAY 1863: VICKSBURG CAMPAIGN. Union Maj. Gen. Ulysses S. Grant wins a number of victories near Vicksburg, Mississippi, a fortified city deemed essential to Union plans to regain complete control of the Mississippi River.

(W) MAY 22, 1863: Maj. Gen. Grant assaults Confederate-held Vicksburg, Mississippi.

(P) JUNE 20, 1863: The western sections of Virginia are admitted to the Union as the new state of West Virginia. A preponderance of citizens in this area have been opposed to secession since the beginning of the war.

(E) JUNE–JULY 1863: GETTYSBURG CAMPAIGN.

(E) JUNE 13, 1863: Confederate Gen. Robert E. Lee defeats Union forces at Winchester, Virginia, and continues north toward Pennsylvania. Union Maj. Gen. Hooker is forced to alter his plans to attack Richmond and must instead pursue Lee.

(E) JUNE 28, 1863: Maj. Gen. Hooker resigns as commander of the Union Army of the Potomac, and Maj. Gen. Halleck replaces him with Maj. Gen. George G. Meade.

(E) JULY 1–3, 1863: BATTLE OF GETTYSBURG. Union and Confederate forces clash near the town of Gettysburg, Pennsylvania. Northern troops under Maj. Gen. Meade outnumber the Southerners and are eventually able to occupy superior defensive positions. The Federal army is victorious but fails to pursue Gen. Lee during his retreat to Virginia. More soldiers die than in any other battle of the war, 3,155 from Northern units and 3,903 from Southern units (more died in a single day of fighting at Antietam, but the most died during the entire three days of Gettysburg). Other casualties include 14,529 wounded and 5,365 missing or captured Union soldiers and 18,735 wounded and 5,425 missing or captured Confederate soldiers. After its defeat at Gettysburg, the Confederacy has its hopes of formal recognition by foreign governments forever dashed.

(W) JULY 4, 1863: SIEGE OF VICKSBURG ENDS. Succumbing to Grant's siege after six weeks, Confederate Lt. Gen. John Pemberton surrenders Vicksburg and thirty thousand troops. Soon thereafter, Union troops capture Port Hudson, Louisiana, bringing the entire Mississippi River under Union control and splitting the Confederacy in half.

(C) JULY 13-16, 1863: DRAFT RIOTS. Sparked by Irish workers angry at being conscripted and unable to afford to pay substitutes, and encouraged by Southern sympathizers, the worst draft riots of the war erupt in working-class sections of New York City. During three days of violence, rioters loot ships, burn buildings (including an orphanage for black children), and attack and kill blacks in the streets. Federal troops have to be called in from the battlefield at Gettysburg to restore order. Anti-draft violence on a smaller scale also erupts in other Northern cities, including Boston.

(E) AUGUST–NOVEMBER 1863: After the Battle of Gettysburg, Union Maj. Gen. George G. Meade engages in a series of cautious and inconclusive military operations.

(W) SEPTEMBER 19-20, 1863: BATTLE OF CHICKAMAUGA. Union and Confederate forces meet near Chickamauga Creek on the Tennessee-Georgia border. Confederate troops led by Gen. Braxton Bragg come close to completely destroying the Union army under Maj. Gen. William Rosecrans, forcing it to retreat to Chattanooga, Tennessee. Casualties include 1,657 dead, 9,756 wounded, and 4,757 captured or missing Union soldiers and 2,312 dead, 14,674 wounded, and 1,468 captured or missing Confederate soldiers (34,624 total).

(W) SEPTEMBER–NOVEMBER 1863: After nearly crushing the Union army at Chickamauga, troops under Confederate Gen. Bragg occupy the mountains surrounding Union-held Chattanooga, Tennessee, a critical rail center.

(P) NOVEMBER 19, 1863: President Lincoln dedicates part of the battlefield at Gettysburg as a national cemetery and delivers his famous Gettysburg Address.

(W) NOVEMBER 23–25, 1863: BATTLE OF CHATTANOOGA. Union troops drive Confederate forces away from Chattanooga, setting the stage for Union Maj. General Sherman's Atlanta Campaign. Maj. Gen. Ulysses S. Grant, called in to break the Confederate ring around Chattanooga, directs a series of brilliantly-executed attacks that destroy the blockade.

(W) NOVEMBER 24: BATTLE OF LOOKOUT MOUNTAIN. In this sideline to the Battle of Chattanooga, troops under Union Maj. Gen. "Fighting Joe" Hooker storm Confederate positions on Lookout Mountain. Casualties of the battle include 408 killed, wounded, captured, or missing Union soldiers and 187 killed or wounded and 1,064 captured or missing Confederate soldiers.

(W) NOVEMBER–DECEMBER 1863: SIEGE OF KNOXVILLE. Taking advantage of the compromised position of the Federal forces following Chickamauga, Confederate Gen. Braxton Bragg sends a force under Lt. Gen. James Longstreet to drive Maj. Gen. Ambrose Burnside's army out of eastern Tennessee. Burnside holes up in Knoxville, which he successfully defends.

(W) DECEMBER 3, 1863: Unable to penetrate the Union defenses of Knoxville, Longstreet ends his siege and withdraws.

1864

Louis Pasteur develops his germ theory that correctly states bacteria can cause disease. Congress passes the Coinage Act of 1864, mandating that the inscription "In God We Trust" be placed on all coins minted as U.S. currency. Montana is organized as a U.S. territory from parts of the Washington and Dakota Territories. Nevada admitted to the Union as the thirty-sixth state.

FEBRUARY 17, 1864: The tiny Confederate submarine CSS *H.L. Hunley* torpedoes USS *Housatonic*, becoming the first submarine to sink an enemy ship. The *Hunely* and its crew are also lost in the action.

FEBRUARY 25, 1864: The first 500 Union prisoners arrive at the southern prison camp at Andersonville, Georgia, after having been transferred a week earlier from Richmond, Virginia.

(E) MARCH–MAY 1864: RED RIVER CAMPAIGN.

(P-E) MARCH 9, 1864: After promoting him to the rank of lieutenant general, President Abraham Lincoln appoints Ulysses S. Grant commander-in-chief of all Union armies.

(E) MAY–JUNE 1864: GRANT'S WILDERNESS CAMPAIGN. Now commander of the Union armies, Lt. Gen. Grant plans to fight Lee's forces in Virginia until they are destroyed.

(E) MAY 5-6, 1864: BATTLE OF THE WILDERNESS. The Union and Confederate armies battle inconclusively for two days. Grant's forces suffer 17,666 casualties. Confederate Gen. Robert E. Lee's casualties, while uncertain, were less than this; unlike Grant, however, Lee receives no replacements for his losses.

(E) MAY 8-12, 1864: BATTLE OF SPOTSYLVANIA. Grant's forces continue to attack Lee's, fighting for five days at Spotsylvania Court House, Virginia. Grant vows to fight all summer if necessary. Nearly 11,000 Union casualties and an uncertain but similar number of Confederate casualties are the price of the battle.

(E) MAY 12-16, 1864: BATTLE OF DREWRY'S BLUFF. Grant's troops continue to battle Lee's. Casualties include 4,160 Union soldiers who are killed, wounded, captured, or missing, along with an unknown number of Confederate soldiers.

(E) JUNE 1-3, 1864: BATTLE OF COLD HARBOR. Grant attacks Confederate positions at Cold Harbor, Virginia, and his forces are savagely repelled. More than 7,000 men on both sides are killed in the worst twenty minutes of the holocaust; total Union casualties are 12,000 killed, wounded, captured, or missing. Although the last clear victory for Lee during the war, his army never recovers from the unrelenting attacks of Grant's troops.

(E) JUNE 15-30, 1864 TO APRIL 2, 1865: SIEGE OF PETERSBURG. Grant hopes to quickly capture Petersburg, Virginia, a vital rail center south of Richmond, then advance on the Confederate capital from the south. This attempt fails, costing him 16,569 casualties, and bogs down into a ten-month siege in which thousands more soldiers on each side are killed or wounded.

(E) JUNE 27, 1864: BATTLE OF KENNESAW MOUNTAIN (GEORGIA). After several days of maneuvering and skirmishing in the rain, Union troops under Maj. Gen. William T. Sherman make three uphill assaults against well-entrenched Confederate forces under Gen. Joseph E. Johnston.

The Union forces are driven back each time with heavy losses, resulting in embarrassment for Sherman and a victory for Johnston.

(E) JULY 1864: Confederate Lt. Gen. Jubal Early leads his troops into Maryland in a raid-in-force in an attempt to relieve pressure on Lee's army. Early gets within five miles of Washington, DC, causing some fear and consternation.

(E) JULY 13, 1864: Union forces drive Confederate Lt. Gen. Early's forces back into Virginia.

(W) AUGUST 1864: ATLANTA CAMPAIGN. Union Maj. Gen. William T. Sherman leaves Chattanooga, Tennessee, and soon encounters Confederate Gen. Joseph E. Johnston, who skillfully holds off the Union force, almost twice the size of his own. Nonetheless, Johnston's superiors decide to replace him with Lt. Gen. John Bell Hood, who is soon defeated.

(W) SEPTEMBER 1, 1864: Maj. Gen. Sherman forces Lt. Gen. Hood to relinquish Atlanta, Georgia, and occupies it the next day. The capture of this vital city greatly boosts morale in the North.

(W) SEPTEMBER–NOVEMBER 1864: Maj. Gen. Sherman's troops occupy Atlanta for two-and-a-half months, resting and accumulating supplies.

(W) NOVEMBER 15, 1864: Before Maj. Gen. Sherman departs Atlanta, he orders his troops to demolish military facilities and set fire to the rest of the city. Much of the city is destroyed.

(W-E) NOVEMBER 15 TO DECEMBER 13, 1864: SHERMAN'S MARCH TO THE SEA. Maj. Gen. Sherman continues his march through Georgia and to the sea, cutting himself off from his lines of supply and forcing his men to live off what they can forage or pillage. Sherman's force cuts a path sixty miles wide and three hundred miles long during its march through Georgia, destroying bridges, factories, railroads, and public buildings as it goes.

(P) NOVEMBER 1864: ABRAHAM LINCOLN IS REELECTED. The Republican Party nominates incumbent President Abraham Lincoln as its candidate for president and Andrew Johnson for vice president. The Democratic Party chooses Maj. Gen. George B. McClellan for president and George Pendleton for vice president. Widespread war-weariness among Northerners makes victory for Lincoln seem doubtful at times, and Lincoln's veto of the Wade-Davis Bill—which called for the majority of each Confederate state's electorate to swear past and future loyalty to the Union before the state could be officially restored—loses him the support of radical Republicans who think he is too lenient. Maj. Gen. Sherman's victories in Georgia, however, boost Lincoln's popularity and help him win the election by a broad margin.

(E) DECEMBER 13, 1864: Maj. Gen. Sherman storms Fort McAllister, Georgia, and orders the fortifications dismantled before continuing northward.

(W) DECEMBER 15–16, 1864: Confederate Lt. Gen. John B. Hood, true to his policy of taking the offensive whenever possible, attacks the Union defenses at Nashville, Tennessee. Union Maj. Gen. George H. Thomas repulses the attack, winning one of the war's most complete victories.

(E) DECEMBER 21, 1864: Maj. Gen. William T. Sherman captures Savannah, Georgia, completing his eastward trek across the state.

1865

Civil War ends. Reconstruction begins in the Southern states. Results of Mendel's first genetic experiments are published. Lewis Carroll's *Alice in Wonderland* is published. Louis Pasteur publishes his germ theory. Joseph Lister revolutionizes antiseptic surgery with the introduction of carbolic dressing. Celluloid is developed. *The Nation* is published for the first time.

(E) JANUARY 1865: Union Rear Adm. David D. Porter's squadron of warships subjects Fort Fisher, North Carolina, to a massive artillery bombardment.

(E) JANUARY 15, 1865: Soldiers, sailors, and marines storm weakened Fort Fisher and capture it. With the loss of this strategic bastion, Wilmington, North Carolina—critical to Southern attempts to circumvent the Union blockade—is cut off.

JANUARY 1865: The South suffers acute shortages of food and supplies due to disrupted rail traffic and supply lines and the tightened Union blockade. Starving soldiers begin to desert the Confederate army in large numbers. In desperation, Confederate President Jefferson Davis approves arming slaves to reinforce the army, but this measure is never actually carried out.

(E) FEBRUARY 1865: Union Maj. Gen. William T. Sherman's army marches north through Georgia, into South Carolina and then North Carolina, destroying almost everything in its path.

(P) FEBRUARY 1865: Confederate President Jefferson Davis agrees to send delegates to a peace conference with President Abraham Lincoln and Secretary of State William Seward, but insists upon recognition of the South's independence. Lincoln refuses and the conference does not occur.

(E) MARCH 25, 1865: Gen. Robert E. Lee attacks Union Lt. Gen. Ulysses S. Grant's forces at Fort Stedman, near Petersburg, Virginia, but is defeated.

(E) APRIL 1, 1865: Union Maj. Gen. Philip Sheridan defeats Confederate Maj. Gen. George E. Pickett at Five Forks, necessitating the evacuation of Richmond.

(E) APRIL 2: Gen. Lee evacuates Richmond, Virginia, abandoning the Confederate capital to the Union army, and then heads west to join forces with remnants of the Army of Tennessee.

(E) APRIL 3, 1865: A smoldering Richmond, set on fire the previous evening by retreating Confederate troops, is captured by Union forces.

(E) APRIL 7, 1865: Lt. Gen. Ulysses S. Grant sends a message to Gen. Lee, calling upon him to surrender and end the war.

(E) APRIL 9, 1865: SURRENDER AT APPOMATTOX COURTHOUSE. Grant and Lee meet at Appomattox Courthouse, Virginia, and agree upon terms of surrender. Lee's command at this point consists of a mere 26,765 men, who are sent home on parole after agreeing not to take up arms against the Union. Enlisted cavalry and artillery men are permitted to keep their horses, and officers their swords and pistols. All other equipment is surrendered to the Union army.

APRIL–MAY, 1865: The last remnants of the Confederate army surrender or are defeated.

(P) APRIL 14, 1865: Pro-Confederate actor John Wilkes Booth, obsessed with avenging the defeat of the Confederacy, shoots President Abraham Lincoln at Ford's Theatre in Washington, DC, during a performance of "Our American Cousin," and then flees through Maryland to Virginia.

(P) APRIL 15, 1865: Lincoln dies from his wounds.

(P) APRIL 25, 1865: Trapped in a burning barn in Virginia, assassin John Wilkes Booth is fatally shot by a Union soldier. Nine other people are determined to have been involved in the assassination, and, of these, four are hanged, four are imprisoned, and one is acquitted.

(E) APRIL 26, 1865: Confederate Gen. Joseph Johnston surrenders to Union Maj. Gen. William T. Sherman at the Bennett House near Durham Station, North Carolina, bringing the war to an end.

(P) MAY 2, 1865: U.S. President Andrew Johnson offers a $100,000 reward for the capture of C.S. President Jefferson Davis.

(P) MAY 10, 1865: Jefferson Davis is captured in southern Georgia.

MAY 12–13, 1865: BATTLE OF PALMITO RANCH. This battle between 80 Union soldiers and 350 Confederate cavalrymen is a victory for the former and the last battle of any size fought during the war.

MAY 19, 1865: Johnson declares that armed insurrection against the Federal government has come to an end.

(E) MAY 23–24, 1865: GRAND REVIEW. A total of 150,000 men from the armies of Union generals Meade (Army of the Potomac) and Sherman (Army of Georgia) march through Washington, DC, to the wild cheers of thousands of spectators.

JUNE 1865: Congress declares that pay, arms, equipment, and medical services for black troops should be equal to those provided to whites.

(P) AUGUST 23–OCTOBER 24, 1865: A Union military commission led by Maj. Gen. Lew Wallace (future author of *Ben Hur*) tries Confederate Capt. Henry Wirz, commandant of the notorious Confederate prison at Andersonville, Georgia. The commission finds Wirz guilty of war crimes and sentences him to death.

(P) SEPTEMBER 1865: Republican Congressman Thaddeus Stevens of Pennsylvania urges that estates belonging to former Confederate leaders be confiscated and divided up into forty-acre parcels for freed blacks.

(P) NOVEMBER 10, 1865: Confederate Capt. Henry Wirz is hanged in the yard of the Old Capitol Prison, the only person to be tried and executed for war crimes in the wake of the Civil War.

(C) DECEMBER 24, 1865: Six former Confederate officers meet in Pulaski, Tennessee, and form a secret society that eventually becomes the Ku Klux Klan.

1866

Laying of transatlantic cable, started in 1858, is completed. A key-opened can is patented. The first-known milk bottle is produced. Machine-made sewing needles are produced.

(P) JULY 24, 1866: Tennessee regains representation in the U.S. Congress, making it the first Confederate state to be full reintegrated into the Union.

1867

Nebraska is admitted to the Union as the thirty-seventh state. Arkansas is placed under Federal military rule. The United States purchases Alaska from Russia. Nobel invents dynamite. Dostoyevsky's *Crime and Punishment* is published. Great Britain grants dominion status to Canada. Joseph Lister performs the first antiseptic operation through the use of carbolic acid. Part one of Karl Marx's three-volume *Das Kapital* is published in German.

1868

Dr. Elizabeth Blackwell founds the Women's Medical College of New York Infirmary and runs it with an all-female staff. Commercially-produced yeast cakes are sold for the first time. Edmund McIlhenny introduces Tabasco Sauce. A.J. Fellows patents a measuring tape enclosed within a circular case. Machines are developed to cut coal. Shoes made of rubber and canvas are introduced as "croquet sandals" for the affluent in New Haven, Connecticut (and are referred to as "sneakers" and "sneaks" by 1873). Carlos Glidden and Christopher Latham Sholes patent the typewriter. The Fourteenth Amendment, preventing states from infringing upon the Constitutional rights of citizens (that is, freed blacks), is ratified. Reconstruction ends in Arkansas, Florida, North Carolina, South Carolina, Louisiana, and Alabama, and they are readmitted to the Union.

(P) JUNE 22, 1868: Arkansas regains representation in the U.S. Congress.

(P) JUNE 25, 1868: Florida regains representation in the U.S. Congress.

(P) JULY 4, 1868: North Carolina regains representation in the U.S. Congress.

(P) JULY 9, 1868: Louisiana and South Carolina regain representation in the U.S. Congress.

(P) JULY 13, 1868: Alabama regains representation in the U.S. Congress.

(P) NOVEMBER 1868: Ulysses S. Grant, former general-in-chief of all the armies of the United States, is elected president of the United States.

1869

The Suez Canal opens in Egypt. Susan B. Anthony and Elizabeth Cady Stanton organize the National Woman Suffrage Association. A gyrator clothes washer, consisting of a tub with rotating blades and a hand crank, is developed. Hippolyte Mege-Mouries patents margarine, made from skim milk and beef tallow. H.J. Heinz markets horseradish in glass jars. Russian Count Leo Tolstoy completes *War and Peace*, which he began five years earlier.

MAY 10, 1869: First U.S. transcontinental railroad is completed with the meeting in Promontory, Utah, of the Union Pacific Railroad line from the east and the Central Pacific line from the west.

1870

The Franco-Prussian War begins with French declaration of war; the Germans employ strategies and tactics influenced by their observations of the U.S. Civil War. Robert Chesebrough patents Vaseline. Benjamin Babbitt introduces baking powder, sold under the brand name Star Yeast Powder. Margaret Knight invents the brown paper bag. The Fifteenth Amendment to the Constitution is ratified. Georgia, Mississippi, Texas, and Virginia are readmitted to the Union.

(P) JANUARY 26, 1870: Virginia regains representation in the U.S. Congress.

(P) FEBRUARY 23, 1870: Mississippi regains representation in the U.S. Congress.

(P) MARCH 30, 1870: Texas is readmitted to the Union after ratifying the Thirteenth, Fourteenth, and Fifteenth Amendments to the U.S. Constitution.

(P) JULY 15, 1870: Georgia becomes the final former-Confederate state to regain representation in the U.S. Congress.

OCTOBER 12, 1870: Robert E. Lee, the general formerly in overall command of the Confederate armies, dies at his home in Lexington, Virginia.

1871

The war ends between France and Prussia with the defeat of the French. The Third Republic is established in France. Bismarck becomes the first chancellor of the German empire. Thomas Adams introduces the first chewing gum, sweetened but unflavored and made from chicle, and called Adam's New York Gum—Snapping and Stretching. A.L. Jones patents corrugated paper.

1872

Elijah McCoy invents an automatic machine lubricator. Amanda Jones develops a vacuum-pressure process for preserving food. Jane Wells invents the baby jumper. Montgomery Ward publishes its first mail-order catalog.

1873

James Clerk Maxwell publishes his *Electricity and Magnetism*. The Dover egg beater is patented. The California Penal Code goes into effect.

MARCH 4, 1873: U.S. President Ulysses S. Grant begins his second term.

JULY 21, 1873: Jesse James and the James-Younger gang pull off the first successful train robbery in the American Old West at Adair, Iowa.

SEPTEMBER 18, 1873: The New York stock market crashes, triggering the Panic of 1873, part of the worldwide Long Depression.

1874

Benjamin Disraeli becomes prime minister of Great Britain (until 1880). Paul Verlaine's *Romances sans Paroles* is published. Robert Green of Philadelphia introduces the ice-cream soda. The St. Louis Stamping Company introduces Graniteware, a lightweight cookware made from enameled steel. Joseph Glidden patents barbed wire.

1875

Congress passes the Civil Rights Act, prohibiting racial discrimination in public accommodations and jury duty. R.J. Reynolds Tobacco Company is founded and begins to produce chewing tobacco, including Brown's Mule, Golden Rain, Dixie's Delight, Yellow Rose, and Purity brands. The first college football game is played.

1876

The United States celebrates its Centennial. Alexander Graham Bell patents the telephone. Mark Twain's *Tom Sawyer* is published. Heinz begins to sell ketchup. Melville Bissell invents the carpet sweeper. Most Sioux are expelled from the Black Hills of South Dakota by the end of the year.

JUNE 25, 1876: Battle of Little Bighorn. Lt. Col. George Armstrong Custer (a former Union army general) is slain in the battle against Sioux forces at Little Bighorn, Montana, the last major Indian victory in the West. Other casualties of "Custer's Last Stand" include his entire command, a regiment of about 225 Seventh Cavalry Regiment soldiers.

1877

Colorado is admitted to the Union as the Thirty-eighth state. Thomas Edison invents the phonograph. Chester Greenwood invents earmuffs. Great Britain's Queen Victoria becomes empress of India. Reconstruction ends in the Southern states.

BIBLIOGRAPHY AND RECOMMENDED BOOKS

Information in this book was drawn from both secondary sources—nonfiction books written largely by scholars—and primary sources, which include regimental histories, diaries, and memoirs of combatants and civilians who witnessed the events of the war, and ships' logs.

Primary sources typically provide straightforward, accurate accounts of day-to-day activities, battles, and incidents often not described in other sources but often lack a broader perspective. Every year, several Civil War diaries, regimental histories, and other primary sources are printed or reprinted, and official documents, such as ships' logs, can often be obtained through the U.S. National Archives and Records Administration or historians' offices of the various branches of the armed forces.

Resources in this appendix are divided into six sections in order to better help readers identify those which would be most useful to them. Books directly used in the compilation of this work have an asterisk (*) preceding them.

PART ONE of this appendix is a selection of notable primary sources.

PART TWO is a list of general sources that are packed with a broad variety of information.

PART THREE is a list of recommended books more specialized than those on the first list that are excellent sources of information about specific aspects of life during the Civil War.

PART FOUR is a list of books not as comprehensive or specialized as those on the first or second lists, but which are still useful resources. It includes a number of titles by the author of this volume written since the initial release of this book that were influenced by his interest and background in the Civil War and which contain material related to it.

PART FIVE is a discussion and list of Civil War literature and novels. No recommendations are implied here, as a preference for one work of fiction over another is largely a matter of taste and opinion. Also, many of the titles, especially classics like *The Red Badge of Courage* and *The Killer Angels*, speak for themselves.

PART SIX is a discussion of Civil War films, documentaries, and other programs.

Part One:
Primary Sources

* *Christ in the Camp; or, Religion in Lee's Army* by J. William Jones (J.W. Randolph and English, 1880).

Co. Aytch: Maury Grays, First Tennessee Regiment or, A Side Show of the Big Show by Sam Watkins (1882).

Corporal Si Klegg and His "Pard": How They Lived and Talked, and What They Did and Suffered, While Fighting for the Flag by Wilbur Hinman (1887).

* *Hardtack and Coffee: The Unwritten Story of Army Life* by John D. Billings (George M. Smith & Co., 1887).

* *How the Other Half Lives: Studies Among the Tenements of New York* by Jacob August Riis, 1890 (Dover Publications, 1971).

* *A Narrative of the Great Revival Which Prevailed in the Southern Armies* by William W. Bennett (Claxton, Remsen, and Haffelfinger, 1877).

* *"Recollections of a Drummer Boy"* by Harry M. Kieffer (*St. Nicholas Magazine*, 1881-1882).

* *Seven Months in the Rebel States During the North American War, 1863* by Justus Scheibert (Confederate Publishing Company, 1958).

Part Two:
General Sources

Armchair Reader: Civil War; Untold Stories of the Blue and Gray by Michael J. Varhola (co-author), et al. (West Side Publishing, 2007).

The Civil War Day by Day: An Almanac, 1861–1865 by E. B. Long, Barbara Long, photographer (Da Capo Press, 1985).

* *The Civil War Dictionary* by Mark Mayo Boatner III (Vintage Books, 1991).

* *The Civil War Society's Encyclopedia of the Civil War* by The Civil War Society (Portland House, 1997).

* *The Civil War: Strange and Fascinating Facts* by Burke Davis (The Fairfax Press, 1982).

The Coming Fury (The Centennial History of the Civil War, vol. 1) by Bruce Catton (Doubleday, 1961).

Days of Defiance: Sumter, Secession, and the Coming of the Civil War by Maury Klein (Alfred A. Knopf, 1997).

* *Don't Know Much About the Civil War* by Kenneth C. Davis (Bantam Books, 1998).

* *Never Call Retreat* (The Centennial History of the Civil War, vol. 3) by Bruce Catton (Doubleday, 1965).

* *A Short History of the Civil War: Ordeal by Fire* by Fletcher Pratt (Dover Publications, 1997).

* *Soldier Life in the Union and Confederate Armies* edited by Philip Van Doren Stern (Indiana University Press, 1961).

* *Sword Over Richmond: An Eyewitness History of McClellan's Peninsula Campaign* by Richard Wheeler (Harper and Row, 1986).

* *Terrible Swift Sword* (The Centennial History of the Civil War, vol. 2) by Bruce Catton (Doubleday, 1963).

PART Three:
Specialized Sources

* *American Country Building Design: Rediscovered Plans for 19th Century Farmhouses, Cottages, Landscapes, Barns, Carriage Houses, and Outbuildings* by Donald J. Berg (Sterling Publishing Company, 1997).

Arms and Equipment of the Confederacy (Echoes of Glory series, vol. 2) (Time Life Books, 1992).

Arms and Equipment of the Union (Echoes of Glory series, vol. 1) (Time Life Books, 1991).

Bloody Bill Anderson: The Short, Savage Life of a Civil War Guerrilla by Albert Castel and Thomas Goodrich (Stackpole Books, 1998).

The Capture of New Orleans, 1862 by Chester G. Hearn (Louisiana State University Press, 1995).

* *Christian History* magazine, issue 33. Kevin A. Miller, ed. (Christianity Today International, 1992).

* *City People: The Rise of Modern City Culture in Nineteenth-Century America* by Gunther Barth (Oxford University Press, 1980).

Civil War Battlefields and Landmarks: A Guide to the National Park Sites edited by Frank E. Vandiver (Random House, 1996).

* *Civil War Medicine, 1861–1865* by C. Keith Wilbur (The Globe Pequot Press, 1998).

Civil War Poetry: An Anthology edited by Paul Negri (Dover Publications, 1997).

* *Civil War Williamsburg* by Carson O. Hudson, Jr. (Stackpole Books, 1997).

* *Confederate Infantryman, 1861–1865* (Warrior Series, No. 6) by Ian Drury (Osprey Publishing, 1993).

* *Confederate Receipt Book: A Compilation of Over One Hundred Receipts, Adapted to the Times* edited by E. Merton Coulter (University of Georgia Press, 1981).

* *Destroyer of the Iron Horse: General Joseph E. Johnston and Confederate Rail Transport, 1861–1865* by Jeffrey N. Lash (The Kent State University Press, 1991).

* *Don Troiani's Soldiers in America, 1754–1865* by Don Troiani, Earl J. Coates, James L. Kochan, and Brian C. Pohanka (Stackpole Books, 1998).

* *Fort Macon: A History* by Paul Branch (Nautical and Aviation Publishing Company of America, 1999).

From Winchester to Cedar Creek: The Shenandoah Campaign of 1864 by Jeffry D. Wert (Stackpole Books, 1997).

Glory at a Gallop: Tales of the Confederate Cavalry by William R. Brooksher and David K. Snider (Brassey's, 1995).

Glory Road (Army of the Potomac Trilogy, vol. 2) by Bruce Catton (Anchor Books, 1952).

* *I Hear America Talking: An Illustrated History of American Words and Phrases* by Stuart Berg Flexner (Simon and Schuster, 1976).

Illustrated Atlas of the Civil War (Echoes of Glory series, vol. 3) (Time Life Books, 1992).

* *Illustrated Catalog of Civil War Military Goods: Union Weapons, Insignia, Uniform Accessories and Other Equipment* by Schuyler, Hartley and Graham (Dover Publications, 1985).

The Life of Billy Yank: The Common Soldier of the Union by Bell I. Wiley (1952).

The Life of Johnny Reb: The Common Soldier of the Confederacy by Bell I. Wiley (1943).

Little Phil: A Reassessment of the Civil War Leadership of Gen. Philip H. Sheridan by Eric J. Wittenberg (Potomac Books, 2005).

Mr. Lincoln's Army (Army of the Potomac Trilogy, vol. 1) by Bruce Catton (Doubleday, 1951).

The Official Military Atlas of the Civil War edited by George B. Davis, Leslie J. Perry, Joseph W. Kirkley, and Calvin D. Cowles, Government Printing Office, 1891 (Gramercy Books, 1983).

Raiders and Blockaders: The American Civil War Afloat by John M. Taylor, Norman C. Delaney and William N. Still, Jr. (Brassey's, 1998.)

Reliving the Civil War: A Reenactor's Handbook (2nd edition) by R. Lee Hadden (Stackpole Books, 1999).

Resources of the Southern Fields and Forests by Francis Peyre Porcher (Ayer Publishing Company, 1970).

Seasons of War: The Ordeal of a Confederate Community, 1861–1865 by Daniel E. Sutherland (Free Press, 1995).

A Shield and Hiding Place: The Religious Life of the Civil War Armies by Gardiner H. Shattuck, Jr. (Mercer University Press, 1987).

Speaking Freely: A Guided Tour of American English From Plymouth Rock to Silicon Valley by Stuart Berg Flexner and Anne H. Soukhanov (Oxford University Press, 1997).

A Stillness at Appomattox (The Army of the Potomac Trilogy, vol. 3) by Bruce Catton. (Doubleday, 1953).

The Story the Soldiers Wouldn't Tell: Sex in the Civil War by Thomas P. Lowry (Stackpole Books, 1994).

The Union Cavalry Comes of Age: Hartwood Church to Brandy Station, 1863 by Eric J. Wittenberg (Potomac Books, 2006).

Union Cavalryman, 1861–1865 (Warrior Series, No. 13) by Philip Katcher (Osprey Publishing, 1995).

The United States Revenue Cutters in the Civil War by Florence Kern (U.S. Coast Guard Historian's Office, 1989).

When the Devil Came Down to Dixie: Ben Butler in New Orleans by Chester G. Hearn (Louisiana State University Press, 1997).

Part Four: Other Sources

Battle Cry of Freedom: The Civil War Era (Oxford History of the United States) by James M. McPherson (Oxford University Press, 1988).

The Battle of Brandy Station: North America's Largest Cavalry Battle by Eric J. Wittenberg (The History Press, 2010).

The Battle of Monroe's Crossroads and the Civil War's Final Campaign by Eric J. Wittenberg. (Savas Beatie, 2006).

A Blockaded Family: Life in Southern Alabama During the Civil War by Parthenia Antoinette Hague (Applewood Books, reprint edition 1995).

The Chronological Tracking of the American Civil War; Per the Official Records of the War of the Rebellion by Ronald A. Mosocco (James River Publications, 1995).

The Civil War: A Narrative (three volumes) by Shelby Foote (Random House, 1974).

Civil War Etchings edited by William Forrest Dawson (Oxford University Press, 1957).

The Civil War Supply Catalogue: A Comprehensive Sourcebook of Products from the Civil War Era Available Today by Alan Wellikoff (Crown Publishers, 1996).

Confederates in the Attic: Dispatches from the Unfinished Civil War by Tony Horwitz (Pantheon Books, 1998).

* *Diary of a Southern Refugee During the War: By a Lady of Virginia* by Judith W. McGuire (University of Nebraska Press, reprint edition 1995).

* *Ersatz in the Confederacy: Shortages and Substitutes on the Southern Homefront* (Southern Classics Series) by Mary Elizabeth Massey (University of South Carolina Press, reprint edition 1993).

* *The Expansion of Everyday Life, 1860–1876* by Daniel E. Sutherland (Harper and Row, 1989).

* *Fighting Men of the Civil War* by William C. Davis (University of Oklahoma Press, 1998).

For Cause and Comrades: Why Men Fought in the Civil War by James M. McPherson (Oxford University Press, 1997).

Ghosthunting Maryland by Michael J. Varhola (Clerisy Press, 2009).

Ghosthunting Virginia by Michael J. Varhola (Clerisy Press, 2008).

Glory Enough for All: Sheridan's Second Raid and the Battle of Trevilian Station by Eric J. Wittenberg (Bison Books, 2007).

Heroines of Dixie: Spring of High Hopes edited by Katharine M. Jones (Mockingbird Books, 1955).

Heroines of Dixie: Winter of Desperation edited by Katharine M. Jones (Mockingbird Books, 1987).

Lee by Douglas Southall Freeman (Scribner, reprint edition 1997).

Lee's Lieutenants: A Study in Command by Douglas Southall Freeman (Scribner, reprint edition 1997).

* *Letters of a Civil War Soldier* by George W. Stilwell (Dorrance Publishing Company, 1997).

Like a Meteor Blazing Brightly: The Short but Controversial Life of Colonel Ulric Dahlgren by Eric J. Wittenberg (Edinborough Press, 2009).

* *The North Fights the Civil War: The Home Front* by J. Matthew Gallman (Ivan R. Dee, 1994).

* *The Official Price Guide to Civil War Collectibles* by Richard Friz (House of Collectibles, 1995).

One Continuous Fight: The Retreat from Gettysburg and the Pursuit of Lee's Army of Northern Virginia, July 4-14, 1863 by Michael F. Nugent, J. David Petruzzi, and Eric J. Wittenberg (Savas Beatie, 2008).

Plenty of Blame to Go Around: Jeb Stuart's Controversial Ride to Gettysburg by J. David Petruzzi and Eric J. Wittenberg (Savas Beatie, 2006).

* *The Price of Union* by Herbert Agar (Houghton Mifflin Company, 1950).

Protecting the Flanks: The Battles for Brinkerhoff's Ridge and East Cavalry Field, Battle of Gettysburg, July 2-3, 1863 by Eric J. Wittenberg (Ironclad Publishing, 2002).

* *Queen Victoria's Enemies (4): Asia, Australasia and the Americas* by Ian Knight (Osprey Publishing, 1990).

* *A Rebel War Clerk's Diary* by John B. Jones (Louisiana State University Press, reprint edition 1993).

* *Redlegs: The U.S. Artillery From the Civil War to the Spanish-American War, 1861–1898* by John P. Langellier (Stackpole Books, 1998).

Rush's Lancers: The Sixth Pennsylvania Cavalry in the Civil War by Eric J. Wittenberg (Westholme Publishing, 2007).

Shipwrecks and Lost Treasures: Great Lakes by Michael J. Varhola (Globe Pequot Press, 2008).

* *Shots That Hit: A Study of U.S. Coast Guard Marksmanship, 1790–1985* by William R. Wells, II (U.S. Coast Guard, Historian's Office, 1993).

Sojourns of a Patriot: The Field and Prison Papers of an Unreconstructed Confederate by Richard Bender Abell and Fay Adamson Gecik (Southern Heritage Press, 1998).

Texas Confidential: Sex, Scandal, Murder, and Mayhem in the Lone Star State by Michael J. Varhola (Clerisy Press, 2011).

* *Three Years With the 92d Illinois: The Civil War Diary of John M. King* edited by Claire E. Swedberg (Stackpole Books, 1999).

* *U.S. Fighting Forces: A Complete History of the U.S. Army, Marine Corps, Navy, Air Force* edited by Mark Lloyd, Robin Cross, Richard Humble, Bernard Fitzsimons, and Derek Avery (Chevprime, 1989).

* *Weapons: An International Encyclopedia From 5000 B.C. to 2000 A.D.* by The Diagram Group (St. Martin's Press, 1990).

* *What People Wore: 1,800 Illustrations From Ancient Times to the Early Twentieth Century* by Douglas Gorsline (Dover Publications, 1994).

Part Five:
Novels and Literature

A great body of literature has been inspired by the Civil War and includes everything from works by witnesses to the Civil War—like Ambrose Bierce and former Union soldier John William DeForest—to history in the form of literature—like the novels of Michael and Jeff Shaara—to the alternative histories of Harry Turtledove and Peter Tsouras.

Many of these can shed light on period attitudes and details of life. Among these are the works of Stephen Crane (e.g., *The Red Badge of Courage*), Bierce (who also produced a body of valuable nonfiction), and DeForest, whose works were to the first on the war to impart a credible sense of realism.

One unfortunate product of Civil War literature is the inflexible, predictable way Civil War leaders are depicted. This phenomena is perhaps more profound in Civil War novels than in any other genre except for mythology or religion, and is subject to the same sort of rigid canon. Just as Jesus or Zeus is only depicted or described in certain ways by the pious, so too are figures from the Civil War. While these dogmatized depictions may ultimately be based upon the actual characteristics of these people, their traits have become exaggerated and their characteristics and motivations are rarely examined critically.

For example, was Robert E. Lee really so very humble, so excruciatingly quiet and cordial, so crushed by bearing the weight of the Confederacy upon his noble shoulders, as virtually every Civil War novelist would have us believe? Did Ulysses S. Grant really chain smoke cigars, as is so often described? Was Joshua Chamberlain really good-naturedly boyish and perpetually bewildered by his own successes, as Jeff Shaara asserts?

Maybe these characterizations are accurate, maybe they are not, but fictionalized, liturgical descriptions of these leaders are not necessarily likely to reveal much that is ultimately true or interesting about them, and people should not rely upon novels or other fictitious accounts as major sources of information.

An uncanny number of the following books are subtitled "A Novel of the Civil War" or something similar. Because this is evident from their presence on this list, such subtitles have been omitted here.

Across Five Aprils by Irene Hunt (Berkley Publishing Group, reissue edition 1991).

Ambrose Bierce's Civil War by Ambrose Bierce edited by William McCann (Wings Books, 1996).

Andersonville by MacKinlay Kantor (Harper and Row, 1955).

Banished Children of Eve by Peter Quinn (Penguin, 1995).

Bring the Jubilee by Ward Moore (Ballantine Books, 1981).

Chickamauga, and Other Civil War Stories edited by Shelby Foote (Delta Publishing, 1993).

Civil War Women edited by Frank McSherry Jr., Charles G. Waugh, and Martin Greenberg (August House, 1988).

Civil War Women II edited by Frank McSherry Jr., Charles G. Waugh, and Martin Greenberg (August House, 1997).

Cold Mountain by Charles Frazier (Atlantic Monthly Press, 1997).

The Confessions of Nat Turner by William Styron (Random House, 1967).

Freedom by William Safire (Doubleday, 1987).

Gettysburg: An Alternate History by Peter G. Tsouras (Greenhill Books, 1997).

Gone With the Wind by Margaret Mitchell (Macmillan, 1936).

The Guns of the South by Harry Turtledove (Del Rey, 1997).

How Few Remain by Harry Turtledove (Del Rey, 1997).

The Killer Angels by Michael Shaara (David McKay, 1974).

Lincoln by Gore Vidal (Random House, 1984).

Miss Ravenel's Conversion from Secession to Loyalty by John William DeForest (Harper and Brothers, 1867).

Oldest Living Confederate Widow Tells All by Allan Gurganus (Knopf, 1984).

The Red Badge of Courage by Stephen Crane (Tor Books, 1895).

Shiloh by Shelby Foote (Dial Press, 1952).

Part Six:
Television and Film

To a large extent, people's perceptions of the Civil War are driven by movies, television programs, and documentaries, which have helped popularize the Civil War and educate people about it. Unfortunately, while many films and documentaries about the Civil War are more-or-less accurate, many have also contributed to some skewed perceptions about the Civil War.

Many Civil War movies and documentaries include scenes of Union and Confederate troops lined up against each other, opposing lines of well-fed, immaculately uniformed blue and gray soldiers, a few of the Southerners wearing straw hats or plaid shirts to reflect that faction's difficulties in fully clothing its men. While there were certainly battles that looked like this, such scenes tend to leave an inadequate impression of how these armies really appeared, as neither were really uniformed or equipped to a high enough cinematic standard (chapter 13 on uniforms and equipment describes what soldiers really looked like). And, while many battles were fought in straight lines in open country, many more were fought by broken formations in forests, swamps, and from within earthworks and other fortifications.

So why do filmmakers show these armies looking better than they really did and fighting differently than they did in actuality? One reason is that historical reenactors frequently fill the ranks of military units in films, and reenactors do not generally like to run around in homespun rags. Naturally, reenactors are also much better fed than typical Civil War soldiers, especially those of the Confederacy late in the war. So, even the best movies, like *Gettysburg*, *Glory*, or *Andersonville*, or the most popular documentaries, like those aired on the History Channel, tend to show men who are better dressed, equipped, and fed than those who really fought in the battles of the Civil War.

Also, to depict the soldiers of either side clothed in rags also begs a lot of questions that many directors and documentarians clearly are not comfortable addressing. It is far easier to sell an audience on a scene of plump reenactors charging into battle in pristine uniforms and falling dramatically in an open field to an anthem of stirring music than it is to show men, ragged as scarecrows, struggling across broken ground, being shot to pieces with no background music but artillery fire and the groans of the dead and dying.

RESOURCES

The array of Civil War information available through a variety of sources is incredible, and a researcher's main challenge is not so much finding information as it is sorting through what is available and identifying what is most useful to him. Following is a sampling of the resources available to anyone interested in a more in-depth study of the War Between the States.

Books

In many years, more books are published about the Civil War than about any other aspect of history, regardless of what is happening in the world or what historic anniversaries are being celebrated at the time. A selection of useful books are listed in Appendix C, which includes a number of classics that have stood the test of time and some specialized sources that can hardly be improved upon. Some of the best sources of information about uniforms, equipment, and other goods, for example, are catalogs (both those published in the nineteenth century and some published by modern manufacturers of reproduction clothing and dry goods).

Interested readers are, nonetheless, encouraged to seek other sources as well. New books continue to be published, too, and writers have many ways of keeping up with what has been released, including best-seller lists and reviews in newspapers and other periodicals (especially Civil War and history publications). Various online booksellers also have information services and will notify people by e-mail of new releases in subjects in which they have expressed interest.

Periodicals

In the United States today, many nationally distributed magazines and other periodicals deal directly with the Civil War. Some of these have been around for several years, while others come and go; what is currently available can be easily determined by a quick perusal of a newsstand or bookstore magazine section. Readers unfamiliar with such magazines should try several to see which have the most enjoyable and useful style of writing and editing, and then, if desired, subscribe to one of them. Those who regularly buy several different genre magazines or subscribe to more than one or two will quickly begin to see the same sorts of material, again and again.

Beyond publications directly concerned with the Civil War, there are many that deal with reenacting, history, or geography that regularly or periodically run stories related to the conflict. Reprints of a number of nineteenth-century publications are also frequently available. *Godey's Lady's Book,* a publication popular with homemakers during the Civil War, can provide those interested with information about diet, recipes, and women's day-to-day concerns. Reprints of it and other period publications are sometimes available, and copies can be found in some libraries.

Web Resources

Researchers today have a vast array of resources available to them through the internet, and dozens of sites are likely to turn up on searches against pertinent keywords. Unfortunately, anything can end up on the web, and some of what is available is poorly written, badly edited, or just plain inaccurate. Be very careful and discriminating when using the internet as a source of information.

Many good websites are available, and the best can do things that conventional books cannot. Many Civil War sites include period music, for example, giving readers a taste of the songs Civil War soldiers played, sang, and listened to.

Official U.S. government departmental and military websites are among the best sites available and contain background information on history, uniforms, ranks, and other subjects of interest. Some of these, such as the U.S. Coast Guard Service and National Park Service sites, are packed with very useful information.

University and college sites also tend to be well written and edited and have fairly extensive, useful content; diaries and other historic texts, often accompanied by period art and illustrations, can often be found on such sites.

Many commercial and private organizations or individuals also maintain useful Civil War sites, many of them run by reenactment groups. It is amongst such sites, however, that researchers should exert the most caution. A few that have been around for some time and have extensive, reliable, and useful content are listed below. Searches coupled with a critical eye can produce many more.

ARCHEOLOGY AT ANDERSONVILLE
www.nps.gov/history/seac/andearch.htm
Explores the site of the Civil War's most notorious prison camp.

CIVIL WAR ARCHEOLOGY
www.nps.gov/history/seac/civilwar/index.htm
A site dedicated to information about historic sites associated with the Civil War.

CIVIL WAR NEWS
www.civilwarnews.com
Website for a current-events monthly newspaper covering Civil War battlefields.

CIVIL WAR REENACTORS HOME PAGE
www.cwreenactors.com
Home to the first forums on the internet dedicated to the Civil War.

CONFEDERATE CIVIL WAR UNIFORMS
www.ushist.com/american_civil-war_uniforms_confederate_cs.shtml
This site includes photographs of Civil War officer and enlisted uniforms used by Rebel soldiers, sailors, and marines.

JEWS IN THE CIVIL WAR
www.jewish-history.com/civilwar
This site includes a database of Jewish veterans of the war and numerous relevant articles.

NAVAL HISTORY AND HERITAGE COMMAND
www.history.navy.mil
This site is part of the official history program of the Department of the Navy helps to preserve, analyze, and interpret naval history.

QUARTERMASTER HERALDIC SECTION AND THE U.S. ARMY INSTITUTE OF HERALDRY
www.qmfound.com/heraldry.htm
Provides information about official government and military symbolic items, such as rank insignia.

UNION CIVIL WAR UNIFORMS
www.ushist.com/american_civil-war_uniforms_union_us.shtml
Includes photographs of Civil War officer and enlisted uniforms of the Army, Navy, and Marines.

U.S. ARMY CENTER OF MILITARY HISTORY
www.history.army.mil
Site for the organization "responsible for the appropriate use of history throughout the U.S. Army" which entails "recording the official history of the Army in both peace and war, while advising the Army Staff on historical matters."

U.S. COAST GUARD HISTORIANS' OFFICE
www.uscg.mil/history
Site for the agency charged with collecting, preserving, and promoting the institutional memory of the nation's oldest continuous-going sea service.

U.S. MARINE CORPS
www.usmc.mil
Appropriate searches on this official service site will turn up some interesting material related to the role of USMC in the Civil War.

VARHOLA TRAVELBLOGUE
varhola.blogspot.com
This official site by the author of this book covers his trips to battlefields and other sites of historical and cultural interest and contains some companion information related to this book.

Historic Sites

Walking across Civil War battlefields and through nineteenth-century buildings, and viewing the objects and clothes carried and worn by the people of the age, can be invaluable to an understanding of the war and its participants. Literally thousands of sites throughout the United States are associated with the Civil War, from major battlefields to the homes of generals, politicians, and common folk. Several are listed next, most of them operated by the National Park Service. Mailing addresses are provided—but note that these sometimes do not represent the physical location of the sites, so those interested in visiting them should obtain directions online or by calling the venues in question.

ABRAHAM LINCOLN BIRTHPLACE NATIONAL HISTORIC SITE
2995 Lincoln Farm Rd., Hodgenville, KY 42748, (270) 358-3137/38
www.nps.gov/abli
In 1808, Thomas and Nancy Lincoln moved into a one-room log cabin near Sinking Spring, Kentucky, and two months later, on Feb. 12, 1809, Abraham Lincoln was born. On July 17, 1916, Congress declared the area was a National Historic Site. Today, the 116-acre site—about one-third the size of the original farm—includes an early nineteenth-century Kentucky cabin.

ANDERSONVILLE NATIONAL HISTORIC SITE
496 Cemetery Road, Andersonville, GA 31711, (229) 924-0343
www.nps.gov/ande
This is the only park in the National Park System that serves as a memorial to all American prisoners of war throughout the nation's history and includes the historic prison site, a national cemetery, and the National Prisoner of War Museum. In authorizing this park, Congress stated that

its purpose is "to provide an understanding of the overall prisoner of war story of the Civil War, to interpret the role of prisoner of war camps in history, to commemorate the sacrifice of Americans who lost their lives in such camps, and to preserve the monuments located within the site."

ANDREW JOHNSON NATIONAL HISTORIC SITE

121 Monument Ave., Greenville, TN 37743, (423) 638-3551

www.nps.gov/anjo

This site honors the life and work of the nation's seventeenth president (from 1865 to 1869), who led the country in the years following Lincoln's assassination and during the beginning of Reconstruction. Features of the site include Johnson's two homes, tailor shop, and grave site.

ANTIETAM NATIONAL BATTLEFIELD

P.O. Box 158, Sharpsburg, MD 21782, (301) 432-5124

www.nps.gov/anti

Established on August 30, 1890, this Civil War site marks the end of Confederate Gen. Robert E. Lee's first invasion of the North at the Battle of Antietam on Sept. 17, 1862, during which more men were killed than on any other single day of the war.

APPOMATTOX COURT HOUSE NATIONAL HISTORICAL PARK

Hwy 24, PO Box 218, Appomattox, VA 24522, (434) 352-8987, ext. 26

www.nps.gov/apco

This is the location of Robert E. Lee's April 9, 1865, surrender to Ulysses Grant, which was authorized as a battlefield site June 18, 1930, and designated a national historical park on April 15, 1954.

ARLINGTON HOUSE AND THE ROBERT E. LEE MEMORIAL

c/o George Washington Memorial Parkway, c/o Turkey Run Park, McLean, VA 22101, (703) 235-1530

www.nps.gov/arho

Arlington House was the home of Robert E. Lee and his family for thirty years and is uniquely associated with both the Washington and Custis families.

BRICES CROSS ROADS NATIONAL BATTLEFIELD SITE

2680 Natchez Trace Parkway, Tupelo, MS 38804, (662) 680-4025

www.nps.gov/brcr

Confederate cavalry was employed with extraordinary skill during the June 10, 1864, battle at this site, during which Union forces attempted to prevent Southern troops from disrupting Federal supply routes.

CHICKAMAUGA AND CHATTANOOGA NATIONAL MILITARY PARK
(Fort Oglethorpe, Georgia, and Chattanooga, Tennessee)
P.O. Box 2128, Fort Oglethorpe, GA 30742, (706) 866-9241
www.nps.gov/chch
America's first National Military Park, established in 1890, honors the Civil War soldiers who fought for control of Chattanooga at the Battle of Chickamauga in September 1863 and the Battles for Chattanooga in November 1863. The park includes two visitors' centers and more than 8,200 acres in both Georgia and Tennessee. Chickamauga was considered the last major Confederate victory in the West, but it was hollow, as Union forces gained control of Chattanooga just two months later.

CLARA BARTON NATIONAL HISTORIC SITE
5801 Oxford Rd., Glen Echo, MD 20812, (301) 320-1410
www.nps.gov/clba
This site commemorates the life of the founder of the American Red Cross. From her house in Glen Echo, Maryland, she organized and directed relief efforts for victims of natural disasters and war.

DRY TORTUGAS NATIONAL PARK
P.O. Box 6208, Key West, FL 33041
www.nps.gov/drto
Built 1846–1866 to help protect the Florida Straits, this is the largest all-masonry fortification in the Western Hemisphere. It served as a prison during and after the Civil War.

FAIRFAX STATION RAILROAD MUSEUM
P.O. Box 7, Fairfax Station, VA 22039, (703) 425-9225
www.fairfax-station.org
This site houses Civil War, Red Cross, and historic railroading memorabilia, along with a variety of artifacts found in and around the Civil War-era station.

FORD'S THEATRE NATIONAL HISTORIC SITE
511 Tenth St. NW, Washington, DC 20004, (202) 426-6924
www.nps.gov/foth
On April 14, 1865, John Wilkes Booth shot President Abraham Lincoln, who had been attending a play at this theater. Lincoln was carried to a small bedroom in the back of the Petersen House, a boarding house across the street from the theater, where he died early the next morning. The theater and house are preserved as national historic sites (the former portion of the site still stages plays) and were recently completely renovated.

FORT DONELSON NATIONAL BATTLEFIELD

P.O. Box 434, Dover, TN 37058, (931) 232-5348 ext. 0

www.nps.gov/fodo/

On February 16, 1862, the Union army in Tennessee, under the command of Brig. Gen. Ulysses S. Grant, won its first major victory of the Civil War. Capture of Fort Donelson and approximately thirteen thousand Confederate soldiers delivered a devastating blow to the Rebel cause, set the stage for the Union's invasion of the deep South and catapulted Grant into national prominence.

FORT PULASKI NATIONAL MONUMENT

P.O. Box 30757, Savannah, GA 31410, (912) 786-5787

www.nps.gov/fopu

On April 11, 1862, defensive strategy changed forever when Union rifled cannon first overcame a masonry fortification after only thirty hours of bombardment. Named for Revolutionary War hero Count Casimir Pulaski, Fort Pulaski took some eighteen years to build and was the first military assignment for a young second lieutenant fresh from West Point, Robert E. Lee. This remarkably-intact example of nineteenth-century military architecture contains an estimated 25 million bricks and 7½ foot-thick walls.

FORT SUMTER NATIONAL MONUMENT

1214 Middle St., Sullivan's Island, SC 29482, (843) 883-3123

www.nps.gov/fosu

On April 12 and 13, 1861, the first engagement of the Civil War took place here. After thirty-four hours of fighting, the Union garrison of the fort surrendered it to the Confederacy. From 1863 to 1865, the Confederates at Fort Sumter withstood a twenty-two-month siege by Union forces, during which most of the fort was reduced to brick rubble. It was declared a national monument in 1948.

FREDERICKSBURG AND SPOTSYLVANIA COUNTY BATTLEFIELDS MEMORIAL NATIONAL MILITARY PARK

120 Chatham Lane, Fredericksburg, VA 22405, (540) 373-6122

www.nps.gov/frsp

About 110,000 men were killed, wounded, or captured in the vicinity of Fredericksburg, Virginia. In 1927, Congress established the site to commemorate the heroic deeds of the men engaged at the battles of Fredericksburg, Chancellorsville, the Wilderness, and Spotsylvania Court House. Today, the largest military park in the world encompasses nearly nine thousand acres and includes the historic structures of Chatham, Ellwood, Salem Church, and the "Stonewall" Jackson Shrine.

GENERAL GRANT NATIONAL MEMORIAL

West 122nd Street and Riverside Drive, New York, NY 10027, (212) 666-1640

www.nps.gov/gegr

Popularly known as Grant's Tomb, this is the final resting place of Ulysses S. Grant and his wife, Julia Dent Grant. Designed by architect John Duncan, the granite-and-marble tomb was completed in 1897 and is the largest mausoleum in North America.

GETTYSBURG NATIONAL MILITARY PARK

1195 Baltimore Pike, Suite 100, Gettysburg, PA 17325, (717) 334-1124, ext. 8023

www.nps.gov/gett

Gettysburg was the site of the largest and bloodiest battle ever waged in the Western Hemisphere. It raged from July 1–3, 1863. More than fifty-one thousand soldiers were slain in a Union victory that successfully repulsed Gen. Robert E. Lee's second invasion of the North. It was Lee's last major effort to take the fighting out of Virginia and into Northern states.

HARPERS FERRY NATIONAL HISTORICAL PARK

P.O. Box 65, Harpers Ferry, WV 25425, (304) 535-6029

www.nps.gov/hafe

John Brown and the Civil War are major themes of this park, which became part of the National Park System in 1944 and covers more than 2,300 acres in the states of West Virginia, Maryland, and Virginia.

KENNESAW MOUNTAIN NATIONAL BATTLEFIELD PARK

900 Kennesaw Mountain Dr., Kennesaw, GA 30152, (770) 427-4686, ext. 0

www.nps.gov/kemo

This 2,884-acre park preserves a battleground where some of the most savage combat of the Atlanta Campaign took place, June 19 through July 2, 1864. Features include historic earthworks, cannon emplacements, and monuments.

LINCOLN BOYHOOD NATIONAL MEMORIAL

2916 E South Street, P.O. Box 1816, Lincoln City, IN 47552, (812) 937-4541

www.nps.gov/libo

Abraham Lincoln spent fourteen of the most formative years of his life and grew from youth into manhood on this southern Indiana farm. His mother, Nancy Hanks Lincoln, is buried here.

LINCOLN HOME NATIONAL HISTORIC SITE

413 South Eighth St., Springfield, IL 62701-1905, (217) 492-4241

www.nps.gov/liho

Abraham Lincoln's two-story home stands at the center of this park restored to its 1860s appearance. Lincoln and his family lived in the house from 1844 until his election to the presidency in 1861. It stands in the midst of a four-block historic neighborhood that has been restored so that the surroundings appear much as Lincoln would have remembered them.

MANASSAS NATIONAL BATTLEFIELD PARK

12521 Lee Highway, Manassas, VA 20109, (703) 361-1339

www.nps.gov/mana

The battles of First and Second Manassas (Bull Run) were fought here July 21, 1861, and August 28–30, 1862. The 1861 battle, in which Confederate Gen. Thomas J. Jackson acquired his nickname "Stonewall," was the first test of Northern and Southern military prowess.

THE MUSEUM OF THE CONFEDERACY

1201 E. Clay St., Richmond, VA 23219, (804) 649-1861

www.moc.org

A great resource for anyone needing information about the South during the Civil War, this site contains the world's most comprehensive collection of artifacts, manuscripts, and photographs from the Confederate States of America.

PAMPLIN HISTORICAL PARK

6125 Boydton Plank Rd., Petersburg, VA 23803, (804) 861-2408

www.pamplinpark.org

This site includes a plantation house restored to its 1865 appearance, walking trails, and the National Museum of the Civil War Soldier.

PEA RIDGE NATIONAL MILITARY PARK

15930 E. Highway 62, Garfield, AR 72732, (479) 451-8122 ext. 227

www.nps.gov/peri

This 4,300-acre park preserves the site of the March 7–8, 1862, battle that saved Missouri for the Union. Elkhorn Tavern, the site of bitter fighting on both days, has been reconstructed on the site of the original tavern. This is possibly the best-preserved Civil War battlefield in the country.

PETERSBURG NATIONAL BATTLEFIELD

5001 Siege Road, Petersburg, VA 23803, (804) 732-3531, ext. 200

www.nps.gov/pete

Petersburg became the site of the longest siege in U.S. history when Lt. Gen. Ulysses S. Grant failed to capture Richmond in early 1864. He settled in to subdue the Confederacy by surrounding Petersburg and cutting off Gen. Robert E. Lee's supply lines into Petersburg and Richmond. On April 2, 1865, 9½ months after the siege began, Lee evacuated Petersburg.

RICHMOND NATIONAL BATTLEFIELD PARK

3215 East Broad St., Richmond, VA 23223, (804) 226-1981, ext. 23

www.nps.gov/rich

From 1861 to 1865, Federal armies repeatedly attempted to capture Richmond, capital of the Confederacy, and end the Civil War. Three of those campaigns came within a few miles of the city. This park commemorates eleven different sites associated with those campaigns, including the battlefields of Gaines's Mill, Malvern Hill, and Cold Harbor. Established in 1936, the park includes 763 acres of historic ground.

SHILOH NATIONAL MILITARY PARK
1055 Pittsburg Landing Road, Shiloh, TN 38376, (731) 689-5696
www.nps.gov/shil
The park was established in 1894 to preserve the scene of the first major battle in the West, fought April 6-7, 1862. This battle was a decisive victory for the Union forces when they advanced on and seized control of the Confederate railway system at Corinth, Mississippi. This park contains about four thousand acres and has within its boundaries the Shiloh National Cemetery.

STONES RIVER NATIONAL BATTLEFIELD AND CEMETERY
3501 Old Nashville Highway, Murfreesboro, TN 37129, (615) 893-9501 and (615) 478-1035
www.nps.gov/stri
A fierce battle took place at Stones River from December 31, 1862, to January 2, 1863, and resulted in Union control of central Tennessee. Although the battle was tactically indecisive, it provided a much-needed boost to the North after the defeat at Fredericksburg. This 450-acre site includes Stones River National Cemetery, established in 1865, with more than six thousand Union graves; and the Hazen Monument, believed to be the oldest to the Civil War. Parts of Fortress Rosecrans, a large series of earthworks built after the battle, still stand.

TUPELO NATIONAL BATTLEFIELD
2680 Natchez Trace Parkway, Tupelo, MS 38804, (800) 305-7417
www.nps.gov/tupe
At this site on July 13-14, 1864, Confederate Gen. Nathan Bedford Forrest attempted to cut the railroad supplying the Union march on Atlanta.

VICKSBURG NATIONAL MILITARY PARK
3201 Clay St., Vicksburg, MS 39183, (601) 636-0583
www.nps.gov/vick
This park was established on February 21, 1899, to commemorate one of the most decisive battles of the American Civil War—the campaign, siege, and defense of Vicksburg, waged from March 29 to July 4, 1863. Located high on the bluffs overlooking the Mississippi, Vicksburg was a fortress guarding the river and was known as "the Gibraltar of the Confederacy." Its surrender on July 4, 1863, coupled with the fall of Port Hudson, Louisiana, divided the South, and gave the North undisputed control of the Mississippi River. The battlefield is well preserved and includes more than

1,300 monuments and markers, reconstructed trenches and earthworks, one antebellum structure, more than 125 emplaced cannon, a restored Union gunboat (the USS *Cairo*), and the Vicksburg National Cemetery.

WILSON'S CREEK NATIONAL BATTLEFIELD
6424 W. Farm Rd. 182, Republic, MO 65738, (417) 732-2662, ext. 227
www.nps.gov/wicr
On August 10, 1861, the battle fought here was the first major Civil War engagement west of the Mississippi River and involved some five thousand Union and ten thousand Confederate troops, and was a nondecisive Confederate victory. With few exceptions, the 1,750-acre battlefield has changed little.

Maps
Many sorts of maps are readily available today, from reprints of Civil War-era battle maps to modern maps that convey demographic or political information. Such tools can be an excellent resource for anyone interested in a deeper understanding of the war. A period map that shows the placement of units on a battlefield and their subsequent movements can be invaluable in helping understand the sequence of a battle. Likewise, a modern map that shows which Southern states seceded from the Union and when can reveal that none of those that actually bordered Union states joined the Confederacy until after the attack upon Fort Sumter.

Heirloom Plants and Seeds
Over the past few decades heirloom plants have become increasingly popular, and those interested in growing them can find them everywhere, from seed companies that offer heirloom varieties, to garden stores that sell heirloom plants of various sorts (tomatoes being especially popular). With this ease of access, there is no reason not to give heirlooms a try, and those interested in the conflict can grow Civil War-era fruits and vegetables for a historically-accurate taste of the era.

SONGS AND POETRY

The Civil War produced a large body of songs that reflected the attitudes of the period and modern readers can go a long way toward understanding the people of the era by knowing the words to the songs they sang. Period songs reflect a wide range of sentiments and emotions, from patriotism and love of country, to derision of the enemy, to the melancholy and suffering that attended life in camp, on the march, and in battle.

Songs that became popular during the Civil War included "John Brown's Body" (whose author is disputed, but which became popular with Northern soldiers upon the outbreak of war), "The Battle Cry of Freedom" (George Frederich Root, 1861), and "Marching Through Georgia" (Henry Clay Work, 1865).

Much poetry was also written about the war, and this tended to be a bit more critical than the songs. For example, "The Picket Guard" (Ethel Lynn Beers, 1861) is a sarcastic response to stories in Union papers about Maj. Gen. George McClellan's inability to advance against the Confederacy in the weeks—and ultimately months—after his defeat at Bull Run.

Poet Walt Whitman was one of the many people to tend wounded soldiers during the Civil War. He served as a volunteer assistant in a military hospital in Washington, DC. In his 1865 book of poems *Drum-Taps*, he incorporated scenes of battle described to him by convalescing soldiers.

Song Lyrics

Dixie's Land

In the early years of the war, many popular songs were common to both sides. "Dixie's Land," written by Daniel Decatur Emmett—a Northerner from Mount Vernon, Ohio—and now associated entirely with the South, was in 1861 widely sung on both sides. As the war progressed, however, and the opposing cultures became more and more separated from each other, songs became more partisan in nature.

CHORUS

His face was sharp as a butcher's cleaver;
But that did not seem to grieve her!
Look away! Look away! Look away, Dixie's Land!
Old Missus acted the foolish part
And died for a man that broke her heart!
Look away! Look away! Look away, Dixie's Land!

CHORUS

Now here's a health to the next old missus
And all the gals that want to kiss us!
Look away! Look away! Look away, Dixie's Land!
But if you want to drive away sorrow,
Come and hear this song tomorrow!
Look away! Look away! Look away, Dixie's Land!

CHORUS

There's buckwheat cakes and Injin batter,
Makes you fat or a little fatter!
Look away! Look away! Look away, Dixie's Land!
Then hoe it down and scratch your gravel,
To Dixie's Land I'm bound to travel!
Look away! Look away! Look away, Dixie's Land!

CHORUS

I wish I was in the land of cotton,
Old times there are not forgotten;
Look away! Look away! Look away, Dixie's Land!
In Dixie's Land where I was born in,
Early on one frosty morning,
Look away! Look away! Look away, Dixie's Land!

CHORUS: *Then I wish I was in Dixie! Hooray! Hooray!*
In Dixie's Land I'll take my stand, to live and die in Dixie!
Away! Away! Away down South in Dixie!
Away! Away! Away down South in Dixie!

Old Missus married "Will the Weaver";
William was a gay deceiver!
Look away! Look away! Look away, Dixie's Land!
But when he put his arm around her,
Smiled as fierce as a forty-pounder!
Look away! Look away! Look away, Dixie's Land!

The Battle Hymn of the Republic

One of the most characteristic and stirring songs of the war, "The Battle Hymn of the Republic" was set to a popular drinking tune usually adapted to far more bawdy lyrics (e.g., one popular version of the time includes the line, "John Brown's body lies a moldering in his grave"). Its moving words reflect some of the fervent beliefs and attitudes that prevailed during the war. Julia Ward Howe wrote it in November 1861 after being inspired by a review of Union troops and deciding the popular tune needed more redeeming words. It was first published in *The Atlantic Monthly* in 1862.

He is trampling out the vintage
Where the grapes of wrath are stored
He hath lossed his fateful lightning of his terrible
swift sword,
His truth is marching on.

CHORUS: *Glory! Glory! Hallelujah!*
Glory! Glory! Hallelujah!
Glory! Glory! Hallelujah!
His truth is marching on.

I have seem Him in the watchfires of a hundred
circling camps,
they have builded Him an altar in the evening dews
and damps.
I can read His righteous sentence by the dim and
flaring lamps;
His day is marching on.

CHORUS

I have read a firey gospel Writ in burnished rows of steel
As ye deal with my condemners,
So with you my grace will deal;
Let the hero born of woman
Crush the serpent with His heel;
Since God is marching on.

CHORUS

He has sounded forth the trumpet that shall never
sound retreat;
He is sifting out the hearts of men beneath his
Judgement Seat.
Oh! Be swift, my soul to answer him, be jubilant,
my feet!
Our God is marching on.

CHORUS

In the beauty of the lilies Christ was born across the sea
With a glory in his bosom
That transfigures you and me;
As He died to make men holy let us die to make
men free,
While God is marching on.

Victory's Band

The following 1861 song by Daniel Decatur Emmett reflects some of the vindictiveness that crept into songs as the war progressed. Sung to the tune of his "Dixie's Land," its lyrics seem coarse and jingoistic when compared to those of the original.

....

We're marching under the Flag of Union,
Keeping step in brave communion!
March away! march away! away! Victory's band!
Right down upon the ranks of rebels,
Tramp them underfoot like pebbles,
March away! march away! away! Victory's band.

CHORUS: *Oh! we're marching on to Victory!*
Hurrah! hurrah!
In Victory's band we'll sweep the land,
And fight or die for Victory!
Away! away!
We'll fight or die for victory!

The rebels want a mongrel nation,
Union and Confederation!
March away! march away! away! Victory's band!
But we don't trust in things two-sided,
And go for Union undivided,
March away! march away! away! Victory's band.

CHORUS

We're marching down on Dixie's regions,
With freedom's flag and freedom's legions.
March away! march away! away! Victory's band!
We're rolling down, a "Pending Crisis,"
With cannon-balls for Compromises,
March away! march away! away! Victory's band

CHORUS

....

Tenting on the Old Camp Ground

Written in 1864 by Walter Kittredge, this song, and many like it, is a striking counterpoint to the earlier patriotic songs. Many commanders prohibited their soldiers from singing such songs, based on the rationale that they lowered morale. Such moves were misguided, however, as soldiers were still thinking the things expressed in the songs, even if they were deprived of an outlet for expressing them. Such prohibitions tended to be ineffective and short-lived, in any case.

We're tenting tonight on the old Camp ground.
Give us a song to cheer
Our weary hearts, a song of home,
And friends we love so dear.

CHORUS *Many are the hearts that are weary tonight,*
Wishing for the war to cease;
Many are the hearts looking for the right
To see the dawn of peace.
Tenting tonight,
Tenting tonight,
Tenting on the old Camp ground.

We're been tenting tonight on the old Camp ground,
Thinking of days gone by,
Of the lov'd ones at home that gave us the hand,
And the tear that said, "Good bye!"

CHORUS

We are tired of war on the old Camp ground,
Many are dead and gone,
Of the brave and true who've left their homes,
Others been wounded long.

CHORUS

We've been fighting today on the old Camp ground,
Many are lying near;
Some are dead and some are dying,
Many are in tears.

CHORUS *Many are the hearts that are weary tonight,*
Wishing for the war to cease;
Many are the hearts looking for the right
To see the dawn of peace.
Dying tonight,
Dying tonight,
Dying on the old Camp ground.

INDEX

Index

Index

Index

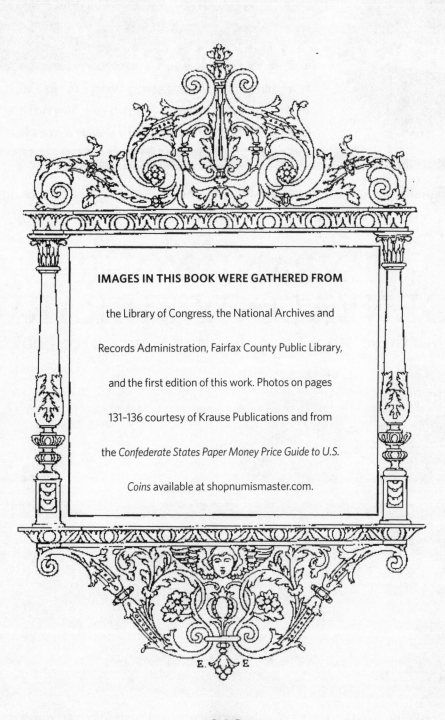

IMAGES IN THIS BOOK WERE GATHERED FROM

the Library of Congress, the National Archives and

Records Administration, Fairfax County Public Library,

and the first edition of this work. Photos on pages

131–136 courtesy of Krause Publications and from

the *Confederate States Paper Money Price Guide to U.S.*

Coins available at shopnumismaster.com.

E. E

featuring a conversation with *Life in Civil War America* author Michael J. Varhola.
Go to <http://bit.ly/civilwaramerica>.

Get **FREE** history and genealogy tips, news, sneak peeks and exclusive discounts!
Sign up for our e-newsletter at <**familytreemagazine.com**>.

EXPAND YOUR GENEALOGY LIBRARY

with these other fine titles from Family Tree Books.

THE FAMILY TREE SOURCEBOOK	FAMILY TREE LEGACIES	FAMILY TREE POCKET REFERENCE	GRAVE HUMOR
From the Editors of *Family Tree Magazine*	From the Editors of *Family Tree Magazine*	From the Editors of *Family Tree Magazine*	M.T. Coffin
paperback	Hardcover	paperback	paperback
#Z9868	#Z4963	#Y0008	#Z9869
ISBN-13: 978-1-4403-0884-0	ISBN-13: 978-1-4403-0134-6	ISBN-13: 978-1-4403-0889-5	ISBN-13: 978-1-4403-0885-7
ISBN-10: 1-4403-0884-5	ISBN-10: 1-4403-0134-4	ISBN-10: 1-4403-0889-6	ISBN-10: 1-4403-0885-3

Available from your favorite bookstore, online booksellers and
<**shopfamilytree.com**>, or by calling (800) 258-0929.